El Norte or Bu

El Norte or Bust!

How Migration Fever and Microcredit Produced a Financial Crash in a Latin American Town

David Stoll

ROWMAN & LITTLEFIELD PUBLISHERS, INC.
Lanham • Boulder • New York • Toronto • Plymouth, UK

Published by Rowman & Littlefield Publishers, Inc.
A wholly owned subsidary of The Rowman & Littlefield Publishing Group, Inc.
4501 Forbes Boulevard, Suite 200, Lanham, Maryland 20706
www.rowman.com

10 Thornbury Road, Plymouth PL6 7PP, United Kingdom

British Library Cataloguing in Publication Information Available

Library of Congress Cataloging-in-Publication Data
Stoll, David, 1952–
    El Norte or bust! : how migration fever and microcredit produced a financial crash in a Latin American town / David Stoll.
      p.   cm
    Includes bibliographical references and index.
      ISBN 978-1-4422-2068-3 (cloth : alk. paper) — ISBN 978-1-4422-2069-0 (electronic) 1. Nebaj (Guatemala)—Emigration and immigration—Economic aspects. 2. Nebaj (Guatemala)—Economic conditions. 3. Microfinance—Guatemala—Nebaj. 4. Ixil Indians—Guatemala—Nebaj—Economic conditions. 5. Quiché Indians—Guatemala—Nebaj—Economic conditions. 6. Emigrant remittances—Guatemala—Nebaj. 7. Illegal aliens—United States—Economic conditions. I. Title.
    JV7416.S76 2013
    330.97281'72—dc23
                                                                    2012039571

Printed in the United States of America

Contents

Maps and Tables

MAPS

TABLES

Preface

This book is about Guatemalan peasants who crashed shortly before Wall Street did. I have been interviewing the people of Nebaj since the 1980s. Never did I expect them to become a leading indicator in the 2008 financial meltdown. Most Nebajenses still cultivate patches of maize on hillsides. They would consider themselves lucky to own a cow. They would like to be known for their hard work, their loyalty to their families, and their faith in God. Their good cheer and animosities, their provincialism and ingenuity, remind me of the nineteenth-century Americans portrayed by Mark Twain and the nineteenth-century Britons portrayed by Charles Dickens. With little to hope from police or judiciary, let alone a state-supported safety net or their community, they are self-reliant, resourceful, and moralistic. When there is no hope, they invent it.

In the international media, the people of Nebaj pop up only as victims of genocide in Guatemala's late civil war (1962–1996). As of this writing, a former chief of state is on trial for the murder of 267 noncombatants by army units operating under his authority.[1] The trial is being attended by survivors and is being followed by other Nebajenses. Usually, however, being victims of genocide is less on their minds than being without work. They have been producing large families for several generations, and they are running out of land. So great is their need for employment that, when they became a magnet for international aid projects, including a generous flow of microcredits, they invested the loans in an enterprise not foreseen by aid experts. They smuggled themselves to the United States. Just as U.S. investment bankers borrowed many times their net worth to produce higher returns, Nebajenses borrowed many times their annual income in order to seek higher wages in U.S. labor markets. Those who couldn't go borrowed to invest in the journeys of those who could. Just as the Wall Streeters relied on the latest technology to minimize their risks, Nebaj's investors had their own high-tech assurances: television to show what life was like in the United States, cell phones to stay in touch with debtors, and bank wires to facilitate transfers. Remittances poured home, and thousands more Nebajenses jumped into the game.

Something began to go wrong in 2006. In a harbinger of the jobs crisis that now affects all but the wealthiest Americans, more and more of Nebaj's migrants were unable to find steady employment. In debates over U.S. immigration policy, most attention focuses on the political theater of anti-immigration forces agitating for crackdowns and pro-immigration forces agitating for amnesties. Overlooked are the millions of underemployed Guatemalans, Dominicans, and other foreigners who continue to pin their hopes on a U.S. job. What are the implications of the U.S. financial crisis, and of the high unemployment rates since then, for people like the Nebajenses who see U.S. jobs as their lifeline?

For readers who do not know Guatemala, I should explain that, according to the most recent available census, 40 percent of the population identifies itself as indigenous. Of these, 50 to 60 percent speak twenty-two different Mayan Indian languages.[2] Eleven of the twenty-two language groups are to be found in the Cordillera of the Cuchumatanes, a mile-high massif that arcs from west to east and cuts off the Guatemalan Altiplano, a plateau to the south, from the Lacandón rainforest and Mexico to the north. This book focuses on the accomplishments and tribulations of the Ixil Mayas and K'iche' Mayas of Nebaj. Nebaj is one of three *municipios* where Ixil speakers predominate. Along with Cotzal and Chajul, the other two municipios in Ixil country, Nebaj is located in the narrow central waist of the Department of El Quiché. To the north, the Cuchumatanes descend to the rainforests which, before they were cut down, used to stretch to the Mexican border. In the valleys south of Ixil country, most of the population speaks K'iche' Maya, the largest of the country's indigenous language groups. K'iche' speakers have been moving into Ixil country for more than a century. Currently they are about 10 percent of Nebaj's population, with nonindigenous ladinos constituting another 10 percent and Ixils 75 percent.[3]

The town of Nebaj, where I do most of my interviewing, has a population of twenty thousand if you count outlying neighborhoods and a few villages within an hour's walk of the town plaza. It is the administrative and market center of a larger jurisdiction, the municipio of Nebaj, which is comparable to a U.S. county and has an estimated 2011 population of eighty-five thousand. Three-quarters of Nebajenses live in ninety-odd hamlets and villages—unless they are working on coastal plantations, in the national capital or the United States. A large majority of Nebaj's migrants to the United States speak Ixil Maya as their first language; most of the rest speak K'iche' Maya as their first language; a few are ladinos who speak Spanish as their first language. The ancestry of ladinos ranges from full European to full Mayan; most are mestizos; what unites ladinos as a category is that they do not regard themselves as indigenous. I will refer to all three groups as Nebajenses, an identity they wear proudly and that often trumps ethnicity in friendship, courtship, religion, and politics.

The simplest explanation for what follows is that Nebaj's Ixil and K'iche' Mayas are not just indigenous, a term which rightly or wrongly we associate with communalism; they are also peasants at the bottom of a class society, which means they compete with each other for resources. Land being scarce, they have become proletarians obliged to sell their labor. Thanks to the marvels of globalization, they have also become low-end financial speculators who leverage their scant assets to smuggle themselves across national borders. One resource for which they are competing is a U.S. job. Another is land back home in Nebaj, the price of which has inflated tremendously owing to remittances. The speculative bubble surrounding U.S. jobs and Guatemalan real estate burst in 2008 when remittances failed to sustain the debts of migrants to relatives, moneylenders, and banks. The collapse revealed pyramid-style investment patterns in which early investors were trying to recoup their losses by transferring them to new investors.

How do I know all this? Because of the stories that Nebajenses tell me. Stories are acceptable currency in cultural anthropology; they are not the strongest form of evidence in other social sciences. Yet what Nebajenses have been telling me about their financial adventures is not very susceptible to the compilation of statistics because so much of it is illegal. Diverting microcredit into human smuggling, or loaning it out again at usurious rates, or sending sixteen-year-old boys across Mexico to join the undocumented U.S. labor force—none of these economic strategies are likely to surface in survey research. So why would Nebajenses share them with me? One reason is that I've been talking to them since the 1980s; I have a reputation as a *preguntón* (someone who asks too many questions) but have never caused enough trouble to be run out of town.

How can I be certain that my sources are telling me the truth? I cannot. But for more important cases, such as the moneylenders and swindlers of chapters 5, 6, and 7, I have interviewed enough sources to distinguish between more and less likely versions of events. The weakness of my journalistic approach is that pursuing particular kinds of stories can quickly lead to false generalizations. Fortunately for my cause, the appearance of two organizations of debtors showed that I was not just documenting my own manias—a growing problem in anthropology. While I had no access to the balance sheets of loan agencies, kindhearted managers shared enough information to allow rough calculations of the number of Nebajenses in the United States and how much money they have been sending. If you lose patience over how representative my storytellers are, jump to the last two chapters.

Undocumented migration can be challenging for Americans to study because of the possibility, in the minds of the people we approach, that we are U.S. immigration officers. Occasionally Nebajenses refused to talk to me, for this or other reasons, but I am eternally grateful to the many who agreed to discuss their affairs. More often than not, I approached people after hearing they had a story to tell. I introduced myself as a social investigator who published a book about Nebaj in the 1990s and was preparing another. My first book was about the war; my second would be about migration to El Norte, indebtedness, and swindles. I emphasized that I was not a political authority, so talking to me was completely voluntary. I also emphasized that I was not an aid organization, so I could not pay anyone's debts. Whenever possible, I took notes, then fleshed them out on a computer. To my embarrassment, I am not a speaker of Ixil Maya, but the people I interviewed were usually capable of explaining their affairs in Spanish. For those who could not, my translator, Jacinto Pérez, provided invaluable assistance.

Except where noted, all interviews were with Nebajenses in Nebaj, in several U.S. locations, and occasionally over the telephone, between June 2007 and June 2012. During this period I spent a total of five months in Nebaj. In keeping with anthropological standards on protecting sources, most people appear under pseudonym, in which case I use only a first name. Public figures, people who have died, and people who have been involved with the legal system are named in full, as are people who said they wished to inform the world of their plight. Except where noted, I have converted Guatemala's currency, the quetzal, to dollars at the exchange rate of Q7.8 = US$1. This is the midpoint in recent fluctuations between 7.6 and 8 quetzals to the dollar. The local unit of land, the cuerda, is .108 of an acre and .044 of a hectare. Thus 9.26 cuerdas add up to an acre, and 22.73 cuerdas add up to a hectare. The "x" in the transcription of Mayan names is the "sh" sound in *shush*, so Ixil is pronounced "ee-sheel" and the village Xexuxcap is pronounced "shay-shoosh-cop." Nebaj is pronounced "neigh-bah."

I owe a lot to scholars who preceded me in the study of migration and debt—the notes should give a sense of how much. Above all I should mention Fred Krissman, Richard Robbins, David Spener, Alexandra Filindra, Pierre van den Berghe, Michelle Moran-Tyler, John Maluccio, and Jan and Diane Rus who read chapters and gave me their reactions. I am very grateful for their suggestions and their challenges, to not all of which I have been able to rise. Brian Stipek caught errors that only a local would be able to identify; Norman Schwartz provided valuable suggestions as well as encouragement when it was needed. So did my colleagues in the Department of Sociology and Anthropology at Middlebury College. I owe thanks as well to the editors of *Latin American Perspectives* for their critical comments and for publishing an earlier version of chapter 5 under the title "From Wage Migration to Debt Migration?" Theresa May and two anonymous reviewers for the University of Texas Press also provided valuable suggestions; I am sorry that my own bad timing and a backlog at Texas became a problem. At Rowman & Littlefield, Susan McEachern and Karie Simpson hoisted me aboard at the last minute—thank you! Also helping with timely reactions and suggestions were Mike and Terri McComb, Steve and Elaine Elliot, Margot McMillen, Paul Goepfert, Courtney Kurlanska, Letty Arroyo, Christine Eber, Andrew Chesnut, Tracy Ehlers, the late and lamented Donald Langley, and, last but not least, my dear wife, Elizabeth Sutton. Responsibility for any errors of fact or judgment is mine alone.

The only source of funding for this study was Middlebury College, to which my gratitude is correspondingly large. I am even more grateful to the migrants, families, moneylenders, loan officers, aid coordinators, lawyers, and officials of Nebaj who made this study possible. I hope the text makes clear how much of my thinking was contributed by them, even if I am solely responsible for any problems of execution. I am sorry that the political realities of the milieu and the topic make it advisable to render most of the Nebajenses who helped me anonymous. I am particularly indebted to the leaders and members of the Organization of Women Affected by the Economic Crisis in the Ixil Area, as well as to the leaders and members of the Integral Development Association for Families Affected by the Economic Crisis in the Ixil Area. I hope they find the Spanish translation a worthwhile chronicle of their trials.

Part I

THE AMERICAN DREAM COMES TO THE CUCHUMATANES

Chapter One

Great Expectations in a Guatemalan Town

Next to an ancestor cross, where elders burn incense and pray, lives a financial speculator in the Guatemalan town of Nebaj. Magdalena Sánchez Hermoso has eight children and sells food in the market. Her first language is Ixil Maya, she doesn't own a motor vehicle but she does have a cell phone, and her story is well known because she has repeatedly apologized for it. In 2005, Magdalena and her husband began asking their neighbors for huge loans. They offered to pay interest of 10 percent and 15 percent per month and presented their house and agricultural land as collateral. Then they transferred the funds to four acquaintances who offered to pay interest of 15 percent and 20 percent per month. Of the four business partners, three said they were loaning the money to men going to the United States. The fourth said he needed seed money to attract an international aid project. And so Magdalena and her husband borrowed some Q500,000 (at 7.8 quetzals to the dollar, $64,000) and turned it over to the four. They expected to reap millions.

What they didn't know was that their partners invested the funds with a Mam Maya priest who promised riches from a volcano. At last report, this spellbinding practitioner of Mayan tradition was the object of an arrest warrant, which was not interfering with his used-car business on the Mexican border. Back in Nebaj, the title to Magdalena's house fell into the hands of a bank. She was about to lose it when the bank agreed to refinance Q225,000 of the debt. She and her family will be able to keep their home as long as they make mortgage payments of Q3,000 a month. The only way they can generate Q36,000 ($4,600) a year is in the U.S. labor market, to which end Magdalena's husband has joined their son in Houston, where the two are washing dishes in restaurants but having trouble finding enough hours. If they hang on in the United States, and if they remit faithfully, their house will be in the clear as early as 2024.

If you told me this story a few years ago, I wouldn't have believed you. How can Guatemalans with household incomes of $1,500 per year make $10,000 loans? How can they charge each other such crippling interest rates? How can they believe that wealth comes from volcanoes? How can their scramble to earn dollars in the United States make them poorer? Answering these questions brings us to two sacred cows in the current pantheon of wishful thinking: (1) microcredit and (2) unauthorized border crossing in search of a better life. The worm in both apples is a certain kind of debt, of the kind that becomes an extractive mechanism.

My first intimation that debt could be the motor of migration came the year before I met Doña Magdalena, on a warm evening in Baltimore. I was visiting a man who had spent a decade in the mountains as a Marxist guerrilla. Now he worked for a Korean grocer seventy-two hours a week and was sending home enough money to build a house. He, two sons, and ten other Guatemalans were living in a three-bedroom apartment in a complex that seemed to include people from all over the world. The complex was heavily patrolled, and usually it was quiet. Suddenly the revolving lights of a squad car flashed across the quad. Burly paramedics were trying to strap a drunk, bawling Guatemalan youth to a gurney. The young man had punched his stepfather in the face, the stepfather had grabbed the phone to call the cops, and the stepson had rushed outside and fallen off a balcony. Or he'd jumped—this wasn't clear. They were quarreling over the debt he owed for his trip to the United States. Unable to find work, he had been talking about killing himself.

Mexican and Central American migration to the United States is generating lots of attention, but only a few journalists and scholars have paid much attention to the necessary underpinning of debt.[1] I say necessary because where else can Central American peasants find the $5,000 they need to get through Mexico and across the U.S. border? If the U.S. labor market needed them, relatives or friends with U.S. jobs would pay for the trip, and they would work off the debt in a matter of months. But many of the stateside Guatemalans I'm meeting do not have stable employment, and it is unclear that the U.S. economy needed them even before the September 2008 credit panic led to a recession. Five months before the credit crisis, in Homestead, Florida, at 7:30 a.m., I counted more than a hundred Guatemalans waiting for work in one location. Worse, there was nothing new about their plight. For several years Guatemalans had been struggling to find work in Homestead, and yet more continued to arrive. Were they dimwitted moths to the flame? Or did they keep coming not because they were pulled by the wages (which in Homestead are often below the legal minimum) but because they were being pushed by debt back home?

One reason for ignoring debt is that migrants can be reticent about it. But in the town of Nebaj, debt has become a very public issue because of the sudden collapse of an economic bubble. For fifteen years, a blissful succession of international aid projects, low-interest loans, and remittances from the United States enabled thousands of Nebajenses to prosper like never before. Credit institutions arrived and gave loans to just about anyone who asked. Loans were so easy to obtain that many Nebajenses took out a second loan, and maybe a third and fourth. Fueled by loans and remittances, local real estate reached astonishing prices. Then, more than a year before the September 2008 U.S. credit crisis, Nebajenses had increasing difficulty paying their loans. In October 2008, as the U.S. financial structure teetered, an association of Nebaj women asked international organizations and the Guatemalan government for a bailout. Unlike Wall Street's biggest speculators, they did not get one.

What follows is a fortuitous window on an obscure subject—how Guatemalan peasants have used formal and informal credit to finance unauthorized migration to the United States and, as a result, are now deeply in the hole. Nebaj is not a typical Mayan Indian town. It has benefitted from an unusual number of international aid projects. Still, I suspect that what I have found in Nebaj has parallels elsewhere. The stories I hear suggest that migration is a highly competitive process, not just in U.S. labor markets but in the sending population, fueled by competition over land, inheritances, and scarce opportunities for upward mobility. The stories I hear also suggest that migration is a process that runs on debt, with migrants indebting themselves and their relatives to the migration stream in ways that many are unable to repay. The debts not only enable migration but pressure more people to go north, in a chain of exploitation that can suck more value from the sending population than it returns.

Mexicans and other Latin Americans have long viewed migration to the United States as a doorway to prosperity. Many Americans agree with them. Even broader claims have been made for microloans, which are supposed to benefit the poor of the Third World, especially women with children, without requiring them to uproot their lives. Enthusiasm over microcredit peaked in 2006 when the Nobel Peace Prize went to Muhammad Yunus and his Grameen Bank in Bangladesh, "for their efforts to create economic and social development from below." Investors celebrated "the fortune at the bottom of the pyramid," to quote the title of a business best seller. Not only could microloans enable poor people to bootstrap their way out of poverty; they could also become a marvelous source of profits for the banking industry and transnational capital.

THE CUCHUMATANES OF WESTERN GUATEMALA

San Rafael La Independencia
○ San Mateo Ixtatán
* **Department capital**

○ Barillas

San Miguel Acatán ○
○ Santa Eulalia
○ **Municipal seat**

La Mesilla ○

○ Soloma

Todos Santos Cuchumatán ○
○ San Juan Ixcoy

Nebaj ○
○ Chajul

Colotenango ○
LOS CUCHUMATANES
○ Cotzal

Huehuetenango *
○ Aguacatán
○ Uspantán

Cunén

Chiché

Santa Cruz del Quiché *
○ Zacualpa

○ Joyabaj

San Marcos *
Totonicapán *
○ Chichicastenango

Quetzaltenango *
○ Almolonga

Zunil ○

○ Panajachel

Chimaltenango *

Santiago Atitlán ○

Antigua *

U.S.A.

ATLANTIC OCEAN

MEXICO

GUATEMALA

PACIFIC OCEAN

BRAZIL

The anthropologist Julia Elyachar has used the term "empowerment debt" to refer to this surprising consensus between bankers and antipoverty activists that poor people can be empowered by lending them money.[2] That defenders of the poor would celebrate credit as a panacea is surprising. It is all too easy to find examples to the contrary, in which debt becomes a technique for separating the poor from their last assets, especially land. By 2010 a storm of protest was gathering around microlenders in India and Bangladesh. They were accused of pushing loans on their clients, charging them high interest rates, and making them poorer. Trouble is also brewing in Latin America.[3] When Latin Americans seek to boost their wages by slipping into the U.S. labor market, many are obliged to borrow heavily and at high interest rates to get across the border. For collateral they put up the titles to agricultural land and houses, either their own or that of relatives, which extends the risk deep into their families. If they fail to pay the debt quickly, they can lose their family's means of production.

CAN YOU HELP ME FIND A JOB?

The Cuchumatanes are a mountain range in Guatemala inhabited by people who, if they had the chance, would ask you for a job. Many would prefer the job to be in your country rather than theirs. "I will do anything," they say. I have been asked if I have a sister available for marriage; I have been greeted by a teenager in her underwear who said, "Take me with you." The inhabitants of the Cordillera of the Cuchumatanes are, for the most part, indigenous peasants. Some practice traditions that are older than the Spanish Conquest; they speak their own languages (eleven of them, all Mayan), but most also speak Spanish; and if you give them your number, they will ring you up on their cell phones. It's not that they want to join the modern world—they have been part of it for the last five hundred years. Instead, they wish to enjoy the modern world like the readers of this book do. They have been watching television, they have been visited by human rights teams, and they have concluded that the only place they can earn a decent living is the United States.

This is not the first time the people of the Cuchumatanes have aspired to a better life. In the 1970s the most dissatisfied and bold joined the Guerrilla Army of the Poor (EGP), a Marxist-Leninist organization that sought to overthrow the Guatemalan government, lead a social revolution, and turn Guatemala into a classless society. Contrary to the EGP's name, it was started by middle-class intellectuals, nonindigenous ladinos rather than indigenous Mayas. Disastrously, the EGP never got its hands on enough weapons to protect the tens of thousands of civilians it organized. The Guatemalan army

arrived and burned down entire villages. Thousands of people died in massacres, most committed by the army but some by the guerrillas. Survivors were
forced to hide in the mountains where thousands more died of hunger, wet,
and cold. Expiring along with them was the revolutionary movement.

Since then the people of the Cuchumatanes have been swarmed by international consultants. First counterinsurgency, and then foreign aid, has brought
new motor roads that switchback up steep ridges and into hundreds of villages. Many people are living in better houses than before, with better walls
made of cement block and better roofs made of metal. Most can catch a bus
or pickup truck to market, most of their children go to school for at least a
few years, and hardly anyone still goes barefoot. Based on such indicators,
I would like to report that the people of the Cuchumatanes are doing better.
Compared to the worst moments of the army–guerrilla confrontation, they
certainly are. But most earn barely enough to clothe and feed themselves.
At the start of the twenty-first century, 96.6 percent of the farms in Huehuetenango Department were officially classified as *subfamiliares*, that is, too
small to support a family.[4]

And so over the last generation, as the war was replaced by aid projects,
more and more people of the Cuchumatanes have become convinced that
their future lies in the United States—either by working there temporarily or
by moving there for the rest of their lives. In this they are not alone. In 2010,
one in eight inhabitants of the United States was foreign born—the highest
percentage since the 1920s. More than half the newcomers are from Latin
America according to the U.S. Census Bureau.[5] Of Guatemalans, there are
850,000, half of whom are in the United States legally, according to the U.S.
census projection. The International Organization for Migration (2011: 52,
63) estimates that the number of Guatemalans in the United States is almost
twice that—1.6 million—of whom a third would be legal residents or citizens.[6] This would mean that one of every nine Guatemalans is in the United
States, legally or illegally.

Why such a fixation on going north? In 2010, Guatemalans in the United
States sent home $4.16 billion, the country's largest source of foreign ex-
change.[7] According to the IOM's estimate, 1.3 million households and 4.5
million Guatemalans (a third of the population) receive remittances. When
Guatemalans are caught entering the United States illegally—30,855 were
deported in 2010—they say they have no other choice.[8] They are quick to
invoke economic necessity. That may or may not be the case—migrants are
rarely the poorest of the poor—but the difference between hourly wages in
Guatemala and in the United States is hypnotic. Agricultural laborers who
earn five dollars a day can earn the same amount, and possibly double or
triple, in an hour. They are the latest converts to the American Dream, the

promise that anyone who reaches the United States and works hard will be rewarded with a better life for himself or his children.

The astonishment of Guatemalan peasants at U.S. wealth is the mirror image of how Americans rhapsodize about Guatemala, at least on their first visit. What they most love about it, apart from the scent of tropical flowers and the chain of volcanoes marching across the highlands, is its picturesque backwardness. Chicken buses go almost anywhere, through verdant highlands shaped by peasant agriculture. Typically Guatemala strikes Americans as a more indigenous version of Mexico. The boundary between the two countries is recent, and life in both is subject to sudden interruption—by volcanic eruptions, earthquakes, and political strife. On closer examination, Guatemala turns out to be a poorer country than Mexico. Nowhere in Latin America is land distributed more unequally. Most of the best land is owned by absentee plantation owners. Malnutrition is widespread, especially among children.

If Guatemalan migrants always invoke economic necessity, human rights advocates are quick to add their need for political asylum. Since the country became independent from Spain two hundred years ago, most of its governments have defended the interests of plantation owners. From 1944 to 1954, reformers were in power and favored peasants, culminating in a land redistribution that upset the United Fruit Company of Boston. The U.S. government was upset too, but more about the communist intellectuals who were leading lights, so in 1954 the Central Intelligence Agency overthrew an elected government. The new administration reversed the land reform and suppressed labor unions. Shut out of the electoral process, radical students and dissident army officers headed for the mountains and recruited peasants for guerrilla warfare. At the height of the confrontation, in 1981–1983, the army massacred thousands of noncombatants. A quarter of a million peasants were terrorized out of their homes and stampeded across the border into Mexico, where many spent a decade in refugee camps.

In 1996 three decades of army–guerrilla confrontation ended with a UN-sponsored peace agreement. The insurgents laid down their arms; an elected government cut back the army and made other changes. Unfortunately, street crime skyrocketed and so has the homicide rate, such that the annual toll of murders now exceeds the annual toll of the civil war. Youth gangs have proliferated and so have extortion rackets. From 2006 to 2010, 630 bus drivers and 201 fare collectors were assassinated for failing to pay protection money.[9] Adding to the uncertainty, the U.S. war on drugs has forced Colombian and Mexican traffickers to find new routes, and they have been welcomed by the gangster wing of Guatemala's elite. No recounting of the country's flourishing criminal enterprises would be complete without ludicrous episodes involving police commanders, politicians, and retired army officers. The police and courts are so unreliable that citizens are afraid to report crimes for fear that the accused or his friends will track them down and kill them. To protect themselves, hundreds of villages and neighborhoods have organized self-defense patrols. When enraged citizens capture suspects, they turn into lynch mobs whose favorite method of execution is immolation.

So great are the uncertainties of life in Guatemala that, arguably, every Guatemalan qualifies for asylum in the United States. Consider the fate of the Soyos family, who one night in the capital were sitting on the sofa in front of the television. The house began to shake, dust rose from the floor, and Mr. Soyos, two of his children, and the sofa disappeared into a sudden hole. Sixty meters below, a storm sewer had collapsed and sucked them to their deaths. In the preceding weeks, neighbors had complained about tremors and rumbles and inspectors had installed a seismic detector, but no one was able to predict the giant sinkhole, a stone's throw from one of the country's busiest traffic arteries.[10] Since then, the sudden appearance of a second giant sinkhole, situated along the same sewer line and portending more to come, has become yet another metaphor for Guatemalans to bewail their national penchant for being overtaken by disaster. Some catastrophes seem like acts of God and others can be attributed to the United States or to drug cartels, but Guatemalans also blame each other—their *egoismo* (selfishness), *descuido* (neglect), *manías* (self-serving obsessions), and proclivity for *relajo* (sowing chaos). In the case of Guatemala City's sinkholes, too much of the storm sewer budget evidently went into the pockets of the politicians who chose the contractor.

Judging from the daily news, all fourteen million Guatemalans are at constant risk from collapsing infrastructure, corrupt officials, and out-of-control criminals. More and more have concluded not just that their country does not function very well, but that it will never function very well, not least because it is inhabited by each other, so they would prefer to leave. The national desire to escape is why the country's leading newspaper, *Prensa Libre*, covers the U.S. immigration debate in greater detail than many American newspapers do, and why Guatemalan peasants are often better informed about the latest crackdown than Americans are. The annual flow of remittances from the United States has become an anxiously tracked index of national well-being. New schemes to escape Guatemala receive prominent coverage, spark rumors, and enrich scam artists who, in exchange for hefty fees, offer foreign visas that never come through. The same day that *Prensa Libre* reported a government warning against illegal migration, its website advertised a scheme to enroll in the U.S. visa lottery.[11] In an election-year ploy, the Foreign Ministry offered up to $5,000 to repatriate the remains of any Guatemalan who died in the United States.[12]

On television news and in newspapers, migration stories vie with stories about drug trafficking, murders, and lynch mobs:

- Two days after returning from the United States, twenty-three-year-old Jafid de Jesús Taque López is assassinated while driving in the capital, with 9 mm bullets shot from another vehicle.[13]
- Twenty-seven Guatemalans are abandoned in Córdoba, Spain, by human smugglers who promised jobs in construction and cleaning. The migrants paid between $2,400 and $5,300 for the trip, and a Spanish public defender is seeking to legalize them on grounds that they were swindled.[14]
- The Mexican police find 164 illegal immigrants, most Guatemalan, inside a truck trailer that supposedly was bringing humanitarian aid to hurricane victims.[15]
- The Pacific port of Ocós has become a port of embarkation for Central Americans, Ecuadorians, and Asians, twenty-four of whom lose their lives when a boat sinks.[16]
- At a graduation of police cadets, President Oscar Berger comments that fifteen gang members deported from the United States are responsible for nine violence zones in the capital.[17]
- Over the telephone, a youth gang demands forty thousand quetzals from a woman in a peripheral neighborhood of the capital. If not, they will kill one of her children. Her husband is in the United States, and she decides not to inform him before handing over the money.[18]
- Josefa Abzún of Quezaltepeque, Chiquimula, pins her hopes on her nine-teen-year-old son who is in Mount Kisco, New York, to pay off the $6,400 debt left by his father, who died in Mount Kisco after taking to drink and being strangled. The deceased paterfamilias was an illiterate plantation laborer; the debt that he left behind is secured by his family's home, which is in danger of being lost because the debt continues to grow at 10 percent interest per month.[19]

IS THERE A HUMAN RIGHT TO THE AMERICAN DREAM?

My first visit to the Cuchumatanes was in November 1982 as a wannabe jour-nalist interviewing war refugees. The easiest place to find them was toward the eastern end of the cordillera in the Ixil Maya town of Nebaj. Speakers of Ixil Maya predominate in the three municipios of Nebaj, Chajul, and Cotzal. The Ixils of each municipio, including its market town and hinterland, speak a different but mutually intelligible dialect. Culturally, they are one of the more conservative branches of the five million or so speakers of Mayan languages in Guatemala and Mexico; their diviners still use the Mayan calendar that dates to the dawn of Mesoamerican civilization. But in 1982 they were in the middle of a war zone because thousands of Ixils had joined the largest of Guatemala's guerrilla organizations, the Guerrilla Army of the Poor. Even more of the population had been conscripted into government civil patrols, a poorly armed militia that the army was using as a human shield against ambushes.

Five years later I returned to Nebaj as an anthropologist, with the aim of writing my doctoral dissertation on whether a boom in evangelical churches was displacing the Catholic Church. As many as fifteen thousand refugees were still in the mountains evading army patrols as their sons and daughters served in small but nimble guerrilla units. But a large majority of the population was now under army control. Many of the latter were seeking haven in born-again Protestant churches, dozens of them, which collectively were now attracting more Ixils than the sixteenth-century Catholic church in the center of town. Nebaj was also starting to become a mecca for national and international agencies helping refugees get back on their feet. Thanks to the stunning photos taken by the American journalist Jean-Marie Simon (1987), Nebaj women with their fire-engine-red skirts and intricately woven blouses were becoming a symbol for the entire country. Even though other areas had suffered equally or worse, no other municipio attracted the number of projects that Nebaj did.

What I wanted to hear about was the war; what the Nebajenses wanted to hear about were aid projects and finding work in the United States. "How much does work pay in El Norte?" they asked. Did I know anyone who could give them work? Helping Guatemalans escape to the United States was not among my research objectives. I do not believe that the United States is the solution to the world's problems; I'm more of the school that the United States is the problem. But if you look at what anthropologists do for a living, mass migration should not be a surprise. We have been coming to Guatemala for the better part of a century, and most of the reasons can be summed up in one word—the Mayas. Ancient stone temples overgrown by jungle, highland peasants speaking pre-Columbian languages, folk Catholic rituals from the Middle Ages, Catholics turning into Protestants, Marxists fomenting revolution, army troops burning villages, refugees starving in the mountains, international volunteers bringing aid projects—Guatemala has been a compelling place to do anthropological research. So many Guatemalans have been willing to help us that we are obviously in their debt.

That the Nebajenses have their own agenda, differing from the agendas of myself and other foreigners who come to their country, is only logical. Anthropologists have long realized that fieldwork is a transaction that is supposed to benefit our subjects as well as ourselves. Over the last generation, the proliferation of nongovernmental organizations (NGOs) has fostered the hope that people like myself and people like the Ixils can work out a shared agenda that serves everyone. But the two sides are so unequal that it is hard to balance the exchange. When I visit Guatemala, I live modestly but spend in a month more than many Ixils earn in a year. With my U.S. passport and round-trip plane ticket, I whisk back and forth over national boundaries, whereas most of my Nebaj friends, unable to secure visas, must borrow several years of income and trek through deserts.

One way of thinking about the transactions between Guatemalans and gringos is what anthropologist Paul Sullivan calls the "unfinished conversation" or "long conversation." Sullivan applies the metaphor to the negotiations between the Bush Mayas of the Yucatán Peninsula and the Harvard archaeologist Sylvanus Morley. To excavate the Postclassic Mayan city of Chichén Itzá, Morley needed good relations with the local population. Eighty years before, the people of this vicinity won independence from the Mexican state in a bloody conflict known as the Caste War. Forced back into Mexico, but still dreaming of independence, the Bush Mayas now hoped the Harvard archaeologist would give them guns. When historian Nelson Reed arrived to interview the last leaders of the indigenous republic before they died, guess what? They still wanted guns, and this was the 1960s.

The dealings between the Mayas and the Americans were amicable but full of mutual misunderstanding and manipulation. What each side wanted was very different. What they told each other was the latest installment in a long conversation that goes back to the Spanish Conquest and that continues to this day, carried on by other people. Unlike a dialogue, which suggests working toward a common goal and eventually reaching agreement, a long conversation is not likely to end in agreement because it has no foreseeable end. It has no foreseeable end because the two sides do not want the same thing. You could call it a long argument, but because the two sides need each other, it never breaks off. The people who started the conversation die, others take their place, and the discussion goes in new directions.[20] In a strange and marvelous way, a conversation that began five hundred years ago, and that used to revolve around European power and Christianity, has evolved into a conversation about human rights. Most recently, the conversation about human rights is turning into a conversation about immigrant rights.

When you join these conversations in poor countries, you have to deal with the contrast between your own ability to cross national boundaries, legally and comfortably, and the inability of your interlocutors to do the same. It is not fair. If we give you permission to visit our country, Guatemalans ask, why don't you give us permission to visit the United States? This is a good question, for which a good answer is: I am not offering to work for their patrón for a lower wage than they do. Yet the issue is painful for anyone with friends or relatives who want to come to the United States. Hundreds of millions of people around the world dream of earning higher wages in America than they can at home. Where I live in northern New England, in the small and politically progressive state of Vermont, many of us pride ourselves on our sympathy for people trapped in poor countries. Supporting generous immigration policies goes without saying. Since few of us make our living as human traffickers, immigration lawyers, or refugee counselors, we do our bit by supporting human rights. But the more we talk about human rights, the more it becomes apparent that human rights will arrive in countries like Guatemala only slowly, if ever. Meanwhile, Guatemalans reason that they will have a better life in El Norte than they ever will in their own country. And so moving to a stable, wealthy country has become a powerful subtext in human rights. Is there a human right to the American Dream?

Human rights advocates emphasize the war as the reason that so many Guatemalans have moved to the United States, as if they had no choice but to flee for their lives. "The first wetbacks were St. Joseph, the Virgin Mary and Jesus," declared the Guatemalan archbishop, invoking the Holy Family's flight into Egypt.[21] The war is indeed one reason why the trickle of people coming north in the 1950s and 1960s turned into a much larger stream in the 1980s. Up to 1.5 million Guatemalans were displaced by the army-guerrilla conflict, especially the army's policy of massacring villages that supported the opposition. Refugees fled across the border into Mexico, and some made their way to the United States. On that basis, U.S. immigration lawyers began to argue that all their Guatemalan clients were refugees. In the view of immigrant-rights advocates, the United States has a moral obligation to admit Guatemalans because, one way or another, they are all victims of U.S. support for repression. Yet most Guatemalans arrived in the United States long after political violence abated in the mid-1980s. Nor were civil wars necessary to trigger comparable migration streams from Honduras, Ecuador, and the Dominican Republic. Are they instead economic refugees? This too is hard to sustain because most migrants are not from the poorest social strata. As a group, Guatemalan migrants are poverty-stricken in relation to their rapidly rising expectations. If that qualifies a person as an economic refugee, then the majority of the world's population qualifies too.

When U.S. authorities arrest Guatemalans for lack of papers, one of the few ways the migrants can fight deportation is to apply for political asylum with the help of a lawyer. To meet the legal standard for asylum, they must be able to document well-founded fear of individualized persecution if they return to their own country. In the 1990s and early 2000s, Guatemalan applicants usually claimed that they were being persecuted by both sides in the civil war. Unfortunately for most of these applicants, they did not leave home until long after the guerrillas vanished. In 2007 I began hearing a new version of the argument—that the petitioner was being simultaneously persecuted by youth gangs and the national police.

A Boston lawyer, through the Guatemalan Scholars Network, asked me to help her with a client who was about to be deported. Ramón was a K'iche' Maya from the mainly Ixil municipio of Cotzal; in his early thirties he entered the United States from Canada. After being arrested, he applied for political asylum. He told the lawyer that, when he was small, a column of soldiers arrived carrying large guns with bayonets. A soldier interrogated his parents, cut off their ears, forced them to eat their ears, shut them inside their house, and burned them alive. Little Ramón was taken to a Catholic orphanage in Nebaj, raised there for three years, and released at the age of twelve. In search of sustenance, he went to the Pacific Coast to work and eventually was earning promotions and raises at the well-known Pantaleón sugar mill. On his way to work, he fell afoul of a youth gang who forced him to pay protection money. One evening in 2006, he was negotiating with the gang when they were suddenly assaulted by men in a pickup truck—a police death squad engaged in "social cleansing." Ramón escaped. Now afraid of the police as well as the gang, Ramón decided that he could not be safe anywhere in Guatemala. So he made his way north to Mexico, the United States, and Canada, then back to the United States.

When the lawyer asked if I could do an affidavit vouching for Ramón, I happened to be in Nebaj. So I offered to substantiate his story if I could. A friend knew the nuns who used to run the Catholic orphanage. The orphanage was tiny, and Madre Roxana didn't remember anyone of that name. My friend was also passing through Ramón's village and ascertained that he was from a well-known family, and not one that was badly off. Then other problems occurred to me. If Ramón had been a prize employee at the Pantaleón sugar mill, owned by one of the most powerful families in the country, why didn't his supervisor vouch for him with the police? His village, San Felipe Chenlá in Cotzal, had not suffered the kind of massacre he described (although others had). Another problem consisted of the bayonets mounted on the soldiers' guns. Bayonets cannot be mounted on either of the assault rifles used by the Guatemalan army—Galils and M-16s—and they were not used by either side in the conflict.

I didn't think Ramón's story was holding up very well and told the lawyer. But bayonets had made their way into the templates used by Guatemalans applying for political asylum. In 2009 the U.S. government received 3,250 applications for political asylum from Guatemalans and approved 155 of them.[22]

DO AMERICANS HAVE A MORAL OBLIGATION TO HELP GUATEMALANS REACH THE UNITED STATES?

Except for a single Ixil woman who married a gringo, the only Nebajenses in the United States in the 1980s were ladinos, who achieved their goal through contacts in Guatemala City and Huehuetenango. When Ixils asked if I could help them get to the United States and find a job, I always said no. I wasn't a patrón and didn't want to become one. Nor did I have relatives or friends who could employ them. But in the early 1990s, a handful of Ixils made it to the United States, typically after working in Guatemala City and meeting someone who could show them how to do it. Scam artists showed up in Nebaj to swindle people hungry for passage to El Norte, but so did genuine smugglers from Huehuetenango. Men began to follow each other north; in 2002 a Belgian aid coordinator studying four villages counted 151 men who had reached the United States. By the following year, local men were going north by the thousands, mainly from Nebaj rather than Cotzal or Chajul.

Since anthropologists are obligated to the people who enable our research, should I help my collaborators migrate to the United States? Is it ethical for me to refuse their pleas for help? Would it be more ethical to help them come to the United States? The most widespread assumption among my colleagues is that it is our moral obligation to welcome Guatemalans, just as Americans have long welcomed (or at least accepted) immigrants from elsewhere. According to human rights advocates who are segueing into advocates for immigrants, the political violence of the 1980s was another chapter in a long history of colonialism that continues to the present. Like so many other Latin Americans, Guatemalans are suffering from the austerity policies of neoliberal capitalism that make it increasingly difficult for them to make a living. Thus their decision to come to the United States is a response to oppression, and any attempt to stop them by enforcing immigration laws is a violation of their human rights.

Consider the following events, which began when an anthropologist asked the U.S. embassy to give tourist visas to a Nebaj weaver and her husband. The anthropologist was impressed by Doña Marta's skillful weaving and by her suffering. Two decades earlier, the army arrested all the men in her family. They were never seen again, leaving behind only women and children. The anthropologist was also impressed by Marta's political activism in the local chapter of a national widow's organization. Actually, Marta was disappointed by the organization because it was unable to help her build a house, and she was beguiled by the idea of earning dollars. So she persuaded the anthropologist to invite her, her postwar husband, and five relatives and neighbors to the United States as a delegation to explain the suffering of their people. The U.S. embassy gave them all tourist visas.

As soon as the human rights delegation reached the United States, it dissolved into a job-hunting expedition. Marta and her husband never had any time for meeting with NGOs because they immediately went to work in a factory. Soon they were in a suburb of Washington, D.C., where hundreds of Ixils have congregated and where the best job they could find was in a Korean-owned supermarket. Here they earned five dollars an hour for twelve hours a day, every day except Sunday, without the overtime pay required by law. Still, Marta and her husband were able to send home enough money to enable their three children to finish high school. Their remittances also made it easier for them to borrow money in Nebaj. A bank accepted the receipts as proof that Marta could repay a large loan, which she spent on building the house of her dreams.

After three years in the United States, around 2004, Marta returned to Nebaj while her husband continued to toil in the Washington suburbs. Neighbors were eager to know what it was like to work in the United States, how much she had earned, and whether they could go too. So many neighbors came to

Negotiating a trip to El Norte

Marta that she decided to help by loaning them the money they would need to go north themselves. She would charge interest of only 5 percent per month—not the 10 percent that other private lenders charged. She also would set them up with a Huehueteco coyote or smuggler who would deliver them to Mexican smugglers for the rest of the journey. Over the next three years, Marta helped fifteen people go north. As a hedge against nonpayment, she and the Huehueteco usually split the Q35,000 ($4,500) investment in each client.

But for three of her clients Marta provided the entire Q35,000. Two were men whom other lenders had turned down. Even though neither was a relative or neighbor, Marta took pity on them. Once in the United States, they refused to pay her a cent. Having failed to sign a contract with either man, let alone obtain collateral, she had no recourse but to wave her investment good-bye. Worse, she had borrowed the Q70,000 from two financial institutions which now held her house and another property as collateral. Her children were angry with her, and so was her husband, who was weary of his lot in Virginia but obliged to continue. To pay off her debts to the two institutions, and to save her new house from foreclosure, Marta had no choice but to return to the United States. She wondered if her tourist visa—valid for ten years—would still work. If it didn't, she would have to borrow another Q35,000 to pay coyotes to take her through Mexico. "This time on foot," she laughed ruefully, "and just to pay off the debt."

We have yet to meet Marta's third client in arrears—her new son-in-law Humberto. Humberto met Marta's daughter in high school where they both hoped to become teachers. Unable to find teaching jobs, they agreed that Humberto should go to the United States before their first child arrived. Humberto managed to join a brother in Los Angeles but could not find work. Only after six months of unemployment did he find a steady job in a chicken-processing plant, whereupon his wife phoned from the Nebaj hospital. She was about to undergo a Caesarean delivery and thought she was going to die. Humberto was overcome with guilt and futility because he never had been able to send her any money. Then he ran into a Guatemalan friend who offered to cheer him up with pizza and beer. It was after accepting several beers that he decided to ascend to his apartment on the fifth floor—the fast way via the fire escape. He lost his grip on a railing, fell several stories, and landed on his head.

At the end of the first month in the hospital, Humberto began to come out of his coma. At the end of the second month, he was able to move the fingers of one hand and speak to his brother, but only at the level of a child. At the end of the third month, he was discharged from the hospital, still paralyzed on one side of his body, with instructions to return for an operation in a year. The reason he would need to return is that half his skull had been removed. But

Humberto's brother could not simultaneously care for his paralyzed brother and earn the money needed to pay rent. So he brought his brother home to Nebaj. Soon Humberto was back at his parents' house in an outlying village, helpless. When we met in April 2008, he was lying in bed under a big American flag tacked to the wall. He wanted to know if I could help him return to the United States for medical treatment. His family asked for donations to this end, without success. His brother returned to the United States but couldn't get his old job back; two years after the accident, he was queuing by the side of the road for day jobs.

But migration sagas have winners as well as losers. While visiting Ixil households in the suburbs of Washington, D.C., I spent an enjoyable evening with one of Marta's friends who had come north with her on the human rights delegation. After many tribulations, she and her husband obtained low-paid but steady employment with Korean grocers. They insisted on showing me a home video. It was of the three-story house back in Nebaj that their remittances had enabled them to build. In the video, holding back tears, Marta's friend conducts viewers through her home, room by room, showing off the appliances and other furnishings while thanking God and a visa-providing anthropologist for her good fortune.

On my next visit to Nebaj, while taking testimonies from a debtor's association, I was approached by an elderly couple who had heard, incorrectly, that a gringo could help them save their house from a moneylender. The couple turned out to be Humberto's parents. They spoke little Spanish and were now Q124,000 ($16,000) in debt, much of it for taking their son back and forth to neurosurgeons in Guatemala City. To actually restore Humberto's cranium, the neurosurgeons wanted another Q80,000. No philanthropy or government agency in Guatemala will pay for such cases. And so, because I was interested in his story, Humberto asked if I could provide the money.

Without the slightest hope, I took Humberto's situation to American friends who directed me to an organization in Addison, Texas, that sends medical teams to Guatemala—but not to handle problems like this. Helps International could not do brain surgery. But its next team would include a neurosurgeon. Good enough. I timed my next trip to Nebaj to coincide with the surgeon's. He took a look at Humberto's head and told us to forget about restoring his cranium. Even if he survived such a risky operation, it could worsen his headaches. Humberto would be better off buying a baseball helmet and doing physical therapy to bring back his left arm and leg. Our luck continued to hold when one of Nebaj's first university graduates returned home with certification as a physical therapist. Treatment and a batter's helmet—this I could afford. By 2010, Humberto's mobility had improved. But his parents were in debt to three financial institutions and two moneylenders for a hopeless sum, so they were losing the last of their agricultural land and their house as well.

At this very moment, I could ring up Humberto for an update, but I don't want to hear about the latest financial emergency. Instead, I will confine myself to the obvious paradox. Guatemalans and other migrants are attracted to the United States by higher wages than they can earn back home. Millions of immigrants have boosted their incomes and consumption levels by coming to the United States. But many of them end up in the most exploited tiers of American society, in work that is not only low paid but seasonal and precarious. The families of Marta and Humberto have penetrated the U.S. labor market only by putting themselves into debt. Any significant interruption in employment and remittance means that they will lose the assets back home that they have pledged as collateral. Paradoxically, migration to labor markets with higher wages can make families even poorer than when they started.

Guatemalans are not the only people in the United States afflicted by massive amounts of debt. Since the 1980s, both Republican and Democratic administrations have jump-started a sluggish economy by deregulating financial institutions. At liberty to milk the public any way they can, banks and other lenders ply American consumers with an astonishing array of schemes to enjoy now and pay later. The sociologist Howard Karger decries a "fringe economy" whose "nonrules" became politically acceptable because they were targeted against minorities, recent immigrants, and other low-income people. Nowadays, the fringe economy is no longer confined to the lower classes because it has also snared millions of heavily indebted middle-class households. They are preyed upon by credit card companies, mortgage brokers, and other seemingly respectable businesses whose double- and even triple-digit annual interest rates used to be outlawed as usury. Among the easiest prey are Latin American immigrants, including up-and-comers who bought homes with deceptive subprime mortgages. The finance industry panders to the belief that everyone can have the American Dream; it is entrenched in all three branches of the federal government as well as in most state governments. But the easy credit offered by the finance industry, Karger points out, is like an addiction that pulls users deeper into debt and strips them of any previous equity. Through credit cards, installment plans, payday loans, and myriad other devices, credit provides short-term relief and long-term entrapment.[23]

THE Q'ANJOB'AL MAYAS OF SAN MIGUEL ACATÁN AND INDIANTOWN

Casino capitalism is an apt description of the U.S. economy in the first decade of the twenty-first century.[24] If Americans have the right to boost their expenditures through financial leveraging, that is, borrowing against future earnings and the patrimony they pass to their children, don't Guatemalans have the same right? To look at the implications, let us go to the towns in Huehuetenango Department, in the western Cuchumatanes, from which Mayan peasants have been leaving for the United States since the 1970s. Huehuetenango's leading industry has become sending workers to the United States. They remitted $342 million in 2007—roughly $342 for every person in the department's population of a million. Anthropologists report astonishing levels of migration northward. In the town of Cuilco, according to Manuela Camus, the most educated members of the population leave as soon as they graduate from high school. Half the households have someone in the United States or Mexico, and 16 percent of the entire population is absent. Accompanying the increasing cash flow in Cuilco is a rise in robberies, kidnappings, threats, and assassinations, in which the victims are frequently women. In the town of Soloma, according to Stephanie Kron, households have an average of two members in the United States. In Todos Santos Cuchumatán, according to Jennifer Burrell, almost a third of the municipio's population resides in the United States.[25]

The majority of migrants from Huehuetenango are speakers of the closely related Q'anjob'al and Akatek Maya languages. Manuela Camus has identified no less than seven previously isolated towns that remittances from the United States have turned into migration hubs.[26] The town from which the Q'anjob'als and Akateks have migrated the longest is San Miguel Acatán. The Akateks were the first Mayas anywhere in Guatemala to make it to the United States as a self-perpetuating migration stream. Like other Q'anjob'als, they live in narrow mountain valleys that are unable to support a rapidly growing population. Many gave their support to the Guerrilla Army of the Poor, whose slender forces took over the area quickly at the end of the 1970s. Until this point, the Akateks had no experience with military occupation; government forces never had any reason to bother them. But in 1981–1982, the army attacked from the ground and from the air, the few actual guerrillas were driven off, their most identifiable supporters were massacred, and thousands of Akateks fled to Mexico. They were far from alone in this regard, but they were the first to keep going and make it to the United States in large numbers. The reason was not that they had suffered more than other refugees. Rather, they were migrating to Mexico before the war, on a seasonal basis for work, and even then some were getting as far as the United States.

Indiantown, Florida, was the first place where Mayan immigrants became a high-visibility population. They were brought there in 1982 by a Mexican contractor to work in citrus groves, winter-vegetable farms, and cattle ranches. So learned Allan Burns, an anthropologist at the University of Florida who helped them get organized. As more Akateks heard about

MAYAN LANGUAGE GROUPS OF WESTERN GUATEMALA

CHUJ

JAKALTEK   Q'ANJOB'AL
AKATEK

Q'EQCHI'

See Inset   IXIL

TEKTITEK   AWAKATEK   USPANTEK
SAKAPULTEK   POQOMCHI'
SIPAKAPENSE
ACHI

MAM   K'ICHE'

Lake Atitlán

KAQCHIKEL   ✷ Guatemala City
TZ'UTUJIL

VILLAGES NEAR NEBAJ

Vicalamá

Palop
Salquil Grande

Río Xacbal

Parramos Grande   Vipecbalám

Tzalbal   La Pista

Nebaj   3

Chortiz
Xexuxcap   Acul

Indiantown, some interpreted the name to mean that it had been set up for the purpose of welcoming them, like the refugee camps in Mexico. In actuality, Indiantown originated as a Seminole settlement in the swamps inland from what is now Palm Beach and the Gold Coast. As Yankee businessmen drained the swamps and created an agroindustrial empire, Indiantown became a barracks for rural proletarians. Far from feeling out of place, the Akateks found Indiantown a very recognizable environment because it was so much like the Pacific Coast of Guatemala where they had long labored.

In both places they worked on plantations; the most important difference was that the pay was a lot better. In half an hour, Akateks and other Q'anjob'als could earn as much as they earned in an entire day back home. By the end of the 1980s, there were at least four thousand Maya speakers living in Indiantown, with more in West Palm Beach. This is not to say they were doing well by American standards. Even in Florida, the demand for agricultural labor fluctuated with the seasons. Wave after wave of new arrivals saturated the labor market, leaving many to wander around Indiantown looking for work. According to Burns, the first waves of Q'anjob'als lived "in cardboard boxes or old buses and automobiles," then moved up to renting space in a "camp"—an apartment building occupied exclusively by farmworkers. Because Q'anjob'als who rented an apartment came under pressure from relatives and friends, they ended up sharing the space with several families or multiple boarders. Living quarters were hot and crowded, partitioned with sheets, and rife with communicable diseases including tuberculosis and dysentery.[27]

Black Americans, Haitians, and Mexicans perceived that the Guatemalans were stealing their jobs and reported them to the Immigration and Naturalization Service. The local Catholic priest came to the aid of the Q'anjob'als, as did Florida Rural Legal Services, the American Friends Service Committee, and the Indian Law Resource Center. "Don't sign anything; don't say anything; call the lawyer" became the watchword, as did the gambit of declining to respond in Spanish and answering only in Q'anjob'al. Eventually a handful obtained political asylum, but most applicants failed. Because Q'anjob'als had come through Mexico, spending months and years there, the United States was not their country of "first asylum." Equally damaging to their claim to be political refugees, political violence in Huehuetenango dwindled after 1983. It became even harder to prove that they were political refugees fleeing persecution when "notaries"—fellow immigrants who claimed to understand the U.S. legal system—boilerplated applications in ways that immigration judges found unconvincing. What legalized the first waves of Q'anjob'als was instead the 1986 Immigration Reform and Control Act, which included an amnesty for agricultural workers.[28]

The influx of Q'anjob'als and other Huehuetecos overwhelmed not just Indiantown but immigrant-rights advocates. As the migration stream brought up more young men, whose pastimes included the consumption of alcohol, there were robberies and murders, shifting the image of Mayas from being victims to being unpredictable. The sheer numbers "stretched the carrying capacity of the community to its limits," Burns reported. "Housing, transportation, health care, waste disposal, and the schools have all been inundated by the tremendous influx of immigrants." In the opinion of local residents and social workers, drunkenness was the number-one problem of the Q'anjob'als—an assessment with which many Q'anjob'als agreed and which led many to join born-again Protestant churches.[29]

Q'anjob'als were slow to learn English, which kept them dependent on advocates who didn't necessarily agree with each other. Underage girls producing babies were especially confounding for American social workers and lawyers. Child protection statutes must be applied not just to an underage mother but to her baby. The fifteen-year-old Magdalena Aguirre apparently consented to give her child up for adoption, but maybe not, because six months later she wanted it back again. It was hard for U.S. authorities to be sure about the wishes of such persons because of their reticence, their apparent lack of Spanish, and the conflicting claims made on their behalf.[30]

Another fifteen-year-old Q'anjob'al girl became a public figure by being charged with first-degree murder. When the journalist Paul Goepfert went to San Miguel to get the Akatek side of the story, he was told that the pseudonymous Eulalia Miguel was a rent-a-girl for an Akatek youth who was home for a visit before returning to Lake Worth, Florida. "Rent-a-girl" is a disrespectful term for what happens when the tradition of arranged marriage (by the parents) meets up with young men who return from the United States loaded with dollars. If a girl has no interest in a boy but the father is receiving payment, she is being sold. If on the other hand the girl and boy start having sex without the permission of the parents, she is being robbed—which however can be rectified with a compensatory payment. Whether it's the parents or the girl who are most attracted by the dollars, neither has much hold on a young man returning to the United States.

In Eulalia's case, she apparently completed three years of schooling before being married off, at the age of eleven or twelve, to a man twice her age. Her father is said to have arranged the marriage while he himself was on a visit home from the United States. When her new husband died unexpectedly, she apparently went to live with another man, who also was home from the United States briefly. Eulalia stayed with the second partner for only a short time, complaining that he beat her, but this is apparently who impregnated her. Soon she herself was mysteriously in the United States, at the age of fourteen and apparently via a San Miguel coyote who also had sex with her. Apparently Eulalia hoped to rejoin the father of her child, but he denied that he was the father, so she moved in with two of her brothers in a Lake Worth apartment. This is where she gave birth without assistance, producing a hemorrhage which led to the emergency room. Her dead baby was found at the apartment, in a wastebasket with a wad of tissue stuffed down its throat. Eulalia spent eighteen months in jail before sympathetic media coverage induced a judge to throw out the case and she was adopted by an American couple who put her in high school.[31]

This is not the only time that Florida authorities have been obliged to sort out many-layered conflicts between Guatemalans, of the sort that never come to public attention unless someone gets badly injured. In 2006 the *Naples Daily News* charged that a thirteen-year-old mother from San Miguel Acatán was a victim of human trafficking. According to the girl, her travails began at age eleven when her stepfather and mother sold her to Fernando Pascual for Q2,000 ($260) and Pascual forced her to move with him to the United States—or so the girl claimed after she ran away from Pascual and reached a women's shelter. When a Naples journalist visited San Miguel Acatán, the girl's mother insisted that it was "pure lies" that she had sold her daughter to Fernando Pascual. Instead, according to the mother, her then-eleven-year-old daughter fell in love with the twenty-year-old Pascual. This occurred one night when Pascual shared the girl's bed prior to driving the stepfather—a Mayan folk healer—to an early morning consultation. The girl and the youth shared candy and started tickling each other, and the girl was happy to go north with him according to her mother. Once in Florida, according to the girl, she was forced to get up at 4 a.m. to cook breakfast, was prohibited from using the telephone or leaving the apartment, and was forced to have sex with Pascual's brother in order to settle a debt between the two.

Who to believe? The *Naples Daily News* attacked the issue tabloid style, with twenty-three stories denouncing human trafficking but repeating what may have been a small number of horror stories that reached the police.[32] Were the U.S. authorities responsible for protecting illegal immigrants from each other? Or were American institutions prejudiced against the marriage practices of in-digenous Guatemalans? Was racism giving rise to an unjustified moral panic? Worst cases, it is important to remember, are not a reliable guide to all the im-migrants who never make the headlines because they are too busy working long hours for low pay. In this respect, low-wage immigrants who remit faithfully to their families are exemplars of family values. But what migration northward does to youth is also a vexed subject in Guatemala.

On my own visit to San Miguel Acatán in 2007, I lost count of the ridges up which my bus toiled. Valleys are so narrow that there is little or no bottom, just a defile, with even the steepest hillsides planted in maize. Even by Guatemalan standards, San Miguel is not just remote but crowded and conflicted. There were no national police and no district judge at the time of my visit. They withdrew after a mob seized an accused robber from the police and lynched him. Yet remittances are transforming San Miguel as they are other Cuchumatanes towns. When the place comes into view, garish mansions and cement highrises tower over the traditional adobe houses and red-tile roofs. On arrival I headed for a six-story hotel in the hope of meeting the owner. Inside it was still a construction site, and not one headed for a successful conclusion: just getting up the stairs required negotiating concrete head bangers, rebar sticking out at odd angles, and a loose banister. After dark the hotel echoed with a cacophony of drinking parties, televisions, and boom boxes. Out on the street, two drunks fought until an older man strode up and bawled them out; they slinked away. The next day I saw young idlers slumping around town in baggy shorts—the *cholo* look from Los Angeles. I also saw many more youth who, affecting the same style, were working up a sweat in gainful employment.

The Eulalia Miguel scandal cast an unwelcome spotlight on San Miguel's relationship with the United States, and I was not the first gringo to arrive with questions. Isn't a boy supposed to get permission from the parents of the girl? I asked mayor-elect Andrés Miguel Francisco. He laughed. "What's most common, he talks to her, she goes with him, and it's a robbery [of the girl from her parents]. Ninety percent are like that. He just takes advantage of the girl and doesn't take her as his wife. She allows herself to be carried away, for ambition." For the money? I asked. "Because she wants to go to the United States. They go together to La Mesilla [on the Mexican border]. He gets across; she doesn't and returns here two or three days later." Because she was arrested? I ask. The mayor laughed again. "Because the man deceived her, took advantage of her, and left her. El Norte is a way to deceive people."

"Twenty years ago it was like that; a boy and his parents would have to ask for the girl from her parents," a schoolteacher told me. "But not anymore. This ended with the arrival of new forms of communication; it became easy to telephone the United States. This is when parents lost control. Pornographic movies, television, and chaotic music arrived. Young men returned from El Norte with money and promised the girls that they would take them north, as their wives. And the girls believed them. In some cases the men fulfilled their promise. In other cases the girl got only as far as La Mesilla and died there, or returned here." Now families are more aware of the dangers, he added, but abandoned children are a problem. Just three months ago a fellow schoolteacher found three children in his doorway—an infant and two toddlers who were not old enough to talk. They were crying and he took them into his house assuming that the parents would appear. No one ever showed up, and now he was taking care of them—after making a declaration to a judge so that he could not be accused of kidnapping.

The parish priest is a native speaker of the closely related Jakaltek Maya language. "In the church, we tell people to stay, but there's not much here to offer them," Padre Dionisio Mateo said resignedly. "Land doesn't suffice anymore. Here there are just steep slopes." Padre Dionisio identified three stages of migration. Some families left for the United States as early as 1970 and never came back. The next wave left because of the violence. "The people in the center of town were relatively educated, and when the violence came, it emptied out; this was a phantom town," he explained. "The army was machine-gunning the hillsides with helicopters, there were many deaths, and these people never came back. Some went to Mexico and then the United States, some just went to Mexico where their refugee camps are now neighborhoods. They're Mexicans now. [Back here] the army gave their land to people who thought like the army, and they have never returned. Sometimes they show up for fiestas, and their kids don't know the language. They don't like the food. It's all strange to them. They're Americans, and they're [physically] large because of American food. The third wave [to leave San Miguel] have been economic migrants. The majority are successful; they achieve something but not much. The minority fail. The reason they come back is that they're not accomplishing much."

Juan Francisco leads an organization that promotes the Akatek Maya language. His friends were finishing their secondary education (the local equivalent of a college degree) and then immediately going north. It was not easy to find work, but some were doing well, to the point of having the time and money to go to the beach and discothèques. Those who were exerting themselves were, within two or three years, building a nice house for their families here in San Miguel. Others were finding another woman and abandoning their San Miguel families. Still others were coming back as addicts, often after being deported. One returnee was drinking pure alcohol. His stomach was out to here and his family was begging him to stop, but he wouldn't listen. Soon he would be dead. Another was sniffing glue. Soon he would be mentally impaired. Unable to stay in the United States and unwilling to work for local wages, such men were unable to figure out any other way to deal with their situation.

Yet at every turn I heard stories of accomplishment in El Norte. "As far as I'm concerned, the United States was a good deal," acknowledged a woman who had just filled my ears with tales of woe. "It treated me well. I didn't suffer from discrimination." She showed me her three-story house, with enough glass on the upper level to be an attractive place to live. Another returnee, the owner of the simple but comfortable pensión where I ended up staying, told me that he spent twenty-four years in the United States as an agricultural laborer from 1978 to 2002. During that quarter century, he came home just three times. Of his seven children, six were in the United States. Two sons were in California, one legally, and between them they had eight Californian children. His four daughters were in Fort Payne, Alabama, and although just one was legal, they were making $300 to $400 per week in a chicken-processing plant and a textile factory. As for mayor-elect Andrés Miguel Francisco with his grim diagnosis of El Norte, twelve members of his immediate family were there; only three remained with him in San Miguel. A quarter of the town's population had gone north, he estimated.

San Miguel may not be a good prediction of what migration to the United States will mean for other Mayan towns such as Nebaj, the town on which we will focus in the next chapter. Thanks to the 1986 Immigration Reform and Control Act, many of the first Akateks won legal status in a way that subsequent arrivals have been unable to. But San Miguel does suggest the siphon-like qualities of migration. Guatemalans typically go north with the idea of working for a certain number of years and returning with enough savings to build a house and start a business. This is what they tell themselves and their families, making them "target earners" in the language of migration scholarship. Then sundry forces conspire to keep them in the United States. Border enforcement makes it more expensive and risky to go home for visits. Once Guatemalans have experienced U.S. wages, it is very difficult to return to the meager purchasing power of Guatemalan wages. Then there are the second families that more than a few Guatemalan men establish in El Norte. As Guatemalans consolidate new lives in the United States, they send fewer remittances, putting their parents and siblings under pressure to send reinforcements. The tremendous contrast in pay pulls a steady stream of new migrants.[33]

Chapter Two

A Town of Many Projects

May God open the spigots of international aid!

—Evangelist at a rally in the Nebaj plaza, 1995

The evangelist who made this prayer did not do so alone, and it was answered in abundance. Nebajenses who were born before the 1980s remember a much smaller and quieter town than the booming commercial center of today. Few buildings were more than one story, and nearly all were built out of adobe and roofed with red tile. There were so few motor vehicles that they and their owners were easy to enumerate. The largest structure in town was the Catholic Church looming over the plaza, and it had been that way since the sixteenth century. Older Nebajenses remember lives that were timed by the Catholic ritual calendar, the growing season for maize, and the annual journey, crammed into the back of a truck, to a lower and warmer elevation to pick coffee for a dollar or two per day. Most Ixil Mayas and their K'iche' Maya neighbors (about 10 percent of the population) lived in dispersed farmsteads next to where they grew their maize, kept their animals, and gathered firewood. There always seemed to be more land available for farming, even if it was on steep slopes or over the mountains to the north.

Actually there were profound changes afoot, but for the most part these were gradual and quiet. This is why Nebajenses date the sudden transformation of their affairs to the arrival of guerrillas and soldiers at the end of the 1970s. When I visited for the first time in November 1982, the town was quiet and scared because it was occupied by the Guatemalan army. Everyone had to be off the streets by dark. One morning I joined a long line of peasants, guarded by soldiers and civil patrollers, who made their way out of town to the destroyed village of Rio Azul to harvest maize from the hillsides before

29

the guerrillas did. A man whom the army had chosen to lead its civilian militia, and who was ordered to butcher suspected subversives in their houses,
moaned quietly to me: "*estamos en medio*" (we're in between). At the town's
airstrip, I interviewed refugees guarded by soldiers; their leader was an evangelical pastor who told me how the guerrillas had killed four of his people.
Then he told me how, on another occasion, the army killed twenty-two more.

Five years later, on my next visit, the army was in firm control of the town,
the war had receded, and the population was breathing more easily. But the
army was still bombarding guerrilla-controlled refugees in the mountains to
the northeast and launching operations to capture them. Knots of refugees
sometimes arrived in the town square, guarded by soldiers on their way to a
relocation camp. Usually Nebajenses seemed more than happy to tell me their
experiences. Often I was the first foreigner to ask. But they wanted something, too—what they at first called *ayudas* (help) and soon learned to call
proyectos (projects). When I arrived in an army-controlled resettlement, the
first question was typically, *de que institución es?* (What is your institution?).
Soon I would be asked, *cuanto se gana en los Estados Unidos?* (How much
can be made in the United States?) Could I get them a job there?

By the early 2000s, Ixil country appeared to be completely recovered.
Signs of destruction were replaced by more and better houses, handsome
public buildings, and asphalt roads. A peace agreement was signed in 1996,
the guerrillas demobilized, the army garrison dwindled to a platoon, and
Nebaj's economy boomed. Thanks to the many aid projects, Ixils and their
K'iche' neighbors replaced their livestock lost in the war. They were growing a more diversified repertoire of agricultural products. Some banged out
textiles on big wooden shuttle looms. Ixils became the majority of the local
teaching profession, most children started primary school (although many
didn't finish), and thousands reached secondary school for the first time. Ixils were in charge of the town hall, the churches, and most aid projects. The
streets were filled with motor traffic and Ixil women with their spectacular
blouses and skirts, some of them in high heels and gabbing on cell phones.
A delegate from the European Union visited Nebaj for the first time, saw all
the new multistory houses going up, and exclaimed, "This has got to be the
drug trade!"

No, it is not the result of the drug trade. The road into Ixil country is an
engineering achievement but a geographical cul-de-sac, so drug traffickers go
elsewhere. The prosperity on display is first of all the result of international
projects, especially from the European Union, in an aid bonanza that began
in the 1980s and shows no sign of ending. The justification for the parade of
new programs is that most of Nebaj's population was displaced by the war.
True, but equally devastated municipios have never been deluged with proj-

ects like this one. What makes the Nebajenses such a magnet for international donors? Well, they live in a majestic mountain valley, they have inherited the faces of the Classic Maya, and they have a knack for ingratiating themselves with foreigners. And so the Ixils have become calendar Mayas in two senses. Their diviners still use the Mayan calendar, and the splendor of their traditional female dress has become symbolic capital for aid organizations. You can't spend a day without meeting an international volunteer, and you can't walk more than a few blocks without passing aid projects and Pentecostal churches. The meek have yet to inherit the earth, but it is pretty clear who has inherited Nebaj.

GUERRILLAS, SOLDIERS, AND MEN OF GOD

A magnet for aid projects run by born-again Christians is not what the Guerrilla Army of the Poor (EGP) had in mind when it embarked on the liberation of Ixil country. In the 1520s the Ixils lived in small, independent chiefdoms when they were conquered by Spanish conquistadores and their indigenous Mexica allies. Contact epidemics devastated the Cordillera of the Cuchumatanes, reducing the human population by something like 90 percent. For the next four hundred years, the survivors and their descendants were a periphery of little interest to outsiders except the Catholic Church. Then, at the end of the 1800s, a coffee-growing boom in Alta Verapaz Department to the east showed that profits could be made in Ixil country, or at least in its lower and warmer valleys. Ambitious men from Mexico, Italy, Spain, and other parts of Guatemala made their way to the three Ixil towns. Some of the newcomers were sufficiently literate and persuasive to win appointment as the municipal secretaries who presided over land records. Practically no one else could read or write. By the 1920s, the outsiders—sometimes referred to as *españoles* (Spaniards) but more often as ladinos, the most common term for nonindigenous Guatemalans—steered the town halls of Nebaj, Cotzal, and Chajul thanks to their dexterity in plying Ixil leaders with alcohol, loaning them money, and overawing them with legal knowledge. They also controlled the best land for growing coffee in the three municipios and were treating Ixils like peons.[1]

The plantation era in Ixil country could have come to a close with the land reform of President Jacobo Arbenz (1951–1954). Under the new legislation, agrarian committees of Ixils petitioned to break up the two largest coffee plantations in Ixil country, the Finca La Perla in Chajul and the Finca San Francisco in Cotzal. Then the U.S. Central Intelligence Agency organized right-wing exiles to overthrow President Arbenz. The new regime reversed his reforms, and the Ixil agrarian committees were carted off to jail. And so finca owners continued to dominate the three Ixil towns. The best arable land remained in the hands of outsiders, and the amount of land per capita shrank because of population growth. In earlier eras Ixils and other indigenous peasants had been drafted into plantation labor; now physical coercion was unnecessary. So many Ixils were running out of maize before the next harvest that they had no choice but to sign up with labor contractors.

In the hot lowlands of the Pacific Coast, labor unions led a massive strike of Ixils and other seasonal plantation workers in 1978. But Ixils spent most of the year in their highland villages, and that is where the guerrillas hoped they could become a logistical base for national liberation. The first Guatemalan guerrillas were led by urban intellectuals and dissident army officers frozen out of the electoral arena by the 1954 counterrevolution. Following several debacles, some of the survivors began calling themselves the Guerrilla Army of the Poor. When its first nucleus of twelve fighters crossed the Mexican border into Quiché Department in 1972, four of the men were of indigenous birth, but the leaders were all ladinos.

The EGP was attracted to the Ixils for several reasons: their deep poverty, their steep terrain, and their social isolation. The mile-high escarpment of the Cuchumatanes, breached by only a single primitive road, walled them off from the rest of the country. Rivers drained north to rainforests and Mexico, which would provide sanctuary. The population of the three Ixil municipios was 90 percent indigenous. It was also disconnected from the national society except by seasonal labor migration, which was brutal, and the Catholic Church, whose clergy in those parts were Spanish. The EGP's founders knew that a secret coterie of Ixils from Cotzal had asked an earlier guerrilla group to support them against the Finca San Francisco, the coffee plantation that controlled the municipio's most profitable land. Recently a Cotzaleño told me how his older brother, father, and uncles welcomed guerrilla leaders and trained for war in a festive atmosphere, without worrying about being betrayed by neighbors. Except for a few military police guarding the Finca San Francisco, the military dictatorship had overlooked Ixil country to this point.

The EGP's commander in chief was the son of an army colonel and a friend of Che Guevara, the Argentine guerrilla who helped Fidel Castro come to power in Cuba and who tried to spread revolution before being killed in 1967. The EGP was supported by Cuba but also hoped to emulate North Vietnam's victory over the U.S. army. Its cadres did not find it easy to explain the Cuban and Vietnamese revolutions to Ixil peasants. To illustrate what the new society would be like, cadres promised equality with ladinos, in which Ixils would be able to ride in cars and airplanes for the first time. They also promised to recover land from ladino plantation owners and stop the abuses of ladino labor contractors.

After the guerrillas were defeated, in my interviews with Ixils in the late 1980s, many acknowledged that they had been awed by the Guerrilla Army of the Poor. They also said that, as the implications of its strategy became apparent, EGP organizers turned coercive. The group's first step was to groom a clandestine network of supporters. Next, fleshed out with students from the capital, an armed column would seize a town or village on market day, proclaim the revolution, and promise victory. The armed column would melt back into the mountains, and the EGP's local clandestine committee would surface in order to assert authority. If village elders resisted, they would be accused of being "ears" for the army and killed. Some Ixils grasped the revolution as a new form of social organization and became dedicated militants, but many were fence-sitters who were soon interpreting the movement in terms of village rivalries. Until the arrival of guerrillas and soldiers, such disagreements had rarely led to homicide. Now there were reciprocal denunciations to the two armed groups, whose assassins could swoop down at any moment.

The army was ill informed and brutal in its response. I lost count of the number of survivors who told me that soldiers killed their father, brother, or uncle because he happened to be in the vicinity when the guerrillas staged a hit-and-run attack. The army's execution of alleged subversives expanded to village massacres in which soldiers slaughtered anyone they could find, including women and children. Soldiers also burned the houses and crops of suspects. With the aim of denying food to the enemy, they applied this policy to the entire rural settlement pattern. The army's violence was so indiscriminate that it seemed to confirm the EGP's claim to represent the population. There is no question that, between 1980 and 1982, support for the guerrillas grew dramatically. But the army never lost control of the three municipal seats. In January 1982, it began conscripting the men under its control into *patrullas civiles* or civil patrols. Anyone remotely of military age was obliged to join; anyone who refused was, by definition, a guerrilla sympathizer, which was tantamount to a death sentence.

Directed by army officers, the civil patrols pressured the majority of Nebajenses to conform to the side that had more force at its disposal. A scorched-earth policy meant repeated offensives against EGP-controlled refugees struggling to plant crops. Burned out of their farmsteads and hiding in the surrounding heights, they could starve to death or they could surrender. If they surrendered, the army forced them to join the civil patrols. The civil patrols were also the only way that people could return to farming their land. Instead of scattering across the landscape next to their fields as they had before, households were required to live together in nucleated settlements. These were the model villages, guarded by constant rotations of civil patrollers to cut off further contact with the EGP. And so Ixil life was refashioned on the army's terms.

Putting a moral face on counterinsurgency was the first Protestant dictator in Latin America—a novelty predicted by no one. Efraín Ríos Montt (1926–) comes from a family of ladino patróns among the Awakatek Mayas who border Ixil country. He worked his way up in the army, from private to minister of defense, and won the 1974 presidential election. Unfortunately, he was running as a reform candidate with the Christian Democrats. His army superiors did not appreciate his maverick streak and imposed their own man as the next president. Ríos Montt was disgraced by his failure to protest. He retired from politics as well as the army, became an evangelical Protestant, and joined an upper-class Pentecostal church.

In March 1982 another questionable presidential election sparked a revolt by junior army officers. Suddenly Ríos Montt was back in uniform and in charge of the new regime, probably by careful planning. Over the airwaves, he informed Guatemalans that God had placed him in charge of saving them from communism. He invoked the wrath of Jehovah and the forgiveness of Jesus, vowed to end government corruption, offered the guerrillas amnesty, and expanded the civil patrols. The previous army regime had become so violent and unpredictable that, in comparison, his manic but amiable expositions reassured some Guatemalans. He lasted only a year and a half in the presidential palace before his many opponents in the officer corps staged another successful coup. But he went on to become extremely popular with voters. Oddly, he was most successful with indigenous voters, against whom human rights groups were now charging he had committed genocide.

To understand this paradox, let us return briefly to 1982, the most devastating year in Ixil history since the Spanish Conquest. Four months after Ríos Montt took power, evangelical missionaries persuaded him to replace a homicidal commander with a personable major who turned Nebaj into a showcase for the army's pacification program. This is why many Nebajenses credit Ríos Montt with restoring peace, at least to them. On the national level, human rights groups accuse him of presiding over an increase in army killing.[2] Certainly there was enough killing to send the guerrilla movement into steep decline. But Ríos Montt's mix of force and persuasion was effective owing to his evangelical reinterpretation of the Latin American tradition of the *caudillo*, the military hero who saves the nation. His rhetoric turned the army–guerrilla confrontation into a showdown between two different conceptions of Christianity: evangelical Protestantism and liberation theology.

The Ixils have been Roman Catholics since the 1560s when Dominican friars supervised the construction of a large parish church at the center of each of the three municipal seats. After Guatemala separated from Spain, resident clergy became scarce. Like other Mesoamericans, the Ixils accepted Spanish practices—especially the institution of *cofradías* or saint societies—but turned them into a Catholic face on their own traditions. Images of Catholic saints, paraded through the streets for religious festivals, took on the attributes of pre-Columbian deities. In the 1950s, Spanish missionaries from the Sacred Heart order took charge of the three Ixil parishes. They were horrified by customs that struck them as idolatrous and decided to train local men as catechists. Also arriving were North American Protestant missionaries who, for the first several decades, had little to show for their efforts. When the war reached Ixil country at the end of the 1970s, there were only a handful of Protestant congregations.

By this time, a small but influential fraction of the Catholic clergy had secretly joined the guerrilla movement. In southern Quiché Department, Jesuits from Spain played an important role in starting the Committee for Campesino Unity (CUC). CUC was led by Catholic catechists. Although not active in Ixil country, it organized an impressive network in several departments for the Guerrilla Army of the Poor. Certain parish priests also collaborated with the EGP before the army forced them to flee. One may have been Javier Gurriarán, the cantankerous but charismatic Spaniard who ran the Nebaj parish in the 1970s. Judging from how Nebajenses debate his role, Padre Javier never told his parishioners to support the guerrillas. But a woman running his house-building program, Yolanda Colom, turned out to be an EGP organizer. Javier was visiting Spain in 1980 when the army assassinated three other parish priests and the bishop protested by closing the Quiché diocese. Soon Javier resurfaced in Sandinista Nicaragua as a founder of the EGP-aligned Guatemalan Church in Exile.

Liberation theology holds that the church's duty is to build God's kingdom in this world rather than the next. Not everyone in the Catholic clergy supported it; exponents tended to be European rather than Guatemalan, and conservative priests viewed it as a front for guerrilla groups. Nor did all liberation theologians support revolutionary violence. But such distinctions were lost on the Guatemalan army, and so it hunted down Catholic catechists, some of whom were involved with the guerrillas and some of whom were not. Evangelicals also died in the army's reactions, including four brothers of Pablo Ceto, a Methodist scholarship student who became the highest-ranking Ixil in the EGP. But the army never targeted evangelical churches the way it did the Catholic Church. Most evangelical leaders claimed to be neutral, which they defined to include submitting to the stronger side. Not coincidentally, evangelical missionaries were the first providers of humanitarian assistance to army-controlled refugees in 1982. With evangelical pastors pointedly refraining from criticizing the army, their churches came to seem like refuges from army suspicion.

Evangelical churches have proliferated everywhere in Guatemala, not just in war zones, so in Ixil country the violence probably only accelerated the inevitable. Of twenty-two evangelical pastors whom I interviewed in 1988–1989, ten were former catechists who began their pastoral careers in the Catholic Church.[3] The popularity of evangelical religion is due to its leadership structure (open to anyone who can preach) and tuneful worship style (which Catholic charismatics now imitate with great success), but also to the demands it makes on personal conduct. Women appreciate the ban on alcohol, which helps men be more responsive to the needs of their wives and children. Among indigenous populations such as the Ixils, evangelical congregations enable members to escape the cost of communal religious obligations while affirming ethnic bonds, if only by using their own language in services.[4]

When I returned to Nebaj for doctoral research in 1987, everyone seemed to want the belligerents to go away. Survivors of the army's pacification process had no interest in rejoining the guerrillas, whose failure to protect their supporters had discredited them. Ixils blamed the EGP for deceiving them, but they had little good to say about the army either. Even Ixils whom the army and the guerrillas had selected as leaders saw no point in continuing the war. The army's civil patrollers resented all the unpaid duty into which they had been drafted. On the EGP's side, its Communities of Population in Resistance—the refugees who continued to hold out in the mountains north of Chajul—were also restive.[5] But war weariness made no impression on the two command structures. For guerrilla commanders whose popular support had vanished, the only way they could claim to represent the Guatemalan people was to continue armed struggle. For army commanders who no longer regarded the guerrillas as a serious threat, the only way they could justify their veto over the country's elected civilian government was to continue the war. This is why, even after the European Union, the United States, the United Nations, and Guatemalan public opinion pressured the army and the guerrillas into negotiations, they dragged on for five years. Only in 1996 did the guerrillas agree to demobilize in return for a smaller army, a range of reforms including equality for Mayan culture, and a truth commission.

By this time, the EGP had merged with three other, even smaller guerrilla organizations to form the Guatemalan National Revolutionary Union (URNG). The URNG and its supporters hoped to build a new left that could take power through the ballot box. Given an earlier chapter in Guatemala's democratic transition—the 1985 victory of the center-left Christian Democrats—the idea of winning a national election was not far-fetched. The majority of Guatemalans have good reason to vote against the current social order. In neighboring El Salvador, the demobilized Farabundi Marti National Liberation Front became the second largest political party and finally won a national election in 2009. In Guatemala, the URNG's supporters hoped that, by recovering "historical memory" of the army's massacres, they could put the perpetrators on trial and attract voters. Truth commissions and exhumation teams documented the army's crimes; human rights lawyers launched genocide indictments in the courts of Guatemala and Spain. But focusing on the army's crimes did not play particularly well with the electorate. While many older Guatemalans had horrible memories of the army, their memories of the guerrillas were not much better. The URNG and other left-wing parties fizzled in the four elections from 1999 to 2011, to the point of almost disappearing from the Guatemalan congress.

In war-ravaged towns such as Nebaj, the peace process was inherited not by the left but by ubiquitous evangelical churches. Jailey Philpot-Munson, an anthropologist who looked at how Nebaj evangelicals interpreted the peace process, found that they distrusted human rights activists.

> Evangelicals' fear of the power of the past, the accumulated force of old resentments, contributes to their suspicion and criticism of national and international human rights organizations in Nebaj. Rather than viewing "human rights" as a non-partisan force with humanitarian goals, evangelicals in Nebaj tend to classify the international human rights movement as ideologically leftist, sometimes going so far as to call it a "tool of the guerrillas" to deceive the Ixils into fighting the army again.

But evangelicals had their own version of the peace process, Philpot-Munson argued.

> All in all, evangelical Nebajenses prefer to leave the difficult task of punishing those responsible for mass death to a God they trust will do the right thing. . . . Evangelical resistance to the internationally recognized peace process does not translate into resistance against the idea of peace itself. Instead . . . evangelicals in Nebaj are re-signifying the concept of "peace" in order to make it fit their subjective experience of the conflict, choosing a "Prince of Peace" over the Peace Accords as the medium of conflict resolution. That is to say, although the dominant discourse of the pro-peace movement demands remembering the past—justice for war crimes, exhumation of mass graves, teaching schoolchildren about the war, etc.—evangelicals espouse forgetting. They wish to neither remember nor relive the past. They maintain that it is not worth the risk to their emotional well-being or the well-being of their community.[6]

The dimensions of evangelical hegemony in Nebaj are outlined in a dissertation for the Jesuit-affiliated university in Guatemala City. In the municipal seat, not including all the outlying villages, Ixil researcher Miguel De Leon Ceto counted thirty-three congregations belonging to twenty-six different denominations.[7] By 2012, the local pastors' association had a list of forty-six congregations belonging to twenty-nine denominations (see my own count in table 2.1). Typically a congregation is started by a man who is formed as a leader in another evangelical congregation and then decides that the Lord is calling him to start a church led by himself. He takes his family and friends with him. Soon the little band is affiliated with one of Guatemala's several hundred Protestant denominations. Except for the Methodists, all the denominations in Nebaj are Pentecostal in orientation or close to it. There are also three evangelical radio stations including Radio Ixil, whose Ixil-language programming dominates local airwaves, and three large evangelical *colegios* or secondary schools. Based on the estimates of Catholic and Protestant observers, De Leon suggests that as much as 60 percent of the Nebaj population identifies itself as evangelical.[8] In 2006 all three mayors of the Ixil towns were evangelicals associated with Ríos Montt's political party. The governor of the department was also an evangelical from Nebaj. Of the ten most influential families in town—six Ixil, three ladino, and one K'iche—only one was still predominantly Catholic.

Critics of evangelical churches attribute their rapid growth to financial support from North American missions. It is true that there are usually one or two U.S. missionaries in Nebaj, but none run churches. Two evangelical organizations provide material aid: one is the Agros Foundation, which has bought a number of ladino-owned properties and turned them into model farming settlements. The other is Food for the Hungry, which helps families improve their food production and nutrition. These are well-funded operations; doubtless they have played a role in the Protestantization of Nebaj and the two other Ixil municipios. But the flow of Protestant donations does not necessarily exceed the flow of Catholic donations: well-off dioceses in Europe have provided the three Ixil parishes with considerable support over the years. Moreover, the leadership role played by evangelicals has spilled beyond church boundaries; they seem to run the majority of nonchurch aid projects. As my colleague Tracy Ehlers remarked of another department in the western highlands, "Evangelicals are now everywhere, at least in San Marcos. And they are us! Everyone I work with, all the professionals, academics, et cetera, are evangelicals."[9]

THE IXIL MAYAS BECOME A
MAGNET FOR INTERNATIONAL AID

When Ixils puzzle over why their homeland became a war zone, and what good this might serve, they console themselves with the fact that, without the guerrillas, they might never have acquired the roads, schools, and other aid projects that began to arrive in the 1980s—first with the army's counterin-

Table 2.1. Evangelical Protestant Denominations in the Town of Nebaj, 2012

Denomination	Date of Formation in Nebaj
1. Iglesia Metodista	1920s
2. Iglesia de Dios Evangelio Completo	1950s
3. Iglesia Asamblea de Dios	1977
4. Iglesia Evangélica Príncipe de Paz	1979
5. Iglesia Dios Viviente	1981
6. Iglesia Evangélica Monte Basán	1981
7. Iglesia Bethania	1982
8. Iglesia El Nazareno	Mid-1980s
9. Iglesia Evangélica Manantial de Vida Eterna	1985
10. Iglesia Evangélica Pentecostés Jehová Justicia Nuestra	1986
11. Iglesia Evangélica Emmanuel	1988
12. Iglesia Evangélica La Voz de Dios	1988
13. Iglesia Evangélica Asambleas Pentecostés	Since early 1990s
14. Iglesia Evangélica Camino Nuevo	Since early 1990s
15. Iglesia Evangélica del Cuerpo de Cristo	Since early 1990s
16. Iglesia Evangélica Elim	Since early 1990s
17. Iglesia Evangélica Elim Iglesia de Cristo	Since early 1990s
18. Iglesia Misión Evangélica El Poder del Espiritu Santo Clinicas de Milagros	Since early 1990s
19. Iglesia Evangélica Familia de Dios	Since early 1990s
20. Iglesia Evangélica Filadelfia	Since early 1990s
21. Iglesia Evangélica Jesús Sana El Verbo	Since early 1990s
22. Iglesia Evangélica La Unidad del Espíritu Santo	Since early 1990s
23. Iglesia Evangélica Lluvias de Gracia	Since early 1990s
24. Iglesia Evangélica Maranatha	Since early 1990s
25. Iglesia Evangélica Movimiento Internacional	Since early 1990s
26. Iglesia Evangélica Nueva Jerusalén	Since early 1990s
27. Iglesia Evangélica Palabra en Acción	Since early 1990s
28. Iglesia Evangélica Palestina	Since early 1990s
29. Iglesia Evangélica Pentecostés Misión Pan de Vida	Since early 1990s
30. Iglesia Evangélica Resurrección	Since early 1990s
31. Iglesia Evangélica Misión Shadai	Since early 1990s
32. Iglesia Evangélica Vida Cristiana	Since early 1990s
33. Iglesia Evangélica Viviente	Since early 1990s

Sources: Stoll 1993: 180–81; De Leon Ceto 2006: 45–46; and unpublished list from the Asociación de Pastores "Holam," Nebaj.

surgency campaigns, and then with an internationally funded peace process. Until the war, the main instigator of development projects in Nebaj was the Catholic Church and its parish priest, Javier Gurriarán. The first groups to provide aid to refugees, only months after the height of the killing in 1982, were evangelical missionaries with connections to Efraín Ríos Montt. The

Catholic Church also provided considerable aid to refugees as soon as its clergy were able to return. Through the U.S. Agency for International Development, the U.S. embassy provided food rations and tin roofing for the army's model villages. The army reasoned that modernization would dissuade Ixils from any lingering impulses to revolt, so it promoted the model villages as "development poles" that would be equipped with potable water, health posts, schools, and electrification.

My first book about Nebaj, published in 1993, focused on Ixil weariness with a war that neither the army nor the guerrillas were very interested in ending. To argue that Ixils were making peace on their own, I borrowed the concept of civil society from political science and described how Ixils were organizing in different ways to regain control of their lives. The appearance of new evangelical churches, the reemergence of the Catholic Church, civil patrol dissidence against the army, and refugee dissidence against the guerrillas were all examples of Ixil civil society reasserting itself against the demands of army officers and guerrilla commanders. Meanwhile, the war was speeding the withdrawal of ladinos from their dominant position in commerce and town government. Thanks to Ixil gains in the town hall, in local commerce, and in the schoolteaching profession, the ethnic majority in Nebaj could be said to control its own affairs for the first time in a century—despite the war and because of it.

I was not alone in placing my hopes in civil society. In the 1990s this became a buzzword in transitions from dictatorship to democracy all over the world. The disintegration of the Soviet Bloc, the collapse of apartheid in South Africa, military rulers heading for the exits—all provided opportunities for a wide range of civil society to enlist in the cause of democracy and human rights. Civil society, to be precise, refers to voluntary social organizations that occupy the space between the family and the state. It is a realm of choice that exists under many (although not all) dictatorships, and it certainly existed in army-controlled Nebaj, in its burgeoning churches and associations for every conceivable purpose. Such organizations were to serve as schools of democracy. Where nothing seemed to work very well—certainly not capitalism or Marxist social revolution—promoting civil society and defending human rights would be an incremental path to a more inclusive and prosperous society.

In the case of Ixil country, it was shunned by nonchurch aid organizations until the late 1980s. The guerrillas were known to have enlisted many Ixils; aid organizations did not want to be complicit in the suppression of a popular insurgency. But large-scale killing ended in 1983, the army proved to have firm control of most of the population, and the arrival of new projects became an avalanche. The internationalist vision for Nebaj and Guatemala combined the binaries of the revolutionary vision—indígenas versus ladinos, poor versus rich, army versus people—with a romantic view of the Mayan communal past and considerable optimism over what the next aid contract could accomplish. Some of the consultants who interpreted Nebaj in these terms had been solidarity activists in the guerrilla movement. Others arrived full of hope for the rather different Maya movement that seemed to be popping up everywhere. Such foreigners wanted to be in solidarity with the poor; the indigenous community was central to their projections, as were their assumptions about Mayan wisdom, harmony between genders, respect for nature, and consensual decision making.[10] The foreigners hoped that, with the help of aid projects, the Nebajenses would recover their vocation as a revolutionary vanguard, or at least become more conscious of their Mayan identity, and help the Guatemalan left win elections.

The thinking behind these projects, I now realize, was based on a pendulum swing between two propositions. The first is that the Ixils and other Mayas have inherited a culture that goes back thousands of years and that will serve them better than rushing headlong into modernity. The second is that they need the help of foreigners and their aid projects to avoid losing their culture.[11] The enchantment of many foreigners with the Mayas has made it easy to juggle the two propositions, with army violence or neoliberal capitalism serving as a convenient explanation for any aspect of Mayan life that fails

A village project

to meet expectations. Prior to all the bloodshed, what attracted foreigners to the western highlands were its archaic Mayan Indian towns. The drama of revolution and human rights became the next attraction. In my own case, I've taken cognitive sanctuary in Nebaj as an escape from the apparent hopelessness of Guatemalan politics on the national level. Because of the physical isolation of the town and its indigenous character, there is a sense of apartness in Nebaj, in the relative self-sufficiency of peasant life, in the town's tradition of self-governance and its distance from the bickering of Guatemalan elites. The crime rate is far lower than in the capital, and most Nebajenses I meet are welcoming.

Since the 1970s, ladinos have lost power, and Ixils have become accustomed to running their own affairs. Even if they sometimes ruin their own affairs, the town and its ninety-odd villages and hamlets are a better place than they used to be. Aid projects are part of the explanation. So, for my first twenty years of acquaintance with Nebaj, it felt like a refuge from the quandaries of Guatemala. While its problems were large, it was full of self-reliant people who knew how to grow their own food and govern their own affairs. It was a functioning democracy, in the imperfect manner of an actual democracy. Municipal politics were occasionally violent, with mobs laying siege to the town hall, but not to the point of political assassination. Since voters were capable of throwing the bums out of office, no single cabal dominated the town for more than two elections. If Nebaj was misgoverned, it was not misgoverned on the unmanageable scale of an entire country. Instead, it seemed like a world of its own in which some of the largest problems could be blamed on outsiders.

As I kept coming back every year, out of affection for my friends and out of fascination with the many layers in local disputes, my feelings about Nebaj became increasingly divided. My discipline's interest in culture, community, and identity has made it too easy for anthropologists—in particular, those of us who are idealistic or ideologically driven—to avert our gaze from individuals and how they compete with each other. Because I wanted to show that the Ixils were capable of running their own affairs without being liberated by the guerrillas or protected by the army, I stressed Ixil solidarity against the two armed groups. My portrayal of a people under siege, their war weariness, and their wish to remove themselves from the conflict accorded with how Nebajenses sometimes idealize themselves—when they are not going to the opposite extreme of denigrating themselves.

In hindsight, I was underestimating how much Nebajenses compete with each other, particularly over land, but more generally over any opportunity for income. I was not taking sufficient account of the rancorous aspects of their lives. These are very social people, but they are riven by tremendous rivalries. It is the rare Nebajense who cannot name his or her *enemigos*—enemies who can be counted upon to take any opportunity to extract revenge for a past incident. In every aid project emerges a tug of war over exactly who will benefit. The community rituals that used to center around the Catholic Church and the town hall, the ancestors and the maize harvest, can still be observed processioning through the streets. But they have been marginalized by a swarm of committees, associations, and institutes seeking to harvest subsidies from the state and international donors. The town hall, church groups, and development associations all compete for funding. No political party, evangelical church, committee, or nonprofit institution for the public good goes for long without a split between competing leaders.

The anthropologist Steve Sampson provides a simple but eye-opening framework for analyzing these situations. Based on his experience with international aid in the Balkans, he argues that three kinds of actors are competing with each other: the state, projects, and bandits. When a state becomes so weak that bandit society and project society compete openly for sovereignty, it becomes a "trouble spot," or a "complex humanitarian emergency," or what Sampson calls a "white-jeep state," in which foreigners drive around in white jeeps attempting to perform basic functions. In practice the state, projects, and bandits are not necessarily easy to distinguish; they can feed off each other, and one can hide behind the other. When bandits succeed in penetrating the state or projects and manipulating them for private enrichment, the result is what Sampson calls a mafia.

At bottom, Sampson warns, the "world of projects" comes up against "a world of kinship, clan and ethnicity." Civil society as foreigners conceive it, idealistically, is in perennial competition with kin structures, other affinities, and intrigues with a strong basis in local tradition. These are the assembled forces of favoritism; they are the true repositories of social trust that enable things to happen; they also fragment the society and lead to feuds. Sooner or later, they will co-opt the transparent bureaucratic mechanisms desired by foreign donors and auditors. "These parallel structures are the true civil society," Sampson says of the Balkans, and I think the same can be said of all but the most idealistic Guatemalans, who are more likely to be found in the middle and upper classes than in the lower. To put this in fewer words, Guatemalans will tend to place their bets on people with whom they have lifelong ties, not with foreigners who arrive in pursuit of their dreams or on three-year contracts.[12]

Applying the term "mafia" to Nebaj could imply that politicians and project coordinators are putting out contracts to assassinate each other. This is definitely not the case; the only assassinations I have witnessed are verbal. But mafia does capture the ruthless, subterranean competition for the spoils of office. If we translate mafia as political party, Sampson's scheme explains why ambitious Guatemalans invest so much time in constructing organizations that, upon attaining office, turn into conspiracies to plunder public resources. Guatemalan parties are organized not around ideology or a stable form of association such as ethnicity or church, but around power brokers. In Mexico these pivotal figures might be called *caciques*, a term that used to refer to indigenous chieftains, but in Nebaj they are referred to as *principales* (Spanish for indigenous leaders) or *b'oq'ol tenam* (Ixil for town leaders). Only by promising specific benefits to supporters can principales and their parties win votes. Guatemala's economy is stagnant once population growth is taken into account, so supporters can be rewarded only by excluding opponents—a simple point with implications for any project that claims to benefit an entire community.

Another helpful translation of mafia is privatization, that is, the corruption of a discourse of public service to serve private ends. The critical social group in Ixil country was starting to emerge before the violence but only consolidated its grip on town affairs in the late 1980s, as the army and local ladinos withdrew. This new group consists of Ixils and K'iche's who have achieved at least a secondary education and then managed to achieve office, either in government or in aid projects. They are known colloquially as "professionals" because, in the Guatemalan educational system, anyone who manages to finish high school has an entry-level qualification for a career in teaching or business (university graduates are still rare in Nebaj). Because the Guatemalan economy offers little opportunity, most high school graduates hope to win an entry-level government job, of the kind from which it is almost impossible to be fired, and the competition for these slots is fierce. So is the competition for contracts with aid projects. In Nebaj the majority of professionals have degrees as *maestros* or primary school teachers, although an increasing number are specializing in business administration. Graduates from the early cohorts of the 1970s and 1980s run the local branches of political parties, the town government, and aid projects. Their salaries alone place them in a different social class than peasants. But starting salaries of Q2,000 ($260) per month are meager when it comes to educating their children and buying consumer goods, so as a group the teachers are anything but well off and disinterested.

Of the four Ixils who have served as mayor of Nebaj since Ríos Montt's coup d'état in 1982, all four have been teachers. Of the four, only one did not become visibly wealthier in property, and he was the first, the one appointed by Ríos Montt. Of the three who have been elected for a total of seven terms—by the Christian Democrats, by the Cotón Civic Committee, by Ríos Montt's right-wing populist party, and by the National Union of Hope—all three have visibly enriched themselves. Judging from town lore, the usual technique is the under-the-table *comisión* or kickback, which contractors offer to any official who might give them a contract.

Meanwhile, aid organizations have found it very difficult to prevent their Ixil coordinators from favoring family and friends. This turns an ostensible communal enterprise into a patronage network. Stealing from aid projects is a different game than stealing from the town hall because, while you can obtain political office only by working through a political party or civic committee, you can move upward in the world of projects only by impressing foreigners. Certain individuals have emerged as power brokers. As they gain leverage, they place relatives and cronies in different offices and projects so that they can make contracts with each other and give each other commissions. They have figured out how to turn the rhetoric of international organizations—Maya culture, the indigenous woman, sustainable development—into a license for private accumulation.

All in all, the Ixil–internationalist marriage has proved to be a bumpy one. What motivates the Ixils to welcome international organizations is their desire to *superar* (get ahead), not their loyalty to the indigenous culture that foreigners so prize. While some Ixils are plaintiffs in genocide indictments against the former dictator Ríos Montt (1982–1983), many more have voted for him and his political party on repeated occasions. Even after Guatemalans voted his Guatemalan Republican Front (FRG) out of the presidency in 2003, the three Ixil municipios elected mayors from this party. Yet Nebaj is so attractive to international donors that they have chosen to overlook its political conservatism and evangelical religiosity.

THE EMPLOYMENT CRISIS

The latest stage of capitalism would appear to be a roaring success in Nebaj just on the basis of all the noise it makes. Throughout the day, the center of town sounds and smells like a truck stop. Nebaj is still a pedestrian town, so the streets are filled with everyone from itinerant vendors to small children to elders hobbling on crutches. But now there are so many three-wheeled *tuk-tuk* taxis, motorcycles, pickups, minivans, and trucks barreling through the narrow streets that making your way on foot feels like being a target inside a video game. A sure sign of progress, or at least of electrification, is heavy-metal music blasting from a shack. Even at my favorite pensión, chosen for its commitment to peace and quiet, dueling sound systems beyond the walls have become a fact of life. There are television programs and boom boxes every day of the week, church services and rehearsals nearly every day of the week, and the occasional political rally. The only relief is that everyone goes to bed by 10 p.m. On the chicken buses that have taken me into Ixil country since the 1980s, the national soundtrack used to consist of songs of romantic loss from Julio Iglesias and the Bukis. Nowadays the drivers are playing more genres—everything from ranchera to Patsy Kline–style lamentations to rap—but if you listen to the lyrics, they always seem to end up invoking the Lord Jesus Christ. During the traditional Catholic fiestas, skyrockets still boom; marimbas and their lonely vocalists still wail through the night. But day to day, evangelical religion has become the soundtrack of Ixil civilization.

For Americans and Europeans who don't have much time for religion, the appeal of evangelicalism to people like the Nebajenses is a source of wonderment. If Nebajenses are so intent on *superando* or getting ahead, why wouldn't aid projects—with their delivery of tangible goods such as potable water and schools—undermine pie-in-the-sky religion? Few evangelical pastors offer handouts to their members. To the contrary, they demand financial contributions, and some pastors live rather well from the Lord's work. Yet evangelical churches have been far more successful at putting down roots and sustaining involvement than have international donors and their aid programs, not just in Nebaj but elsewhere in the Third World (cf. Pfeiffer 2004). Even more impressive, people often stay involved in evangelicalism despite the collapse of particular congregations and leaders. Amid the rise and fall of so many competing agendas and projects, why is enthusiasm for evangelical religion so resilient? Why in the last generation have evangelical churches captured the imagination of so many Nebajenses?

One explanation is precisely the demands that evangelical churches place on members. In contrast to aid projects, which are defined in terms of material or social benefits, the distribution of which sets off competitive scrambles, evangelical congregations impose a family-like hierarchy that demands reciprocity in the form of participation, contribution, and submission. Just as many Nebajenses appreciate the rigor of the evangelical ban on alcohol, I think they also appreciate the clear chain of command. God avows the authority of the pastor over the congregation, of elders over youth, and of men over women. But men are responsible for serving the needs of their families, and if they don't, they can be ignored. Family hierarchy is a comforting theme for people on whom many changes are being imposed. Just as a matter of ritual reinforcement, it would be hard to find a better way of sustaining a sense of obligation, in a pleasant and inviting way, than by meeting several times a week to a tuneful beat and going into a mild collective trance.

Another explanation for the resilience of evangelical churches is that they have effective techniques for, not just sustaining obligation to the group, but accommodating individual ambition. The Catholic Church and most aid projects assume a community framework that, in practice, is often disrupted by competition between families and social networks, if not by outright robbery. But in the evangelical scheme, each person is responsible for his or her own salvation. This confers legitimacy on an individual's struggle for success; it also allows space for the bane of every community project—factionalism. Whereas legitimacy in the Catholic scheme requires an ordained priest appointed by the bishop, in a hierarchy of appointment stretching back to Rome, in the evangelical scheme, anyone who believes the Lord is calling him to start his own congregation is free to do so. The majority of these spirit-led enterprises are flops, but in the meantime, the kin-based factionalism so typical of villages and projects has been accommodated by what amounts to an evangelical marketplace.[13] It allows dissension and puts a moral face on it.

The purpose of this chapter has been to give you a sense of the different visions and agendas competing for the loyalty of the Nebajenses since the 1970s. It is easy to cluck about opportunists who steal community funds, or poor people who buy large televisions, but peasants live tough, uncomfortable lives and what they want is some of the comfort that they see other people enjoying and that has always been denied them. Prior to the war, virtually all Ixils lived on dirt floors. Thanks to aid projects and remittances, this is changing. But most men have spent their lives pushing dirt and hauling loads up mountains until they are too tired to do anything else. Most women have spent their lives performing even more monotonous household tasks. So you can talk about heaven, historical memory, or justice, but can you deliver a cement floor?

Only a small fraction of Nebajenses enjoy the prosperity on display in the streets of the town. Most Ixils and K'iche's live in mountain villages that look more picturesque from a distance than they do up close. The diet of most people is still very monotonous—maize three times a day, with astonishingly little besides. In all my years of learning about Latin America, the most instructive moments have been sitting down to eat the best that an Ixil peasant family has to offer. Then there is the weather, which is often overcast, chilly, and damp. Yet there is much to be said for Nebaj: the topography is dramatic, nature seems green and abundant, and life is intensely social, in contrast to the privacy, if not isolation and loneliness, of so much life in the United States. Walking down the street, it is hard not to bump into several people you know, and at least one version of the latest imbroglio. Households are run by maternal hierarchies, often three generations strong, with teenagers and children providing a jokey atmosphere. Even a cold, drizzly afternoon can suddenly become *alegre* (fun) with troops of youngsters laughing and tumbling. This is how I like to picture my friends in Nebaj, in gatherings of men and women surrounded by their progeny; this is where I like to visit them, and this is where I would like to see them have long and satisfying lives.

But if the joy of Nebaj is its children and youth, they are also its quandary. Thanks to vaccination campaigns and potable water projects, most children are surviving to adulthood. Nebaj parents have been slow to reduce their pregnancies, and the population has reached five times what it probably was before the Spanish Conquest. Even though at least four thousand inhabitants of Ixil country died in the violence, and possibly many more, the impact on population growth is difficult to see.[14] Since Ixil parents usually apportion their land among their children instead of choosing just one heir, landholding has become so fractionated that most Nebajenses do not inherit enough cropland for subsistence. Most local jobs pay four to eight dollars a day, which is enough to feed a family but not enough to pay for the consumer goods that Nebajenses now admire and want.

When international donors fell in love with Nebaj, they took on a mission with no foreseeable end. Before the war, most Ixils engaged in below-subsistence farming in which they made up for their lack of land by migrating to coastal plantations for several months a year. The majority of Ixil children did not attend school, and most Ixils lived and died without modern medical care. Self-sufficiency ended when the army burned down their farmsteads in the early 1980s. The majority of Ixils became refugees and learned how to stand in line for rations. They also learned that an array of *instituciones* could be petitioned for an array of needs. *Que proyecto trae?* (What project do you bring?) became an acceptable opener with foreigners. As for all those aid agencies, they could hardly confine themselves to restoring the status quo. Before the war, the majority of Ixils lived in adobe or wood huts without running water, latrines, or electricity. So all these necessities of modern life would have to be provided for the first time. Moreover, because Ixil women still bear an average of six children who begin reproducing in adolescence, every year Ixils start hundreds of new households. Every year, some combination of government agencies and donors is being petitioned to finance housing, electricity, potable water, roads, schools, and health care for the equivalent of several new villages sprouting across the landscape.

Despite all the projects—sustainable agriculture and nontraditional exports; marketing cooperatives; a veterinary association and village pharmacies; food supplements and education for mothers and small children; medical teams from the United States and Cuba; and a model justice center with legal aid, mediators, translators, and sociologists to resuscitate traditional community law—how many times have I heard young Ixils lament, why do none of these organizations really help us? If we look at Nebaj as an economy of desires and attempts to meet those desires, what Ixils want has changed dramatically over the last fifty years. Because they are Native Americans, international donors would like to believe they are guardians of the earth, keepers of ancient wisdom, and faithful defenders of their culture. There are Ixils who fit this description; many do not. About their culture, Ixils tend to feel the way that Americans of my generation feel about the 1950s. Sometimes we feel nostalgic about the 1950s; sometimes we do not. Getting drunk in honor of the saints, subsisting on diets of maize and beans, trying to stay warm in traditional cotton clothing—Ixils have good reasons to turn their backs on many traditional ways. They are proud of who they are and where they come from, but they are also eager for the bright lights of modernity and the creature comforts that they can attain only by abandoning many of the practices that attract tourists.

Isn't the goal of foreign aid to help people develop new sources of income so they can become self-sufficient? Dozens of Nebaj projects have tried to do just that. There have been successes, such as two associations that help hundreds of families sell their coffee at higher prices. Families in favorable microclimates are producing new export crops such as French beans. But most Ixils do not have the right kind of land for such strategies. Even if the area's remaining large holdings were broken up (many already have been), small cultivators would still not have enough land to be self-sufficient. According to a study by French agronomists, Ixil country is too steep and has too little soil to provide the agricultural income needed to motor the area's development.[15]

What about factories? Factories across Central America are struggling against low-wage competition from China. As for retail commerce, every category has multiplied to the point of saturation. So has motor transport—the streets are clogged with vehicles whose owners are barely making their loan payments. Certain kinds of artisan production such as furniture and textiles provide employment, but not of the kind that satisfies aspiring consumers. Nor can these endeavors absorb the tens of thousands of Ixil youth without enough land to farm. So Nebaj's most important product, its principal export, continues to be surplus labor.

Chapter Three

Nebaj Goes North

What I earn here in a month, I earn there in a day.

—Returned migrant, 2008

If everyone in Nebaj can agree on a single proposition, it is that their most serious problem is a lack of income. Despite decades of aid projects, the majority of the population is trapped in below-subsistence agriculture that fails to provide what they need and want. What they want extends far beyond subsistence due to their growing acquaintance with consumption levels elsewhere, as promised to them by a succession of outsiders who have shown up with the idea of helping them in some way. Not just aid consultants, but guerrillas, soldiers, and missionaries have all, in one way or another, offered Nebajenses the blessings of modernity at every level, from sanitation to diet to electric guitars for their church services. Unfortunately, no local cash crop offers a stable income that could sustain a higher level of consumption—nor does any local industry for that matter. Only occasionally do the prices for the area's main cash crop, coffee, rise above breaking even. New export crops such as garlic can be very profitable, but only for the small fraction of the population that owns land in suitable microclimates. Family planning is still a novelty for the majority of couples, especially out in the villages, so the average number of children per woman is still high, a subject to which we will return in chapter 8. This means that most Ixil youth will never inherit enough land to feed themselves.

In the 1990s there were two new ideas to make the people of Nebaj self-sufficient. The first idea, conceived by aid consultants, was to lend them money so that they could become entrepreneurs. We have all heard how microloans can help the poor beaver their way out of poverty. Even if that is not actually the case, making it easier for poor people to borrow money is not necessarily a bad idea. The Mayas were a busy commercial civilization before the arrival of Europeans. After the Spanish Conquest, they continued to operate their own commercial networks; market day is the highlight of the week in any municipal seat. Mayan peasants are eager for a safe place to park their savings. They are also eager to make large purchases. And some actually succeed in starting new businesses and creating jobs. For aid agencies, meanwhile, lending money to individuals and small groups avoids the endless accountability problems of communal projects. Lending money to the Nebajenses seemed like such a good idea that, by 2008, they could borrow from at least twenty-three different banks, credit associations, and revolving-loan funds within a few minutes' walk of the town plaza (see table 3.1).

One problem to which the lenders didn't give enough attention was, exactly what were Nebajenses going to do with all that credit? Presumably they were going to start businesses, which is why Nebaj now features hundreds of retail outlets—corner groceries, school supply stores, hardware stores, pharmacies, ice cream parlors, shoe stores, Internet cafés, and market stalls—without enough customers. Opening modest lines of credit to Nebajenses was a good idea. Pumping large amounts of credit into a crowded mountain environment with little potential was, in retrospect, not such a good idea. No one has been able to come up with a game plan for turning Nebaj into a high-productivity consumer economy.

The most exportable commodity that Nebaj produces is labor. And so the second way to make the people of Nebaj self-sufficient—this one conceived by Nebajenses rather than aid consultants—was to seek a more advantageous market in which to sell their labor. Ixils have plenty of experience with selling their labor on disadvantageous terms. Before the war, the majority migrated to coastal plantations at least once a year to make up the difference between what they could harvest on their own land and what they needed to get through the year.[1] Those who failed to obtain land from their parents—because of losses to moneylenders, sibling rivalries, or displacement by another village faction—were likely to move to the coast and lose their ties to Nebaj. Even now, when a family runs out of maize before the next harvest, the most obvious solution is to go to a coffee plantation—not so much for the pay, which is minimal, but for the food ration. To earn money faster, up to eleven dollars a day, Ixil men go to coastal plantations to cut sugarcane, but not everyone is fit for this brutal job. A third alternative is Guatemala City and its burgeoning periphery; here thousands of Ixils have become factory workers and street vendors, only to find that living expenses are so high that many come home without savings.

Table 3.1. Loan Agencies Active in Nebaj to 2012

Institution	Year Began Lending	Source of Capital/Credit Type
1. Asociación de Asentamientos Unidos Area Ixil (ASAUNIXIL)	1996	Nonprofit agricultural association with revolving-loan fund (asaunixil.wordpress.com)
2. Asociación Chajulense Va'l Vaq Quyol (Una sola voz–with one voice)	1999	Nonprofit coffee-buying association with revolving-loan fund (headquartered in Chajul, www.asociacionchajulense.org)
3. Asociación Civil Guatemalteca Grameen Credit (ACGGC)	2011	Nonprofit Grameen Trust Build-Operate-Transfer (BOT) in cooperation with Banrural and the Whole Planet Foundation of Whole Foods Market
4. Asociación de Desarrollo Integral de Productores de Café de la Aldea Sujsiban Loch B'al (ADIPCASAL)	1999	Nonprofit coffee-buying association with revolving-loan fund
5. Asociación de Desarrollo Integral Lochb'al Tenam (ASODILT)	2001	Nonprofit agricultural association with revolving-loan fund
6. Asociación de Desarrollo Local (ADEL-IXIL)	1993	Nonprofit agricultural association with revolving-loan fund, started by a United Nations Development Program contractor and incorporated as an association in 2000
7. Asociación de Mujeres Mayas Ixiles de Nebaj (AMMI)	1995	Nonprofit savings and loan association
8. Asociación de Promotores Agropecuarios del Triángulo Ixil (APAPTIX)	1994	Nonprofit veterinary association with revolving-loan fund
9. Asociación para el Desarrollo Raíz (RAIZ)	2004	Nonprofit microfinance association (www.redimif.org/24.0.html?&tx_galileoaffiliated_pi2[id]=2)
10. Asociación T'al Ka'b (Miel or Honey)	c. 2003	For-profit multiple services association including high-interest loans
11. Bancos Comunales del Fondo de Integración Social (FIS)	c. 2000	Government-sponsored microcredit program replaced by Red de Mujeres Ixiles
12. Banco de Café (Bancafé)	Early 1990s	Commercial bank which went bankrupt in 2006 and was absorbed by Banrural
13. Banco de Desarrollo Rural (Banrural)	1998	Commercial bank whose shareholders include Guatemalan state and which replaced the state's Banco de Desarrollo Social (BANDESA), which operated in Nebaj from early 1970s (www.banrural.com.gt)

(continued)

Table 3.1. *(Continued)*

Institution	Year Began Lending	Source of Capital/Credit Type
14. Banco de los Trabajadores (Worker's Bank)	2009	Commercial bank (www.bantrab.com.gt)
15. Banco Granai & Townson	2006	Commercial bank
16. Cooperativa De Ahorro y Crédito San Miguel Chuimequená (COSAMI)	2007	Nonprofit savings and loan cooperative (www.cosami.com.gt)
17. Cooperativa Los Tejidos Ixiles (COINTEX)	2007	Nonprofit savings and loan cooperative
18. Cooperativa Integral de Ahorro y Crédito Multiplicador	1997	Nonprofit savings and loan cooperative
19. Cooperativa Maya Inversiones Futuras (COMIF)	2008	Nonprofit savings and loan cooperative
20. Cooperativa Agrícola Integral Santa Maria	1970s	Nonprofit beekeeping cooperative with revolving-loan fund
21. Cooperativa Agrícola Integral Todos Nebajenses (COTONEB)	1989	Nonprofit multiple services cooperative, especially savings and loan
22. Banco Azteca Guatemalateca (previously Punto Azteca and Credimax)	2007	For-profit enterprise offering easy-access, high-interest consumer credit (Grupo Salinas of Mexico, www.bancoazteca.com.gt)
23. Fundación Agros	1989	Nonprofit agency focusing on agricultural development (office in Cotzal, www.fundacionagros.org)
24. Fundación Centro de Servicios Cristianos (FUNCEDESCRI)	1999	Nonprofit agency supporting food production (funcedescri.org/funce)
25. Fundación de Asesoría Financiera a Instituciones de Desarrollo y Servico Social (FAFIDESS)	2000	Nonprofit microfinance agency sponsored by Rotary Clubs of Guatemala City (fafidess.org/main.asp?clc=306)
26. Fundación del Quetzal (Fundación para el Desarrollo Rural y Servicio Social)	2005	Nonprofit microfinance agency started by 17 Nebajense donors
27. Fundación Génesis Empresarial (Genesis Entrepreneurial Foundation)	2005	Nonprofit microfinance agency (www.genesisempresarial.com)
28. Puente de Amistad (Bridge of Friendship)	c. 2003	Nonprofit microcredit agency focusing on indigenous women (www.friendshipbridge.org)
29. Red de Mujeres Ixiles (Network of Ixil Women)	2004	Women's organization, previously Bancos Comunales of the Fondo de Integración Social
30. Semilla: Créditos para el Desarollo Empresarial (Seed: Credits for Entrepreneurial Development)	2006	For-profit microfinance agency started by a business-school student with Banrural loans

Source: Faceta Central Desarrollo Empresarial 2002 and author's interviews.

And so Nebajenses had a better idea—why not invest my loans in export-ing the single product that I possess in abundance to a distant market where this product will be in demand? And so they exported themselves to the United States. *Me urge ir a los Estados Unidos*, men told their wives. Al-most without exception they have gone *mojado*, the Spanish term for "wet," which refers to the gambit of swimming across the Rio Grande. "Wetback" is a derogatory term in English, but Nebaj's migrants are proud to claim their status as *mojados*, even though the majority reach the United States through the Sonora-Arizona desert.

The first researcher to study Nebajense migration to the United States was a Belgian aid volunteer. While I was still avoiding the subject, Cécile Stever-lynck did structured interviews in four villages, two of which were mainly Ixil speakers (Parramos Grande and Palop) and two of which were mainly K'iche' speakers (Chortiz and Xexuxcap). Their location along the municipal boundary with Huehuetenango Department suggests the source of the inspi-ration. The first man from Palop went north in 1996. Six years later, when Steverlynck did her interviews, sixty of Palop's 121 men between the age of twenty and forty-four were in the United States. Of the four villages' 360 men in this cohort, 151, or 42 percent, were in the United States. They were paying between $3,500 and $5,000 to get there; some were being financed by an already-arrived relative who was helping them find work. If they fell into the hands of U.S. immigration authorities, their anchor relative in the north could finance their next attempt, such that "failure is nearly impossible and reaching El Norte is almost guaranteed."[2]

Initially these men saw the United States as an alternative to seasonal plan-tation labor, which paid as little as fifty dollars per month. The most visible signs of success were their new cement-block houses and agricultural plots, often at lower and more productive altitudes. So many achieved these goals that they began looking at El Norte as a better way of life. There was so much money there, men reported back in wonder, that even hens and dogs were treated with respect. Conscious that they were siring more children than could ever support themselves as farmers, they began to view their future in terms of sending contingents of relatives north. Men from the four villages scattered to Ohio, North Carolina, Illinois, Florida, and Colorado.[3]

As Steverlynck did her interviews, the daring and success of the four vil-lages was producing a quiet but unstoppable migration fever elsewhere in the municipio. How many Nebajenses have gone can only be estimated. In April 2008, the two largest credit institutions in Nebaj handled 2,653 remittances from the United States. If we add an estimated 1,225 remittances through other agencies, the total number of remittances from the United States would be 3,878. This is not the number of remitters—some are sending money only intermittently while others are sending it once a month or more. Assuming a typical distribution, and assuming that a quarter of Nebajenses in the United States are not sending any money at all, I estimate 4,041 Nebajenses in the United States in April 2008.[4] That would be 5.5 percent of the municipio's estimated 73,216 population that year.

A large majority are males between the ages of fifteen and forty-five.[5] The remainder consist of older men, women joining their husbands, and unmarried girls in their late teens who are typically joining brothers. My impression is that at least half the males are leaving behind wives and children, or at least pregnant girlfriends, but I have no hard evidence. Nebajenses often refer to male migrants collectively as *muchachos* or boys—adolescents and twenty-somethings who will not necessarily meet all the expectations of adult behavior. Whether a migrant will live up to the financial obligations needed to place him in the U.S. labor market is, as we shall see, a perennial question.

Only a handful of Nebajenses have managed to enter the United States legally—usually by obtaining tourist visas, which have become increasingly hard to obtain because so many of the recipients jump into the workforce. Additionally, I know of one Ixil who married a U.S. citizen; another who went to work for Guatemalan diplomats in Washington, D.C.; and another who went on a student visa and has since returned. Everyone else has made a deal with one of the many smuggling networks that promise to deposit Guatemalans safely in the United States. The networks are customarily referred to as coyotes, after the wily beast of this name, and will occupy much of the next chapter. For now, let it suffice that most of the networks operate through Huehuetenango Department to the west. The Huehuetecos employ Nebajenses as recruiters; pay them a commission for every migrant they *enganchar* or "hook"; and deliver Nebajenses to the Mexican networks that take them through Mexico and across the U.S. border.

Crucially for what follows, most of the capital at risk in these ventures comes from fellow Nebajenses, either relatives or moneylenders. Between 2007 and 2012, the typical cost was Q40,000, with lowball estimates at Q38,000 (warnings attached) and *viajes expresos* (express trips) at Q45,000 to Q50,000. Depending on the exchange rate with the dollar, Q40,000 means around $5,000. Many although not all Nebajenses pay an *anticipo* (advance payment) of Q15,000—close to $2,000. Upon reaching what is known as a safe house, stash house, or drop house, most often in Phoenix, Arizona, the family in Guatemala pays the remainder. The rewards of this system have been enormous. I have only fragmentary data on remittances, but I estimate that in the peak year of June 2007–May 2008, Nebajenses sent back as much as Q213,404,000, or $27,359,000.[6] That would be $374 for each man, woman, and child in the municipio.[7] Since annual per capita income in Ixil country was probably less than this beforehand, remittances must have been a tremendous multiplier of the money in circulation.[8]

Adán was one of the first Ixils to go north, at the start of the 1990s. He is from the municipal seat, not an outlying village. His father died when he was young, but an older sister gave him enough financial support to go to high school. When a cousin who worked in Guatemala City was able to reach Florida, Adán saw his chance.

"There was still army conscription at the time, and I did not want anything to do with the army. I don't even like to touch a firearm," he told me. "My mother and I borrowed five thousand quetzals to pay a coyote, and three weeks later I was in the United States, in Harlingen, Texas. The worst was fourteen hours in a small boat in the Gulf of Mexico, from the rolling waves. On the American border at the time there was just a Migra vehicle in the distance.[9] It was easy to find a way to cross. Now it is very different. Now there are many vehicles, there are helicopters, dogs, infrared devices, and it is a lot harder.

"In Harlingen I lived in the Rio Grande Refuge for six months. I asked for political asylum because I was young and there was still military conscription. I met a very good lawyer who is known for helping migrants. But my five thousand quetzal debt had increased to fifteen thousand, because of the ten percent interest per month. My mother was calling me on the telephone, crying that we owed lots of money. At the refuge we worked half a day on chores, plus two more hours to pay the lawyer. We grew vegetables so that the refuge could be self-sufficient. But we were not supposed to go out to work, so I could not send my mother anything to pay the debt. Once a man from San Pedro Jocopilas and I sneaked out to work. A Mexican asked us, 'what are you doing in the street? Don't you know that the Migra is going to grab you?' But the Migra didn't grab us and we earned seventy dollars each.

"The next day I left the refuge for the Greyhound Terminal and bought a ticket to Houston. I didn't know anyone there. In the entire United States I knew only my cousin, and he was in Miami. I was astonished by the buildings downtown. At the time, roads in Quiché Department didn't even have asphalt. But what surprised me the most, what motivated me more than anything else, was to see a black woman driving a bus. Here we never see a woman doing the work of a man. My bus ticket had cost me forty dollars, so I didn't have much left. I told a taxi driver that I had just eight dollars left—because I also needed to eat—and asked him to take me to the Casa Juan Diego. There I lived for three weeks. After breakfast, we went out to a big patio, and they closed the door behind us. Maybe because the Casa belonged to the Catholic Church, they said the Migra could not enter. But people looking for workers could. They paid me forty to fifty dollars a day. When I saved three hundred dollars, I went to Western Union to send it to my mother.

"The next time I saved money, I went to the airport and bought a ticket to look for my cousin in Miami. By this time I had my work permit and a Social Security number, even though I never received political asylum. In Miami my big shock was that people did not speak English. My idea had been that no one in the United States was going to speak Spanish. This is why I had studied English in a correspondence course and could speak it 30 percent. One day in Miami a Cuban asked me, 'why are you speaking English? Here we speak Spanish.' Miami is where I spent three years, bought my first car, and managed to save the $3,000 I brought back to Guatemala.

"This was the inspiration for many, when I returned with my car and went from a house of wooden planks to a house of cement block. Going to the United States became all the rage. People here think there are no poor people there; they didn't believe me when I told them about people who live in cars. There's a saying that you can't enjoy two glories at the same time. There, if you want to buy a car, you buy it. If you want to buy a nice jacket, you buy it. But there is no family there; it is not your pueblo, and there are many strangers. You don't even know who is in the next apartment, even after living there a long time. Here is your family, here is your pueblo, but for lack of money, there are many things that you cannot buy. I stayed here [in Nebaj] two years, or a year and a half. I couldn't stand it, and so I returned to the United States. It's a characteristic of the migrant that, being there, I want to be here. Returning here, I want to go back there."

In the end, Adán spent a decade in the United States and was arrested on more than one occasion for illegal entry or lack of papers. To bail himself out and continue working, he hired a lawyer, but his quest for legal status ended with a judge who ordered deportation. The judge allowed him to choose voluntary departure, a liberal element in the U.S. approach to illegal immigrants. Rather than being led away in handcuffs, spending a month in an immigration prison, and being sent home with a planeload of deportees, Adán agreed to leave at his own expense, giving him time to wrap up his affairs. The night before the flight home, he and his equally illegal wife, also from Nebaj, agonized over whether they should go or stay. Staying would mean living in constant fear of being stopped, identified, and carted off to prison. They decided to go.

Adán's story illustrates how the first Nebajenses to go to the United States were not the poorest of the poor invoked by the Emma Lazarus poem affixed to the Statue of Liberty—"Give me your tired, your hungry, your poor." Many were from a rapidly growing cohort of high school graduates who earn entry-level degrees in fields such as teaching and accounting but cannot find desk jobs. Others were sons of village leaders who had land that they could sell or borrow against to finance the trip. Still others were ex-guerrillas who had been off in the mountains in the 1980s when their siblings divvied up parental land. Ex-combatants were often landless, without so much as a toehold in the smallholder agriculture of their parents, but they were also models of energy and determination.

Some of the first men to go north were very successful. If we compare Adán and nine others who returned to the municipal seat with enough savings to become beacons of prosperity, one shared trait is that they went north earlier than most Nebajenses. Another is that they won the trust of Anglo employers, more often than not construction contractors, who spoke little Spanish but who were so impressed by their Guatemalan employees that they provided stable employment, pay raises, and friendship. For such bosses, Guatemalans were not just more reliable and productive than the Americans they could hire. They were even better than Mexicans. "They asked me, where are you from?" a Nebajense recalls of his arrival in the Bay Area.

Modern youth

"'I'm a Guatemalan,' I answered. 'Very good,' they told me, 'we have work for you.' If I told them I was a Mexican, they would not have given me work because the Mexicans demand their rate of pay, they demand the hours they want, they ask for a break and everything, even lunch."

Guatemalans like Adán know how to work hard, they are undistracted by families because their families are thousands of miles away, and they can be trusted to supervise other Latin American workers. One Nebajense worked as a detail painter on remodeling jobs in upscale Marin County, north of San Francisco. He started at ten dollars an hour, then went to fifteen dollars an hour and ultimately twenty-seven dollars an hour because he was a perfectionist. Another went north, not in his teens or twenties like the others, but at the age of sixty-four. I interviewed Marcelo Canel at his home in Chortiz, 3,200 meters above sea level. It is too high to grow maize so, like other K'iche' Mayas who live at this altitude, he pastured animals and grew potatoes. Marcelo lost his wife and all but one of his children in the war, started a new family in the 1990s, and went north with his one surviving son in 2004.

He and his son's first jobs were in a packing plant paying $8.40 an hour in Omega, Georgia. The son settled nearby in Tifton, but Marcelo went on the road through northern Florida, the Carolinas, and Virginia with an agricultural crew of fourteen Guatemalans and Mexicans. They harvested tobacco and other crops and planted melons and tomatoes. The contractor was a gringo named Wilbur who paid seven hundred dollars a week, provided transport and lodging but not food, and prohibited heavy drinking. Marcelo was obviously an old man, and Americans asked him if he wasn't ready to retire. But this was easier work than hauling loads up to his village. Marcelo envisioned that he would stay in the United States for eight years. But he returned after just two and a half years, in early 2007, because his wife was having trouble taking care of their ninety-eight sheep. With his earnings and his son's, he had already bought three mules, one chainsaw, thirty-two cuerdas of pasture and ten cuerdas of mountainside for milpa—1.8 hectares in all. He also built himself and his family a snug house.

IMMIGRANT EMPLOYERS, FAMILY WORK GROUPS, AND ETHNIC NICHES

Most Nebajenses never find an ideal Anglo patrón. Unlike better-connected migrants whose relatives have attained legal status, few have any jobs awaiting them. All too often they enter the labor market by standing on a curb, in the company of dozens of other Central Americans and Mexicans. With luck, short-term jobs turn into more stable jobs, often in (depending on the locality) stoop agriculture or construction. Other typical starting jobs are dishwashing in ethnic restaurants, stock work in ethnic groceries, and low-wage factory work, most often in slaughterhouses or textile mills. Only in industrial plants are Nebajenses usually working for Anglo employers. In agriculture, construction, restaurants, and groceries, they are more likely to work for fellow immigrants who have attained legal residency or U.S. citizenship.

In my circle of acquaintance, one family migration chain has been locating jobs through Chinese labor brokers who, on more than one occasion, have been prosecuted by the U.S. government for Social Security fraud and conspiracy to harbor, transport, and entice illegal aliens. All over the eastern United States, Chinese restaurants rely on labor brokers in Chamblee, Georgia, an Atlanta suburb and ethnic enclave, to send them Central Americans.[10] According to a Nebajense working in Syracuse, a Rust Belt city in upstate New York, his Chinese employer prefers to hire Guatemalans because they work harder than his Chinese employees. Another Nebajense working in Bennington, Vermont, is paid $1,500 a month for washing dishes seventy-two hours a week. For 288 hours a month, Alfredo is earning $5.20 an hour, almost three dollars below the state's minimum wage. The saving grace is that his Chinese patrón gives him a place to live, within easy walking distance, and also pays for his electricity and cable television. Thus Alfredo is able to send home most of his pay, making this the best job he has ever had, and more remunerative than most Nebajense jobs in the United States.

Back in Guatemala, Alfredo has enough education to teach primary school, but the best job he could find was in a carpentry shop for sixty quetzals ($7.70) per day. Before reaching Bennington, he worked in two Chinese restaurants in Alabama and three in Mississippi, all through a labor broker in Chamblee. The final Mississippi job was the best—the owner paid him $1,700 per month, gave him a place to live rent free, and provided all the Chinese food he could eat. But the cashier was an old lady from Oaxaca, Mexico, and the other employees were all related to her. She wanted Alfredo's job for another member of her family, so she made his life hell. Realizing that he was outnumbered, he telephoned Chamblee one more time. The broker sent him to Bennington. Alfredo paid his own bus fare, and the broker's commission of $180 was deducted from his first week's pay. When he decided to leave eight months later, he gave notice on Thursday evening, and two replacements were on hand by Sunday morning. They had been sent up from Georgia by the Chinese broker in Chamblee.

The ideal work schedule for a man like Alfredo is as many hours as possible, on as many days as possible. Nebajenses who are being paid on the books and whose employers don't wish to pay for overtime—confining them to forty hours a week—are on the lookout for jobs with longer work weeks. I have a friend in the town of Uspantán, not far from Ixil country, who went to Denver and began his workday with an eight-hour shift at a McDonald's franchise; then, every evening, he walked a mile to a second eight-hour shift at another McDonald's franchise, for a total of eighty hours a week. But I know an ex-guerrilla from Nebaj who has been working even longer hours. He does thirteen hours a day at a Korean supermarket from Wednesday through Sunday, for a total of 65 hours. On his two days off, Monday and Tuesday, he works nine hours at a Dominican supermarket, for a total of eighty-three hours a week.

Since most new arrivals from Nebaj lack a promised job, the next best alternative is to head for the address of a relative or neighbor. "Coyotes can falsely promise work when there isn't any," explains a successful returnee. "That's why it's best to join family, because they will feed you while you're looking for work." At a time when U.S. employers are shredding their commitments to employees by turning to contractors, subcontractors, and other forms of temporary labor, Nebajenses are sending up family work groups— networks of siblings, cousins, nephews, and in-laws who finance each other's trips north, live together and often work together, and, as they told Cécile Steverlynck, reduce each other's risk of failure.[11] As to how well they are served by this strategy, the clearest answers are in three U.S. localities where enough Nebajenses have found employment to create stable populations. In each of these labor markets, Nebajenses occupy ethnic niches. The niches are occupational categories that are easy for them to enter but, for lack of English and legality, difficult for them to leave.

Homestead

Homestead is an inland Miami suburb that originated as a railroad depot for a frost-free agricultural district where crops grow all year long. Ever since, Homestead has housed labor for hundreds of nurseries and other agricultural operations cut into the wetland Everglades of southern Florida. In the 1980s and 1990s, Cubans, Puerto Ricans, and Haitians settled in Homestead, followed by Salvadorans and Guatemalans, the latter of whom currently provide the bulk of agricultural labor. The Anglos who were the first employers have been supplanted by a rainbow of entrepreneurs from Cuba, Mexico, Colombia, Brazil, and elsewhere. The jobs they offer are attractive only for undocumented immigrants who lack a Social Security number, the ability to speak English, and any path to nonagricultural labor. In Homestead, undocumented immigrants can find work with a Spanish-speaking patrón who has no interest in their legal status because he is paying them off the books and in cash. Of the various Ixil colonies, Homestead provides the closest approximation to agricultural labor on Guatemalan plantations.

The first Guatemalans here were apparently Q'anjob'al Mayas from Hue-huetenango. According to a man from Parramos Grande, he and a friend from Tzalbal were the first Nebajenses to reach Homestead, in 1998 when he was sixteen. There was lots of work then. He started out waiting at the side of the road but soon found reliable employment for sixty dollars per day. Aside from four-season agriculture, especially nurseries that grow palm trees and other ornamentals for landscaping, Nebajenses have found better-paid but in-secure employment in the construction industry, which is converting agricul-tural land along the Florida Turnpike into housing and shopping complexes. Some Nebajenses live in the nurseries themselves, in primitive conditions but with very low expenses; others live in bare-bones two-story apartment buildings off Krome Avenue, the old downtown, which has been devastated by big-box shopping centers and so has been renamed the Historic District.

When Nebajenses wish to escape Homestead, the closest exit is West Palm Beach, where Guatemalan settlement seems to have been pioneered by Hue-huetecos from Indiantown. Nebajenses in West Palm Beach hail particularly from the village of Acul. They rent houses for as little as seven hundred dol-lars a month off Broadway Avenue between Twenty-Fifth and Fifty-Third streets. One attractive feature is that they can walk to the beach on the Inland Waterway in fifteen minutes. Employers include Anglos, Cubans, Mexicans, Colombians, and Venezuelans, particularly in landscaping, remodeling, roof-ing, and vegetable packing.

Dover and New Philadelphia

In Homestead and West Palm Beach, Nebajenses and other Guatemalans are part of large Latino populations. Small towns in Ohio are a different proposition. New Philadelphia and Dover adjoin each other in southeastern Ohio, between the decaying industrial city of Akron and the coalfields of West Virginia. New Philadelphia originated in the late eighteenth century as a Moravian mission to the Delaware Indians and a German agricultural settlement. Dover began a bit later as a canal and mill town. A man whom I will call Lucas says he was the first Nebajense to come here. He is a K'iche' speaker from Xexuxcap, and not a poor man by Nebaj standards. He already had a government job, but he wanted to buy a truck. His first stop was Home-stead, but it didn't agree with him ("I'm no good in a field; I have a bad foot and my abdomen hurts when I stoop for tomatoes; my stomach hurts"). So Lucas and four other men paid three hundred dollars each to a Huehueteco from Soloma to take them to Ohio. They paid the Huehueteco another three hundred dollars each for Social Security numbers. Then they went to work at the Case Farms chicken-processing plant in Winesburg.

Case Farms is famous for union busting and appears in labor historian Leon Fink's *The Maya of Morganton*, about a strike at its plant in North Carolina. Many of the Morganton workers and strikers hailed from Huehuetenango, especially Aguacatán, which is just over the mountain from the Nebajenses and home to many of the smugglers who take them north. It would be interesting to know more about Case Farms' system of labor procurement, but according to my friend Lucas, his bosses never asked him to recruit more workers from home. Instead, whenever he learned that the plant was hiring, he informed his relatives in Guatemala and they showed up. He soon became an assistant supervisor for an Anglo named Jeremias who didn't speak Spanish but picked it up quickly and gave orders that Lucas passed to other workers.

When Lucas started at the Winesburg plant in 1998, the pace of the chicken-processing line was much slower than it later became. During his first months, workers on the line still included Americans. By the time Lucas left, line workers consisted mainly of Guatemalans from Quiché Department, especially Nebaj and Joyabaj. Even Mexicans couldn't stand the pace, Lucas claims. According to another Nebajense, an Ixil from Parramos Grande, by 2008 the pace of the Winesburg, Ohio, line increased from twenty or thirty chickens per minute to sixty per minute, and the Americans couldn't take it. "Once they put an American next to me in the line. She cried on the first day because she couldn't do the work, and after three days she didn't come back."

By 2008 there were hundreds of Nebajenses in Dover and New Philadelphia, especially K'iche's from Xexuxcap and Ixils from Parramos Grande. They worked at meatpacking plants as well as at factories producing plastic, wooden pallets, and fertilizer, usually requiring a long commute by car. According to a Nebajense who worked at several of these places, the fertilizer plant was the best. During the busy season he earned six hundred to seven hundred dollars per week with an hourly wage of nine dollars rising to fourteen dollars with overtime. "One really great boss named Jeff gave us debit cards to buy food at Walmart. We were hired only for four to five months, during the busy period, and we didn't get paid vacation. But if I'd been able to stick around and get a permanent job, they would have given me paid vacation. I was the first Guatemalan there. The boss asked me, do you have more Guatemalans? And so I brought twenty more. In other plants most of the workers are already Guatemalans, only the people in charge are still gringos. They told me that if I spoke English, I could become a line supervisor in five months."

Pleasantville

One of the largest Ixil Maya colonies is in a suburb of Washington, D.C., that I will call Pleasantville. A nineteenth-century crossroads has been obliterated by shopping centers, townhouse complexes, an interstate, and other highways. Country roads have turned into six-lane viaducts because everything has been supersized to accommodate the traffic flows pulsing between the District of Columbia and its far-flung suburbs. Few human beings are in evidence unless you count the solo drivers buzzing past in cars. Of the few pedestrians, most are Guatemalans. The place seems almost deserted in the morning; then it comes to life in the afternoon and evening as commuters get off work and drop by to shop. Yet in this seemingly inhospitable place, the antithesis of a highland Indian town, several hundred Ixils have found employment and residence. Some can walk to work in five minutes.

The first Ixils found their way to Pleasantville because there was a hiring location for day labor—a go-slow avenue in the middle of a new commercial complex. Here they found work with building contractors, landscapers, and homeowners, many of whom turned out to be Koreans who also owned many of the new businesses. In 2002 a Korean supermarket opened, and Ixils became half the workforce. Then they went to work for other stores in the same chain throughout the Washington and Baltimore suburbs. Ixils also went to work for Korean restaurant owners. Complementing this occupational niche, they found a place to live in a row of townhouses which they dubbed Apartamentos Las Cucas in honor of the cockroaches. It was home until the buildings were demolished to make way for condominiums. Fortunately, the Ixils were able to reestablish themselves in an adjoining neighborhood of townhouses. It houses an American racial panoply, is well maintained, and is very peaceful. It is also the only place in the United States where I have seen a few Ixil women wearing their traditional garb.

Even though Pleasantville is surrounded by suburbs in which Anglos predominate, many Nebajenses have little contact with white people, whom they term *Americanos*. Their progress with English seems minimal. One morning in 2008, Francisco was waiting in front of a public library along with several other Guatemalans, hoping that someone would stop to offer work. "Our main problem is that we can never talk with Americanos," he told me in Spanish. "You're the first one to talk to us. The Americanos who hire us don't speak Spanish and are overjoyed when we produce a bit of English. 'Oh,' they say, 'you speak English!'" Francisco and his companions interrogate me about English-language slang that has backfired, including "buddy," "guy," and "honey." They also want to know how to ask basic curbside questions such as "What kind of job is this?" I decide that language-learning tapes would help, so we drive to the nearest bookstore. Francisco is of the opinion that Americanos make the best employers. But now his best-paying employer, an American building contractor, can hire him only two days a week, so he's standing beside the road. "We almost don't want to work for Latinos because they treat us bad and pay us bad," he claims.

Nebajenses have little good to say about the Koreans either. The very fact of paying workers $400 to $500 for a seventy-two hour week constitutes wage theft because it does not include overtime pay. Nor do the Koreans provide rent-free apartments like many of the Chinese restaurant owners. Since few Koreans speak Spanish, and since no Nebajenses speak Korean and few speak English, the two ethnic groups rely on hand signals and one-word commands to communicate. This could be one of the reasons why the Guatemalans have a hard time locating the Koreans' sense of humor.

Gilberto lived in Pleasantville until 2007 when the construction industry slowed, prompting him to return to Nebaj. He remembers it as a safe place to live because it was untroubled by Immigration and Customs Enforcement (ICE), and there was little crime. Gilberto counts himself lucky to have first a good gringo patrón and then a good Korean patrón. But the Korean was the only good one, Gilberto claims. "Koreans are not like the North Americans. They only pay by the day, not by the hour. You have to work from 6 a.m. to 8 p.m., for twelve hours [*sic*], and they only pay $80, which is like $7 an hour. They don't give you a soda, they don't give you lunch; you have to bring your own lunch. The Vietnamese are the same. The Chinese are the same. A Hindu . . . worse. I worked for a Hindu for three months, and he only paid me for one."

Despite this harsh assessment, Koreans are the most reliable employers the Ixils have found in the Washington suburbs. Crisanto used to work himself to exhaustion for $250 to $300 a week. But this last week his paycheck was for $400 because a Korean contractor was paying him thirteen dollars an hour. "They're not all bad," Crisanto told me. "If you trust in the Lord, you will be rewarded. The Koreans are better bosses than Hispanics because they pay the agreed amount. Hispanic bosses are bad because they don't keep their word." Equally important, Korean supermarkets and other businesses provide stable employment that held up against the 2007 downturn in the construction industry and the 2008 financial panic.

I soon learned to recognize Nebajenses' residential niche in the Washington–Baltimore corridor. They live in apartment or townhouse complexes behind shopping centers. A three-bedroom unit is shared by eight to twelve people, mostly from Nebaj and mostly male. Except for Nebajenses with steady work in construction, their wages are in the vicinity of the legal minimum. Since housing units rent for $1,500 to 1,700 monthly, the most obvious way to maximize remittances is to pack the residence with as many wage earners as possible. This divides the rent into smaller fractions, resulting in two or three persons per bedroom (usually kin) and several more out in the living room.

Bachelor pads have almost no furniture except for a plastic kitchen table, a few plastic chairs, and a big-screen television in each bedroom. In the absence of mattresses, residents sleep on the carpet with a blanket and pillow. Bathrooms lack soap or toilet paper because each resident has his own supply. But in two apartments commanded by Ixil matrons, I am pleased to report, the bathroom was stocked with essentials, there were beds, and there was furniture on which to sit. Computers and sound systems are ubiquitous. Printed matter is almost nonexistent except for a few bills and landlord notices. When I asked for a phone book at one apartment, I was told that it had been thrown out. Everyone has at least one cell phone, usually on monthly plans which allow lengthy conversations. Sometimes my interlocutor carried on two conversations simultaneously, one via the cell phone in Ixil and the other with me in Spanish.

To lower per capita expenses and meet savings goals, Nebajenses not only pack apartments but bring up relatives and neighbors. I visited one such family work group at the apartment of Candelario and Juliana in Pleasantville. Candelario has been in the United States since March 1999. In the first years, he moved from North Carolina to South Carolina, then back to North Carolina and all the way to Colorado, in vain attempts to make more than two hundred dollars a week. In 2002 he reached Pleasantville and has been working for the Korean supermarket ever since. At one point the Koreans were paying him five hundred dollars for sixty hours per week, but with the 2008 recession, they cut him back to $420. He lives in a well-kept townhouse with shiny white floors, a glass table and five chairs in the dining area, and two sofas arrayed before a television in the living room. His wife Juliana also works a twelve-hour day at the supermarket. As soon as she returns home at ten at night, she whips up a big group meal. They preside over an assortment of sons and nephews. On a rare day off, Candelario drives youth to and fro in his old but spotless sport utility vehicle. No good deed goes unpunished: when one of the kids plugs in his personal electronics, it knocks out the television, and another kid inadvertently takes off with Candelario's key to the apartment, locking him out.

But Nebajenses don't just bring up relatives to share expenses. Some families are trying to bring up every male sibling, and sometimes every female sibling as well, in the belief that each will need remittances to establish a household back in Nebaj. Diego and his brother Pedro are grandsons of one of the great Ixil *principales*, a political and ceremonial leader in the first half of the twentieth century who controlled large tracts of land but lost most of it to ladino bar owners and moneylenders. Diego and his brother spent years in the mountains with the Guerrilla Army of the Poor; he was a *responsable* administering civilians, and his brother was a lieutenant in the Ho Chi Minh Front. Both survived their surrender to the army and in the 1990s became involved in resettlement projects. But the Q60 ($7.70) per day that they could earn in their capacity as aid coordinators was not enough to meet their needs.

So in 2003, at the age of forty-eight, Diego sold fifty cuerdas of land (2.2 hectares) to raise the Q36,000 needed to go north. His first job was in a Korean restaurant in Pleasantville; he worked twelve hours a day and six days a week for three hundred dollars in cash. After a month he moved to a Korean supermarket for four hundred dollars a week. Several months later he moved to a painting contractor who paid him ten dollars an hour for up to sixty or seventy hours a week, weather permitting. As winter shut down that job, Diego went to work for a builder of backyard patios. One day in March 2004, he and the crew were searching for an address in the winding streets of Arlington, Virginia, when they blundered into the gate of a military installation. The sentries demanded identification. Three members of the crew could provide it, but Diego and three others could not; they were turned over to the Migra. And so, just as he was starting to make money on his investment, he was deported back to Guatemala.

By the time I met Diego in 2007, three of his four sons had replaced him in the United States by working for Chinese restaurants. On the basis of 7,200 hours of dishwashing and cooking per year, two of his sons built two-story houses back home. The third son, after two years of work, was picked off a Greyhound bus in Rochester, New York, and deported home. He was not able to build a new house and was feeling left behind, but he was about to try his luck again. Elsewhere in the family panorama, Diego's brother Tomás was picked off a Greyhound bus as he traveled to a Chinese employer in Buffalo. A nephew who went north at the age of sixteen had also been arrested, but because of his juvenile status, he was released to a foster parent and allowed to attend an American high school near Pleasantville. A second nephew whom Diego helped go north with a loan at 5 percent interest per month (half the normal rate) was successful in working at a succession of Chinese restaurants. A third nephew was in Homestead doing field labor for a Cuban employer. Scorecard for Diego and family: he, a brother, three sons, and three nephews had gone north, resulting in three deportations, one foster arrangement, and four workers as of 2011.

FAILING TO FIND ENOUGH WORK

The Nebajenses who have benefitted most from migration to the United States went early, found stable and sometimes high-paying employment, and returned with their savings intact. Some have glowing assessments. "As far as America, North America, is concerned, I have nothing bad to say," one successful returnee told me.

They received me well, they paid me well, the North Americans are very good. The first year was good, magnificent. The second year was magnificent. I worked with a gringo who remodels houses: tiling, painting, plumbing, drywall. We worked only from eight to four, and if you are inexperienced, he pays $10 an hour. He picked me up at my apartment and left me there at the end of the day. There were breaks. He gave us a soda and crackers. He gave us lunch. Everything was fine. Then I worked with a Korean who also was fine, a painter. As far as America, North America, the gringos are concerned, I don't have any complaint. I went and saw that it is very different there.

Some returnees endorse the entire country as a better way of life:

The United States is a good example for us because everything is organized and they don't quash the law; instead the law comes first. Here [in Guatemala] it's how to manipulate the law. Here a murderer kills five people, posts bail, and walks free. Here the police ask for your license to extract a bribe. There, if you drive carefully, there's no problem. In five years in the United States, they never bothered me. The police know that we're undocumented but don't bother us if we drive well. I never had problems with the police. I was really lucky. The patróns were good to me. I didn't lose my money; my wife is a good person and kept all my savings. The majority [of wives] run around with other men, but not her. The United States was a blessing for me. I flew back from San Francisco. It was my first flight, and I felt the airplane rising in the air [spreading his arms with a big smile]. When we reached a certain altitude, I said out loud, "God bless the United States!" The people next to me said that's the first time they'd heard anyone talk like that.

More often, however, returnees express disappointment. *Más o menos* (more or less), *un poco de éxito* (a bit of success), and *me fracasé* (I failed) are the most common responses when I ask Nebajenses how they fared. Some were deported before they paid off their travel debt; others managed to pay their debt but came home soon after because the pressure to search for work was so unrelenting and stressful. Of Homestead in particular, Nebajenses have nothing good to say, to the point that I wondered why any were still there.

In 2007 a Nebaj pastor stopped in Homestead to visit members of his church. He was shocked by how desperate they were. "It was like Guatemala," he told me. "In one service we met with 100 or 125 people, then with a smaller group of 15 or 20. The first time we stayed in a little hotel, the second time in two tiny apartments crammed with 25 people sharing a kitchen and a bathroom. We had to get in line to use the bathroom. Beds here, beds there, bunk beds. The people were crying because there wasn't any work. The patróns pay very low. And the blacks—they're very afraid of the blacks; they say they're bad and rob them. 'What should we do?' they asked me.

"What could I do?" The pastor gestured helplessly. "I told them to pray to the Lord. I told them, 'Work as hard as you can for the patrón, to convince him to keep you in the job rather than fire you, and look for something else.' And I told them to look for another place where people are not crowded together. In Homestead there are Guatemalans everywhere. Here, there, all you see are Guatemalans. They have to make telephone calls to other places. They have to look for work in other places where Guatemalans are not piling up."

Homestead, it would appear, had become too much like home. Should Guatemalans be blamed for recreating the conditions they hoped to escape? I don't think so. Most Guatemalans in Homestead are orderly and hardworking, and they contribute more than their share to Miami's boom-and-bust economy. Away from the crowded and hot apartments where they live, there is prosperity galore. New shopping centers, new condominiums, recreational extravaganzas, and stately rows of palm trees line the routes to the Florida Turnpike. But much of the labor force in landscaping, plant nurseries, and winter-vegetable farms is undocumented, which means that workers are powerless and wage theft is common. Wage theft is abetted by off-the-books payment in cash, and it includes "shaving" hours, delaying payment for weeks, not paying the agreed-upon wage, and paying below the minimum wage. When two investigators from Florida International University interviewed Homestead workers in 2007, the majority could not name the minimum wage. Many are illiterate; the most indigenous have limited fluency even in Spanish. And because they fear being deported, they are very challenging to organize.

Alejandro Angee and Cynthia Hernández report that "although workers are hardest hit by wage theft, businesses that comply with fair wage and labor laws are also undercut by the lower overhead and an environment of dishonesty created by competitors who ignore the law. The deregulation of business, specifically the lack of enforcement of wages and hours standards, makes these workers more vulnerable. At a local level, Miami-Dade's power dynamics also play an important role as Miami has become a magnet for immigrants from Latin America and provided a form of labor that is easy for employers to exploit. . . . The success of some immigrants in Miami means that employers who exploit workers are just as likely to be Latinos as they are Anglos."[12]

According to Jonathan Fried, a labor organizer who runs a workers' center called We Count!, wage theft around Homestead is worse than in any other corner of Dade County. He guesses that 90 percent of the victims are Guatemalans, because they're the most recent arrivals and work for the most marginal employers. He has been on the scene for a decade and thinks employment has been going downhill since 2006. By 2010 the construction industry, which provided the best jobs for Guatemalans, seemed completely dead. There were so many foreclosures that a rebound seemed unlikely. The collapse of new construction meant that the nursery trade was also depressed. Many Guatemalans had gone home or gone elsewhere in search of work.

When I visited Homestead in April 2008, Alejandro Angee and I counted 110 men along a half mile of Mowry Avenue at 7:15 a.m. The first men we approached were from Huehuetenango, but they quickly connected us with several knots of Nebajenses. One man was from Parramos Grande. He estimated that, from his village alone, forty or fifty men were in Homestead. He had been there for two years and agreed that employment was diminishing. He and his companions could only cover their rent, not save or remit.

Another of the Nebajenses, a twenty-eight-year-old, had been in Homestead longer and remembered better times. There was lots of work when this second man arrived in 2002; two years later, the men waiting on Mowry Avenue vanished because everyone had a job. During this period of glory, he made sixteen dollars an hour with a painting contractor. Then so many Guatemalans showed up that work became scarce. After months without stable employment, he was now pinning his hopes on a Chinese grower who would need him in June. Waiting for this good patrón, who would pay eighty dollars a day plus overtime, struck him as preferable to taking his chances with labor contractors from the Carolinas who were hiring workers but might be telling lies. In the meantime, men who had been out of work for weeks were accepting as little as fifty, forty, or thirty dollars a day, just in order to eat. He had not seen his wife and two children in six years.

Now that he knew what it was like, I asked, would he do it again? He looked away. "No," he said. "Living there is better. You have your little house, you don't have to pay rent or buy food. Here everything has to be paid for—rent, food, transport." "Are youth from Parramos Grande still coming?" I asked.

"Yes."

"You don't tell them that there is no work?"

"Yes, but they think this is a lie. We send money and they think it's easy to earn it. They think that life here is easy. But we spend more than we send."

In January 2010 I arrived at nine in the morning and counted upward of 150 men on Mowry Avenue. This time it was harder to locate Nebajenses—most of the men I approached said they were from Huehuetenango, especially the town of San Juan Atitán. Then I located a knot of Nebajenses. Of the four men with whom I spoke, three of the four said they were still in debt for their journey north after being in the United States an average of 4.75 years. There were still many Nebajenses in Homestead, they said. But if they were not standing on Mowry Avenue, they had jobs. So I was talking to men in the worst straits, not a representative sample of the Nebaj population in Homestead.

That same January, I also visited Nebajenses in the suburbs ringing Washington, D.C. At eight locations, including Langley Park, Maryland, and Annandale, Virginia, I counted 465 men waiting for someone to come by and offer them work. The men included Mexicans, Salvadorans, and Hondurans, as well as Guatemalans, most of whom were not from Nebaj. Most of the men I approached had been in the United States for at least a year and said they had experienced better times, mainly in construction. They were hoping that construction would spring back to life in April. The sight of so many men without work is disturbing, but I cannot quantify the larger population from which they are drawn—how many other men in these migration streams have jobs? Even for men waiting for work, we would have to know their work history—how much they've earned and how long they have been idle—to know how badly off they are.

One place where jobs still seemed to be available in 2010 was southeastern Ohio. So why weren't all the Nebajenses going there? "Because they don't like the cold, because they're accustomed to Florida, and because they don't need papers there," was the answer of one veteran. In Ohio, to qualify for factory work, everyone had to buy papers from Puerto Ricans or Chicanos. Getting a job in Ohio also entailed driving to factories in other towns, filling out an application, and waiting. This required not just a high degree of confidence, but relatives or friends who would provide lodging, food, and transportation until the job came through.

ASSAULTS, CAR WRECKS, AND COMING HOME IN A WHEELCHAIR

One of the most resonant arguments in the U.S. immigration debate is that immigrants take jobs from Americans. An equally resonant response is that Americans who reject high levels of immigration are racists. Only occasionally did I hear Nebajenses refer to friction with American workers. One possible reason is that, since so many Nebajenses work for immigrant employers in ethnic enclaves, few of them actually work alongside Americans. But in Ohio, some Nebajenses have learned to be apprehensive.

"They bother us, they corner us with the forklift truck, rushing toward us," one returnee told me, "because we don't take breaks, work twelve hours a day, and collect $600 checks, while they work eight hours and get checks for $400." This same man was also targeted by vandals. One evening he discovered adolescents in the yard yanking out his television cable. He called the police. They brought him to the station to check photos of local youth; he could not identify anyone. While he was at the station, someone slashed the tires of his car and his brother's car. He decided to change his address because of the attack, and because his housemates were consuming too much alcohol.

Nebajenses are short by American standards—men average five feet six inches—and they are afraid of being attacked by criminals, whom they usually identify as blacks, followed distantly by Mexicans, fellow Guatemalans, and whites. The riskiest locale is Homestead. Thus far I have met three men who, after criminal assaults there, came home as cripples. Jacinto Ceto had worked in Homestead for three years when, one evening, his apartment was hot and he was sitting outside. Suddenly the lights went dark, and there was a cry that the *morenos* (black men) were coming. Still in his chair, he was hit in the temple with a baseball bat. "From the first I realized that the place was not good, that I could not go out at night because they could attack," he told me. "If they find a Guatemalan walking in the street alone, they attack." A U.S. hospital equipped Jacinto with a glass eye at the cost of his $2,500 in savings, but the bone below his temple was still fractured and he was having a hard time making a living.

Jorge Oxlaj had been in Homestead for two and a half months when, walking down the street with a newly purchased soda, two men shot him in the leg with a pistol from a distance of ten yards. He'd never seen them in his life, and as in the previous case, there was no robbery. They ran away when the police showed up. A U.S. hospital removed the bullet, but now he had a severe limp and his leg hurt when he walked, limiting his ability to work. A year later I was visiting Homestead and introducing myself to day laborers on Mowry Avenue when one turned out to be Jorge's cousin. The reason he was clinging to Homestead despite being jobless was that a second member of his family had been felled by criminals.

In November 2007, his twenty-two-year-old nephew Juan Oxlaj was returning from work at 7:30 p.m. when men shot him in the chest. Another Oxlaj relative had a different version of events; Juan was a drinker and was coming home at 1 a.m. when he was shot, probably for resisting a robbery. During the operation that saved his life, his brain lost its blood supply for five minutes and six months later he was still in a coma. At the two year mark, Juan regained consciousness but was semi-paralyzed; he could neither see nor speak, and judging from the noises he made, he was in distress. His uncle and his mother wanted to bring him back to Guatemala but could not get permission from U.S. authorities.

Some months later, I was standing in line at the Nebaj hospital when I met yet another gunshot victim from Homestead. Two months before, Pedro

López had gone to the store at eight o'clock at night to buy a phone card to call his wife in Guatemala. A man asked him for money. When Pedro said he didn't have any, the man gave chase and shot him in the arm. Now that he was home in Nebaj, his arm was still in a sling and he was unable to move all his fingers. According to the labor organizer Jonathan Fried, Guatemalans are the most frequent victims of strong-arm robberies in Homestead because they don't have cars, they walk or bike to work, and they don't have bank accounts. Most dangerous are the environs of a liquor store presided over by a squat, suspicious Q'anjob'al Maya named Mario. Taped to the bullet-proof glass of the cashier's cage are Polaroid snaps of Mario's least-favorite customers—a leering pantheon of the Guatemalan working class. Each is scribbled with a caption such as "I stole a pack of beer" or "I am a thief" or "I'm a big testicle [*huevón*]."

Nebajenses in the United States have also been crippled by traffic ac-cidents. If employers realize they are liable, they are quick to offer cash so the victim will sign away his rights to a larger settlement. Now and then, thanks to American tort lawyers, injured Guatemalans receive large damage awards. Or their heirs do. But this is a mixed blessing because, back home, the money attracts extortionists who threaten to kidnap the beneficiary or his children. Winners of settlements are exceptional; the majority of victims and families receive nothing. Lacking legal status is a big disadvantage, as is the fact that many Guatemalans work under an assumed name. What enables some victims to collect settlements is timely intervention by ambulance chasers, to which end Spanish-speaking *en-ganchadoras* or hookers—in Miami typically Cubans—work the trauma wards signing up plaintiffs.

To convey the flavor of wheelchair cases, I will outline a case elsewhere in the Cuchumatanes. Luis Alberto Jiménez was an illegal immigrant from the remittance boomtown of Soloma, Huehuetenango. Through no fault of his own, in a highway accident caused by a drunk American driving a stolen vehicle, he suffered irreparable brain injuries. Two Guatemalans were killed, and two were seriously injured. Since the thief had no insurance, Luis' lawyer tried to recoup the cost of his medical care from the company from whom the vehicle was stolen. That did not work. An American hospital saved Luis' life twice but received only $80,000 in compensation from Medicaid. After three years and $1.5 million in expenses, the hospital negotiated an agreement with the Guatemalan government, which agreed to take custody of Luis and then flew him home in an air ambulance. When interviewed by a Guatemalan journalist, Luis thought he was still in Florida and failed to remember that he had a wife and two children. Instead, he wanted gold fillings in his teeth so that he could attract a girlfriend.[13]

Within weeks a government hospital discharged Luis to another government hospital, where he was found in a corridor on a stretcher, lying in his own excrement. His family brought him home to Soloma. Back in Florida, a cousin sued the American hospital for false imprisonment, punitive damages, and the cost of his medical care in Guatemala. Florida judges ruled in favor of the nearly $1 million lawsuit on two occasions before a Florida jury, without any Hispanic jurors, let the hospital off the hook. When Luis' American legal team hiked up to his off-road hamlet in the Cuchumatanes, they decided that his quality of life there, cared for by his family, was better than in an American nursing home. But his seizures were getting worse, and he probably did not have long to live. His advocates were firm that his care was the responsibility of the U.S. government.[14]

RUNNING AFOUL OF THE U.S. LEGAL SYSTEM

However apprehensive Nebajenses feel about U.S. criminals, they are equally or more apprehensive about being arrested by U.S. immigration authorities— as they well might be, given that virtually all of them have broken the law to enter the United States. Unfortunately, I have no way of quantifying how many have been arrested for illegal entry, how many have been arrested for lack of legal status inside the United States, how many have been arrested for criminal activity, and how many have been deported back to Guatemala. But the number of detainees and deportees surely runs into the many hundreds just for Nebajenses. In 2011 alone, the U.S. government deported and flew home 30,855 Guatemalans.[15] Because border crossing and its financial repercussions will occupy the next chapter, here let's consider the wide spectrum of harshness, leniency, and oblivion that Nebajenses encounter in the U.S. legal system.

Nebajenses who have Social Security numbers are often being paid under an assumed name. Many of the numbers seem to be genuine and belong to U.S. citizens or legal residents with Hispanic names whose numbers have been stolen or who have chosen to sell their numbers. The advantage of selling your number is that, apart from the cash, anyone who works under your name will contribute to your retirement.[16] Since the September 11, 2001, attack on New York and Washington, D.C., the U.S. government's get-tough attitude toward document fraud has included checking Social Security numbers. Yet I know of just one Nebajense who has been prosecuted under this kind of enforcement.

Miguel is the ne'er-do-well brother of one of my friends. He was in the United States for four years without paying off his smuggling debt, which meant four years of anxiety for his family rather than the remittances that were supposed to improve their life. One night in Ohio, Miguel had too much to drink and got into a fight with his girlfriend, whose housemate called the police and accused him of robbery. It was after pleading guilty to aggravated burglary and spending four months in jail that the police turned him over to Immigration and Customs Enforcement (ICE) for deportation. This was when it emerged that he had been working under someone else's Social Security number. A federal prosecutor decided to charge him with theft of the number, with a mandatory sentence of two years, in the hope that he would cough up information about who sold it to him. The prosecutor wanted to go after corporate employers who were hiring large numbers of workers with false identities.

It turned out that Miguel was being paid under the name of a man whose Social Security number was being used by nine people, all of whom were apparently contributing to his retirement while he resided in prison. I don't know whether Miguel told the prosecutor anything useful, but at the suggestion of his public defender—a lawyer in a nearby city—I wrote a clemency plea from his brother in Nebaj, in English for the judge and including an explanation of my role. Miguel's brother and I explained his circumstances: one of six siblings, he inherited almost no land and was trying to support a wife and four children. We assured the judge that Miguel's family would help him pay his debts and prevent him from returning to the United States. Thanks to the public defender, the prosecutor allowed him to plead guilty to a lesser offense, and he was home four months later. Unfortunately, Miguel's failure to save money during his first four years in the United States meant that he was now $13,000 in debt. So, little more than a year later, he went back to Ohio, where he is now supposedly working and staying away from alcohol as he pays off $18,000 in debt.

Nebajenses have no end of stories about getting deported, but they also have stories about getting into serious trouble and getting off the hook. Such is the case of one of Miguel's relatives, a veteran of the Guatemalan army who went north and seemed to be earning large amounts of money in Washington, D.C., but who suddenly stopped communicating. With great difficulty, his family learned that he had been in a car crash and was facing up to eighteen years in prison. After less than a year behind bars, he was home again.

Here is the story that Julio Vicente Toc told his family. In his first six months in the United States, Julio made lots of money—supposedly in a furniture factory—and instead of paying off his smuggling debt, he bought a new car. Then he bought a more luxurious car, started hanging out with Mexicans, and seriously injured an American in a traffic accident. He fled the accident and took refuge with his Mexican friends, only to have police bust the apartment and seize him, along with marijuana and lots of cash. That's why he was prosecuted not just for the hit-and-run but for drug trafficking. Julio threw himself on the mercy of the court. He convinced the judge that he was an orphan, that his siblings were suffering, and that they depended on him for support (in actuality, two of his brothers were rising rapidly in the Guatemalan army). Julio also fooled the judge into accepting his false identification papers as genuine, such that he was treated as an American citizen. Two public defenders helped him plea-bargain, resulting in a suspended five-year sentence that enabled him to go back to work in a furniture factory where his wages would be garnished to pay the victim of his car accident. Once back at work, Julio realized that his payments to his victim meant that he would not be able to save any money for himself. What was the point of that? So he asked his mother to send his Guatemalan identification card, he went to the Guatemalan consulate to obtain a passport under his true identity, and he returned home. "Who knows how much I owe there!" he told his family. His mother sold land to pay off Julio's debt in Guatemala. At last report, she was doing fine because two more of her sons had gone to the United States.[17]

Nebajenses have become attentive students of the difference between U.S. immigration authorities, local police who turn them over to the Migra, and the many local police who do not. "There were police everywhere and of four different kinds," a shocked Ixil told me of his unhappy stay in Buford, Georgia, an Atlanta suburb full of Latin American immigrants. This was quite a contrast to the relaxed policing to which he was accustomed elsewhere. Driving cars is often the occasion for meeting the constabulary, and not just for lack of a driver's license or driving skills, but also because the drivers are performing logistical functions for other migrants. "Everyone who drives falls into the hands of the police," a returned Ixil elder told me. "But not for lack of a license—it isn't difficult to obtain a license. My son always took people where they could obtain legal documents such as Social Security numbers. He was always taking people, always taking people, until the police took him away."

Another returnee from Ohio claimed to have had repeated encounters with law enforcement, none of which led to deportation. Benedicto made his best money not in factories but as a *raitero* (ride giver), ferrying new arrivals between Ohio, Virginia, and Florida. He charged $1,000 for a trip to Florida, or $1,200 for two passengers. In 2004, Ohio police caught him driving without a license and identifying himself as a Mexican with a different name. Upon learning that this other individual faced a serious traffic charge, Benedicto disowned the identity. A judge fined him $300 and let him go. On another occasion, Benedicto's brother borrowed his car and immediately collided with another driver. By this time Benedicto had a driver's license, but it was a Mexican license that he obtained by buying a Mexican birth certificate;

the judge punished him by taking away his license, impounding his car for a month, and making him buy new plates.

In contrast, Benedicto's brother succumbed to his first traffic stop, by a "racist cop" who arrested him and sent him to the Migra for deportation. Benedicto's escapades occurred between 2004 and 2007 while his brother's misfortune occurred in 2008, after an outcry over a vehicular manslaughter. The Guatemalan driver who caused the death did not have a license; on a previous occasion he had been caught driving drunk under a false identity and ICE promised to deport him, but he was soon back. Even after this second and more serious offense, through a quirk in Ohio law, the Guatemalan could be charged only with a misdemeanor, not a felony, and got off with little more than a year in jail.[18] That same winter, two Nebajenses named Adán Felipe Raymundo Gallego and Luis Pastor Herrera died on an icy Highway 250 in two separate accidents, nineteen days apart, as their carpool drivers sped to work.[19] "It comes from driving after drinking," a Nebaj elder told me. "What happens is that they drink, they go to sleep late, and they sleep until it's time to start work. Suddenly they wake up, look at the clock, jump in the car, and drive too fast."

Another occasion on which Nebajenses become acquainted with the police is when they make too much noise. Many Guatemalans tolerate levels of noise from boom boxes and televisions that many Americans do not. As one returnee observed, "North Americans live in silence." Still another occasion is excessive consumption of alcohol. In Ohio a youth was living next to gringos on one side and Guatemalans on the other. One day while in his cups, he became confused and knocked on the door of the gringos by mistake. A woman came to the door and he tried to excuse himself, but she called the police and accused him of abusing her. The police sent him to ICE and he was deported. From such incidents, some Nebajenses have concluded that it's better not to live next to Americans, or even to have American girlfriends. I know of three men in Ohio who have moved in with American women, sired children, and helped the women care for their previous children. But the arrangements seem to last only a few years, and the men have learned that it is risky. "If she gets crazy, she's going to denounce you to the police," warns a returnee. He had a child with a gringa who then left him for someone else and cut him off from his son.

Nebaj men are more likely to become involved with women from their town, from elsewhere in Guatemala, or from Mexico. Even here, however, they run into forms of law enforcement that are new to them, such as protection against domestic abuse and requirements for child support. On one such occasion, an Ixil couple in Nebaj asked me to help their son escape New Jersey. It seems that Domingo was living in an apartment with three other men when, according to his mother, "a woman showed up. We don't know from what country, but she's from there. She was drunk, became pregnant, had a baby, and she is now suing our son because she says that it is his child. Every week she's bothering him even though he now has a woman, he lives with her and her parents, and they have a child." Worse, Domingo's mother informed me, his new in-laws became upset when they learned that he might have impregnated another woman.

What did Domingo have to say for himself? I asked. There were two other males in the apartment, his mother explained; he was drunk and didn't remember what happened. The door was open and this nuisance of a girl walked in. Now she couldn't get at the other two youths because they had moved away, so she was focusing on poor Domingo. Everyone was awaiting the results of the paternity test. If the test shows that Domingo is the father, I explained to his parents, his wages would be garnished until the child is eighteen. They were horrified—he was supposed to be sending his savings to them. And so they had another question. If the paternity test identified their son as the father, could I help him come home with his other woman and child? The only problem was that their son was out of work and didn't have any money. Did I know of any *fondo* (fund) or *proyecto* to help people in this predicament?

Lack of legal status makes Nebajenses extremely vulnerable to their partners. Reinaldo is not indigenous and went north through a Huehueteco friend in 1992. He landed a job with ConAgra in Omaha, Nebraska, and rose to the level of a supervisor making $52,000 a year. In 2003 he married a Mexican woman from Durango who also arrived illegally but obtained U.S. citizenship through a husband from whom she was now divorced. She made much less money than Reinaldo did, so he made the payments on both their vehicles, as well as on the house they bought, and he also paid the lawyers who were sorting out their legal situation. Years earlier, upon reaching the United States, Reinaldo had obtained temporary protected status (TPS) on the basis of claims suggested by a notary; this gave him permission to work, but it had to be renewed every year and ICE was asking too many questions. He knew his time was running out. So now a lawyer suggested starting over again, with the help of his Mexican wife who was now a U.S. citizen. In 2007, Reinaldo declared his past illegal entries, returned to Guatemala, and had a reassuring interview with the U.S. embassy. Now all he had to do was wait for the paperwork to come through, enabling him to return to Nebraska with legal status—until a nightmare telephone conversation with his wife. She had never approved of the large remittances that he sent his mother and siblings. Now she was upset that he was giving his mother $26,000 from the sale of a Nebaj inheritance. "If you want to be with your family," she said, "stay with your family." She cut off communication, canceled her application to bring him to the United States, and invited another man to live with her in his house. The U.S. embassy refused to give Reinaldo a visa to return. If he were to return illegally, his wife would report him and he could spend years in jail. So Reinaldo said good-bye to his life in the United States.

Chapter Four

Indenture Travel

I don't have the economic resources to finish high school. I will do any job; I don't care what job. I will break stones, chop down trees, clean toilets, I don't care what job. I will do anything to earn well.

—*Tuk-tuk* driver in Nebaj, 2007

For many of us involved in the U.S. immigration debate, enforcing the Mexican border against job seekers is senseless and unjust. If Latin Americans seek work in the United States and if employers want to hire them, why go to so much trouble to stop them? To arrest, jail, and deport migrants is to violate their human right to cross borders, improve their lives, and support their families. This is the moral baseline for those of us horrified by the human cost of border enforcement, and our most potent symbol is the undocumented border crosser who dies in the Arizona desert. Since the federal government began fencing border towns in 1996, obliging unauthorized crossers to make longer circuits through deserts, as many as five hundred a year have perished—and these are only the bodies that have been recovered.

In Nebaj, whenever I asked if migrants had died on their way north, all I heard about were migrants who died after they arrived. They were killed not by border enforcement, but by their destination, especially Florida. My list includes six Nebajenses who died in traffic accidents caused by someone else. A seventh met his end driving under the influence, an eighth died in a construction collapse, and another three were shot and killed by criminals. There also have been one alcohol-related asphyxiation, one alcohol-related suicide, and one knife murder by fellow Nebajenses who were drunk, for a total of fourteen deaths, eight of them in the Sunshine State. The mortality of Guatemalan males who stay in Guatemala may be no higher, but for the families, these are tragedies with sharp financial repercussions. "The family expects money and gets a cadaver," commented a returnee. "They sacrificed so much for the muchacho to get there, only to have him die."

One night in the suburbs ringing Washington, D.C., I finally heard about a youth who died in the Arizona desert. My host was not certain of the name but had an idea where the mother lived, in an outlying *cantón* of the municipal seat, so I was able to locate her and ask what happened. Jacinto Ceto Raymundo was nineteen years old when he went north in 2004. He had already spent four years working in a factory in Guatemala City and concluded, "Life here doesn't provide much; maybe I'll do better in the United States." His parents helped him arrange a loan. According to the coyote, Jacinto was in one of two vehicles being chased by the U.S. Border Patrol. During the panic, he jumped or fell out of the vehicle that was carrying him and was run over by the next vehicle.

Soon I heard about a second possible death in the desert. Antonio Pastor Raymundo was also nineteen when he went north in May 2006. He was one of nine siblings whose parents owned 1.5 hectares of land. He worked as a street vendor in the tourist spa of Antigua Guatemala and tried selling clothes, then ice cream and bread; next he started a store that failed, leaving his family in debt. "Since there's nothing here, I'm leaving to make money," he told his father, who helped him set up the trip. According to the coyote, Antonio's foot became swollen; he was unable to keep up with the others and said he would stop to rest at a hut. That was the last that was ever heard from him.[1]

A few Nebajenses have wangled tourist visas that enable them to arrive in the United States legally on an airline. One man bought a passport in Costa Rica that allowed him to fly under another name. Others report being floated across the Rio Grande, then marched through the thorny scrub of South Texas to a waiting vehicle. But from 2007 to 2012, a large majority of Nebajenses have been walking through the Sonora-Arizona desert. Their coyotes truck them out of the fabled town of Altar de Sonora in the evening, lead them through the desert for several nights or more, then have them picked up in vans and taken to safe houses in Phoenix.

In the U.S. immigration debate, one argument against the next costly investment in U.S. border security (more fences, more technology, more detention centers, and more personnel) is that they never seem to work. People who are prevented from crossing in urban areas simply undertake more arduous and dangerous journeys through the desert. Those who are caught usually try a second time, and if necessary a third time, until most get through. By 2007, Nebaj's coyotes were even offering three tries for the price of one. If migrants were caught in Mexico or the United States, they simply reconnected with their coyote upon release. He would arrange a second trip, and if necessary a third. A large majority of Nebajenses seemed to be making it into the United States on their first or second attempt. But not everyone. Some were so shaken by a near-death experience or detention that they didn't want to try again.

Pablo is one such *fracasado* (failure) who has returned to this merciless label. It is the middle of the day, in the middle of the week, and he is slouched on a sofa watching sexy women cavort on a large-screen television. In 2007, Pablo made it across Mexico in a passenger van; the coyotes for his group were so skillful, or at least so well connected, that they were never stopped by the Mexican police. They crossed the Rio Grande, spent three nights in the desert, and were in McAllen, Texas, when they fell into the hands of the Border Patrol. Pablo recalled,

> The Migra asked us where we were from. We told them that we arrived out of necessity, because of poverty, to work. "This is not your country," they answered. "What are you doing coming into a country that is not yours without going through the port of entry?" First we were taken to a checkpoint, then to other places, and we were fed just once a day—a ham sandwich with water. There were toilets and showers and so much air conditioning that we were cold; they didn't give us blankets. It was a jail without windows. They treated us like objects, like savage animals, worse than criminals. They had us chained up when they transferred us to a new place, even though we came only to work for the North Americans. We crossed the border to work, not to commit crimes. The food gave us illnesses; there wasn't any food to which we were accustomed. It was as if they were trying to punish us so that we wouldn't try crossing again. "This is what you get when you break the law," the guards said when we complained.

Pablo had two more chances to cross with his coyote, but on his second attempt, he was captured and deported again. At last report he was out in a village teaching school.

However many Nebajenses have been arrested by U.S. authorities, and some by the Mexican authorities as well, I have yet to hear of anyone who has died in custody. If Guatemalans convince the Border Patrol that they are Mexican, they are simply taken back to the Mexican border, facilitating their next attempt to cross. If they fail to pass as Mexican, they spend more time in custody until they can be placed on a deportation flight that takes them back to their own country. A few are not spit out in the predictable span of a few days to a few months. In such cases, one possible reason is asking for their right to legal counsel and a deportation hearing, which can add half a year to their limbo.

When migrants fail to communicate with their families, it produces deep anxiety. If I happen along, the family asks me to help. I never met Jacinta in person, but she was a forty-year-old mother of four who, along with a group of other Nebajenses, reached a safe house in Phoenix. Assured of their arrival, the families wired tens of thousands of dollars to the usual coyote bank accounts in Mexico. Soon after leaving the safe house, they were all arrested. Her companions who admitted to being Guatemalans were deported and soon home again. Her companions who claimed to be Mexicans were deported to Mexico, and on their second try they made it to their U.S. destinations. But from Jacinta, not a word. Someone had seen her in detention, crying. Alarmingly, she was not on the Guatemalan consulate's list of detainees.

The person who brought me into the case was Jacinta's sister-in-law. She was now in charge of Jacinta's four children, the oldest of whom was ten. Jacinta had never said good-bye to them, let alone informed them of her plans, and they were so distraught that they were suddenly failing at school. Perhaps, the sister-in-law suggested, Jacinta could not give her name to the U.S. authorities because she didn't speak Spanish? This I doubted—I've never met an Ixil who cannot respond to basic questions in Spanish. More likely, Jacinta did not want to give her real name because this was the second time that she had been arrested for entering the United States. The year before, she spent a month in custody before being deported back to Guatemala, losing her Q10,000 ($1,300) advance payment. Doubtless the Migra had warned that if she was caught again the punishment would be worse. But she was desperate to join her husband in Florida. While he was in the United States sending her money, she had been so flagrantly unfaithful that he found out. Now she was so afraid of losing his remittances that she was determined to join him in Florida, regardless of the repercussions for her children—all this according to the sister-in-law, who did not have a high opinion of Jacinta's judgment.

After two months, Jacinta was still not showing up on the consulate's list of detainees. And her children were falling apart. So I asked the sister-in-law if I should contact Immigration and Customs Enforcement (ICE) with her real name. The sister-in-law asked the rest of the family, and they said yes. So I e-mailed a letter to the detention center where I guessed that she was being held, in Florence, Arizona. My letter invoked her children and provided her real name. There was never a response, but several weeks later Jacinta showed up on a deportation flight to Guatemala City. At first she was defiant and insisted that she would go north again. But now she and her husband were $6,000 in debt for her first two trips north; a third trip would add another $5,000. The last time I asked, Jacinta was still with her four children and her in-laws.

The drama of the border, its conferral of life and death, has attracted enormous attention. But getting through the border, while always an adventure and sometimes traumatic, turns out to be less a challenge for Nebajenses than paying for it—the reason I have titled this chapter "Indenture Travel." Unlike Chinese immigrants who indenture themselves to Chinese gangs and employers in the United States by signing contracts to work off their debts in brothels, sweatshops, and restaurants, Guatemalan migrants do not indenture themselves to stateside employers in any formal sense. But they must borrow so heavily that they indenture themselves, their relatives, and their property to their vision of a better life.[2] The rest of this chapter explores the relationship between Nebajenses and the smuggling networks that take them through Mexico and across the U.S. border.

THE CASH-ON-DELIVERY SYSTEM

Mexican coyotes do not get much favorable press in the United States. They make their living by outwitting the Border Patrol. When they make headlines, it is usually because their strategies to evade the law have led to the injury or death of their *pollos* (chickens, i.e., customers). Yet the majority of Nebajenses who hire coyotes seem to reach their destination. The efficiency of the best coyotes is legendary: one man told me how, after being arrested on his first crossing into the United States, he and his fifteen companions spent thirty-two days in custody before being deported. Waiting for them at the Guatemala City airport was Francisco Ortiz, brother of the most renowned coyote in these parts, Santos Ortiz of Aguacatán. Twelve days later, thanks to the good offices of the Ortiz brothers, our man arrived safely in Homestead, Florida.

For Nebajenses determined to go north or send their children, coyotes are an invaluable resource. Thanks only to coyotes, not to unhelpful gringos like myself, thousands of Nebajenses have been able to enter U.S. labor markets. Consider the events of July 3, 2007, when three men armed with M-16s and a grenade kidnapped a coyote. The victim was a Huehueteco from Aguacatán, and the kidnappers—Ixils judging from their speech and stature—planned to hold him for ransom. They trussed him up and marched him into a forested canyon where the national police, few in number and wedded to their vehicles, would never venture. What the kidnappers failed to anticipate was the reaction from the surrounding villages, where most men above the age of thirty have military experience with the civil patrols, the army, and/or the guerrillas. Alerted by cell phone, men from Salquil Grande, Tzalbal, La Pista, Vipecbalam, Xepiun, and Cotzol dropped what they were doing and descended into the canyon—three hundred of them, I was told. When one of the posses came upon the kidnappers, the latter fired warning shots, jumped into the river, and escaped.

Shortly thereafter a vehicle of masked men carrying pistols and a bullhorn descended on the Nebaj police station. They believed that the police had custody of the kidnappers, and this was a lynching party. Fortunately the police were in possession only of the rescued coyote, prompting a spontaneous rally that was taped by Radio Ixil.

"Do you have anything to tell the population?" an interviewer asked the coyote in Spanish. "Do you realize how many people mobilized to rescue you?"

"We would just like to thank people," responded the coyote. "We are very grateful to you. Señores, we are not from here. We are from elsewhere, but we thank you for helping your neighbor. They think that we carry money. But, señores, we have debts in other places to help those persons here who have needs. Señores, we want hardworking people; we don't want worthless ones. I would like to thank you a great deal. Perhaps I cannot pay you for your time, but God will pay."

The applause was light, but the next speech, from a rally organizer, drew rousing cheers. Here are the phrases in Spanish that I picked up: "We are men with balls. That is to say, we are not *huevonazos*. We are *hombres hombres*.[3] We know how to fight. . . . We need to unite to have our organization. It's better that the people apply their own justice. We're cleaning up the youth. We have to clean up. We have to keep going, to struggle against those who do evil to their neighbors. We call the police, and they don't show up. Let's start organizing ourselves. We're seeing that we're united. They're getting a salary from the state, but they're not doing anything. Let's clean it up ourselves. The people united will never be defeated!"

Despite this moment of solidarity, Nebajenses have complicated feelings about coyotes.[4] When an expedition turns out badly, disappointed migrants and investors accuse the coyotes of swindling them. Consider the following affidavit, filed with the district court in Nebaj in 2006 by a widow named Juana Brito Gallego:

> On October 3, these señores [two Ixils named Miguel and Francisco] deceived my sixteen-year-old son Raúl González Brito [into thinking that he could] go work in the United States of North America. They offered him easy work in the United States, and because he's a minor and lacks experience, he accepted their proposition. Next these men demanded the title to my land near Las Violetas and, without my consent, took me before a lawyer and obliged me to put my thumbprint on a document whose content I did not understand, in the first place because I cannot read or write and in the second place because they didn't explain it to me.
>
> Since October 3, the date on which my son left for the United States, they are charging me ten thousand quetzals plus 10 percent interest per month. But the

truth is, never did they give me a single cent, nor to my son, and I do not understand why they are charging us for money that we have not received, which I consider a robbery or swindle. When I ask where my son is, they tell me only that he is now in the United States and they demand more money or another property document, they say in order to take out a loan from the bank in my name. When I insist about my son, they threaten to kill me or do something to me and my family. Last week a señora called who said she is a migration worker and who informed me that my son has been arrested by U.S. Migration and that in three months he will be deported to Guatemala. Meanwhile, these señores are demanding more money from me, or another property title.

When I met Raúl a year later, in 2007, he was eighteen years old but could be mistaken for fifteen. Now he was home again with his mother, four younger brothers, and his grandmother. They lived together in a hillside shack. The father of the oldest three boys died of illness; the father of the youngest two took off. As a kid, Raúl went to the plantations with his mother every year to pick coffee. Then he tried cutting sugarcane—a grueling job for anyone, let alone a slip of a youth like Raúl. Yet he learned to cut as much as eight tons a day, for seven quetzals (a little less than a U.S. dollar) per ton. A cousin showed him how to take an antidepressant and painkiller called Tramal (tramadol hydrochloride) to ignore the pain, and something called Sin Sueño (apparently caffeine tablets) to ignore his weariness. When the harvest was finished, a Nebaj furniture maker hired him for forty quetzals (five dollars) a day. That was his wage—not a bad one for a teenager—when he heard about all the money he could make in the United States, and two men who could help him get there.

Contrary to his mother's affidavit, Raúl now told me, it was he and his mother who approached the coyotes. To pay for the trip, his mother put up the deed to their ramshackle dwelling. Although on a steep hillside, it is only fifteen minutes from the center of town, making it valuable. On Raúl's journey, getting across Mexico was the easy part. His coyote gave him an identification card, with the name Alfredo Baudilio Orozco, that enabled him to get through police checkpoints. The U.S.-Mexican border was another matter. On his first try, a boat ferried him and dozens of others across the Rio Grande near Harlingen, Texas. They walked through the desert for three hours before being intercepted by the Border Patrol. Most were captured. Raúl escaped and managed to get back to the river. Swimming was new to him; his backpack pulled him down and he thought he was drowning. But a coyote helped him stagger onto the Mexican bank and he just lost his pants, not his life.

The second time, they crossed the river in the dark and walked the same route, but this time for the entire night. Following a day of sleep in the shade of cacti, they set off again under cover of night and reached a road where they found a passenger van and a pickup truck. Raúl boarded the van which the coyotes loaded until it contained thirty people (which I find hard to believe, but I have seen Nebaj drivers load theirs with more than twenty). The driver took off at high speed until a rear tire blew, whereupon he slammed on the brakes and the van rolled four times. Three passengers were killed; most of the rest were injured. Raúl's head swelled up, and he couldn't stand straight. Migra helicopters arrived with searchlights, followed by the local police. Raúl tried to hide but was found by a search dog and arrested along with everyone else. He and four others were allocated to local law enforcement who took them to a hospital emergency room. Suddenly, at three or four in the morning, he and two others without serious injuries were free to go. There were no cops around, let alone the Border Patrol, and at the age of seventeen, Raúl was walking up the street to his future in the United States of America.

"I was with a muchacho who was twenty-two years old, not from Nebaj but from Quiché, and he began to cry," Raúl said. "I wanted to look for work, but he couldn't take it anymore. A police car stopped; he told them that he was a Guatemalan and that he wanted to return to his country, and he asked the police to call Migration. I got angry with him. I wanted to escape, but lots of police and Migra cars were arriving and I couldn't." Because Raúl was a minor, he ended up in a youth center. Over the next six months, he enjoyed more schooling than he ever received in his own country. They made sure that he didn't have any tattoos on his body, which would indicate gang membership, and he never told them his real name. Back in Guatemala, his mother had no clear information and was frantic with worry, both about him and about the coyote debt that could take her hillside shack. Once Raúl had several months to think about his mother's need for income, he asked for deportation. When he told me his story in November 2007, he was again earning a decent wage by Nebaj standards. The difference was that he and his mother had yet to recover the title to their home. They were still afraid of losing it. Could I help him go back to the United States?

I don't know if Diego Velasco Matom was really the biggest coyote in town. He may have been merely the most visible coyote in town because of his air of importance and the three-story house rising above his neighbors. Before I could ask Diego for an interview, he was suddenly dead, and I could only attend his funeral in the mountain hamlet where he was born. It was the biggest funeral I've ever attended. Three sound systems were going simultaneously. From a double blaster on the back of a pickup truck came a stately but hopeful funeral march. From the Full Gospel Church of God, whose cement-block walls were raised by Diego's generous contributions, came his funeral service in Ixil Maya. From the third loudspeaker came Diego's life and works, mainly in Spanish. He was "a good man—hardworking, honorable with people, a good Christian" said the eulogist. "At seven years of age he went to the Finca La Perla to pick coffee with his father. He suffered poverty but surmounted it. At the age of eight he began to trade in *panela* [the raw sugar used to distill bootleg alcohol]. At the age of twelve he went to cut sugarcane at the Finca Madre Tierra." Next he became a buyer and seller of cattle. Oddly, the eulogist kept cycling back to these stages in Diego's career instead of advancing to the next. He never got around to describing how Diego became a labor contractor, recruiting Ixils to work on plantations, and then a coyote, recruiting Ixils to go to the United States.

The day Diego was shot at his three-story house a few blocks from the Nebaj plaza, Radio Ixil arrived well before the police did, and the most memorable feature of the broadcast was the heart-rending wail of Diego's women. Two young men had arrived on a motorcycle, asked for his house, walked up the stairs to the second story, and pumped three bullets into him. It was the middle of the day, on a busy street with numerous witnesses, but no one would tell the police or the family what the assailants looked like. What if the killers came again and retaliated? It looked like a contract killing, but who paid for it? I never found anyone who offered more than conjecture. Maybe Diego had been too hard-nosed in forcing someone to sell property to

Diego Velasco Matom's funeral

pay a debt. Maybe he had charged a high price for a trip that turned out badly. Maybe he had antagonized the coyote network that took his clients.

The most popular explanation, however, consisted of Diego's love affairs. Here too there was a coyote angle. When killed at his townhouse, he was with his new woman, not his wife back in the village. His new woman or *casera* (literally a housekeeper, colloquially a mistress) was much younger than his wife, and he was said to have taken her from one of the men he sent north. This was the explanation that made the most sense to Nebajenses, with two variants: either the offended husband had paid for the hit, or the second wife (not the first) had paid for it herself. The reasoning behind this final conjecture was that, since little money had been found in Diego's house after the murder, the *casera* must have taken it. Running through most theories was a common thread: *debía algo a alguién*—he owed something to someone. His murder was due to his own failings, the usual premise in Nebaj's merciless rumor mill.

Coyote networks are not easy to study, and research on them is scarce. For many years, the only book in English was the journalist Ted Conover's *Coyotes*, about his misadventures crossing the U.S. border with migrant farmworkers. In the 1990s the sociologist David Spener began fieldwork with Mexican migrants from San Luis Potosí and other states in northeastern Mexico. No other scholar has spent as much time on the subject. *Coyotaje* is a Mexican category older than the Spanish Conquest, Spener points out, with many different connotations. Three connotations particularly relevant for us are, not just crossing the border surreptitiously, but bribing officials and placing migrants with employers. Some scholars use the term "migration industry" to refer to this hive of activity, but Spener portrays a very decentralized endeavor, in which the mutual-aid networks of generations of Mexican migrants have given rise to networks of independent contractors. Because these networks grow out of kinship, friendship, and shared geographical origin, it can be very difficult to distinguish between coyotes and their customers. Thus when U.S. prosecutors indict coyotes and persuade them to name collaborators, they tend to implicate aunts and uncles.[5]

Looking at this system from farther south in Guatemala, my biggest question is how coyotes and their clients develop enough confidence in each other to make it all work. In my first interviews in Nebaj, I heard one story after another of coyotes (or of people who claimed to be such) swindling would-be migrants. Victims invariably paid the coyote in advance, or gave him a large down payment, only to be abandoned far short of their destination, in a seedy pensión in a strange city. The father of one migrant told Cécile Steverlynck that he and his son had gone Q200,000 ($26,000) into debt for five attempts to go north.[6] So payment in advance didn't work very well, and not only for the clients, as Spener points out, because it creates a perverse incentive to abandon clients at the first moment of difficulty, the repercussions of which then cut off the flow of new clients.[7] On the other hand, if the migrant pays only after reaching El Norte, what really obliges him to fulfill his financial obligation? Soon I was listening to Nebaj moneylenders bewail all the borrowers who, after arriving in the United States, claim that they are unable to pay and stop answering their cell phones.

Moreover, if this is how Ixils treat members of their own ethnic group, whom they will continue to meet in social encounters, how do smugglers and migrants from different ethnic groups and countries become reliable business partners? Nebaj coyotes deliver their clients to Huehueteco coyotes, who deliver their clients to Mexican coyotes in the state of Chiapas, who relay the migrants through Mexico to coyotes specializing in crossing the border, who deliver the migrants to the coyotes running safe houses in Phoenix. Only at the safe houses does the network obtain final payment. By what miracle is the $5,000 from each Nebaj migrant being equitably and reliably partitioned among so many business partners along a 1,500-mile route?

David Spener's ethnography of Mexican coyote networks casts light on this question. He refers to its critical feature as COD or "cash on delivery," which fits how Nebajenses describe their arrangements. Evidently cash on delivery was invented by Mexicans who imparted it to the Huehuetecos who have imparted it to the Nebajenses, and over the years it has evolved into a remarkable apparatus for moving unauthorized migrants north. The question is, if coyotes are always subject to arrest and other sudden interruptions, if they are often forced to improvise, how do they sustain the complicated business relationships that are necessary to deliver their clients to the United States? Through violence and threat of violence? Not when Spener did his research (prior to 2006) and where he did it (along the Texas border). There, at least, U.S. law enforcement rarely found guns on the coyotes it captured; Hollywood-style violence was atypical.

The only way these wily rule breakers can succeed at what they do, Spener argues convincingly, is by trusting each other. The coyotes must trust each other, and they must also establish trust with their clients. In Spanish, the most popular term is *confianza*; in scholarship, the most popular term is "social capital." Successful coyote networks abound in confianza and social capital, which according to Spener comes from four different sources:

1. altruism toward family and friends;
2. solidarity with fellow townspeople against external threats;
3. reciprocal exchange with fellow townspeople, in expectation that the favor will be returned; and

4. enforceable trust, that is, fear of stigma and financial loss if contractual obligations are broken.

How can trust be enforceable in a decentralized underground industry? If coyotes victimize their customers and partners, Spener points out, someone else will be hired for the next trip north. If migrants fail to pay what they owe, coyotes will not help their relatives come north in the future. As for the coyotes running safe houses on U.S. soil, should they become too heavy-handed, they can be denounced to the local police or the Border Patrol—which occurs when U.S. citizens and legal residents accuse coyotes of kidnapping their relatives for ransom, setting the stage for a human-trafficking indictment.[8]

In Guatemala, the most experienced towns in Huehuetenango and San Marcos Departments are developing their own smuggling networks. In San Juan Ixcoy, for example, migrants are said to travel together in groups, fifteen to twenty-five at a time, and to cross Mexico without coyotes. If so, they are taking charge of their own payoffs to police, their own navigation, and their own transportation, which means they have become their own coyotes. Nebajenses, in contrast, continue to rely heavily on smugglers from other towns. No one seems to pay the full price in advance anymore. The usual down payment is Q10,000 or Q15,000.

But even the cash-on-delivery system does not protect Nebajenses from paying for failed journeys, the cost of which they will not recoup unless they undertake the risk and debt of another trip north. Arrest and deportation after leaving the safe house but before paying off the debt has befallen many Nebajenses.[9] Others are ruined by putting their faith in the wrong coyote network, one taking advantage of the opportunities for extortion along the U.S. border.

Consider the fate of Mateo, an experienced bus driver in his mid-thirties. Except for weekend bus runs (Q50, or $6.40, per day), he has been reduced to driving someone else's three-wheeled taxi (Q40 per day) and stealing firewood from other people's land (Q20 per load if you escape; confiscation of your axe if you don't). In December 2009, Mateo went north with a well-known Ixil recruiter in the village of Cambalám who turned him over to Huehueteco smugglers from Soloma. To get through Mexico, the coyotes taught him to talk like a Mexican and sing the Mexican national anthem; they also gave him an ID card with a photo that resembled his own face. Crossing the desert from Altar de Sonora became a nightmare of interdiction. The guide was a Guatemalan from San Marcos Department; no matter what route he chose, they ran into the Border Patrol. On the fourth night the guide ditched Mateo and his companion, who survived only by finding a power line and following it until they reached the Border Patrol. Not only had Mateo given the Cambalám coyote Q10,000 in advance; in Altar a member of the same network extracted another Q25,000 from him. After he was deported home, the Cambalám coyote blamed him for stupidity, claimed to have also paid for the trip, and demanded that Mateo repay him. Now he and an aunt were failing to keep up the payments on a Q35,000 loan, and they were in danger of losing two parcels of land.

Crossing the Arizona border between 2007 and 2012 has been a more dangerous proposition for Guatemalans and other foreigners than crossing the Texas border was for Mexicans in earlier periods. When David Spener did his research prior to 2006, smuggling people and smuggling drugs were separate businesses, even if low-level independent contractors hired themselves out to both kinds of operations.[10] Since then the border has become more violent because of escalating conflicts for control of the drug trade. Mexican drug gangs engage in mass kidnappings and extortions of migrants. On one occasion, they murdered seventy-two migrants for refusing to pay, and on other occasions almost two hundred more, just in the town of San Fernando, Tamaulipas, and they did so with the connivance of men in police uniforms.[11] Unfortunately, the small-town social ties that pressure Mexican coyotes to behave respectfully toward their own migrants imply that migrants from elsewhere are fair game. When Nebajenses report being kidnapped or extorted by rival bands of coyotes, one possibility is that these are billing disputes over previous trips, with the aggrieved party attempting to collect from the transgressor's next human cargo.

EXACTLY WHO ARE THE COYOTES IN NEBAJ?

Nebajenses refer to anyone involved in sending people north as a coyote. But I have been able to identify just one Nebajense who has personally guided clients all the way to the United States.[12] Otherwise, Nebaj coyotes confine themselves to recruiting people for the trip north, arranging the loans they need to pay for it, and assembling them for the first stage. More often than not, Nebaj coyotes are working with Huehuetecos from the neighboring municipio of Aguacatán, but also Huehuetecos from Soloma and the city of Huehuetenango, and occasionally from the Department of Quetzaltenango. Diego Velasco Matom was a coyote because he recruited migrants for Huehueteco coyotes and arranged the loans that paid for the trip. In local parlance, he was an *enganchador* (hooker or recruiter) and *prestamista* (moneylender) rather than a *contrabandista* or *traficante* (the actual smugglers).

I can't say that Diego Velasco Matom was a typical Nebaj coyote because the coyotes I have met defy generalization. I have interviewed a coyote who turned out to be an evangelical pastor, another who repairs shoes, another who sells snacks from a pushcart in front of the courthouse, and another whose house is painted with slogans from Spanish solidarity organizations. Still another is a cooperative organizer who appropriated his group's bank account to loan it to migrants (he is now a former co-op organizer). Other coyotes are shopkeepers and back-strap weavers. All told, I have interviewed thirty-one people whom Nebajenses identify as coyotes, although some of the interviews were brief. All thirty-one are Nebajenses except for one Cotzaleño; all are Ixils except for two ladinos and two K'iche's. Twenty-one are men and ten are women, including two married couples and a mother and son. Since I was meeting them through personal contacts, they are not necessarily a representative sample. Seventeen of the thirty-one agreed to talk to me when I was accompanied by my translator Jacinto Pérez, although all spoke sufficient Spanish that he had to intervene only occasionally.

How did this assortment of people become coyotes? Their stories suggest four different roads into the business:

1. Working as a labor contractor for Guatemalan plantations, as did Diego Velasco Matom. Until the war, labor contracting in Nebaj was a business dominated by ladinos, not all of whom had good reputations and not all of whom survived the arrival of the Guerrilla Army of the Poor. Nowadays all the labor contractors seem to be indigenous.
2. Being recruited by out-of-town coyotes who perceive that you will be a persuasive and clever intermediary—this is how several market women have become coyotes.
3. Returning from wage labor in El Norte with the idea that the easiest way to make money there is to send others, starting with your own sons and nephews and proceeding to neighbors.
4. Tapping into the projected earnings of migrants by lending them money at high interest rates.

Of the thirty-one coyotes I have interviewed, the scale of their operations varies widely, from sending a few migrants per year to dozens per month. None operate on the scale of Santos Ortiz of Aguacatán, who supposedly sent as many as a hundred migrants a month during the peak years of 2003 to 2006. But several of my interviewees were among the recruiters and moneylenders feeding that operation. Recruiters don't need capital, just sales ability, and they can be more threadbare than their clients. For example, the single Cotzaleño in my sample told of spending two years as a *sheetrockero* in Orlando, Florida. Because he was finding employment only three days a week, he headed for Texas. A cop pulled him over for speeding and arrested him for driving without a license. His deportation cost him a $6,000 car and a $1,500 computer. Now he was back in Cotzal, repairing shoes in a shack, but he still owed half his own smuggling debt from two years before, at 10 percent monthly interest. Why didn't he shift the debt to a lower-interest bank loan? Because he and his father didn't own any real estate they could use as collateral. Still, they were advertising trips, jobs, and U.S. wages on Cotzal's evangelical radio station, even though their own situation was hardly a good advertisement.

Judging from the coyotes I was able to interview, the local branch of the profession hits a lower average than their business partners in the U.S.-Mexican badlands. Nebaj coyotes are more likely to be novices than veterans, and at least a few are so lacking in acumen and luck that, instead of making money, they have lost their houses. Of the thirty-one coyotes in my sample, as few as five of the men and three of the women have personal experience in the United States. But these eight were early migrants and have become an inspiration for many others. Seven of the eight returned to Nebaj after only a few years in El Norte, adducing the need to care for their families and believing that they could make more money by sending relatives and neighbors. They do not view themselves as exploiters because, in their view, they are providing the opportunity of a lifetime. If migrants fail, it is their own fault.

"I tell them, to go to the United States is not to have a good time," one migrant-turned-moneylender told me. "It is to work. It is to send money to the family. If one goes just to have a good time, he returns without money and the family here suffers. So why go? It is not for drunks. What happens is that beer is just nine dollars a carton—it's really cheap—and muchachos fall into vice. Then they don't show up on Monday. If they don't arrive another Monday, they're sent away. Then they go to another company. The same thing happens again; now they're in the computer and they cannot find work. My rules are—don't go to bars or dances."

Now consider the case of Manuel, who received no land from his parents. During the war, his siblings took advantage of his absence to cut him out of his share of the inheritance. The only way he could support his wife and children was by spending much of the year cutting sugarcane on the coast. He went to the United States in 2000. His first job was cleaning oil from looms in a textile mill in Ashford, North Carolina, for $250 a week. Even though Manuel has a wiry physique, stooping and crawling under the machinery was difficult for a man approaching forty years of age. His next job was in a slaughterhouse, which also was very taxing for little more than minimum wage. To escape factory work, Manuel moved to Homestead but lasted only four months; the heat and humidity of field labor was too punishing. His next stop was a chicken-processing plant in Columbia, South Carolina, for two and a half years, until he was able to go to work for Korean grocers near

Washington, D.C., for $460 a week. Five years later he was working for the same employer at the same rate of pay, from 8 a.m. to 8 p.m. six days a week.

In constant communication with his wife, Manuel has built a substantial house, bought two three-wheeled taxis and agricultural land, and financed secondary education for his sons. But he has never been free of debt, and the struggle to pay it off has generated more debt. To earn money faster than the $6.38 an hour he was making from the Koreans, for example, Manuel invested Q120,000 ($15,000) in bringing his wife and two sons to the United States. One son got lost in the desert and fell into the hands of the Border Patrol. Because he was under eighteen, the authorities released him to Manuel under court supervision—his own legal status never came up. The other son was going through a dumpster behind a store when he attracted a police helicopter from which he fled—producing a second arrest that did not lead to deportation. Manuel's wife was able to work for a while but then became ill. For medical treatment she could afford, she returned to Guatemala, as did the two sons because they were not finding enough work.

Meanwhile, Manuel was also recruiting other Nebajenses to go north and loaning them money. This, too, backfired. Manuel's friend Alfonso was so enthusiastic about the prospect of earning U.S. wages that he sent three of his sons north. They moved in with Manuel, who kept an eye on them, but they didn't fare well in the 2007 job market. The oldest son took seven months to find a stable job. The middle son took three months to find a job. The youngest son went to work for a fellow immigrant who stole part of his wages. More interested in enjoying adolescence than laboring, the youngest son returned to Guatemala without paying his debt and began drinking heavily. Alfonso was now afraid of being bankrupted by his huge 10 percent per month loan from Manuel. So he paid it off with an equally huge $22,000 loan from Banrural, at 2 percent interest per month but secured by the title to his house. The Banrural loan will cost him and his sons $450 a month for ten years, for a grand total of $54,000. If his two sons stay in the United States, if they stay faithful to the family project, and if they continue doing so for ten years, Alfonso won't lose his house. In 2008, Alfonso was incensed at Manuel for leading him into this trap. Four years later, happily, his two older sons were still hard at work in El Norte, and he thought it all might work out.

In the meantime, Manuel and his wife were regretting their coyote investments. Their last five loans, each of Q45,000 ($5,770) to five migrants at 5 percent interest per month, had not gone well. All five were now in the United States, and all five alleged that they could not find work. One had the excuse that she had just produced a baby, a family obligation which would postpone repayment into the indefinite future. Back in Nebaj, Manuel's wife was staggering under three different loans from Nebaj financial institutions on which they owed $1,500 per month—the lion's share of Manuel's wages. He needed someone to come north immediately to help him earn money faster, but all available hands in Nebaj were either caring for newborns or in school. As of 2012, I am pleased to report, two of Manuel's sons were at work in the United States, and he himself was finally home for a well-deserved rest.

For years, confianza or social trust enabled coyotes and their clients to pump unauthorized migrants to the United States, but this trust evaporated in the case of Manuel and Alfonso. Their plight suggests how easily the obligations of kinship and friendship can be overwhelmed by the implicit indenture of migration debt. Ultimately their trust in each other depended on the viability of their business model—that is, of steering their sons into enough employment to pay off large investments. They were not alone in riding the ups and downs of the immigrant employment cycle. From the moment that I began meeting Nebaj coyotes in 2007, the majority complained of having trouble collecting payment from their borrowers. Luis is one of the better-known moneylenders in town. Like the majority, he has never been to the United States, or even Mexico. Instead, it was the departure of his father and brothers for Ohio that brought him into the coyote industry. Young, charismatic, and smart—the brains of the family—Luis stayed behind to manage the remittances, which he decided to leverage by investing in loans to neighbors who wished to join his father and siblings. He seemed to be doing so well that other people asked him to invest their savings as well. He paid his investors 5 percent a month and charged his borrowers 6 or 7 percent a month (or so he told me—10 percent is the norm). And so Luis became a broker in the underground railroad moving thousands of Nebajenses north. He brought together stay-at-home lenders, borrowers going north, and coyote connections that supposedly would enable a steadily rising number of Nebajenses to find work in Ohio. This is how the dense social connectivity of an indigenous town became a business venture.

Even in 2007, when the U.S. horizon had yet to darken, Luis told me about all the risks he faced. The majority of Nebaj coyotes seem to be junior partners to Huehuetecos, but Luis said he was sending his clients to a Mexican network that moved them across Mexico. Then he was negotiating with a different Mexican network to get his clients across the U.S. border. The drawback was that the Mexicans who moved his clients through Mexico demanded to be paid even if the next set of Mexicans failed to get the migrants across the U.S. border. His most serious problem, therefore, seemed to be the jailing of his borrowers by the Migra. Some of his customers were sufficiently shaken by their month or two in detention that they didn't want to try again, but the expenses that Luis had incurred on their behalf might already exceed their advance payment. "If the muchacho is returned to Guatemala and does not want to continue, I talk to him about his commitment," Luis told me. "Because if he does not want to try again, I lose what I spent on him. This is a commitment, I tell him. You can't go up there to drink or fall into another bad habit such as drugs. You have to pay back your loan."

Another problem with the American Dream, Luis discovered, was the opportunity it provided to disown one's obligations back home. "They get there and start to drink. Or they get there and do not send money. Or the value of the property in the document they gave me is less than the value of the debt. It might be a no-good property that is worth two thousand quetzals. So people think it would be better to ditch the property and not pay the debt."

Had Diego Velasco Matom been pressuring deadbeats before he was murdered? I asked. Luis didn't know, but he did recall a final conversation with Diego on precisely this subject. "How's business?" they asked each other. The conversation quickly turned to debts and how to get migrants to honor them. People who can't pay, who are in danger of losing their property, need to be treated with consideration, Luis now told me. "There are lenders who impose and order people around—do this, do that. You can't act like that." He himself was becoming accustomed to receiving threats, so it was important to treat overdue borrowers with kid gloves.

Couldn't he take nonpayers to the courthouse? I asked. Yes, he could, because he had a lawyer draw up contracts for his loans, with real estate for collateral. But the district attorney at the courthouse could turn up his nose at the contract, or the property title could be bogus, or the land that it represented could be worthless, turning his legal expenses into another financial drain.

Well, I asked, why not inspect the property before he made the loan? Maybe if it was close to town, Luis replied, but usually it was up some mountain. Getting out there and back would kill a day; he would be running all over the place. So he had learned that he could operate only on the basis of confianza or trust. Without a personal relationship, either through long acquaintance or through an equally trusted third party, you could only expect to get screwed. In one such case, he came into a property through default, only to be told, "If you go out there, you won't come back. They will machete you." So if borrowers cannot pay, Luis explained, "you have to reason with them and work out a solution. Some people I've taken over to the bank to help them fulfill the requirements to take out a loan. They pay their debt with me and they remain with a debt to the bank at a lower rate of interest."

That was the theory. In the absence of meaningful collateral, however, the same supposed confianza which enabled moneylenders to use their personal ties to extract remittances from borrowers could also make it easy for the borrower to turn the tables on the lender. When I sought Luis again in 2009 and 2010, he had retreated behind an imposing cement-block wall surrounding his new house at the edge of town. He never seemed to be at home and was said to be spending lots of time with his cattle in the Ixcán, two days' journey from Ixil country. "Yes, he owes a lot," a relative told me. "He said that he owes a million and a half, or half a million, or a million ($128,000) to Banrural and that he has to come up with Q25,000 ($3,200) a month. But he's not afraid; he says that he's going to pay."

Luis was not the only coyote from whom I heard warnings of failure and loss even in 2007. One morning, thanks to my translator Jacinto Pérez, I met an Ixil man who refused to tell me his name but left no doubt that he was a coyote. He was in his late thirties, slight in stature but lean and erect, with a direct gaze suggesting that he was accustomed to frank assessment of the human material before him. Like Luis and many of the coyotes I interviewed, he said that he does not have to recruit anyone because the migrants come to him. "It's a trip with many risks, with many dangers," runs his standard warning. "You can lose or you can win. If you lose, you can lose house, land, family—you can lose everything. You can end up more poor than before. If you win, you can win a job that pays well, you can build your house or buy a car." Only 30 percent [*sic*] were making it across the border, he claimed. Like other coyotes, he argued that he shared the risk: "If the migrant does not arrive, he loses all his money. But he that loans the money, he also loses because he does not have the backing of the law. [The loan agreement] is only verbal. We too lose when they don't manage to enter [the United States], because in any case we have to pay the Mexicans."

WHO BENEFITS, AND WHO DOES NOT

Fracaso económico (economic failure) is a familiar topic in Nebaj. Like *éxito* (success), it is easy to find examples. The most telling stumble past or sprawl unconscious a few steps from the shops selling *trago* (distilled alcohol), which have become as prolific as evangelical churches. Usually males, their clothing is ragged and their skin is grimy; their relatives have tired of the fruitless task of coaxing them home if they even have one; and their incapacity for work reduces them to begging. The local assessment is that they have succumbed to *vicio* (vice). But if alcoholism is the easiest folk explanation for economic failure, this can occur in other ways as well, through an accident that cripples one's ability to work, or by trying and failing to obtain a job in El Norte, or just by borrowing money and getting into debt. Economic failure is less obvious than economic success or late-stage alcoholism, but it is pervasive.

Some of the people who are worst off in the new Nebaj are ex-guerrillas—not former political cadres who have schooling, or at least the skills of persuasion, and who have the connections to run aid projects and seek public office, but rank-and-file combatants who, while away in the hills, were jostled out of their slender land inheritance. Pedro López Chel joined the guerrillas in 1979 at the age of seventeen. He served first with the Ho Chi Minh Front locally, and then with the Ernesto Che Guevara Front in Huehuetenango. After twelve years as a combatant, he went to a refugee camp in Mexico before coming home to Nebaj in 1995 with other returnees. While he was off in the mountains fighting for a better Guatemala, his nine siblings carved up their father's three hundred cuerdas (13.4 hectares). He ended up with eight cuerdas of steep land (.35 hectares). Along with his wife and three children, he lives in the yard of one of his brothers in a structure that lacks four walls, from which he hangs blankets to keep out the night chill. Aside from farming his eight cuerdas, he works as a laborer for Q35 ($4.50) per day. He also sometimes works for an association that brings together parents and children separated by the war. Not only does he have no money for going north, he has nothing against which to borrow to go north.

This chapter has looked at how the border issue leads to the issue of coyotes, and how the issue of coyotes leads to the issue of debt. Debt is the subtext of every conversation about going north. Failed migrants are even easier to find than failed moneylenders. Consider Ricardo, who is clearly embarrassed about his time in the United States. The only reason he agreed to talk to me is that I have known his father for years. His first job was in Galleton, Tennessee, near Nashville, where he worked in greenhouses raising flowers. He made $7.50 an hour and worked many extra hours without overtime pay. But the worst was the competition for jobs. There were too many immigrants showing up, Ricardo said, and he was lumped together with them. Of the Americans he met, 5 or 10 percent treated him like a human being; the rest acted like racists. In this they were not alone. There were lots of Mexicans who did not like the Guatemalans, and there were lots of Guatemalans who did not like the Salvadorans.

According to Ricardo, the majority of his friends who have gone north have learned the same lesson that he has—that the opportunities for employment are so limited, and the pay so poor, that it is a terrible struggle to pay for the trip and send money home. But each of his friends sets out with high hopes, sometimes over the opposition of mothers and wives, and many are still there, because when they come home they will not have much to show for it. They will be labeled a *fracasado* or failure. Setting off with illusions and coming back without them is no defense against the scorn of peers who still believe in the great dream of El Norte. In the case of Ricardo, his sociological analysis of what went wrong did not prevent him from blaming himself. Why did he fail if others succeeded?

"Our mind travels," Candelaria told me.

A dollar equals seven quetzals; it's better than Guatemalan money. We think that life in the United States is very different from here, that it's more comfortable, but it is not like that. Life there is only for working. He who does not work does not eat. People like me do not have qualifications there; our studies don't matter. I have a Salvadoran friend, a very Christian woman from El Salvador. In her own country she worked as a secretary. When she went to work in the United States cleaning toilets, she cried. There was nothing else because she did not speak English. There English is everything.

Candelaria went to the United States with her brother. It took her two months to find work near Washington, D.C., and when she did, it was "pure exploitation." She made three hundred dollars a week, paid in cash by a woman named Missy, who put her through an exhausting schedule of cleaning houses and cheated her out of wages. After six months, Candelaria's mother became ill, and she returned home to Q25,000 ($3,200) in unpaid travel debt.

I was starting to wonder, what if El Norte doesn't benefit the majority of Nebajenses who go there? It is not easy for Nebajenses to argue with the purchasing power of remittances, but many decry the social cost. Adán, the pioneer I quoted at the start of chapter 3, has become quite a student of the Nebajense dream and where it goes wrong. "It's characteristic of the migrant that he expects his pueblo to stay the same while he is abroad," he told me. "But it's not like that. This happens with my friends. They left here seven years ago and they keep asking about their girlfriend, because they think that everything here remains congealed. Many people here are against the migrants, because they have no one in the United States and so their economy [purchasing power] is limited.

"A woman here asks to buy a house lot, and the owner says that the price is Q80,000 ($10,260). She mentions her plan to a friend, and the friend mentions it to her son who is in the United States. He advises her to offer Q100,000 or Q120,000. The emigrants are making the same mistake as the aid institutions. We have contributed to elevating the prices here. If a woman has a husband in the United States, she pays Q2,000 or Q3,000 ($385) for a *huipil* (hand-woven blouse). Many outsiders show up and criticize women here for abandoning their traditional dress and their culture. If a huipil costs Q2,000 to Q3,000, what can a woman do without a husband in the United States? Walk around in a good huipil or eat? She has to eat. It's a lot cheaper to go to the *pacas* [stores selling used clothing from the United States] and buy a nice blouse there."

Francisco Marroquin Velasco is rare in having nothing good to say about El Norte. But then he leads the most successful peasant development association in Nebaj. "It's a disaster when all the youth go to the United States," he told me with his customary decision. He doesn't like to deal with villages that seem to consist entirely of women, and he doesn't like to see families who are bitter because a youth may never return. "Whenever employment is generated, the people view it as very positive, even if there are negative effects in the long run. I don't want them to stay there. Staying there will end up being a vice, with the culture of there, and community values will be destroyed. If the youth stay there, if they marry and have children there, then people are going to think that life there is better.

"We don't see everything that happens. It's an uncontrollable epidemic. Many people have come back and say that there's no work. There are times when there is work, and there are times when there isn't work. They're standing around for a week, by the side of the road begging for a chance. It breaks them away from the family. The parents go into debt; sometimes they don't have the capacity to pay and must sell the little that they own. And the youth up there get into bad habits. Some die, others fall into depravity, others return with debts that they cannot pay. The time comes when the migrant breaks ties with his family and the wife seeks another man."

The ambivalence I hear from Nebajenses is also expressed by the K'iche' Mayas of southern Quiché Department. In 2007, anthropologist Patricia Foxen took life histories in a village called Tuluché, which supported the Guerrilla Army of the Poor in the early 1980s and experienced three army massacres. Even after the survivors were forced into submission, they held together against a murderous civil patrol leader and eventually managed to send him to prison. In the peace process of the 1990s, Tuluché attained ownership of its land, but the cost of living has risen, villagers feel poorer than before, and the older generation is demoralized by the younger generation's rush to go north. Many of Foxen's interviews were filled with "desperate discussions about K'iche' youth, who (their parents state) either claim not to believe that the genocide happened, or do not want to hear about it, and are more concerned with leaving for the United States and acquiring material goods, thus fragmenting families further and abandoning community norms for a more global materialistic culture." Illustrating the "sad vacuum between the generations" is the Tuluché elder who laments, "The youth today . . . they don't want to be educated about our poverty, you try to get them to a meeting to talk about these things but they don't come. . . . What interests them is vices, cell phones, televisions, motorcycles."

Foxen has spent years studying the migration stream from this corner of Quiché Department to the capital of Rhode Island. "In search of Providence," to quote the title of her book, many repercussions are felt back home: there are *envidias* (resentment), *chismes* (malicious gossip), and *brujería* (witchcraft) over exactly who will receive and control remittances. In a municipal seat near Tuluché, the price of land has inflated to as much as Q50,000 per cuerda (.044 hectares); in hamlets, it has inflated as much as five hundred times the price in the early 1980s. In the late 1990s, the trip north was costing $3,000 to $4,000, which men were borrowing from ladino moneylenders for as much as 20 percent interest per month. This could easily leave their families back home in a precarious state.[13]

In a comparison of different Guatemalan populations, Matthew Taylor, Michelle Moran-Taylor, and Deborah Rodman Ruiz have noticed migration dollars pushing nonrecipients off their land. That is, recipients of remittances have been buying up land from nonrecipients.[14] But no one seems to have really focused on indebtedness until it confronted Jan and Diane Rus in a Tzotzil Maya village in San Juan Chamula, in the Mexican state of Chiapas. When the couple began research in the pseudonymous Ch'ul Osil in 1973, it numbered some 690 people. Twenty-five years later, the population was 1,525—not counting another 575 people who lived elsewhere. The people of Ch'ul Osil experienced a few years of hope in the 1990s when the Zapatista uprising induced the Mexican government to flood the area with economic projects. But the projects carried heavy political obligations to the state and did not halt the steady decline in their purchasing power. Having lost considerable land to plantations a century earlier, most men in Ch'ul Osil were now completely dependent on migrating elsewhere to work—at first to plantations and then to urban areas where wages barely provided subsistence. Even the village's small entrepreneurial elite, those producing flowers and vegetables as cash crops, were going deeper into debt.

So by 2001, the young men of Ch'ul Osil were ready to join the Mexican migration stream to the United States. Four years later, fifty-seven migrants were sending forty-five households steady remittances that collectively added up to 756,000 pesos of income ($69,000 at eleven pesos to the dollar). But how was this income distributed? For more than 80 percent of the households in Ch'ul Osil, there was no direct remittance income from the United States. Of those who did go to the United States, a typical debt for the cost of being smuggled into the United States was 18,000 pesos ($1,600). More than 60 percent of the loans were at 10 percent interest per month, with another 25 percent of the loans at 5 percent interest per month. Paying off the loans was an uphill battle that could easily take several years and cost three times as much as the original amount.

Judging from the interest rates being charged, in 2005 the stateside workers of Ch'ul Osil were paying as much as 54,000 pesos ($4,900) per month in interest—out of total remittances to their households of 43,000 to 63,000 pesos per month. Hence most of the money earned in the United States was

flowing to ten lenders, and most of that to just three. The most obvious beneficiaries of migration to the United States were the lenders and two coyotes
who soon had new houses, new cars, and—in one case—a prestige-boosting
second wife. Once families broke out of debt, they were using their remittances to lend money to nonremittance neighbors who, when they couldn't
pay, were turning over their land. Thanks to debt and remittance, migration
to the United States was acting like a machine to concentrate land in some
families and take it from others.

This is not the first time that remittances have been caught in the act of
stratifying a sending population in Mexico—that is, differentiating a single
class of smallholders into landlords and tenants. Anthropologists have been
reporting this phenomenon for more than thirty years. In Las Animas, Zacatecas, Richard Mines reported, the land purchases of migrants led to "extraor-
dinary inflation," which excluded "all but those with a high-wage U.S. job
from the village land market."

In Guadalupe, Michoacán, Joshua Reichert found, almost two-thirds of
current land tenancy was based on remittances from the United States. Real
estate inflation put nonmigrants, and even illegal migrants, at a "competitive
disadvantage" with men who had attained legal status in the United States.
Sixty percent of the local land base was owned by eighty-two migrant families who comprised only 18 percent of the population. Instead of undertaking
productive improvements, most of the absentee owners were renting out their
land, turning it over to sharecroppers or using it to pasture cattle.

In Acuitzio, Michoacán, reported Raymond Wiest, tension between migrants and nonmigrants escalated to the point of gunfights. Remittances were
turning migrants into absentee landlords at the expense of neighbors who
were becoming sharecroppers. Adopting a term coined by Reichert, Wiest argued that the "migrant syndrome" perpetuated dependency because remitters
"earn considerably more than they could earn in Mexico, must continue to
migrate to sustain a higher standard of living, and have patterns of consumption which induce still others to migrate." In such towns, the journalist Sam
Quinones remarks, there is a "culture of departure" in which "people leave
out of economic necessity, but leaving has also become a culture."[15] One
symbol, very visible on the mountainsides of Huehuetenango but less so in
Ixil country, are the big, empty houses into whose construction migrants pour
their remittances and to which many of them will never return.[16]

As to which men gain from the migration stream, and which men do not,
a critical issue is whether there is enough demand for their labor when they
arrive in the United States—a variable that can change quickly. Consider Jan
and Diane Rus' summary of Ch'ul Osil experience since the 2005 survey.

Whether it pays or not depends a lot on the historical moment. Many of the guys from Ch'ul who came before 2004–2005 eventually did okay. The ones who came later when the tighter border made it more expensive, and especially when work really died after 2007, didn't do well at all. Migration occurs in a rapidly changing historical context. The guys I know who came in the 1990s and early 2000s were in general well pleased by their experience in the U.S. They even talked about what a surprise it was to find police—and even migration agents— who treated them honestly. Those who were still here in 2007 and later talked more about hunger, sleeping under bridges, and having white guys throw stuff at them out of pick-up trucks.[17]

Much of the research on undocumented migration focuses on towns in northern Mexico that have been sending their youth to labor in U.S. agriculture for generations. Migrants from these towns were in just the right position to benefit from the amnesty provision in the 1986 Immigration Reform and Control Act (IRCA). Since then, they have used their legal residency to become U.S. citizens and to bring up relatives and neighbors—some legally and some not.[18] Thanks to two decades of modest but crucial legal advantages for these sending populations, many of their migration sagas can be told with a happy ending.

But the good fortune of Mexicans and others amnestied by IRCA has encouraged two other trends to which we will return in chapter 8. First, the most enterprising amnesty recipients have been able to rise into the middle class by becoming employers of more recent immigrants. But second, the many new arrivals encouraged by the IRCA amnesty have driven down wages for immigrants. This is where too many Nebajenses find themselves. Like many other migration streams from central and southern Mexico, Guatemala, and Honduras, they arrived too late to qualify for the IRCA amnesty. Some have found good employers who pay good wages; many have not. How the challenges Nebajenses face in the United States have reverberated back home is the subject of the next three chapters.

Part II

THE NEBAJ BUBBLE
AND HOW IT BURST

Chapter Five

Borrowers, Moneylenders, and Banks

When Nebajenses go north, their relatives wait for the remittances to pour home. The majority have been disappointed. Why isn't he sending money? they ask. Or why is he sending just a few hundred dollars a month, barely enough to pay back the loan for going there? For wives, the most obvious answer is that their husband is screwing around. Doña Feliciana is a weaver who borrowed heavily to buy a comfortable house that she is about to lose. She is about to lose her house, she informs me, because her husband is in Minnesota getting drunk and chasing women instead of sending money. Oh, I respond brightly, what's his number? I'll call him when I get back to the United States! Out pops the cell phone and, before I know it, Doña Feliciana has me on the line with her no-good husband. "Tell him he has to send us money or you're going to get him deported!" she hisses. And so I talk with Feliciana's husband, who has been away for seven years. An injury put him out of work at a meatpacking plant. After an idle period, he has started a new job in a bakery at the lower wage of $6.50 an hour. He and three other men are paying $1,000 a month for an apartment in which the pipes have frozen, so there is no running water.

How Ixils fare in the United States depends on what they call their *suerte*, their luck or destiny. Will they make it through Mexico and across the border? Will they find enough work to pay the cost? Will their earnings be cut short by arrest or injury? Some have been able to send home enough money to buy a lot and build a house, or at least to buy a motor vehicle. Some are still sending back handsome remittances of $1,000 or so per month. But while going north is an obvious way to obtain a higher price for your labor, there are enormous risks that could easily leave you poorer than before.

To be successful, Nebajenses must juggle three major obligations: the $5,000 they owe for being smuggled into the United States, their living expenses (always higher than expected), and only then the sustained income expected by their families. Unfortunately, finding enough work to earn all this money means competing with other Guatemalans and Mexicans who have arrived in the same labor market with the same idea. The worst-case scenario is to be arrested and deported after you pay $5,000 to reach the United States but before you can work off the debt. Such an amount is almost impossible to repay from working in Nebaj. The only way to climb out of the hole caused by your previous trip north is either to sell land (if you have any left to sell) or to borrow another $5,000 for a second try, doubling your wager on El Norte.

Now for an obvious question. Where do Ixils borrow the equivalent of several years' income to buy their way into the United States? The most fortunate have a stateside relative with a steady job who is willing to finance them. That brings the debt into the family. Alternatively, if they still have a bit of land, they can sell it—at the risk of never recouping it and ending up poorer than before. This leaves two other possibilities. They can borrow the money from a local coyote—which in Nebaj refers to recruiters (*enganchadores*) and moneylenders (*prestamistas*) more than the actual smugglers (*traficantes*) who take them across borders. Unfortunately, Nebaj moneylenders typically charge 10 percent interest per month. Even though interest is not compounded, the debt will double in less than a year and triple in less than two years.

The other place to borrow $5,000 is from one of the twenty-three banks, credit unions, and revolving-loan funds I counted in 2008. Their purpose is not to finance illegal migration; if anything, easy credit is supposed to help Guatemalans stay home and earn their living locally. Officially, no Nebaj institution will accept a loan application for going to the United States. But until recently, most did not view the diversion of their loans to human smuggling as a serious problem. The largest lenders accepted remittances as evidence of the ability to carry large loans that could never be repaid from Guatemalan income. And so they took on investments in the American Dream, importing into their balance sheets a tangle of complications that I call the wives-and-mothers problem. Fathers and uncles are involved, but the majority of people who borrow money to send their wage pilgrims north seem to be female. They remain behind with the debt, and if the migrant fails, they pay a large share of the consequences.

Once in debt Q40,000 ($5,100) for a trip north—or double or triple that amount, because siblings often go together—families become accustomed to chronic uncertainty over their future, akin to sending a man off to war. Their future hinges on whether remittances arrive, as well as on phone calls that have become very cheap and very dangerous, because they enable the instant transmission of misfortune and distrust. Thus the proverbial phone call from the husband who has gotten drunk because he lost his job—or who has lost his job because he got drunk—and who accuses his wife of infidelity. When remittances fail to arrive, families wonder whether their man has relapsed into drinking or set up a new household with another woman. I have no way of quantifying, but everyone in Nebaj agrees that illegal migration is hard on marriages. According to the International Organization for Migration, 36 percent of the families of Central American migrants disintegrate.[1]

Illegal migration is also hard on revolving-loan funds. When wives and mothers lose a wage earner to El Norte, one way to compensate is by borrowing money from credit institutions at 2 percent monthly interest (the most common rate) in order to loan it to neighbors at 10 percent monthly interest. They hope to live off the difference. Of the ten women I have interviewed in the Nebaj coyote industry, at least seven have borrowed money from institutions in order to lend it to migrants at 10 percent a month. Typically they began by lending money to close relatives and confidants, who paid them back, before lending to acquaintances, who were less reliable. By 2009, all seven were saddled with nonpayers from whom they had obtained no collateral, or collateral that turned out to be worthless. They tried to keep their head above water by obtaining more loans.

The most resilient of the moneylenders seemed to be Doña Maria. The majority of her family was massacred by the army when she was a child. From the age of fourteen to sixteen she was a combatant in the Guerrilla Army of the Poor. In the late 1980s, Maria was among the thousands of EGP-administered refugees who were targeted by army offensives and forced to surrender. She had several close calls because, once the army took possession of her, it demanded that she return to no-man's-land to bring back more refugees. To save her life, she escaped to factory work in Alta Verapaz Department. When Ixil country settled down, a relative asked her to come home and help him administer projects for women. She received a salary and eventually a house for herself and her two children. "It's good to show that it's not just men who have capacity, that we women can get ahead as well," she told me. "Sometimes men don't know how to handle money; they waste money drinking in bars and chasing other women. In contrast, women are responsible for children. We're more responsible. We can provide education for our children and get ahead."

While buying project animals in Huehuetenango, Maria met a coyote who asked her to help him recruit migrants. She was not the first aid coordinator in Nebaj to discover that international migration was more profitable. Between 2004 and 2008, she sent forty people north, paying for each trip as far as Guatemala's border with Mexico but no farther. When her customers reached a safe house in Phoenix, she wired a bank transfer to the "señor coyote" in Comitán, Chiapas. By 2009, Maria had two problems:

1. She lost Q72,000 ($9,200) on two migrants who, only a few days after she paid for their safe arrival, were arrested and deported.
2. Every month she had to make four payments, totaling Q11,200 ($1,400), to four different credit institutions. Keeping up with such relentless payments would require sending more migrants north, but job seeking there was going so badly that some would turn into deadbeats.

CREDIT HISTORY

This is not the first time that Ixils have had trouble repaying loans. During the coffee boom in the early 1900s, ladino entrepreneurs began importing large amounts of *aguardiente* or firewater. Ixils had long honored their patron saints by inebriating themselves during fiestas. Now they could do so faster with the assistance of ladino cantina owners and moneylenders, who then took the land pledged as collateral. Once the land was gone, a celebrant could be marched off to debt peonage on a plantation. In 1966, Benjamin Colby and Pierre van den Berghe were told that moneylenders were mainly ladinos and charged as much as 10 percent interest per month. In 1973, Horst Nachtigall heard that labor contractors were adding 10 percent monthly interest to the cash advances that they gave Ixils for their next trip to the plantations, for work that paid a dollar a day. The advances were small and for no more than a few months, so the amount of interest may have been small. But Nachtigall also heard that many borrowers were unable to pay their debt by the end of the season, leaving them in hock for the next year. He also heard that they could lose land in this way.[2]

In the 1970s, Ixils and K'iche's began to establish themselves as labor contractors, displacing most ladino contractors by the end of the 1980s. This might be how 10 percent monthly interest came to be the norm in loans between Ixils, but most Ixil moneylenders have never been labor contractors, and they are far from the only ones to charge 10 percent monthly interest— moneylenders all over the world impose this rate, if not higher. According to standard economic rationality, high interest rates are the result of, and provide insurance against, high default rates. Even if half the loans made at 10 percent monthly interest are never repaid, the other half earns 120 percent a year, for an overall return of 10 percent a year. Another explanation for high rates of interest is that administrative overhead for small loans is essentially the same as for large loans. If a small loan is repaid within a few months, then 10 percent monthly interest resembles an administrative fee.

Still, I was surprised that Ixils could charge each other such punishing interest without inviting censure. The rate has long been illegal in Guatemala, but the people who charge it are never prosecuted. Indeed, I have yet to detect a local term with the negative connotation of "loan sharking" (*usura*, the Spanish term for usury, I have never heard from an Ixil). A monthly rate of 5 percent is regarded as generous, and only monthly rates of 15 to 20 percent are perceived as unneighborly. But until recently such rates would have applied to much smaller amounts than they do now. Most loans between Ixils would have been for a few hundred quetzals or less, many would not have been secured with property documents, and repayment would have been subject to moral negotiation owing to the social ties between lenders and borrowers. According to two old-timers, 5 percent monthly rates were more common than 10 percent.

Three developments multiplied the amount of credit available to Nebajenses. First, an Italian contractor of the UN Development Program, the Program for Displaced People, Refugees and Returnees in Central America (PRODERE), discredited itself by lavishing most of its large budget on itself. To make everyone feel better, PRODERE left behind revolving-loan funds that soon disappeared into the pockets of Ixil administrators and borrowers. Second, the newly arrived gospel of microcredit assured the next wave of aid organizations that they could set up more credit programs and, armed with the latest development lingo, ignore what had happened to their predecessors.[3] Third, many donors decided to focus their credits on women. They reasoned that mothers tend to be more responsive to children's needs than fathers. Mothers were less likely to sink a loan into an unrealistic business scenario, alcohol, or some other form of status consumption. And women were supposed to be better repayers than men. So lenders decided to organize women's borrowing groups. Some decided to lend exclusively to women, producing today's portfolios in which female borrowers outnumber male borrowers even though Mayan culture is unapologetically patriarchal—an issue to which we will return in chapter 7.

Under the banner of credit as the key to development, an array of agencies have opened their doors. Nebaj's institutional lenders include

- national commercial banks;
- nonprofit savings-and-loan cooperatives which pledge to serve the community but must protect the savings of their members;
- nonprofit development associations which channel capital from international donors into revolving-loan funds;
- nonprofit microfinance associations which must also recover their donated capital;

- nonprofits focusing on women such as Puente de Amistad (Bridge of Friendship), to which Nebajenses sometimes refer as Fuente de Amistad (Fountain of Friendship); and
- Banco Azteca, a Mexican company offering consumer credit within twenty-four hours at up to 87 percent interest per year.

For the sake of brevity, I will sometimes refer to Nebaj loan agencies collectively, the way the Nebajenses do, as *bancos* or banks. Most charge between 18 and 30 percent annual interest—low by Guatemalan standards. The two largest are the Rural Development Bank (Banrural), a well-known national enterprise, and the Todos Nebajenses Cooperative (Cotoneb), a local Ixil-run credit union. Along with several smaller banks and credit unions, Banrural and Cotoneb lent Q50,000 ($6,400) or more at a time. They accepted remittance stubs from the United States as proof of the capacity for repayment. They required collateral in the form of property titles. Some loan officers suggested setting up a credit bureau to detect multiple borrowers, but higher-ups nixed the idea. Some clients built up debts of Q300,000 ($38,500) and more, especially to Banrural.

Meanwhile, smaller organizations busied themselves with actual microcredits of Q10,000 ($1,280) or less. Instead of asking for collateral, such agencies followed the example of the Grameen Bank in Bangladesh and required their borrowers to join solidarity groups. In a solidarity group, no one can obtain a second loan until everyone has repaid the first. But villagers can define solidarity very differently than aid coordinators think they should.

THE CASE OF DOÑA INGRACIA

In Nebaj, a particular case put loan officers on notice that many of their credits would never be repaid. In 2007 a fifty-two-year-old inhabitant of Salquil Grande named Ingracia Velasco Corio organized more than fifty women into solidarity groups. But these were not solidarity groups of the kind visualized by microcredit agencies; Doña Ingracia and her associates had a different approach. Instead of going to the lenders as a group, each member applied for credit as an individual and then turned the money over to Ingracia in exchange for a *regalo* (gift) of up to several hundred quetzals. She promised each group that, aside from giving each member a cash gift, she would pay off all their loans. That same year, Doña Ingracia approached more than a dozen neighbors and asked them for loans, too—but each as individuals and in the secrecy in which peasants normally conduct their finances.

No one grasped the scale of Doña Ingracia's borrowing until five agencies in the municipal seat realized they had more than fifty borrowers in a single village who denied that they had any obligation to repay their loans. Instead, they all pointed to Ingracia, who on December 17, 2007, loaded her possessions and chickens on the early-morning bus and left for Guatemala City. When I showed up a few months later, one of the first doors on which I knocked led to a meeting with six of Ingracia's creditors who had loaned her a total of Q122,000 ($15,600). Just one of her solidarity groups—the twelve women of Las Rosas (the Roses)—gave her Q115,000. If these are average totals for the seventy-five victims who stepped forward as of May 2008, Ingracia managed to borrow Q978,000, or $125,000—equivalent to the annual income of a hundred poor households.

What could she have done with so much money? When I caught up with Doña Ingracia, she was hospitable but declined to speak with me as soon as she grasped the reason for my visit. Her Spanish is minimal, she has never gone to school, and she does not know how to read or write. She has no criminal record, and like so many Ixils seeking to *superar* (get ahead), she belongs to an evangelical church. Her only remotely suspicious antecedent is that she belonged to a "community bank" (*banco comunal*); that is, a solidarity group set up by a microcredit agency. When asking victims for loans, she pointed to the new house she was building (a handsome three-level affair) and a son studying to be a lawyer in Guatemala City. Construction and education were her stated reasons for wanting to borrow; remittances from her husband and another son, both in the United States, were how she would repay.

In actuality, like so many Ixils gone north, Ingracia's men were failing to earn the money they expected. This, apparently, was another way to finance the house of their dreams. Three months after Doña Ingracia fled, a village delegation found her living near the capital. Instead of turning her over to the police, they brought her back to Salquil Grande. According to Ingracia, it was all the fault of her husband in the United States, who had taught her how to duplicate property deeds, and of her son studying law in Guatemala City, who was the one who had instructed her to organize women into multiple borrowing groups. She had given her husband and son all the money. Their response was to sue her for defamation. Victims could not take possession of the house because, while it was being built by Ingracia, it was titled to one of her sons. Nor could victims sue that son, the other son, or the husband because the only one who owed them anything was Ingracia. My guess is that the budding lawyer figured out how to take advantage of legal loopholes that would make his mother's debts unrecoverable. Eventually Ingracia went to jail, but her husband and sons did not—none of the loans were recovered.

Soon Doña Ingracia was not the only credit sinkhole being peered into by Nebaj loan officers. At least four other women used their social skills to orchestrate loan rings channeling money to themselves. Then there was a much larger number of borrowers who decided to meet those burdensome monthly payments by taking out a second loan with another institution, then a third loan with a third institution, and so on. No one knew how many borrowers had resorted to this strategy. New institutions arriving with fresh capital have never been lacking because Nebaj is the town where every aid organization in Guatemala wants to work. And so microcredit quickly evolved into debts that were no longer micro, because of the ease with which borrowers could pay off initial loans by taking out more loans, and pay off these loans by taking out still more, until the banks stopped handing out money in 2008.

In my interviews with Nebaj loan officers, they were quick to acknowledge that many of their borrowers were in arrears. Aside from the borrowers themselves, the managers blamed competition between institutions (i.e., each other) for fostering a culture of nonpayment. Several loan officers were especially critical of the most philanthropic institutions—nongovernmental organizations (NGOs) with a social mission who do not have to recover capital for their funders, who therefore never get around to confiscating property pledged as collateral, and who tend to prioritize loans to women. Since loan officers tend to be men, this chain of reasoning leads to blaming the señoras. Here is what Doña Ingracia's first loan officer told me with an air of I-told-you-so: "Her attitude changed. She became one of these señoras who walks down the street with her cell phone, talking of her movements, always with her deals. Maybe she's involved in a fraud. Cell phones are for emergencies and businessmen. The [señoras] always want to borrow larger amounts. I saw the change and told myself, the next time the loan will not be paid."

"There's confusion over what a credit is," another Ixil loan officer told me. "Other institutions of social welfare have arrived that give donations, or they have funds that they give out in the form of loans but without demanding repayment. So people arrive here, and although I explain that it's a credit and they will have to repay it, they leave thinking that they're not going to pay. Before, there weren't many female moneylenders; then in the 1990s all the NGO groups wanted to work with women. They're more responsible, they repay better than men—this is what was said. And so it was until now. Now many don't want to pay."

Mayan women, it turned out, were not the ideal beneficiaries envisioned by NGOs. The Guatemalan reincarnation of Mother Courage was, like the original character of this name, tempted by profit. She was dreaming of remittances and, in the words of a bank manager, "imagining that it would be possible to pay any loan. Then the migrant doesn't find work, or doesn't send money for another reason, and doesn't have the capacity to repay. A loan of Q50,000 ($6,400) is very difficult to pay here in Guatemala. I have a client who borrowed this quantity to go to the United States. Of course, he did not tell us this was his plan. Going to the United States is a big wager. We don't accept it for loans. Two or three months later, the wife comes to us because he's still not sending money, and she's falling behind. She has no way to repay."[4]

The dream of remittances was not just a folly that overtook borrowers. It was also indulged by lending agencies. They did not wish to hear that their money would be used to go to the United States, at least not in so many words. But the majority were more than willing to finance migrants after the fact. With so many migrants rushing north on loans at 10 percent monthly interest, their relatives were the most eager applicants for less onerous institutional credit. Without much thought, loan officers assumed that such borrowers would receive several thousand or more quetzals every month for the life of the loan. They assumed that the remitters would enjoy steady employment, that the U.S. government would refrain from deporting them, and that the U.S. economy would continue to provide jobs. If any of these assumptions proved wrong, their borrowers would never be able to repay.

Another practice that encouraged overlending was the *comisión de colocación* or bonus that agencies such as Génesis paid their loan officers for surpassing their monthly quota. This created a financial incentive, not just to overlook signs of insolvency, but to exaggerate the collateral and cash flow of applicants. At some institutions the bonus took the form of a "commission" or "tip" which the applicant paid the loan officer under the table to exaggerate his qualifications. Thus a man who owned a pig became a pig-raising enterprise. At the Granai & Townson Bank, auditors arrived to check the paperwork and collateral for each bad loan. Many had been approved by a single employee, who was fired.

Overlending was not just due to crooked loan officers or remittance-hungry bank managers, however. It was multiplied by borrowers who went from one lender to another, persuading each to issue a loan secured by what turned out to be the same piece of property. A property title is supposed to guarantee ownership and transferability. In a Mayan Indian town like Nebaj, most land is held not through the national title registry but through the *ejido municipal*, the holding granted to the town's inhabitants by the Spanish crown or the Republic of Guatemala. A municipal grant might sound like collective property, but in Nebaj all land has long been privatized. Sales and inheritances are supposed to be registered through the town hall, but there is no actual registry. All that exists are thousands of documents squirreled away in drawers and under mattresses. Friends sell land to each other but decide to save

the trouble of documenting the sale. Heirs sell property that, on a future occasion, other heirs will claim belongs to them. Owners claim to have lost their
document and ask the town hall to give them a new copy. In exchange for
a fee, lawyers and notaries draw up elaborate declarations of ownership and
transfer without verifying their accuracy. I will occasionally refer to a "title"
or "deed," but in Nebaj these are usually just *papeles* (papers) or *documentos*,
easy to duplicate, on the strength of which the same piece of land can be sold
or mortgaged more than once.

THE WOMEN'S DEBT COMMITTEE

Less than a year after Doña Ingracia fled her creditors, so many other Ixil
women were in financial distress that they organized a committee to plead for
rescue. "We are victims of the Internal Armed Conflict which brought poverty
and hunger to our children and families," their October 2008 petition begins.
"After the signing of the peace accords, we were left without material goods.
All that remained was our house lot. This obliged some families to journey
to the United States to pursue the American Dream, but unfortunately some
of us have not had the luck to attain it, with the result that we return home
with empty hands."[5] According to the petition, seventy-six individuals—all
but eleven of them women—owed a total of Q5.4 million, or $692,000. This
was an average of Q71,000, or $9,100, per household, in a town where many
households get by on $1,500 a year or less.

When I became acquainted with the committee in January 2009 and returned in May, it was in more or less permanent session. A stream of women
who spoke little Spanish pulled loan documents from their blouses and
requested my help to decipher them. The executive committee consisted of
women proficient in Spanish. Two men had helped start the group, but there
had been a split, with rosters, funds, and legitimacy going in different directions. This side of the split was an all-woman organization, to be more appealing to donors, and the meetings consisted almost entirely of women. But
the first meeting I attended was opened by a Pentecostal pastor and closed
by another Pentecostal pastor, both males who led the group in loud appeals
to the Almighty.

Gringos also have a certain magical quality in Nebaj, so I too was welcome
to the deliberations. Even though I reiterated that I did not represent an aid organization, could not pay their debts, and was only doing a study, my presence
signified that well-heeled internationalists cared about their plight. Queues of
women formed to tell me their stories, and I produced a compilation for the
group's next delegation to Guatemala City. Forty women (all but a few with

husbands), a man, and a couple explained their situations to me. The average debt they reported was Q126,500, or $16,200, per household. Thirty of the forty-two said that they had lent money or property titles to others. The purpose, in twenty-five of the cases, was to send someone to the United States. Eight of the twenty-five deals had been undermined by deportation, two more by the death of the migrant, and three more by incapacitating injuries. Ten of the forty-two family heads I interviewed had already lost their houses, either to foreclosure or to a debt-forced sale. Unfortunately, Guatemalans do not have the right to declare bankruptcy and shield their house from confiscation.

The president of the committee, Doña Julia, is a small, bustling figure who in January 2009 had the reassuring air of a fairy godmother but who by May was being ground down by her fate. Ixil women are known for their intricate weaving, and this is how Dominga Julia Marcos Bernal used to make her living. She was a protégé of Padre Javier Gurriarán, the Spanish priest who introduced liberation theology to Nebaj before he was driven out by the army, and she has participated in a succession of projects to empower women. Liberation theologians and feminists are horrified by evangelical Protestantism, but Doña Julia is now an evangelical Protestant like most other Ixil leaders.

"We all have our work before the Lord," Julia told me at her large but sparsely furnished house on the outskirts of town. "The people here are very poor, and my work is to help them with their journeys. My husband was drinking, he didn't support me, and I was weaving to earn my living. But I was really getting tired, and my legs were affected. So five years ago I switched to this kind of work. The gentlemen at Banrural gave me a hand and I gave a hand to those who travel north. That's why I lent them money for the trip—yes, at 10 percent interest per month—until they have their own remittances and can take out their own loan from the bank."

Doña Julia was borrowing money at 2 percent interest per month in order to loan it to migrants at 10 percent per month. She was also getting a commission from the coyotes for bringing them clients. In the first three years, Julia estimates that she earned double her investment in each migrant she sent north. When I asked how many, she showed me her accounts. They consisted of tattered school copybooks in which she had jotted down names, phone numbers, and arithmetic in no apparent order (she has two years of formal education). Of all the people she sent north, by her account, only five had failed to pay her, but these five had sunk her. Once in the United States, they either could not find work or decided that repaying her was not a priority. When she approached the father of one deadbeat, his response was, "Tie me up and kill me if you want, but I cannot pay."

By the time I met Julia, she was going through hell. She showed me a bag of pills she was taking to get to sleep. According to the October 2008 petition, she owed four different institutions a total of Q160,000, or $20,500. But according to Julia herself, she owed four times that amount: Q300,000 ($38,500) to Banrural and another Q300,000 to at least six of her neighbors. I say "at least" because rarely did a day go by that I did not hear something new about her tangled affairs. Functionaries at three additional institutions alleged that she also had borrowed from them—but through intermediaries, on their own property documents. If the accusations are true, Julia borrowed from at least seven different institutions. She was able to keep up her monthly payments to Banrural only by persuading neighbors to loan her money or property titles, which she used as collateral for new bank loans. Many of the new deals cost her 10 percent per month, with each supposedly guaranteed by the imminent repayment of a previous deal. One creditor stripped Julia's kitchen of its appliances. Another creditor put a lien on the salaries of her daughter and her husband. She wanted to sell her two-story house but was getting no offers, and Banrural initiated legal proceedings to take it.

By January 2009, Doña Julia's group had grown to 221 members. Of the forty-two family heads I interviewed, none had as many creditors as she did, but the majority echoed her sad story in the following ways:

1. They borrowed large amounts of money from institutions at low rates of interest.
2. They turned around and loaned the money to someone else they thought they could trust.
3. The person they trusted was usually going to the United States or sending a husband or son there.
4. They hoped to live off the difference between the two rates of interest.

The debtors' committee accused loan agencies of failing to verify their ability to pay—that is, failing to detect that they were engaging in multiple borrowing. According to the same petition, the seventy-six households were indebted to an average of 3.1 institutions each, with twenty-nine reporting debts to four or more institutions. When serial debts collapse, agricultural land is usually the first to be seized or sold, then the house, and then the property of relatives and neighbors, although some relatives and neighbors lose their house before the borrower does. In one of many deals gone awry, Doña Julia persuaded her daughter-in-law to use the title to her house to borrow Q25,000 ($3,200) and give Julia the money. Julia managed four payments on the loan before she went into arrears and penalties more than doubled the debt. The daughter-in-law had not consulted her husband before putting up their house as collateral. When he found out, he beat her so badly that she had to go to the hospital. In a compromise, a judge gave the couple four months to come up with Q38,000 ($4,870) to save their home.

A single failed trip to the United States was enough to start a vicious cycle that could take a household's property and that of its most trusting kin. One of the women I met at the debt committee was Esperanza. She and her husband borrowed Q50,000 from Banrural to send their son to the United States and also to build a house. Their son was drinking and driving when he broke his skull; instead of paying for the cost of his trip north, he ended up in a hospital and required an additional Q20,000 to come home. As the interest and penalties on the Banrural loan mounted to Q100,000, Esperanza plugged gaps by borrowing from moneylenders at 10 percent per month. When she and her husband sold their house for Q300,000 ($38,500), this should have put them in the clear. But so many creditors wanted payment, and the money went in so many directions, that by 2011 the penniless Esperanza and her husband were still in debt Q35,000 to Banrural, Q35,000 to Cotoneb, and Q65,000 to a migrant in the United States. All three of these obligations ($17,300 in all) were secured by the property of in-laws, who were in danger of losing three houses and two agricultural plots.

"Please tell the internationalists that there is no peace because the institutions take advantage of women who cannot read or write," Doña Julia told me. "We beseech international human rights to protect the rights of Ixil women." The committee's trips to the capital led to a Spanish organization that offered an income-generating project, of the weaving and vegetable variety, that would not generate enough income to save houses from foreclosure. Brushing aside doubts within the committee, Julia persisted in looking for a bailout. "They say they are going to give us a project, but we do not need projects. What we need is to speak with the First Lady Sandra [de Colom] so that she will speak with the bank. What we need is a fund to pay our debts." But the First Lady turned them down, members accused Julia of taking their membership dues, and the committee disintegrated.[6]

WHY TAKE SUCH RISKS?

Peasant farmers have a reputation for being cautious. One school of thought holds that they are governed by moral economy, a risk-averse ethic of safety first, which prefers to invest any surplus in strengthening social ties rather than seeking monetary profit (Scott 1976). Being partial to this view myself, I was astounded to learn that so many Ixils were enmeshed in financial speculation.[7] When Latin Americans depart to the United States en masse, hometown critics refer to *fiebre de migración* (migration fever), *manía* (mania), or *contagio* (contagion). According to this diagnosis, the migrant is so enchanted by his prospects in El Norte that he is overcome by what a psychologist would call a compulsive disorder. He loses the ability to judge his own best interest; he could harm himself and his family. In anthropology, we try to avoid explaining cultural patterns in terms of psychological dysfunction; we prefer to find the method in the madness. In this case, Ixils are peasants who, in their competition for increasingly scarce land and jobs, have schooled each other in the precise calculation of self-interest. Doña Julia and her peers are savvy market women; many of the migrants are obviously energetic and intelligent.

Economists and political scientists begin with the assumption that human beings are rational actors. Yet they have learned much to undermine this assumption, as have I in Nebaj. For example, if Nebajenses are rational actors, why would they borrow from moneylenders at 10 percent monthly interest when they could borrow from loan officers at 1.5 to 3 percent per month? It isn't as if coaxing loans out of Nebaj's financial institutions was all that difficult before 2008. When I present this conundrum to Ixil loan officers, they say their people feel more comfortable dealing with moneylenders than with institutions. Borrowing from a moneylender will usually be conducted in their own language, with someone they know from their neighborhood or church. Negotiations are conducted in the reassuring, singsong of *confianza* (trust), a flattering form of address that Guatemalans can produce at the drop of a hat, in which each party is a person of honor and all concerned will benefit. In a study of rotating-credit circles among Mexicans, the anthropologist Carlos Vélez-Ibáñez explains that confianza grows out of reciprocity.[8] You cannot have confianza with a bank because it demands intimate knowledge of your affairs without offering a personal relationship in return. Ixils assume that a friend who can be flattered, supplicated, and pressured will be more manageable than a rule-bound official. Then, too, borrowing from a bank requires more contact with the tax system than many Ixils wish to have.[9]

Perversely, large flows of cheap institutional credit not only failed to reduce loansharking; they encouraged Ixils to borrow even more money at high rates of interest. How could commercial and philanthropic credit not only fail to undermine personal moneylending, but increase it? Peasants struggle with so many deficits and unmet needs that, given the opportunity to borrow, they can quickly go over their heads even without the allure of El Norte—just by investing loans in educational expenses, medical emergencies, and consumer durables.

How many people here have debts? I asked a village leader in La Pista in 2010. "The majority owe the banks," he responded, "and they also owe individuals. They borrow Q10,000 or Q15,000 [$1,280 or $1,920] to buy a radio, a bicycle, and other things that don't provide income. Then they borrow from individuals to pay the bank. And when they can't pay the individual, they take off," he laughed. "The bank says, if you pay it off this month, you'll get your title back. But there are people who owe Q50,000, Q60,000, Q100,000, Q150,000 [$19,200], and this is why they fled; they can no longer pay. We don't know where they are, if they are in the capital or somewhere else." Of the 450 families in La Pista, he guessed that 60 or 70 have lost their houses to debt.

Finding a productive use for capital in a town like Nebaj is no small challenge. All conceivable retail outlets have multiplied beyond the effective demand for their services, as have all conceivable forms of motor transport, giving rise to the following reasoning: if loans are supposed to be invested in an activity that pays the interest and generates a profit, and if I cannot identify any such activity, why don't I give the task of paying the interest and making a profit to someone else? Give her the money and let her figure it out! Even if the borrower doesn't think of this herself, the idea is certain to come walking up in the form of a relative or a neighbor who has a *necesidad* (need) and pleads for help. And so the borrower invests the loan by passing it to someone else at a higher rate of interest.

Some moneylenders were returned migrants, or migrants still in the United States, wondering how to multiply their meager savings. Aware of the many storefronts without customers, they decided to invest their capital in the next wave of migrants, either directly or through a relative or neighbor acting as broker. Other moneylenders were bystanders who had no experience in the United States, nor anyone sending them remittances, nor any savings, but who were determined to catch up. Why not go to a credit institution, make up a story about needing money for something else, and invest the loan in a migrant? Then there were all the relatives of yet-to-be-successful migrants in El Norte, staggering under 10 percent monthly interest, who were now eager to switch to a lower rate. And so the cheap credit from financial institutions was drawn into the migration bonanza. By increasing the amount of cash that Ixils could loan each other, cheap credit had the paradoxical effect of increasing rather than undermining high-interest moneylending. The result was chains of debt, the funds for which originated in remittances and institutional credits, which were then farmed out in idiosyncratic person-to-person deals at higher rates of interest until they were almost certain to collapse.[10]

Arguably, this is all rational choice. Irrational choice is equally easy to find in Nebaj: borrowers and lenders who lack basic arithmetic and who fall for ludicrous pitches. There are obvious limits to rational calculation when people are weighing immediate benefits against future costs—a shortcoming that is hardly confined to Guatemalans. Two additional explanations for high-risk borrowing emerge from the stories I have heard. Call them perverse incentives if you will:

1. Once Nebajenses have staked a house or agricultural land on a trip that fails and that is about to swallow their property, the only way to save it is to redouble their quest for U.S.-level wages. Thus the riskiness of going

north generates pressure for further borrowing, however badly past borrowing has turned out. This is the sunk-cost trap, also known as throwing
good money after bad, to which we will return in the next chapter.
2. All the new sources of cash—from aid projects, loans, and remittances—
have had a ferocious impact on the price of land in Nebaj. The scholarly
literature on sending communities includes many terse references to this kind
of inflation, which on closer inspection turns out to be astronomical.[11]

REAL ESTATE INFLATION

Sometimes I couldn't believe my ears. One day I panted a thousand meters up
a ridge to the cloud-wrapped K'iche' village of Chortiz, an early sender to the
United States. Here I met a man who, upon his return, purchased 32 cuerdas
(1.4 hectares) of good pasture. It was the price he quoted for the pasture that
I couldn't believe—Q160,000 ($20,500), which means Q5,000 per cuerda,
$5,900 per acre, and $14,600 per hectare.[12] I suspected exaggeration, but
other men told me that good agricultural land was selling at this level. Inflation of the price of house lots was even more shocking. House lots are a major
issue for families with five, six, or seven children surviving to adulthood,
most of whom will reproduce and need a new dwelling. House lots acquire
even more resonance for peasants who have lost all their agricultural land;
this becomes their last claim to the resource defining their cultural heritage.

Because cropland and firewood are more available away from the town of
Nebaj, three-quarters of the population continue to live in villages and hamlets, but even there the price of house lots has shot to intimidating levels. In
the outlying village of Vicalamá, an elder told me, land cost Q10 per cuerda
before the war (US$10 or Q78 at today's exchange rate). When the village
was rebuilt in the late 1980s, a cuerda (.044 hectare) was still fairly cheap.
Even in the late 1990s, following considerable population growth, a cuerda
still cost only Q200 to Q300 ($26 to $38). But by 2007, a cuerda for building a house cost as much as Q50,000 ($6,400). Background inflation in the
Guatemalan economy accounts for some of this; the only likely explanation
for the rest is the impact of credits and remittances.[13] In the migration hotbed
of Xexuxcap, house lots went for as high as Q80,000, and at La Pista for as
high as Q125,000.

More often, prices of this kind were for building lots on the outskirts of
the municipal seat. For centrally located real estate, within a few blocks of
the town square, knowledgeable Nebajenses claimed that prices were reaching the level of Guatemala City. An evangelical pastor offered Q2 million
($256,000) for a four-cuerda vacant lot near his church and school, on the

premise that he could sell his current property for that much and erect a better building. But the younger brother of another pastor grabbed the property for a higher price.

Who could pay prices like this? The buyers consisted of migrants, relatives of migrants, and real estate speculators who were investing profits from previous deals but also possibly taking out large bank loans. According to frustrated buyers priced out of the market, the migrants and their agents would pay anything for land. "There are more and more people, and everyone wants to buy land. Those who have land will sell it only for a high price. And people who have gone to the United States have no hesitation to pay any price," a project coordinator told me. "When people who have gone to the United States are offered a property, they just throw themselves at it," another coordinator claimed. "They don't bargain. They just pay whatever is asked."

Rapid inflation is threatening because it tells everyone that they are in danger of falling behind. In this case, it put every household in Nebaj under pressure to send someone north. Not every household did so, and not every household would, but every household was thinking about it. Thus the prosperity of some Nebajenses has meant deep anxiety for others. Remaining faithful to the routines of peasant subsistence meant being left behind. "This is producing more poor people because not everyone can go; there are more families that stay than go, and they can no longer buy land," one of the coordinators added.

In Florida I met a former guerrilla cadre for whom the decisive moment was bidding on a neighbor's lot; the neighbor sold it to someone else, who has a son in the United States, for Q300,000 ($38,500). "Where am I going to get money like that?" he asked plaintively. And so he borrowed Q40,000 ($5,100) from a credit union to venture north in 2005. His first year of labor paid for the trip north, but the next two years it was harder and harder to stay employed. When we spoke in 2008, he had just lost another job, and his savings were minimal. Now he was grappling with the fact that, in return for all his work and three years of separation from his family, he had gained nothing.

Back home, other Nebajenses who wagered on El Norte were losing their last shreds of property. I came across a woman who was trying to subdivide her steep one-cuerda house lot in an outlying cantón into two separate sales. For the half cuerda of land that was more or less unoccupied (12 × 12 meters), she wanted Q7,000 ($900). For the other half cuerda, she wanted Q45,000 ($5,800) because it included the hut in which she lived with her five children. Why did she want to sell her habitation? Her husband went north two years earlier. Because he wasn't sending money, the property against which he had borrowed at 10 percent monthly interest was about to be lost; it belonged to his brother. She was hoping to save the brother's property by selling her own.

I heard stories of children who weren't getting enough to eat because their father had gone north, of a woman who was confronted by a collection agent and fainted, and of another who abandoned her children to hide in the fields.

Loan officers holding land and houses as collateral were convinced that, if they took pity on the most innocent and needy defaulters, the bulk of their clientele would stop paying. That is what happened in the 1990s when Nebaj's first generation of revolving loans vanished. After some borrowers stopped paying, entire villages followed suit. Even then, some borrowers had been required to put up real estate as collateral, but loan agencies declined to confiscate it. The ostensible purpose of the first loan programs had been to educate Ixils about repayment. The programs were indeed educational, but not as envisioned by the planners. What Ixils learned is that they didn't really have to repay the loans because, despite the rhetoric, lenders would not really grab their collateral. European Union administrators wanted to help Ixils, not profit from them. Taking their property seemed immoral. And so, without intending to, donors accustomed Ixils to the idea that any debt with an institution would ultimately be forgiven.

In 2004 a scornful Ixil administrator told me that every Ixil-controlled organization giving out loans was an accounting disaster. The fundamental problem, he asserted, was that borrowers did not feel any compulsion to repay. "It makes me angry," the same man said of the women's debt committee five years later. "If the president were to show up and pay their debts, they would do the same thing over again! There's an attitude here that never changes. The problem is here," he pointed to his head. "Along the road to Salquil there are fields ready to plant, but they don't do anything. Later on, in March, they'll plant maize. But for four or five months they don't plant anything! They could sow French beans to recharge the nitrogen and they don't do it. How many talks have I given, in the high schools, in the associations, and in the villages? And they don't change. They don't change because they expect this!" He cupped his hand to receive a handout. "They're waiting around for financial compensation for the violence, they receive it, and they spend it on televisions. They get loans and spend them on buying cars. And on trips north, with the wife and children waiting for the papa to send them money. Everyone thinks that the United States is going to open the door and that they will all find work there."

THE BUBBLE BURSTS

By the end of 2007, Nebaj's bankers and moneylenders were becoming aware of two unfortunate facts. First, more and more of their borrowers were falling behind on payments. Second, these borrowers were in debt not only to them but to multiple other lenders. Over the next year the bankers and moneylenders became aware of a third unfortunate fact. All the bad news from El Norte—migrants losing jobs in the construction industry, enforcement of immigration laws, a recession, and then the September 2008 liquidity crisis—was cutting deeply into the remittances upon which so many of their borrowers depended. Thanks to years of aid, credit, and remittance inflows, Nebaj had become a bubble economy in which two key assets—illegal migration to the United States and local real estate—were overvalued.

More precisely, Nebaj was now a dependent inflationary economy. Its economy was dependent because, although the main livelihood was still peasant farming, it was unable to produce enough food to sustain itself, so it depended on exporting labor to the outside world. Nebaj's economy was inflationary because the inflow of aid donations, credit, and remittances led to a price bubble for a basic productive resource that is in fixed supply: land. As the supply of money in Nebaj increased, the price of house lots and agricultural land spiraled upward. The only way that youth could hope to buy real estate was to leave for El Norte. And so the bubble in real estate led to a second bubble, in all those loans to migrants going north, which could last only as long as more distant bubbles in the U.S. economy did.

In the second half of 2008, remittances plunged. Judging from remarks at various agencies, they may have dropped by as much as half. Default rates climbed into double digits, and dozens of foreclosures clogged the docket at the local courthouse. Nebajenses were still going north, but in smaller numbers, apparently because they grasped the lack of jobs, and even if they didn't, it was much harder to raise the necessary Q40,000 ($5,100). The real estate market froze, making it impossible for creditors to recover their capital. And so the Nebaj bubble turned into its own version of the global credit crisis, in an uncanny echo of the U.S. credit derivatives bubble and how it burst.

I knew change was afoot when I found used televisions for sale at a microcredit agency. The manager acknowledged that the majority of his solidarity groups had fallen apart because the women were not making sales and had no income. Since his agency had not asked solidarity groups for collateral, it was in the lurch. The mediation service at the courthouse was no help: when borrowers learned that "for debt there is no jail," they felt relieved of the last pressure to pay. As for larger loans for which the agency did have collateral, the same property title often turned out to guarantee a loan from another institution. "If we sue them," a loan officer at another microcredit said, "they don't have anything to pay us. They say, 'we don't have anything,' put their hands in the air, and think we ought to let them off the hook. If we don't, they say we're abusing them. But they also abuse us. There are threats when we show up to collect."

For lack of remittances and other woes, a loan officer at a third microcredit told me, 45 percent of his borrowers were in arrears by mid-2009—more than twenty times his arrears rate of 2 percent just a year and a half before. A year later the agency had coaxed a third of its nonpayers into resuming their installments, with the result that only 30 percent of the borrowers were in default—mainly members of solidarity groups who had no property at risk. The agency's best hope for recovering capital lay with *fiadores* or cosigners—a relative or friend of the borrower, in Nebaj usually a government employee with a salary that could be garnished if necessary.

In 2008 I found just one loan manager who thought he was escaping the default crisis. The Granai & Townson Bank gave loans only to people with businesses whose dimensions could be verified. Two years later, up to 70 percent of the manager's portfolio was in arrears. First one payment was late, then three or four, then payments stopped. The suddenness of the change, in October 2009, long after the business slowdown began, suggested that defaulters were acting in concert or at least imitating each other. But Granai & Townson was avoiding foreclosures. "Seizing property isn't business," the manager explained.

> The bank doesn't want properties; it wants its capital. First I call people to remind them that they are late. That is, to appeal to their conscience. We're willing to give them more time and stretch out the payments. They say there's no business or my family member was sent back from the United States. But there are people with prosperous businesses who are late and say they can't pay. The next step is that a lawyer calls them, with words that aren't so sweet. Right now I'm talking with the higher-ups about our next step. We have to get our loan principal back.

Is there a culture of nonpayment here? I asked.

> Chajul and Cotzal are now a red zone for us; we won't make more loans there. Nebaj is suspended for new credits and will be a red zone next year unless we recuperate 50 percent of our arrears. What we're realizing is that people here have very little left. Three different institutions find themselves foreclosing on a single house and fighting over how to split it in three.

One institution that had a lot to lose, and that was using the legal system to recover collateral, was the Rural Development Bank. Banrural is the largest financial institution in Guatemala, and by far the largest in Nebaj. To protect itself from multiple loans on the same property, Banrural set up a mortgage registry with the town hall—which then failed to stay current or extend to the new loan agencies opening for business. Critics attribute its careless lending to the fact that it was receiving low-interest trust funds (*fideicomiseos*) from the U.S. Agency for International Development and the European Union.

Banrural's manager, a local man who knows Nebaj well, conceded that his officers loaned out too much money between 2005 and 2008. But default was minimal until February 2008, he claimed. For borrowers falling behind, Banrural was now offering longer payment periods. After borrowers were three months behind, Banrural put a lawyer on their case. But it hoped to avoid going to court and seizing the collateral because the procedure was time consuming and costly. It also did not want to be saddled with a property that, in a depressed market, could not be sold for enough to recover its losses. Because many of the initial loan agreements were looking unwise, Banrural was also willing to settle for the initial loan amount, to the point of pardoning interest and late penalties, but only if the borrower could come up with a lump sum. The manager never admitted to more than a 5 percent default rate.

Soon Banrural was processing dozens of borrowers at the local courthouse. In June 2011, the judge in charge of foreclosures told me that Banrural had brought seventy-five to ninety cases before him in his three years on the Nebaj bench, but only about twenty had gone through, and perhaps ten from other lenders. In the cases that were dropped, either Banrural worked out a deal or desisted because of a procedural hang-up, such as collateral that was fictional or claimed by multiple owners. Tacked to the courthouse bulletin board I found thirty-five pending cases. Twenty-nine were from Banrural, another five were from the San Miguel Chuimequená credit union, and they dated back as far as November 2008.

The second largest lender in Nebaj is the Ixil-run Todos Nebajenses ("We're All Nebajenses") Cooperative, a credit union started by Ixil teachers, businessmen, and pastors in the 1990s. Cotoneb began as part of a wider movement called Cotón, named after the red dress jacket trimmed in black that Ixil elders wear on ceremonial occasions. With the slogan "Everyone together," Cotón's accomplishments included an organization to defend Ixil culture; one of the town's first secondary schools; and a civic committee, a way to run candidates for the municipal government without joining a national political party. Cotón's proudest accomplishment was electing an Ixil schoolteacher to two terms as mayor, from 1996 to 2004. Unfortunately, Pedro Raymundo Cobo succumbed to the temptations of office. When Don Pedro insisted on running for a third term, the civic committee split, and a Riosmonttista won election as the next mayor.

Cotón's credit union survived these vicissitudes and grew rapidly, but it was always plagued by bad loans. A 2002 study pegged its default rate at 14 percent.[14] Five years later Cotoneb had Q31.7 ($4.1) million in loans against Q13 million in accumulated capital and Q17 million in local savings. The

portfolio of loans ranged from as low as Q1,000 to as high as Q200,000
($25,600) at an interest rate of 18 percent a year. It was processing more than
Q1 million ($128,000) per month in remittances and administering a U.S.-
funded food security program for the Ministry of Public Health. Cotoneb was
not apologetic about going after defaulters because it was run by Ixils whose
legitimacy was impossible to question. After three months without payment, borrowers heard from a lawyer and then the courthouse. In May 2008,
Cotoneb's president told me that it had seized many properties but never a
house. Eight months later he said that Cotoneb had seized fifty-six properties
worth Q1.6 million ($205,000), only two or three of which included houses.
He acknowledged a default rate of 10 percent, but an in-house critic claimed
that it was as high as 25 percent.

According to the same in-house critic, Cotoneb's origin in the civic committee and the "everyone together" ideal meant that it was slow to recognize
business realities. Feelings of fraternity did not necessarily encourage the
repayment of financial obligations. Late penalties swelled the size of its loan
portfolio to Q38 ($4.9) million against Q33 ($4.2) million in deposits, capital, and obligations from other institutions. Cotoneb's president turned out
to have made inappropriate loans to himself and relatives; he was replaced.
Poor administration also included bad collateral—unsellable, nonexistent, or
multiple-claimed property put up by borrowers who were now in the United
States and whose loans would have to be written off. Last but not least,
property values had fallen fifty percent since 2008. Banrural, Cotoneb, and
other credit unions were choked with bad properties they could not sell. Soon
Cotoneb was giving late payers six months before going to court to foreclose
them. It was also letting the previous owners stay in foreclosed properties
until a buyer was found.

The debt crisis also pulled down the town's development associations—the
only hope for improving the income of peasants as agricultural producers
rather than as migrants in distant labor markets. Sustainable peasant agriculture is popular with international donors, but these are very conscious of the
need for local initiative, leadership, and accountability, so they are eager to
connect with grassroots organizations. Unfortunately, funding can become a
Midas touch when it turns activists, full of energy and idealism, into employees whose priority becomes perpetuating their salary. Philanthropy can also
be fatal when it enlarges revolving-loan programs. In theory, a revolving-loan
program is equitable and sustainable, but in practice it can quickly become
a division of the spoils, and the recriminations can quickly hollow out a
membership. In Nebaj, one example of this cycle is Apaptix, a development
association that started as a veterinary service and became known for its
spirited volunteers.

In 2005 an energetic new president decided to make Apaptix bigger by expanding the revolving-loan program. International donors were giving Banrural low-interest capital for precisely this purpose; some of it would now flow to Apaptix. The funding would cost Apaptix 14 percent annual interest, and Apaptix could loan it to producers at 36 percent annual interest, supporting itself in the process. Ultimately Banrural extended a total of Q2.5 million ($320,000), and Apaptix abandoned restraint. It increased loan amounts, loaned to townspeople (speculators) as well as producers, stopped inspecting properties before accepting them as collateral, and put its insiders on salary.

After four years of this, Apaptix board members asked me if I could find a forensic accountant to help them figure out where the money went. Borrowers had stopped making payments, but Apaptix still owed more than Q1 million ($128,000) to Banrural, which seized its donor-financed building. "Thanks to Banrural's loans," an aid consultant told me, "a voluntary association swelled into an NGO from which all this money was extracted. Now that it has shrunk again, into bankruptcy, is it a cadaver or is it still alive? All the directors and employees became accustomed to high expenses; I doubt that they can return to the status of volunteers." What was left of Apaptix—the pharmacy for village veterinarians—retreated to a humble storefront. In 2012 it was in cheerful operation and hoping to be refloated with a new contract from the Ministry of Agriculture.

The borrowers who lost their property fastest were the ones who signed a *compra-venta* (literally, "buy-sell") document. Here the borrower only receives her loan after signing a notarized document in which she sells her collateral to the lender. The sale is nullified only if the borrower is able to repay the loan and interest, most often 10 percent per month. Otherwise the lender takes possession of the property without the delay and expense of a court-supervised eviction. If the borrower resists vacating her property, the lender can present the compra-venta to a judge as a sale, without reference to its origin as a loan at an illegal interest rate. For unscrupulous moneylenders who can afford notaries and lawyers, compra-ventas are an excellent technique for fleecing the poor. But in a milieu so ridden with default, they are easy to defend as a necessary guarantee. Cotoneb uses them, and so does another local operation called the T'al Ka'b Association, which between 2008 and 2010 could be counted upon to grab a defaulter's house faster than any other lender.

"T'al Ka'b" is the Ixil term for honey, the marketing of which was the association's initial purpose. A Peace Corps volunteer helped start it, and the organizers included a war orphan raised by Catholic nuns. Despite these philanthropic antecedents and the reassuring name, T'al Ka'b's name kept popping up in the eviction stories I was collecting. So I was surprised when its address turned out to be the house of my friend Pedro Onofre Bernal Guzmán, an accountant and loan officer who was always good for an analysis of Nebaj's comedy of errors. I knew Onofre from his job at one of the town's microcredit agencies, whose loans were always under a thousand dollars and which didn't ask for property titles as collateral. Unbeknownst to me, Onofre had his own operation at T'al Ka'b, in which he and the former war orphan were lending to borrowers who were already deeply in debt, charging them 5 percent interest per month and grabbing their houses at the first opportunity.

One of Onofre's clients was Sebastián Marcos Pérez, an easygoing agriculturalist who would prefer to trust people in the belief that it will all work out in the end. Several years earlier, Sebastián borrowed heavily to go to the United States along with his son-in-law. He was grabbed by the Migra and deported back to Guatemala. Then his son-in-law was grabbed by the Migra, and Sebastián made his biggest mistake; out of concern for his daughter, he borrowed an additional Q60,000 ($7,700) from T'al Ka'b in order to wire the money to the United States and bail out her husband. The son-in-law was released from jail and was never heard from again. Soon Sebastián was unable to keep up payments to T'al Ka'b. He told Onofre that he would sell his house in order to pay the debt and put the rest of the proceeds toward building a new house. While Sebastián was away working on the coast, Onofre sent a crew of men to the house, pressured Sebastián's children to come into the road, and then immediately knocked it down and put the land behind barbed wire. This was illegal, but Sebastián never went to the courthouse to make a complaint. When I asked why, he said that he didn't have the money to pay a lawyer. Just to get started on a case, lawyers ask for thousands of quetzals. If an overdue borrower refuses to vacate a property, a moneylender can hire a lawyer and take the borrower to court, where he will be told he needs a lawyer he cannot afford. In at least two cases, T'al Ka'b's lawyer has persuaded a judge that the compra-ventas are legitimate bills of sale.[15]

Even with these versatile documents, moneylenders are not always able to seize collateral—not if they are so overextended that they cannot afford lawyers, and not if the property documents are phony. Consider the fate of Gregorio, one of the founders of the women's debt committee who left to start a rival group. Like many other project coordinators in Nebaj, Gregorio's career with nongovernmental organizations began as a capable young refugee. Due to his skill in negotiating on behalf of older men with less Spanish and less confidence, he helped organize the first successful coffee-marketing cooperative in Ixil country. Then he started a rival organization before leaving that one as well, each time taking members and funds with him. Parallel to his activities as an organizer and disorganizer, Gregorio became a moneylender. By

Sebastián and family showing where their home used to be

2009 he was the secretary of yet another organization, which proposed to help people pay their debts by soliciting new loans for agricultural production.

But now every bad loan was yapping at his heels. Migrants going north were his source of profit and ruin. Of the borrowers, Gregorio told me, some twenty had repaid him in full. Another fifteen had not—five of them from Cotzal, the others from Nebaj villages—and collectively they owed him Q400,000 ($51,000) in capital, not counting the 10 percent monthly interest that they had agreed to pay. Most of the fifteen were still in the United States. Before making each loan, he had paid lawyers Q450 to turn the written agreements into compra-ventas, but now he was learning that many of the underlying property documents were useless. They were either duplicates or to someone else's land or to none at all. Confirming which documents were valid, taking possession of the properties, and selling them would require large payments to lawyers. Even if successful in taking possession of the properties, he would have a hard time finding buyers for anything like the value of his loans. As for his own house and properties, these were in hock to three financial institutions and five individuals, for a total of Q320,000 ($41,000) in loans that he had no way to repay. The collateral for one of the loans was the house of a friend, who was now losing it to Cotoneb and suing him for fraud.

DEBT PRESSURES MORE NEBAJENSES TO GO NORTH

Despite financial disaster at every turn, Nebajenses continued to hatch schemes to get themselves to the United States. When I expressed misgivings, they said they had no choice. Some were pressured by debts from previous attempts to reach the promised land. The only solution, as far as they could see, was another expedition. Lucia is a leader of the women's debt committee and lives in a two-story house near the center of town. Her husband is from a successful family but failed in his own career as a labor contractor. At his peak he owned trucks, recruited as many as 250 workers to cut sugarcane, and gave out cash advances of Q200. He was ruined by *saltistas* or "jumpers"—workers who collectively defect to a patrón offering higher pay, leaving the contractor in debt to the plantation that provided his cash advances. After overdue bank loans took the last of his trucks, he learned from a coyote that good jobs were available in the United States. And so, approaching the age of fifty, he went north with the idea of working as a *chófer* or driver, the kind of job befitting a man of his seniority.

"There were already lots of people there," Lucia says of her husband's experiences in Florida. "It was the worst moment of his life. We receive Americans well here. They used to come here to learn how to weave. But when we arrive there, they treat us like brutes. They are racists. Why is this, if we receive you so well? My husband says that 99 percent of the Americans are bad. He didn't know how to read or write, or to speak English, and no one respected him. He wanted to work as a driver, 'but you don't know how to read,' they told him. 'You don't know how to write, and you're too old.' He was humiliated. At last he found work as a helper on a trash truck in West Palm Beach, but he had to run a lot and his old war wound opened up and he became sick. He hurt his back, they fired him, and when he came back to ask for help, the company didn't want anything to do with him. There was no worker's compensation. He became disabled and no one helped him. They're very racist there."

As a labor contractor and truck owner, Lucia's husband had plenty of experience with debt. He borrowed to buy his trucks, he borrowed from plantations for the cash advances that he paid workers, and of course his workers had been in debt to him. This was the debt chain that enabled his career as a labor contractor. Now another debt chain sucked his wife's remaining assets all the way to Florida. "I began to borrow from individuals to send my husband to the United States," Lucia explained. "It took him a month to get through Mexico. I was paying the debt while the interest mounted at 10 percent a month. It was horrible. He never had a good salary and could not send money. He explained that he had to pay rent, transport, and lunch, leaving him with nothing, and he got sick. Instead of getting ahead, we just sunk into debt."

To support her failing husband, Lucia borrowed additional funds to send her brother Jeremias north. Jeremias was able to work for two years until one evening he was shot by criminals outside his apartment, putting him in the hospital for two months. Using her house as collateral, Lucia now borrowed Q165,000 ($21,000) from Banrural to send rescue money north, to pay for her children's schooling, and to invest Q50,000 in a get-rich-quick scheme (see chapter 6). The money evaporated, but not the obligation to repay it; the monthly installments were brutal. And so to stay abreast Lucia obtained still more loans—from neighbors, from the Quetzal Foundation, from the Association of Ixil Maya Women, and from Cotoneb—for the last of which she used one of her mother's properties as collateral.

By the time I met Lucia at the debt committee, Cotoneb had seized her mother's property and she was four months behind with Banrural. The bank advised her to sell the house before it went to auction. Unlike most people in this situation, Lucia was approached by a buyer because her house is in a prime commercial location, but she turned him down on the grounds that selling it would traumatize her children. Fortunately for Lucia, she was more adept in Spanish and more resourceful than most members of the debt committee. A month before Banrural's deadline, she won the ear of an aide to First Lady Sandra Torres—but only for herself, not the group. The aide rang up the bank, and the bank offered easier terms: it would drop her annual interest rate from 22 percent to 13 percent and her monthly payments from Q4,200 ($540) to Q2,200 ($280).

Lucia spoke of the First Lady reverently. The refinancing was the Lord's answer to her prayers. And she still had possession of her house. But even monthly payments of Q2,200 were killing her, and now they were staring her in the face every month for the next ten years. Her husband was home from the United States as an invalid. Her brother was still there but was sending nothing. So now she decided it was her turn to go north. This was her only hope, and she wanted me to help her. "You cannot help me?" she asked, fixing me in the eye. I stammered that I couldn't. I explained that I live in a small town within a hundred miles of the U.S. border, where the U.S. Border Patrol has authority to stop anyone it pleases. I knew too many people who were struggling to find employment, and there were sixteen million others in the same position.

That wasn't what she meant. "My niece works for a Guatemalan woman in Los Angeles, she makes three hundred dollars a week, and the woman says that she can give me work too." But Lucia did not want to go through the desert; it was too dangerous and expensive. She wanted to go legally, on an airplane.

"You'll be a live-in maid," I shot back, "a *muchacha* [girl] who works from morning to night. $300 a week is below minimum wage. You say Americans are racist, but this is an immigrant exploiting fellow immigrants."

"That doesn't matter," Lucia said. "I'll do anything for my children! And I have a nephew who is in charge of a company in Washington. The owner is asking him to bring more Guatemalans. They only need visas; they cannot be wetbacks. Can't you help me get a visa? Can't you write a letter for me?"

"The embassy doesn't even look at the letters anymore," I responded. "That's what the chargé d'affaires told me. No matter what the letter says, they know the person will look for work. So now all they care about is your bank account, whether or not you have a car, land, a house, et cetera. Moreover, even if you get a tourist visa, you'll be illegal as soon as you go to work. And you'll learn the same lesson as your husband, that working without papers will put you deeper in debt!"

"That doesn't matter, I just want to work for my children!" Lucia cried. "Instead of giving to my children, I'm giving everything to the bank. I'll do any kind of work for my children. I don't care what it is!" Now we were arguing. A downpour clattered onto the tin roof above our heads and drowned out the sound of our words. We were shouting at each other.

The goal of wage migration is to earn higher wages and a better life. But if Lucia's most urgent need is to pay the debts generated by her previous investments in El Norte, a better term might be debt migration. She is caught in a debt trap generated to a considerable extent by El Norte, the solution to which she believes is another expensive and risky trip north. It is a cruel fact that, even if Nebajenses gain a foothold in the U.S. labor market, most find themselves in the same position as their parents and grandparents on Guatemalan plantations—at the bottom. Shouldn't they have known better? In the early 2000s, they didn't have to read the *Wall Street Journal* to absorb the zeitgeist. The sky was the limit for the U.S. economy: busts, recessions, and depressions were being exorcised from the economic cycle by deregulation and financial ingenuity. Not without reason, Nebajenses assumed that U.S. demand for their labor was unlimited. Wall Street investment bankers made similar assumptions. What differs dramatically is their social class. While limited-liability incorporation allows upper-class speculators to leverage other people's capital, divert gains into safe havens, and offload losses onto clients and taxpayers, Nebajenses must wager their only productive resources, their bodies and their land. The only people on whom they can offload risk are their own relatives and neighbors.

Chapter Six

Projects and Their Penumbra—Swindles

Missionaries, guerrillas, soldiers, and politicians have all, in their different ways, promised Nebajenses the rewards of modernity. When such benefits actually arrive, it is usually in the form of a project—typically a projection by outsiders of how Nebaj could become a better place if only the Nebajenses would organize in a certain way to carry out certain improvements. Since Catholic and Protestant missionaries introduced this model in the 1950s, the Nebajenses have taken to it with vigor and ingenuity. They have organized themselves in many ways—as Christians, revolutionaries, voters, and Mayas, as women, violence victims, and solidarity groups. Their hopes in projects reached an apogee with the 1996 peace accords. Thanks in no small measure to projects, most Nebajenses are now better shod, housed, doctored, and schooled than before. But they place fewer hopes in projects, and one of the reasons is the difficulty of distinguishing between projects and swindles.

This is not just a challenge for illiterate peasants. In cooperation with the U.S. Agency for International Development, or so she thought, an experienced Ixil organizer collected Q25 quotas from women to start a weaving cooperative. She added Q800 of her own and delivered Q2,500 ($320) to a Guatemalan employee of USAID. He was never heard from again. When she asked USAID, it informed her that he was no longer an employee. A former mayor of Nebaj told me how, in 1990, when fifty quetzals was a substantial sum, a K'iche' aid coordinator arrived in town announcing a project to supply roofing and other building materials. The mayor and 150 other Nebajenses each handed over Q50. On the appointed day, they chartered vehicles to Tecpán, Chimaltenango, to take delivery. Here they found themselves in a crowd of five thousand people. The aid coordinator never showed up.

Swindles such as these are a mirror image of village-level aid projects, the kind that stress participation, and the way they resemble such projects

is not very flattering. In both projects and scams, as Jan and Diane Rus
have observed in southern Mexico, a central role is played by the *promotor*
or intermediary—the villager who signs up neighbors for free or low-cost
benefits. To receive the benefit, villagers must attend meetings and provide
unpaid labor. Most attractively for swindlers, villagers must also pay *aportes*,
or contributions, to demonstrate that they are not just lining up to receive a
handout.[1] Other parallels include

- the largesse that comes from a distant and mysterious source;
- the rhetoric of democracy ("grassroots" in English, *popular* in Spanish),
  even though donors have made key decisions beforehand and will prevail
  in case of disagreement; and
- the rhetoric of community, even though the most aggressive and menda-
  cious individuals collect disproportionate rewards and are rarely punished.

You might think that the failure to deliver on promises would be a firm,
unmistakable distinction between swindles and aid projects. Many projects
in Nebaj have indeed delivered new roofs, potable water, and other goods.
But there are enough disappointments that this is not a firm distinction in the
minds of peasants. The fantasies encouraged by aid projects are suggested by
Nebaj's *proyecteros*, a term for people who seek to make their living from
them. Every cantón and village in Nebaj seems to have proyecteros. Housing
programs are a frequent source of inspiration because, while heavily subsi-
dized, they require sweat equity and an advance payment, which must be collected by a local promotor. One day my translator Jacinto Pérez took me to
meet a proyectero, but it was Sunday and the man's womenfolk decided that
he was too drunk to deal with a gringo. By way of substitution, we looked up
another proyectero, Don Alejandro, who turned out to be a pleasant man in
his early sixties, living in a simple tin-roofed house surrounded by the detri-
tus of peasant life. I introduced myself as a student of projects, as well as of
swindles, and asked him what his project was about.

"It's a housing project for people who have been crippled, for people affected by the armed conflict, and for people with few resources," Alejandro
told us. "But everything is legal with Señor Government. For contributions I
ask little, just for expenses, the trips that I pay out of my own pocket. Right
now lots of people are coming, but enrollment has closed. Some three hundred have signed up. They all have to be authorized by the top leaders in
the government. There's lots of auditing because right now there are lots of
swindles; there's lots of auditing to investigate if these people really exist. I
put down their name, the number of their identity card, whether they want
a house or a business, and there [in the capital] it's all put into a computer.

Everything depends on the project managers of FOGUAVI [the Guatemalan Fund for Housing]."

I expressed sympathy. "For two years we've been organizing," Alejandro continued. "There's no discontent; the people realize that projects take time. Nothing is given away for free. Managing a project requires a lot of formality. One has to be legally honest, because many do it to enrich themselves, and that is a sin. No, there's no name for this project. There's no committee. Last time I formed an association with a committee and the committee began to ask for money; I didn't like that. The committee began to demand money from the beneficiaries, and then they disappeared. They asked for five quetzals from each person. That's why it's just me. I like to be sincere. If not, the people call me a liar, they call me a swindler. If not, I'll end up on bad terms with people. I don't want to play with the people's feelings. And I don't want to swindle the people. One eats well and dresses well but is discredited."

Discredit is precisely what has befallen Alejandro. This is the usual fate of proyecteros—to be perceived as failures at best and swindlers at worst. I have no grounds to contest Alejandro's sincerity—he was helpful and candid about the pitfalls of collecting money for projects that, in his case, never arrived. He achieved the form but not the substance. In this he is hardly alone; projects inspire many imitators. Is this just evidence of peasant gullibility, to be remedied by further education? No, because it is the result of education by the aid industry. This is precisely what it seeks to achieve through "institution building," that is, teaching beneficiaries how to apply for grants and make careers out of these routines. The idea is so appealing that it has become pantomime, a theatrical routine for attracting funds which flourishes beyond the boundaries visualized by donors and administrators.

In Nebaj, the perpetual-donation machine has an identifiable origin. It was set in motion by an Italian organization called the Development Program for Displaced Persons, Refugees and Returnees in Central America (PRODERE). PRODERE operated under contract from the United Nations Development Program and was active in Nebaj from 1989 to the mid-1990s. It was also the first organization to arrive in Nebaj bearing the blue emblem of the United Nations. Guatemalans have such a low opinion of their own institutions that when PRODERE's first personnel arrived in white jeeps with the UN global emblem, they were received like a long-awaited relief column. The group's lavishly funded endeavors in Nebaj were led by a tall, charismatic Bolivian of indigenous ancestry named Iván Arizcurinaga. His first move was to mobilize all the government employees in Ixil country. He instructed them to visit each village, call an assembly, and ask the people what they wanted.

Tell us what you need, Iván said; we will respond to the priorities. It wouldn't come from the government. The community itself would manage the project. There would be community funds, multifamily enterprises, and self-determination. The funds were there, he said; all that needed to be decided was how to invest them. As months turned into years, questions arose such as, "When are the resources actually coming?" Iván and his personnel always responded with pregnant expressions such as "Pending further study," "First we have to plan," and "Soon there will be a diagnosis." For those who insisted, the inevitable response was "PRODERE doesn't give anything away" and "the people have to be educated."

In the end PRODERE confined itself to pilot projects and studies which it refused to share with other organizations, with the result that it spent the major part of its budget on consultants, trips back and forth to the capital, and other forms of administration—that is, on itself. To avoid handouts, PRODERE and its successor program from the European Union encouraged Ixils to start development associations whose first priority would be to solicit projects from other international donors. The raft of new organizations was couched in the language of sustainability, such as the revolving-loan fund which in theory would refinance itself. Since revolving-loan funds rarely do so, and since nothing else these organizations did was likely to be self-supporting, in practice they were in perpetual competition for new sources of funding.

The best example of the mimetic principle in the aid industry, and its shadow the fraud industry, is AVIDESGUA, the Spanish acronym for the Association for the Life and Development of Guatemalans, and its companion organization APRODESGUA, the Association for the Life and Sustainable Development of Guatemalans. AVIDESGUA and APRODESGUA came to Nebaj in a motor vehicle driven by Licenciado Rolando Reyes y Reyes.[2] Given how many engineers, consultants, directors, and *licenciados* have passed through Nebaj, Reyes did not stand out from the crowd, except perhaps in the drama of the offer that he made. Seventy-eight million dollars were left over from the international financing for the 1996 peace accords, he told peasant leaders. He didn't want the money going back to the European Union, so he and his organization were going to build five thousand houses for people who needed them. I first heard about Reyes from Diego Tránsito, an ex-EGP combatant and cadre who spent seventeen years in the mountains, who lost his parents to the army, and who lost his land to his neighbors. By way of compensation, the peace accords taught Diego to navigate the world of projects, and he played a leading role in several. By 2010 his luck was running out.

I made Diego's acquaintance at the house of Doña Julia, the president of the women's debt committee. A half moon of fifteen men and women was standing at the entrance to her house in the pouring rain. Whatever held their attention was worth getting soaked. Pinned in the doorway were Diego Tránsito and Doña Julia's husband, and the discussion was not going their way. The two men had collected Q650 ($83) quotas from several dozen neighbors for a housing project that never materialized. Now the neighbors wanted their money back, but the two men didn't have it; they had given the money to Licenciado Reyes. Later that evening, after I invited Diego to supper, we passed another half moon of petitioners. They were the same men and women as before, but now they were at the police station. Before I could even turn to him, Diego vanished.

We caught up with each other at the Association for Integral Development Lajba'l Tenam (ASODILT), where Diego was vice president. The organization claims 952 members and occupies a well-equipped office on the way to several other organizations with similar offices. But the office is completely lifeless, and the most obvious reason is that it has no further money to lend. Capitalized by the European Union, ASODILT offered loans up to Q30,000 ($3,800) for economic betterment. Some of the loans went into businesses that failed; others went into moneylending at higher interest rates. A board member finishing his education to become a licenciado made off with Q105,000 ($13,500); at last report, he was moving upward in a government agency that helps peasants with their land titles. However, what finished off ASODILT's credibility was collecting sign-up fees for the housing project being organized by Licenciado Reyes. Judging from the receipts that Diego showed me, his organization collected Q300 from 394 members and gave Q118,200 ($15,200) to the licenciado in cash. That was the way he wanted it.

ASODILT was not the only development association that collected advance payments for Reyes. All told, he received money from more than three thousand Nebajenses in at least five different organizations, typically led by ex-insurgents like Diego Tránsito who were now taking the blame. Petitions for schools, fertilizer, land titles, and other desiderata required still more advance payments, which were turned over to the licenciado. Adding insult to injury were all the trips that Diego and his fellow leaders made to the capital, each journey full of hope and requiring more contributions from their members in Nebaj. A K'iche' leader recalled,

> There were big, beautiful plans on the wall of how he would build the houses. He promised ASODILT a new office. He offered electric plants to the villages. What the people wanted, he offered. An office that was too fancy he offered us. There would be a cellar, offices on the second floor, and a hostel and diner above. The plans for the houses, also beautiful—two bedrooms each, a kitchen, a dining area and a corridor, made of cement block and with a good metal roof. At the end of the meeting he offered bags of food to each person—bags full of incaparina [nutritional supplement], oatmeal, canned fruit, canned beans and

dried beans, corn flour, and pasta—two bags of five pounds each, how they weighed! Our directors were really happy when they received the bags. The licenciado said that, when construction began, there would be a weekly bag of food for everyone. The beneficiaries would only have to level the site for their new house and help the builder.

Licenciado Reyes made it known that he was an ex-guerrilla commander. In actuality, he was a schoolteacher with a drinking problem and a university degree in psychology. An Ixil leader gave this account:

After a while we began to suspect fraud because of all the delays. "All that's lacking is a document," he would tell us. "Once that's done, we'll begin next week." There was always another step. "The plan is going to arrive at such and such a date," he would say. There's the prequalification, the bond, the supervision. Every time we arrived, there was something else. "I'll call you next week," he would tell us. "That document didn't come, which is why there is another delay, but we're almost ready!" How many times we went to him in Guatemala City! A trip a month for four years—some sixty trips.

"He took everyone's certified documents—the originals," Diego told me at the ASODILT office. "People are really angry with us. 'Why don't you coordinate with the town hall?' we asked him. 'No,' he said, 'because they will ruin it with political favoritism.'" To demonstrate the project's legitimacy, Reyes sent a technical team that toured villages and produced a handsomely bound, two-hundred-page study. Some villagers were so eager for their new house that they tore down the old one and leveled the ground to prepare for construction. At a climactic conference at the end of 2009, Reyes organized the Nebaj leaders into commissions, told the building contractors to buy material, and declared, "Now we're going to begin!" But the contractors demanded an advance payment. Reyes promised forty thousand dollars the very next day—barely enough to start fifty houses. "'You're going to have problems with the people,' an Ixil leader warned. 'There will be a check tomorrow at 10 a.m.,' the licenciado vowed. At ten there was no check; at twelve there was no check. 'It will come tomorrow,' he told us. This went on for seven days."

After three and a half years of being played for fools, the delegates checked with foreign embassies to see if they knew anything about Reyes. The answer was no. They went to the judicial system, and he was arrested in May 2010. Reyes refuses to disclose where the money went, and the Guatemalan government has little capacity to trace it. The longest sentence he can get is five years—not enough to pressure him into talking.[3] Whatever Nebaj's development associations wanted, he offered. If they asked for schools and fertilizer, he offered schools and fertilizer. If they wanted electric generators, he offered that as well. All the petitions and promises recapitulated a golden moment when the United Nations arrived in white jeeps and offered the people of Nebaj everything they wanted.

THE PROYECTEROS OF CANTÓN JULÁ

I was tired of hearing about *confianza*. In my conversations with moneylenders, with failed moneylenders, and with trusting souls who handed over their property titles in order to get rich quick, confianza came up every time. It was the all-purpose excuse. "But I trusted her!" Judging from this line of reasoning, Nebaj had been brimming with confianza, and now there was none. "Before, people gave loans all over the place," a woman told me. "Everyone gave loans. Now they won't lend you a tortilla." In the stories I was hearing, confianza took on a new meaning—gullibility. I never heard the word more than in a small neighborhood called Cantón Julá, on the outskirts of Nebaj, where the town gives way to cornfields and pastures. A lane climbs a hillside, past small farmsteads to two rustic dwellings that stand empty and forlorn.

Until 2007 the houses belonged to two brothers, peasant farmers who were unschooled but eager to improve their lot. The older of the two, Pedro Aviles Cobo, hungered for a development project so that he and his family could have a better life. He was always looking for a *proyecto*, which meant showing up at countless meetings, affixing his name to countless petitions, and ponying up contributions for the next delegation. One day Pedro heard about a new government agency with the entrancing name of Fondo Tierra, the Land Fund. Its purpose was to buy plantations for peasants! Pedro became a believer. He made trip after trip to Guatemala City, he enrolled neighbors who each contributed Q300 for expenses, and in the end he came back with nothing.

In 2005, Pedro's wife Elena Marcos began asking her neighbors for loans, one at a time and quietly. Three years later, my questions about Elena and her husband brought six women into the lane. Belying the appearance of a tight-knit indigenous community, some of what they had to say surprised each other as well as me. Two neighbors said they had loaned Elena their house titles, which she used to borrow Q38,000 ($4,900) from moneylenders. The others loaned her large amounts of cash. One neighbor claimed to have given her Q80,000. Another said she had loaned Elena Q50,000, another Q5,000, another Q40,000, and another Q65,000, for a total of Q240,000 ($31,000). Such amounts could come only from remittances, loans, or sales of land at inflated prices. But of the ten Cantón Julá victims I've interviewed, just one admitted to receiving remittances. Most of the capital they gave Elena came from financial institutions or their own neighbors and relatives, who obtained their capital from . . . I'm not sure where. All I know is that everyone was trying to *superar*, the ubiquitous Guatemalan phrase for "getting ahead," through the borrowing and lending of money. Now the empty houses of the two Aviles brothers were surrounded by wider circles of loss and ruin, victims of chain defaults that reverberated through the town.

Why did Elena say she needed to borrow money? For relatives, her story was that she had to pay off the debt for her two daughters' arrival *mojado* (wetback) in Virginia. For neighbors, the story was that her husband had found a new project, the best project of all—an interest-free loan of a million quetzals to plant coffee and other cash crops. When interest-free cash failed to materialize, she told her creditors about yet another project—an office in the department of Quetzaltenango that was full of money. What about receipts? I asked Elena's neighbors—do any of you have receipts? Astoundingly, none of them did. Why not? "We don't know how to read very well" was one answer. Another was that Elena was a person of confianza, as demonstrated by

1. her promise to return the money or title in a matter of days;
2. the fact that she was an evangelical who belonged to the Assemblies of God; and
3. her offer of 10 percent monthly interest.

Elena had approached each neighbor individually and sworn her to secrecy—a normal precaution for peasants who know that any hint of potable wealth will attract robbers. Later, when Elena's creditors insisted on being repaid, she would tell them to be patient—soon the project would come through and they would get their money—but not if they lost patience and started making accusations.

Next to Pedro and Elena's empty house stands a second empty house, where Pedro's brother Tomás Aviles Cobo and his wife, also named Elena, used to live. This couple, too, were sending their progeny to the United States. The first son found work and began repaying his loans, only to break his arm and become unemployable. Their next son was arrested and deported, after they had paid the coyotes but before he could earn money. Only on his third attempt did he manage to find work. Tomás and Elena now sent their daughter-in-law north, only to have her deported as well. Then they sent a son-in-law who failed to find work. Sending four youth to the United States would cost a minimum of Q160,000 ($20,500), a sum that the setbacks would only have increased, so Tomás and his wife were now deeply in debt. Among their many creditors was Elena's own mother, sister, and brother. When I talked to Elena's family in 2009, they were still in their home but no longer owned it. Elena had persuaded them to post it as collateral for a Q22,000 ($2,800) loan from the San Miguel Chuimequená credit union. She made the payments for five months before taking off. Now San Miguel had sold the house to an Ixil lawyer, who was giving the family a grace period to relocate. Six other families in the neighborhood were supposedly in danger of losing their houses because of the two Elenas.

Such stories have become common in Nebaj. Not only do Ixils say they have been victimized by *estafas* (swindles) and *engaños* (frauds); they often blame their own relatives, and El Norte is usually somewhere in the picture. Competition over inheritances is a frequent issue, with the United States serving as a convenient exit. Consider the following story from a couple in their sixties, very *campesino* in their manner (*humilde* or humble is the usual description in Spanish) and requiring my translator, Jacinto Pérez. The couple's son Jorge was twenty-eight years old when he went north in 2006. To pay for the trip, his mother loaned the document for her house to her daughter-in-law, who used it to borrow Q70,000 ($9,000) from Banrural. Jorge found work in the United States but never sent money to pay off the loan, which rose to Q100,000 ($12,800) before the bank took possession of his mother's house in August 2008. This was the very house in which he grew up.

Jorge had been a good son, his parents told me, and a church member who avoided alcohol. Something changed after he married their daughter-in-law. A month after losing their house, they watched his wife go to the United States to join him. Since this must have cost another Q40,000 ($5,100), it apparently was where Jorge was investing his savings. His parents didn't know his location in the United States because, when they called his cell phone, he didn't answer. Jorge's two children were with his mother-in-law in another cantón; she wouldn't tell Jorge's parents anything because she knew that he took their house to pay for his promotion into the U.S. labor force. "No son or daughter can be trusted because times are changing," Jorge's mother told me. Interjected his father, "I told her, don't hand over the document because they can take the house. My son deceived his own mother and ate all the money."

Sometimes the escape to the United States fails, and the inheritance-grabber falls back into the Nebaj crab bucket. Consider the following tangle of family rivalry, title duplication, and migratory failure. In 2000, Eduardo borrowed Q40,000 ($5,100) to go to the United States but only got as far as a Mexican jail. This was in the bad old days before cash on delivery, so Eduardo paid the trip's full price in advance and lost it all. On this sum he was paying 10 percent monthly interest, forcing him to sell twenty-two cuerdas (one hectare) of precious land. Determined to recover the land, in 2004 he used the municipal document to a second property as collateral for a second loan and a second trip, through a coyote from Salquil Grande. This time Eduardo reached the United States but never found enough work to pay off the debt, or so he said. After four years his wife asked him to come home. "It's all the same to me," she said. "You're not sending money, and I'm not getting anything out of this."

Eduardo returned on a bus rather than on an airplane, another sign of failure. Any peace of mind about his return suddenly vanished when, out of the blue, he was arrested on a warrant from the courthouse. According to the Salquil coyote, he was owed Q90,000 ($11,500), and Eduardo had ignored seven summonses. Now he was in jail for fraud. This forced his family to hire a lawyer who required an advance payment of Q5,000 ($640). It turns out that the property which Eduardo used to guarantee his second trip north—a plank house in one of the army's model villages—belonged to his siblings as well as him. Fortunately for Eduardo, the document he had given the coyote was fraudulent, having been duplicated by Eduardo's father when (in secret, after a family quarrel) the father decided to sell the house to Eduardo rather than apportion it to all his children. Ownership was so ambiguous that the lawyer was able to persuade the coyote to drop charges in return for getting some of his money. But the losers now included Eduardo's three siblings, who gave up their shares in the house to rescue him.

Such family conflicts may seem hopelessly complicated. But the existence of competition within families, and between families, merits attention. It needs to be underlined because of the still widespread assumption that Native Americans are better persons than the rest of us, that they have a strong cultural disposition to place the interests of the group ahead of the interests of the individual, and that they are inherently communal and unselfish, at least until corrupted by Western civilization. If this was ever the case, it no longer is. Rapid population growth has made it impossible for Ixils and most other Mayan peasants to survive on traditional agriculture. Many are bearing too many children to support even with high-tech agriculture; it requires more land than they have. They are also bearing too many children for a comfortable urban future, which requires more investment in education than they can give an average of six children. So competition between siblings, half siblings, and other relatives over family land can become intense.[4]

By itself, cheap credit has provided little relief because, even in the booming Nebaj of the last two decades, it has done little to increase productivity. The number of retail outlets competing with each other has multiplied, but not the amount of production. Once cheap credit helped Nebajenses reach the United States, this provided a welcome escape from competition over the municipio's very limited resource endowment. The first cohorts earned far more than they ever could back home. But the flow of credit and remittances had unsettling results. As neighbors stood in line to collect remittances and then bought land at prices that stay-at-home Nebajenses could never afford, the disparities between migrant and nonmigrant households became painful to behold. And so, with the wave of prosperity came a wave of envy and anxiety, in which many Nebajenses realized they were being left behind. This is what has made so many of them vulnerable to get-rich-quick schemes, in which they convert their social ties into cash and then lose it, devastating themselves, their family, and their friends.

MAGICAL ENRICHMENT THROUGH ZAHORÍNS AND HOLISTIC DOCTORS

The two Elenas of Cantón Julá, and their respective husbands Pedro and Tomás, left Nebaj after receiving threats from creditors. "You don't know the people here," one of their victims told me. The large amounts she loaned Pedro's wife came from moneylenders. "If we don't pay up, they're capable of killing us. They might put out a contract on us and have us assassinated." "People say that if you don't pay, they're going to burn or lynch you," a woman in another cantón added. "How she berates me," she complained of her most persistent creditor. "She shows up here insulting my children, saying that I am fat on her money. She comes to the house, and I tell her it's not appropriate. She's a schoolteacher and should be an example for people."

The two Elenas and their husbands were said to be in the K'iche' Maya town of Almolonga, in the department of Quetzaltenango. Their victims presumed that the two couples were prospering thanks to sons in the United States who were presumably earning well, to daughters in the United States who were producing babies there, and to still other offspring who were said to be driving passenger vans and getting educations. According to other sources, however, the two couples were actually in dire straits, living hand to mouth, because of the strangest aspect of this story—they had given all the money they borrowed to a Mayan *zahorín* who promised them riches from the sacred volcano above Almolonga.

This was not the first time I had heard of zahoríns—a term usually translated as priests, diviners, or healers—liberating their clientele of assets rather than ailments. One well-known victim of a zahorín was a woman I will call Catarina. She lived on the periphery of Nebaj and its economic boom, like the two Elenas and their husbands, and like them she was hungry for projects. In 2005 she belonged to a women's microloan group when she met a zahorín who could go to a *cerro* (mountaintop shrine) and bring her money. "You have need," he told her, looking into her eyes and swearing her to secrecy. "There is a señor who gives gifts. He is going to give you a box with lots of money." And so Catarina paid the zahorín to take her to the Cerro Quemado, a volcano above Almolonga frequented by Mayan holy men. Only after repeated payments and trips did the zahorín finally give Catarina the box. She and her family were to spend eight days praying to it, burning candles to it, and asking it for *perdón* or pardon, an ubiquitous term in Mayan prayers. Only then were they to open the box.

After eight days of religious exertion, Catarina and her family opened the box. Inside they found seventy-five quetzals and some rags. For a year the pitiful Catarina showed up at the zahorín's house and begged him to return part of her money. The baby she had been carrying died, and in 2007 she finally went to the courthouse. "Poor Doña Catarina is denouncing me," the zahorín confronted her one day. "This is why people are no longer coming to me. Señora, if you continue to accuse me at the courthouse, I'll send frogs into your belly. Your baby has already gone to sleep. Any of your children could die." At the courthouse, the prosecutor needed receipts; Catarina didn't have any. A zahorín cannot be asked for a receipt because the offering is to a god, and gods don't give receipts. According to Catarina, she entrusted him with a total of Q155,000 ($19,900). Microloans from four different agencies provided Q21,000 ($2,700); the rest she assembled from neighbors to whom she gave, as collateral, the documents for her house and three plots of land. By the time I found Catarina at a relative's house in 2007, she had satisfied most of her creditors, but only by selling her house, selling the three plots of land, borrowing Q35,000 ($4,500) from a brother-in-law in the United States, and borrowing an even larger amount from a brother, who obtained the money by mortgaging his house to Banrural and who was having trouble making payments. The equity of three households had vanished into the hands of the zahorín.

Catarina's case follows a familiar story line: the foolish woman who borrows from her nearest and dearest to give to a swindler who promises riches. Misogynistically, the man who took the money never seems to be the focus—even though this particular zahorín is local and, until recently, lived a block from the bus terminal. Zahorín is a K'iche' rather than an Ixil category. Traditionally, Ixils have *baalbastixes* (prayer makers) and *aa'qii* (diviners) who appeal to ancestors in the hills surrounding Nebaj, preside over group rituals, and are consulted in health crises and other emergencies. Zahoríns, in contrast, invoke the sacred volcanoes of Quetzaltenango and a pantheon of occult powers worshipped across Mesoamerica. Anthropologists tend to be deferential toward folk healers as incarnations of religious traditions that merit our respect, but Mayan peasants have mixed feelings about them. Traditionalist Catholics distinguish between good ones and bad ones. I used to hire a baalbastix to say prayers for me and my family; he was an old dear who charged very little, and I never heard a negative word about him. The sign of a bad healer is that he charges high prices and fails to save the patient. Disillusion has motivated many a conversion to evangelical Protestantism; evangelical pastors tend to dismiss all Mayan priests and healers as charlatans. Yet the evangelical boom in Nebaj has not ended their appeal.

The zahorín in question, Antonio Sánchez Ixim, has a K'iche' mother but inherited his vocation from an Ixil grandfather who served San Simon—a Guatemalan saint who originated in Mayan towns, not the Catholic Church, and is associated with Judas Iscariot. When I went to see Antonio, he was too inebriated to be at the top of his game. Catarina was still terrified of him and had forbidden me to raise her case, so I told him I was studying migration. He scrutinized my business card, acknowledged that he is sought by muchachos going north, and within a few minutes took a call on his cell phone. Serendipitously, someone in Miami needed his help. Antonio broke out his Tarot deck and, for my benefit, switched from Ixil to Spanish. "Do you have a bit of debt?" he asked the caller. "Your woman getting you down? What are you giving your first woman? What are you giving your other woman? What is your religion—evangelical? Do you have a pain in your belly and legs? I have a friend here, please call me again tomorrow at eight."

Like Ixil traditionalists, Antonio had an altar of statuettes decorated with candles, empty liquor bottles, and flowers, but with fewer Christian saints

A traditional procession

and ancestor crosses. Instead, he placed his bets on a plump red Mexican with an odd double-brim sombrero. This was Diegito, also known as Juan Diego or Duende (goblin), who helps with business and love affairs. There was also Santa Muerte, the skeleton who has become the patron saint of Mexican drug gangs, and San Simon in his guise as a nineteenth-century undertaker. San Simon is the relevant authority for going north, Antonio informed me. When a muchacho comes to him, Antonio asks him questions which San Simon then answers, again through Antonio. Reportedly he charges men going north Q1,000 ($130)—half in advance and half upon arrival—with the understanding that if they fail to pay the last half, they will never get home alive. According to Antonio, however, he charges Q25 per question and Q150 for spiritual protection. "I'm known in many places!" he exclaimed. "In Zunil! In Huehuetenango! In Quiché! In the Ixcán!" A sign on the wall read:

> As you treat me,
> I will treat you.
> Because your money is as valuable,
> As my work is sacred.

Akin to zahoríns, but not Mayan or even local, are itinerant healers to whom Nebajenses refer, with much uncertainty, as *naturistas* (naturists) or *médicos holísticos* (holistic doctors). Coming and going in groups of two or three, they rent storefronts, invoke Catholic icons, and sell herbal medicines and protective amulets. The Hermanos de la Buena Esperanza (Brothers of Good Hope) put up a sign identifying themselves as the Clínica Médica Milagrosa (Miraculous Medical Clinic), but Nebajenses also referred to them as the Virgin of Guadalupe because they put her image in the window for added appeal. The brothers, who said they were from Puerto Rico and Costa Rica, reputedly charged between one and two thousand quetzals for cures. Among the ailments they treated were *fracaso económico* (economic failure) and *preocupación* (worry). For trusted customers, the ones who could keep a secret, they offered to turn Q100 bills into Q500 bills and Q1,000 bills into Q10,000 bills. Where could their threadbare clients obtain seed money to duplicate? By selling land and borrowing from banks. A loan officer believes that one of their clients was Doña Ingracia of Salquil Grande, whom we met in the last chapter. If so, this is probably where part of her fortune vanished. The brothers departed soon after she did. Unlike her, they have never been located and brought back to Nebaj.

I had a hard time finding a victim to interview until I was rescued by Doña Lucia, the same confident matron who, at the end of the last chapter, wanted me to help her become a live-in maid in Los Angeles. Around 2006, Doña Lucia rented space to a Centro Naturista. Her house looks upon a sacred location in the town's Catholic topography, where processions end and where Ixil priests pray to the ancestors, so the naturists attracted a stream of visitors. They were very kind people who showed genuine concern for one's problems, Lucia recalls. "People arrived here one by one; there were no group meetings. In the shop they sold medicines and cured people. A señora arrived who could not walk, and she managed to walk. Why did I give them Q50,000 [$6,400]? They said they could duplicate money. You gave them a bill of one hundred [quetzals] and they gave back two. They put a liquid on the bill, and two appeared. They said that they wanted to help me so that we could get ahead. They inspired confianza."

Then my translator Jacinto Pérez located two other households with similar experiences. In both cases, the healers offered to spend the night praying over Q300, gave their patients Q600 the next day as proof of their powers, and then suggested that they borrow large amounts for an even more beneficial outcome. A recovering alcoholic borrowed Q50,000 from a credit union so that a naturist could double it. When he realized he had been swindled, the only way he could deal with his rage was by going back to drinking, and he was soon dead. Four years later in 2012, after many payments and missed payments to the credit union, his widow and step-son were hoping to stave off eviction by taking out a new Q59,000 ($7,600) loan. Another couple borrowed Q150,000 ($19,200) from Banrural for the same purpose; they were evicted from their house in 2011.

Lucia believed that the naturists who swindled her were Mexicans because of their accents, but the owner of a radio station who ran their advertisements had a different assessment.

> The groups seem to be different but they belong to the same network because they share meals. They are extraordinarily pleasant, very polite, kind. They've been coming for three years, and I believe they extract Q100,000 a month. It's not just people from villages who come to them, but also people from town and even schoolteachers. Problems with the wife, any illness—they say they can cure cancer. Our people are very naive. They even say, bring me Q30,000 and in ninety days I will give you Q90,000. They said they are Costa Ricans, but I know they are Colombians. They constantly change telephones, their number stops working, and they also change names. We give a [tax] receipt to every customer, but they didn't want a receipt because they didn't want to give their name.

"Why don't you and the other victims go to the police?" I asked. "Because they have a license from the government as a naturist clinic. And because we're embarrassed—some of the victims are teachers."

THE SUNK COSTS OF VICTIM/COLLABORATORS

I learned where Cantón Julá's loans went only after I met Guadalupe, the one woman in the neighborhood who seemed capable of organizing the victims and explaining the swindle to a judge. Guadalupe used to work in a factory in Guatemala City, her Spanish is confident, and she is quick to volunteer what a fool she was. In 2005 her husband went north on Q40,000 ($5,100) in loans from moneylenders at 10 percent monthly interest. It was the staggering interest every month, then conversion of the debt to a Banrural loan, which made her receptive to Pedro's wife, Elena. "It was a project for a million [quetzals] to sow coffee, *pacaya*, and banana. The project was not going to charge interest. We were going to sow and harvest first, and pay only after five years." Elena told her that she needed Q80,000 ($10,300) for only eight days—but then month after month she failed to repay. Eventually Guadalupe accepted an invitation to learn more about the project and was taken to headquarters, which proved to be in Almolonga, the same K'iche' Maya town at the foot of the Cerro Quemado where Antonio Sánchez Ixim fleeced his victim Catarina. Guadalupe found herself in a strange house where Elena, along with twenty-two other Ixils and K'iche's, lived under the tutelage of a man named José Carlos.

"It's when I arrived in Almolonga that I realized it was a fraud," Guadalupe told me. "When I looked José Carlos in the eyes, I saw that he was a swindler and said so to Elena. 'Shut up,' she told me. 'You're going to make us lose the project and fail.'" The next thing Guadalupe knew, José Carlos was boring into her eyes and challenging her: "Why are you calling me a thief? You don't have any proof." That's when she realized that José Carlos could read her mind and was also a *brujo* (witch). If Guadalupe denounced him to the authorities, José Carlos said, he would impose a Q30,000 fine on Elena. But if they provided him with another gift, they would receive an even larger gift in return.

Only now did Guadalupe understand where her and many other people's money had gone: "The money was a gift that we had to bring to a house at the volcano. I saw that he was a *hechicero* [sorcerer] because of all the things that he burned: candles, incense, something else that I don't know what it was, as well as meat, beans, and sweets. There were lots of things that he burned. He talked about Satan and said, 'That is who I serve.' He also talked about San Simon and San Sebastián. I don't know where he lives because, when I visited, he only came to the house that Elena and the others rented, at midnight when they gave him a knapsack with Q400,000 ($51,000)."

Back in Nebaj, as I met other fraud victims, the names of Elena and Pedro of Cantón Julá kept coming up, as well as a man named Tomás Ramírez

Sánchez and several brothers and cousins from Sacapulas with the surname Lux. They all had been living together in the mysterious house in Almolonga. But José Carlos' most persuasive confederate in Nebaj was a woman named Susana Filomena Quiñones. Given all the stories I had heard about Susana, I did not expect to find her at home, scrubbing clothes in a washbasin and greeting me with a big gold-capped smile. I only had to mention my interest in loans for Susana to volunteer that she owed Q500,000, or maybe a million, she wasn't sure. I offered to do a tally, and she reeled off one debt after another until the figures added up to Q1.55 million ($199,000). All the debts were to individuals, including Q130,000 ($16,700) to a son and Q250,000 ($32,000) to her husband, who was still in the United States after six years. According to Susana, most of the money had gone to one man—José Carlos—whose real name proved to be José Domingo Sánchez. He hailed from the Mam Maya municipio of Colotenango, Huehuetenango; he used the Cerro Quemado in Quetzaltenango Department to perform his ceremonies; and now Susana thought he was selling trucks near La Mesilla, a contraband hub on Huehuetenango's border with Mexico.

By Susana's account, I was astonished to learn, José Domingo Sánchez was the third Mayan priest to whom she had entrusted large amounts of cash. The first was Antonio Sánchez Ixim, whom we have already met and to whom she gave Q27,000 ($3,500) for three arduous offerings atop Cerro Quemado. The second was a Miguel Pérez García from San Sebastián Retalhuléu to whom she and a confederate gave Q150,000 ($19,200). Accompanied by five bodyguards, Miguel instructed her to organize a fiesta to receive a box of money from the Cerro Quemado. She went to considerable expense to put on a lavish celebration; he never showed up. Only after these disappointments did she fall victim to José Domingo Sánchez.

"'Don't worry,' he told me, 'because you're going to have your money.' That's why he bought us big votive candles and vases for beautiful flowers. We bought liquor, beers, sodas, juices. Each of us gave Q30,000 ($3,800), and José gave us liquor. He brought us to the Cerro Quemado, and we brought birds and turkeys to sacrifice." He didn't speak Spanish very well, and he didn't know how to read or write, but he did know how to count money. Ultimately almost two dozen disciples gathered around José Domingo, living together in the house in Almolonga and, on four occasions, giving him enormous sums of cash—seven million quetzals in all ($897,000) according to Susana.

How did she hit up her relatives and neighbors for loans? I asked. "Do me a big favor—lend me money because there's an office that's going to give a large quantity of money, and I'll pay you 20 or 25 percent interest," Susana says she told them. Her more astute targets were told that she would invest their funds in loans to migrants. But the office full of cash seems to have been her most appealing pitch. "You're poor," a victim reports that Susana, Elena, and Pedro told her. "We're joining a good institution which is going to bring us many millions, and you're going to be able to buy a house, car, motorcycle, furniture. Through God's grace it is going to fall into our hands. It is not like those institutions that send many millions; they buy car and house and motorcycle and computer, and very little remains for the poor. Through God's grace we have found an institution that can really help us."

By Susana's reckoning, she met José Domingo in 2005, spent two and a half years in his service, and became disillusioned in 2007. He levied many fines including Q5,000 ($6,400) for refusing to drink a bottle of liquor. Susana became disillusioned when he instructed his followers to organize a big fiesta, then failed to show up, and stopped taking calls on his cell phone. He never talked about Satan, according to her. But his patron saints did include Juan Noj, Juan Diego, Nicolás, San Sebastián, San Simon, and María Candelaria, as well as the virgin Lorena Morales and the virgin Ana María. The roles of María Candelaria and Lorena Morales were incarnated by José Domingo's wife and daughter.

After many comings and goings—to Nebaj to borrow money and to Almolonga to deliver it—Susana and the others were reduced to day labor on vegetable farms for Q30 ($3.85) a day. By 2007, some of José Domingo's followers were demanding their promised reward, while others were still in thrall, and the two factions collided. One fracas occurred in the plaza of La Democracia, Huehuetenango. The police arrested the loyalists as swindlers but let them go after imposing a Q35,000 ($4,500) fine. On another occasion, the dissidents cornered José Domingo's wife and daughter as they drove a car through La Democracia. They were arrested and released after paying another large fine.

By the time I met Susana, in 2009, a court in Quetzaltenango had a warrant out for José Domingo's arrest. But a lawyer said that executing it would cost Q25,000 ($3,200). As soon as they had the necessary funds, Susana informed me, they would go to Panajachel to file a lien against the house that José Domingo owned there. Then they would go to Quetzaltenango, to ask the court to seize his motor vehicles, and then they would be able to pay off all the people they owed. In the meantime, Susana and her collaborators were in danger of losing their dwellings—if their creditors could sort out who had the right to seize what. Susana always seemed to be upbeat. But one day, in between the calls that she and her teenage son were taking on their cell phones, she remarked, "I'm really screwed. There are days we don't know where we're going to find food."

I was amazed that, after failing to repay so many people, Susana was still to be found at home. That she hadn't been arrested was no surprise. No one familiar with the Guatemalan legal system would be surprised by that. But why hadn't she run away like her confederates in Cantón Julá? "I don't go to the market because people might grab me," one of her male collaborators told me. "The people we owe could lynch us," said another. No one had borrowed from more people than Susana. "So many people are crying on account of this señora," a victim told me. "She took the property documents of many people in Pulay and Xolcuay," another said. Yet when I visited Susana, she was always socializing with one or more victims, who also proved to be her collaborators. They would tell me how they borrowed large sums from an organization, or a stateside son's bank account, or an evangelical pastor in order to give it to Susana, thanks to which they were now in the process of losing their house. Holding back tears, they would then join Susana in heartily blaming José Domingo.

How could Susana have failed to learn from her first disastrous experience handing large sums of money to a zahorín? Or from her second, third, or fourth experience? That José Domingo made a point of inebriating his followers at key moments is significant—drinking in honor of the saints is a Mayan tradition and makes it easier to part people from their money. It is also significant that the magic portal has become an office or factory full of cash. This may sound very naive. But once you try to reason out the "full faith and credit" of the U.S. government, a vault becomes a reasonable inference about the source of all the aid that has rained down upon Nebaj. The largesse from Western Europe and North America has been little short of miraculous for peasants who, from early childhood, are schooled in the strict and divinely ordained finitude of resources. In a peasant culture premised on what the anthropologist George Foster (1965) calls "the limited good," prosperity can come only at someone else's expense, often supernaturally through a pact with the devil. This is a thaumaturgical interpretation of capitalism, in which people use a religious frame of reference to understand the mysterious multiplying power of capitalist production and finance.

Still, I didn't understand how victims could repeatedly hand over large amounts of cash to a person who was not paying them back. Once, yes, but why repeatedly? Enlightening me on this point was a village leader named Tomás Ramírez Sánchez. Unlike anyone else in this panorama, Tomás was actually arrested and spent thirteen months in jail for presenting a phony land title as collateral. Like many others, Tomás blames Susana for his troubles, although he has a mixed reputation of his own that goes back to his time as a war refugee and guerrilla cadre. According to Tomás' version of events, Susana approached him for Q30,000 ($3,800) to send her son north, then another Q30,000 to send her husband as well. He gave her the loans, which came from the remittances of his own sons in the United States, for which he charged 10 percent per month. A year later, after Susana was falling behind on payments, she told him that she would make good her debt, and enrich him many times over, with a big international project. Having lost his sons' remittances, Tomás now began mortgaging their real estate and turning over the proceeds, in installments of Q10,000 and Q15,000, to Susana and two of her accomplices. He also began using duplicate documents to borrow repeatedly on the same property. Only after he was in over his head, with no possibility of repaying all the money he had borrowed, was he taken to Almolonga. Here he joined the group waiting upon José Domingo, in hope of a large reward that never came.

As Tomás recalled the steps on his road to ruin, I realized that he was in a sunk-cost trap, also known as throwing good money after bad. Once he had borrowed more money than he would ever be able to repay, and once he had made himself complicit by borrowing money under false pretenses, his only hope was that the zahorín would finally deliver the box full of cash. But to stay in the game, he would have to make further contributions. If that were not enough, José Domingo's followers were physically afraid of him—several referred to his magical powers. If anyone showed signs of impatience, the zahorín was quick to respond with a threat. "Whoever crosses me will regret it," he would say, pretending to pull a trigger with his finger.

In 2011, I learned that Elena and Pedro of Cantón Julá had returned to Nebaj, although not to their old neighborhood. Instead, they were living in a hut on a disputed finca, at the behest of a ladino patrón who promised them ten cuerdas (.4 hectares) if they would help him hang on to his property. Elena proved to be a diminutive woman with a steady gaze. It was easy to see how she had inspired confidence. Her husband Pedro was anxious and repentant; he attributed his downfall to alcohol. He had been an evangelical for two decades when José Domingo penetrated his defenses.

Why did you keep giving him money? I asked. "He always startles you about money," Pedro explained. "'If you don't pay me,' he says, 'there will be a problem with the money that you already gave me. Either you pay my debt or we're blocked. This takes money!'" And so Pedro found himself in the sunk-cost trap; his only hope of escape was a volcano. He and his wife showed me a list of thirty-two names, each with a location and amount that added up to Q862,000 ($111,000). This was the capital that the two had received, mainly from individuals to whom they offered to pay 10 percent per month. Once they started giving large amounts to José Domingo, the only way they could hope to repay their debts was by giving him even more.

Elena and Pedro fled back to Nebaj after the police arrested their confederate Tomás. Their life in Almolonga had been one of misery, they said. Stories of their children's success were grossly exaggerated, they claimed, and I could see that they and their sons were living in shacks with dirt floors. Elena was eager to join a delegation to the courthouse to denounce José Domingo. But Pedro was afraid that he would be the one to get arrested. While waiting for the bus back to his humble abode, he hid in a doorway so that he would be less visible to passersby. Here was one reason that Susana had not been hounded out of town by her creditors—a good number of them were afraid of the same fate from their own creditors. The web spun by the zahorín had entangled victims by turning them into victimizers.

Swindles by folk healers and holistic doctors might seem to wander from our central issue—how migration generates debt—but the victims' need to pay for children going north, and the credence they put in the office full of money, suggests that swindles prey upon the same state of mind that migration fever does. The simplest and most satisfying explanations for how capitalism multiplies wealth, to say nothing of how it widens the gap between haves and have-nots, are magical in nature. If the secret of success is available to the initiated or to the faithful, then it is within the reach of anyone who is sufficiently determined. This is the message of the prosperity gospel in Christianity, and it is also the message of zahoríns who have become swindlers. For people who are disconnected from any actual engine of wealth, it is a source of hope.[5]

THE ASSOCIATION TO SUPPORT NEEDY PEOPLE OF A SINGLE HEART AND FAITH

The most successful swindle in Nebaj is one in which many victims may still believe. It is led by campesinos rather than licenciados, and the reason for its credibility is that it is a new religion. Like cargo cults after World War II, in which Pacific Islanders marched and prayed to bring back the logistical extravagance of the U.S. Navy, this religion is a reaction to, and an attempt to appropriate the magic of, international capitalism. The Association to Support Needy People of a Single Heart and Faith (ANECOF) requires a sign-up fee of Q500 ($64), followed by smaller levies for operating expenses. For peasants weary of the conditions attached to aid projects (applying for funds, hosting consultants, organizing community workdays, electing village committees, filing reports, and doing it all again next year), ANECOF is the project of their dreams because it promises the most versatile benefit of all—a big pile of cash.

In Mexico, where the scheme began in the late 1990s, organizers inform new members that they will each receive 700,000 euros. In Guatemala, organizers have more modestly promised Q500,000 ($64,000). Members receive an official identity card with their name, photo, and number, and they also receive a votive candle to which they pray. The candles are a Catholic custom, rejected by evangelical churches, but many of ANECOF's members are evangelicals. I heard about all-night prayer vigils and found the well-appointed house in the municipal seat where they were held. But I couldn't score an interview—two committee members, a car mechanic and a schoolteacher, turned me down. Nebaj's aid coordinators have rarely refused to explain their programs to me, so I assumed they had something to hide.

Then I met Victor. Victor is a farmer and has a ninth-grade education, which is a lot for an Ixil born in the 1960s. He lives in La Pista, the village at the town's airstrip which originated as a refugee camp and which, after many aid projects, has become a well-appointed but debt-ridden suburb of the town center. Reluctantly, Victor ushered me into a room piled with moldy documents, from which he selected documentary proof of ANECOF's legitimacy. He showed me its registration as a nonprofit association, its exemption from value-added tax, and typewritten rules against slandering and threatening the organization's leaders. In the year 2000, I was fascinated to read, members voted to raise the payout that each will receive to Q750,000 ($96,000). Members who lacked faith and questioned the association would receive just Q1,000 ($128). On a hand-drawn chart, an arrow pointed downward from the European Union and Germany to the directors, then to the subdirectors, and then to the community. A dog-eared sheet of frequently asked questions included, why will they give us so much money? "Because of international compassion, they have world banks." Another FAQ was, how do they know about us? "Through international migration . . . some of us reach other countries and explain conditions."

Victor was such a soldier of patience that I peppered him with questions. How did ANECOF begin? I asked. "When the peace agreement was signed, there were refugees in Campeche [Mexico] who met with interviewers," he explained. "The interviewers promised them nongovernmental help, explained the requirements, and offered a *regalo* (gift) for everyone who fulfilled the requirements. The Guatemalan government promised to bring the list of people who needed help, but different administrations came and went and none of them did. The rich became richer; the poor became poorer. ANECOF arrived to seek out the people who needed help." Why are people here so poor? I continued. "It's the Spanish who arrived to enslave us economically and politically," Victor replied. "The government has gone to other governments, soliciting support for the poor, but the support has stayed in the hands of the rich." Why are people here in such debt? I asked. "The banks give loans," Victor replied. "There are people who have built their houses and bought land; they've become accustomed to borrow money from the bank, then they go to another bank and take out another loan to pay the first loan.

But now the banks aren't giving more loans and the people can no longer pay."

Why is the project taking so long? I asked. "There is an agreement of fifty-two years with Europe and Germany. It has arrived in other countries, but I can't find the paper that says which ones," Victor explained as he sifted through documents. "They know the answer in San Juan Ixcoy." San Juan Ixcoy is the town in Huehuetenango Department where ANECOF is headquartered. "Many people don't believe, saying that no one is going to donate so much money," Victor acknowledged. But he had not stopped believing, which was why he was about to undertake a long bus ride to the next conclave. Victor was all too aware that ANECOF had gone up in smoke in southern Quiché. In the K'iche' Maya town of Zacualpa, disillusioned members from several municipios attacked the head of the scheme, a man who has gone into legend as El Millonario.[6] The mob burned the gas station that he owned and seized four of his accomplices; their release had to be negotiated by the national police, and he is presumed to have escaped to Mexico.[7]

By Victor's count, ANECOF had two hundred members in La Pista, seven hundred in the municipal seat, and another eight hundred in Salquil Grande. Two years later, he was still leading the La Pista branch but was beset by doubts. "In 2010 the leadership said that the money would arrive on March 3, 2011," he told me in June. "It didn't. I went to a meeting with the president in Mexico, Manuel Garcia Silvestre. Now he says it's going to arrive on January 28, 2012. I really hope it comes. The truth is that all this waiting is very difficult, not everyone has the patience. The money will come if God wills it, if it's not a swindle they are doing. People lose hope, but if [the money] comes, those who stopped hoping are going to be sorry. We have legal registration. We are registered with the tax system. We're paying. We're confident. But it's true there are bandits who are incorporated. It depends on God's will." If all that cash arrives, I asked, won't it attract robbers? "Yes," Victor acknowledged, "this is a problem that we have presented to the administration. It would be very difficult for us to go there and bring the money back. It would not be easy to make it home when there are so many criminals on the way. This is why it has to arrive in each municipio, and that's how they're going to do it."

A year later, in June 2012, Victor was fed up. "By dribs and drabs the people have given lots of money: first Q500, then a Q50 bill, then another Q50," he told me. "If there are 300,000 members in Guatemala and 300,000 members in Mexico, how many millions have the directors received? If the money doesn't arrive, they're the ones who owe us. I'm not afraid of the people here; they know I go to work with a chainsaw." The Guatemalan directors, Victor informed me, were touring the municipios to rally their members. At a mass meeting in Nebaj in December 2011, local schoolteachers belonging to ANECOF took down every word of the visiting leaders and had them sign it—the evidentiary basis for a future lawsuit. At a May 2012 meeting in southern Petén Department, Victor related with amusement, thousands of members captured six ANECOF directors and turned them over to the police as swindlers.[8] Now the money was to arrive in June and July of 2012. If it didn't, Victor said, his members would decide whether to hire a lawyer.

So what should we make of the Association to Support Needy People of a Single Heart and Faith? What of the zahoríns, holistic doctors, proyecteros, and Licenciado Reyes, with his Association for the Life and Development of Guatemalans? All of these swindles appeal to a touching faith engendered by Christian ethics and aid projects. It is faith that peasants can produce large families, without worrying overmuch about the amount of land their children will inherit, and that someone else—wealthy foreigners, or maybe God—will rescue their children from becoming paupers. What the different schemes also have in common is an evil alchemy, the conversion of confianza or trust into cash, which is then siphoned from gullible intermediaries and sucked out of Nebaj. Much of the social trust being lost is between relatives, friends, and neighbors. In the case of AVIDESGUA, it is the social trust holding together development associations led by ex-insurgents.

Loosely speaking, these can all be classified as pyramid schemes. They share a pyramidal structure, with a visionary at the top recruiting confederates who are then persuaded to recruit their friends and relatives, either as new members (AVIDESGUA and ANECOF), new patients (holistic doctors), or new investors in an international project or Mayan ceremony (the zahoríns), or simply as creditors loaning money for labor migration to El Norte. Another shared trait is that contributions move from the base of the pyramid to the apex before vanishing. But there is a notable difference in the amount of financial devastation that can occur. AVIDESGUA and ANECOF claim to be community projects; they operate more or less publicly, appeal to many households at once, and ask for no more than a month or two of earnings. In contrast, the zahoríns and holistic doctors offer magical solutions, operate under veils of secrecy, ask for huge payments, and can make off with a household's entire equity. Still, none of the swindles in this chapter are pyramid schemes in the strictest sense. In pyramid schemes, also known as multilevel marketing schemes, investors in the middle layers recoup their investment from later investors in the lowest layers.[9] Only the bottom layers lose their investment. In the swindles described in this chapter, the middle layer is usually not recouping its investment from the bottom layer.[10] Thus in the house at Almolonga, the zahorín's confederates—Susana, Tomás, Pedro, and Elena—claim to have lost everything to their spiritual adviser. Judging from their current threadbare condition, they are telling the truth. If so, the zahorín who took their money was not running a pyramid scheme.

But pyramid schemes are alive and well in Nebaj, and they can be respectable. The oldest goes back as far as the Spanish colony in Guatemala, to the Romans, and perhaps further. It is the Guatemalan state, through the sale of political offices and government contracts. In the most corrupt administrations, the top of the pyramid consists of the president, his closest relatives, and his contributors, with the sale of offices extending downward as far as schoolteachers and policemen. Income flows to the top of the pyramid, with midlevel appointees recouping the cost of buying office by extracting income from their own appointees, who recoup their own costs by extracting income from the population. A few years ago, three former Guatemalan presidents were simultaneously fugitives from justice.[11] Locally the most ostentatious monument to this kind of corruption is the four-story Hotel Villa Nebaj and an equally resplendent four-story gasoline station down the street. "To God be the glory," proclaims a banner on the gas station. Both belong to a man who never displayed the slightest entrepreneurial talent except to leave for the United States, in the usual unlicensed manner, and return as the town's most liquid real estate investor. In some Guatemalan towns, the two buildings would be called coyote palaces; in others they would be called narco palaces. But in Nebaj, they are most likely owned by politicians who will never be identified.

Three other pyramid schemes are open to a much wider share of the population. In chapter 8, I will show how chain migration to the United States can become a pyramid scheme—by enabling migrants to recoup their losses through the recruitment of new migrants who, on average, will face even more difficult conditions than they did. I will also show how credit can become a pyramid scheme—when it enables borrowers to increase their rate of consumption by taking out new loans to pay off old loans or by passing on their loan capital, together with the obligation to repay, to a new borrower. Finally, I will argue that having a large number of children, in the hope of turning them into wage earners at a tender age, can also be analyzed as a pyramid scheme. But first, in the next chapter, let us take a closer look at the challenges facing women who have been left behind by Nebaj's still largely male migration stream northward.

Chapter Seven

Losing Husbands to El Norte

I am a single mother
I need a man, call me at [1111-1111] San Cris[tobal] Toto[nicapán]
I am not a whore nor a lesbian nor a homosexual,
I am the mother of two children
My husband took off for the North
He doesn't send me money
I need a man to make love to me
100 quetzals [a woman's name]

> —Scrawled in a toilet stall on the Pan-American Highway near
> Quetzaltenango, October 19, 2007

One day I was talking to an Ixil weaver who lost her husband to El Norte. "All the women have been abandoned," she exclaimed. This is hyperbole, but it is the worry of women who send their husbands north, and it is easy to come across wives and mothers who are fending for themselves. Sometimes I did not even have to ask. One afternoon I was looking for a neighborhood swindler and stopped to inquire at a cantina. Two Ixil women, resplendent in their Sunday best, were presiding over an amiable collection of drunks. As I explained my project (i.e., "I'm looking for people to tell me about migration to El Norte, indebtedness, and swindles"), the proprietor's daughter identified herself as a *viuda* (widow) because her stateside husband had cut off contact.

What did he say when he left? I asked. "He didn't say anything when he left. He just went." Hadn't he even said that he was leaving? "No. After sixteen days he called us to say that he was in the United States."[1] Only after five months did he begin sending money—but less than $100 every two months. When he phoned, it was only to talk to his two daughters, not to their mother. After five years, he stopped calling and remitting. Now he has another wife—an Ixil

163

woman whom the first wife knows because she grew up a few blocks away—
and they live together near Washington, D.C.

A second marriage in the United States is particularly tempting if the new
spouse has legal residency or citizenship. Marriage is just about the only way
that a Nebajense can gain legal status. This is how Sierra Desidora Mendoza
Cardona lost her husband. He went north in 1999. They had a five-year-old
boy, with a second child on the way. "I lived in the house of his parents in
Chiul," Sierra told me. "He sent all the remittances to them, and they gave
only a small part to me. With his remittances they were building a two-story
house when my mother-in-law kicked me out. She hit me, and I came here
[Nebaj]. If I had stayed, they would have buried me. Later my in-laws obtained visas; every year they go to the United States for six months and come
back for six months."

In Florida, Sierra's husband married a woman from his own village of
Chiul, who gave him legal status and with whom he has two children. By his
first wife's count, he has two wives and three different identity documents,
according to one of which he is still single. "Sometimes, when he feels like it,
he still sends money, Q1000 or Q700, never more than Q2,000 ($256). From
time to time he telephones and we fight. Our son is in eighth grade, and I
don't have the money to pay for it. I have to borrow from my sister and father.
When I insist, he says, 'I have my woman here. I have my children here who
I'm supporting!' He gets angry, calls me names, and says he wants a divorce.
Supposedly he has another house in Palín [on the Pacific Coast], and he says
that he's going to give me the house of his parents but he never does."

Sierra told me her story in the house of her father and brother. They asked
if I had any suggestions. You have a choice, I said. You can make do with the
money he sends or you can sue him for child support. You could even try to
get him deported back to Guatemala. But lawyers want tens of thousands of
quetzals for a challenging case. If it is difficult to extract child support from
fathers living in Nebaj, what are the chances of extracting it from a father in
Florida? Either way, I couldn't see that they would get more money out of
him. So Sierra, her father, and her brother asked if I could call him up when I
returned to the United States. Could I find a lawyer to pressure him? I said no.

Matea Ingracia Ceto y Ceto is a vendor of Ixil weaving. She has a stall in
the Casa de Cultura, a handsome, donor-financed building which lacks only
tourists to buy the weaving. Her first husband was one of the hundreds of men
arrested and murdered by the army in the early 1980s. Her second husband,
whom she married in 1991, is known for his blood-curdling accounts of his
career as an army assassin before he became a born-again Christian. In 2004
he took out a Banrural loan to go north. In Florida he came to the attention
of a contractor who renovates condominiums, enabling him to live rent free

on site and save most of his wages. The first year he sent home as much as Q3,000 ($385) a week and paid his coyote debt quickly. Then the remittances dried up. He would be under the influence of alcohol when he called home, and he claimed to be out of work. He also met a woman from El Progreso, a ladina with a visa, which enabled her to shuttle between Guatemala and the United States.

"When I challenged him, he said, 'Don't preach at me because I already know about that.' He never admitted there was another woman, but I found out they are now married—even though he is married to me. When I go to the courthouse, they ask me for his address, which I have no way of finding out. I don't know when he comes back to Nebaj. He comes to visit his children but doesn't give them anything for school. It's said that he has some kind of job here, but I don't know where he spends the nights. He says he's a Christian [evangelical], but I told him, this is not Christian. He became angry, put himself like this [holds herself rigid], and said, 'Don't sue me because I don't have anything.' Maybe he gets like this because of what he did in the army. Perhaps everyone who went through the army became violent. Who knows what they did, and it's still visible in their faces. Perhaps my husband became enraged because he doesn't live in peace. I can only ask God to help me."

A question that nags wives in this position is when exactly they should consider themselves abandoned. When remittances dry up? Men who fail to remit say they are failing to find work, which could be true. Only when wives learn of the existence of a new wife in El Norte can they be certain, and this is usually kept from them for years. It took Tomás Pérez Terraza three attempts and Q90,000 ($11,500) in debt to establish himself in the Washington area. He had no property of his own, so his wife Magdalena Brito Chel and her family secured the debt with their own property. He never sent enough money to reduce the debt; instead it grew, and amicable telephone conversations ended after two years. One day, five years after his departure, Magdalena phoned and a woman answered. "Now he's my husband and please don't bother us," the new wife told her. Wife number 2 spoke some English that Magdalena couldn't understand, but her Spanish sounded like that of Quiché Department. When Magdalena said she had Tomás' son to support, the woman responded, "Your son is like a little dog that you can feed with a tortilla." Then Magdalena was run over by one of Nebaj's many speeding motorcycles, this one driven by a minor who could pay for only a small fraction of her medical expenses. "Why are you calling me? Why are you bothering me?" Tomás responded to her request for help. "Now I have my life here, and you have your life there." By this time, the debt necessary to attain his new life in the United States had risen to Q135,000 ($17,300). To pay it off, Magdalena was forced to sell her house.

One woman still in limbo is Feliciana Matom Ramírez, who lives in a shack at the back of a bulldozed lot that she lost to Banrural in 2008. The property used to belong to her husband. Next door is a crumbling adobe house, with a backyard filled with junk, that still belongs to her husband's brother. Feliciana's husband was working in a factory in Guatemala City, but the high cost of living prevented him from supporting his family in Nebaj. Worse, he had a problem with alcohol and spent fifteen days in jail. So in 2004 he went north, to finance which Feliciana borrowed Q50,000 ($6,400) from Banrural with the house as collateral. Her husband made it to Baltimore but could find work only one day and not the next. His remittances were occasional and small, just one or two thousand quetzals, which could not keep pace with monthly payments of Q1,500 ($192). So Feliciana lost her home to the bank, which sold it to a new owner who dismantled the dwelling and has offered to sell the empty lot back to her for Q100,000 ($12,800). She hasn't heard from her husband for a year, which she blames on the slanders of his brother next door. On one occasion the brother punched her in the mouth and she went to the police; they took a look at her bruised face and jailed him for a day. Her most pressing problem is supporting her four children aged eleven, nine, seven, and three.

LOOKING FOR MR. REMITTANCE

Judging from their remarks, Nebajenses are not surprised when spouses separated for long periods become unfaithful. According to a woman who lost her husband to a second wife in El Norte,

> Many there become involved with another woman. Because they live with other men, the others inform the woman [here in Nebaj]. The women here, some go out with another man. But perhaps only because the men phone from the United States and accuse them. Sometimes the mother-in-law engages in slandering the wife. And the wife says, if I'm being accused, why shouldn't I go ahead? Sometimes [husbands] themselves say, look for another spouse. We don't matter to them anymore. Or there were problems before they left and they don't want to keep trying. It's better that there isn't much communication because, over the telephone, they just berate us.

Women can find El Norte as tempting as men do, but with the disadvantage that it expedites the disappearance of their Romeo. Candelaria was recovering from her own failed trip to the United States when she found herself under siege from an old boyfriend who claimed to be breaking up with his Ixil wife in the capital. Nicolás had been in the United States since

2003, returning just long enough to impregnate his wife on two visits home. But now he told Candelaria that the marriage was disintegrating. One promise that played well with Candelaria was that he would take her back to the United States with him. Following a one-night stand, Nicolás returned to the United States and Candelaria became pregnant. When she informed him by telephone, he was surprised, reminding her that he already had a family in the capital. But he reiterated his offer to bring her to the United States. That was the last she heard from him; he is now said to be drinking, and she is raising the baby with the help of her parents.

Every year Nebaj women ask me to help them go north, jokingly or in earnest. The most obvious reason is that they need to earn money quickly, and the impetus for that urgency is debt.[2] Even teenage girls may step into the breach. Daniel is a man of warmth and insight who was abandoned by his parents. He was befriended by the parish priest and has become a respected schoolteacher and evangelical elder. His son Julio also trained as a schoolteacher; but, like many other high school graduates, he lacks the political connections necessary for a government job, so he set his compass north. After three years in the Miami suburbs, Julio was in charge of an after-hours cleaning crew that went from store to store, enabling him to send home as much as Q11,000 ($1,400) per month. On the basis of Julio's remittances and a Q420,000 ($53,800) loan from Banrural, Daniel built a house with a ground floor large enough to garage two trucks. Then disaster struck in Florida. As Julio got off a bus, he was picked up by the Migra and held for months.

Over the phone from Guatemala, Daniel asked if I could figure out where his son was being held and why he wasn't coming home. I had no luck. Julio was still somewhere in the detention archipelago when I arrived in Nebaj two months later. Imagine my astonishment when Daniel informed me that he now had three children in the United States—not just Julio but his two younger sisters, high school girls who had just gone overland through the Sonora-Arizona desert. Why did you do that? I asked, dumbfounded. "We owe for the house." Daniel gestured toward the unfinished construction surrounding us. A relative in Miami had dreamed that the two girls were with him. Then the two girls also dreamed they were in Miami and decided they wanted to go. "We asked the Lord. He told us the girls ought to go, and they went," Daniel explained. "There were no problems in the road, not even crossing the North American border. They spent four days in the desert. They stuck to the guide and never saw the Migra. They suffered only from weariness, nothing more. Only in Atlanta did they run into the Migra. The Migra stopped them but let them go after five minutes. I have faith that everything is going to turn out right."

To pay for the two trips, Daniel invested Q20,000 ($2,600) that he received from a government program compensating violence victims, plus another

Q60,000 ($7,700). To assure me that his daughters were fine, he rang them up on his cell phone. "No, there's no work," one told me from Miami. "Work is scarce. Our uncle is working in a store and we're applying, but we have to be patient." Daniel: "All they need is patience because they arrived just eight days ago. The problem is, there's a bit of debt. We had to ask the Lord because there is no other solution." "They are going to study English and computers," Daniel's wife added hopefully, "and with that they will get the degree that helps them find work."

After three months of detention, Julio returned to Nebaj, tight-lipped about his experience and thinner than before. Within months he was back in Miami, one sister had a job at Kmart, and the other was earning $50 a day on a cleaning crew run by an Ecuadorian. Two years later, all three were still at work; their father had paid off much of his debt, and he was finishing a large house, the first floor of which was already rented to a newly arrived microloan agency.

Few Ixil women in the United States wear their spectacular indigenous clothing except on special occasions such as church or the Saturday expedition to Walmart, if then. But Nebajenses estimate that hundreds of their women are in El Norte. The majority seem to be in their late teens and twenties, but I meet older women who wish to go, or who already have done so and returned. Women in their thirties and forties go north not just to join their husbands but also because they have been abandoned by their husbands. In one expedition of five women, all were in their thirties or forties, each with as many as six children, but just one was joining her husband. The others had been abandoned for one reason or another (not just migration), and they were parking their children with relatives.

One woman who lost her husband to El Norte decided that, instead of trying to follow him, she would become a coyote. Photos of the husband looking young, confident, and handsome still adorned her wall nine years after he left in 1999. For the first three years he sent back money so reliably that she was able to build the house in which she lives with their three children. Then her husband took up with a Nebaj woman in the United States, had two children with her, and stopped sending money. Fortunately for wife number 1 back in Nebaj, he was remorseful and authorized her to put the house in her own name so that his own blood relatives could not grab it and evict her. For the first five years she stayed at home, caring for the children, but she tired of being shut up like a dog (her expression). So in 2004 she began to send people north, not as a moneylender but as a recruiter who receives a commission for each customer. She has so little idea of U.S. geography that, when I pointed to a photo of her husband standing in a snowy parking lot, she identified the location as Miami.

The most obvious reason that women hesitate to go north is their fear of rape on the U.S.-Mexico border. Local coyotes offer special arrangements for women, but Nebajenses have learned that such commitments must be taken with a grain of salt. Even on a trip that goes smoothly, migrants are passed from one relay of smugglers to the next. Nebajenses tell stories in which Mexicans extend a helping hand at a crucial moment and save the day, but they also tell stories in which Mexicans take advantage of them. For all the trepidation about rape, I have heard of only two cases involving Nebaj women. But this is not a subject on which I would expect my sources to be forthcoming. Still, rape is not standard operating procedure in the coyote industry because it would disrupt the flow of future customers. The danger of rape escalates when rival gangs get into billing disputes and then turf wars, kidnapping each other's migrants to extort them.

Given women's subordinate status at home, El Norte can increase not just their income but their control over their lives. But it is still an uphill battle because their lack of English and legal status makes them very dependent on other migrants from their hometown, who are still overwhelmingly male. The resulting pressures are illustrated by a woman who went north in 2003 and who says that she was raped not just by coyotes but by the Ixils who received her in the Washington, D.C., suburb I am calling Pleasantville. "They gave me a welcome meal, and I don't know what they put in the juice but it put me to sleep," Catalina told me. "When I woke up, I was on the floor. According to what I heard later, all eight raped me." After six months on a cleaning crew, by Catalina's account, she felt horrible and escaped to Charlotte, North Carolina. Here she moved in with a fellow Nebajense who went north at the early date of 1998. Juan had a wife and five children not far from Catalina's house in Nebaj. He worked in the Carrier factory making air conditioners and earned eleven to twelve dollars an hour plus overtime on Saturdays, for as much as $3,000 per month.

Not once but twice, Juan went to jail for hitting her. "He became angry when he found out that I was sending money to my children. The first time, the court told him to take some classes about why family violence is bad. He went to the classes and continued hitting me. He went to jail a second time, and the court and I pardoned him." Why did she stay with a man who hit her? I asked. "I wanted someone to protect me," Catalina answered. They were together in Charlotte for two years before she became pregnant. He called her his wife, but she decided that she did not want to give birth in the United States. "'We're going to build a house on my lot,' he told me. 'I'll send you money so that you can buy the materials and build it. The money won't be lacking. I don't want you to work. I want you to rest.' But when I came back to Nebaj, his wife showed up and hit me. I couldn't go out because I was afraid. He sent only a bit of money, and after my daughter was born, nothing."

The infant girl wasn't healthy; she went into fits. Physicians said she had encephalitis and would die. When Catalina informed Juan, he explained why he had stopped sending money. It was the fault of an American woman who had taken up with him, persuaded him to buy her a $25,000 car, put the car in her own name, and then driven off in it, never to return. As Juan received further reports from the home front, doubtless supplied by his first wife, he decided that he was not the father of Catalina's daughter because he was very brown and the daughter was very white. Catalina threatened to bring the girl to the United States, ask for a DNA test, and force him to pay child support. Juan said he was finished with Guatemala and would be able to stay in the United States thanks to the new amnesty law.

And so Catalina decided to bring her daughter north. U.S. medical specialists would save the child's life, and the U.S. legal system would qualify her for child support. But their journey ended badly. At the U.S. border, Catalina claims, a coyote demanded that she hand over her daughter to smuggle cocaine, that she and the child were separated for five days, and that when they were reunited back in Mexico, coyotes kept them captive for twenty-six days until a Mexican woman took pity and helped them escape in a hail of gunfire—leaving me to wonder if Catalina experienced some of these episodes on television.

What I do not doubt is that unattached females in the United States face lots of pressure from Nebaj males, some of whom have wives and children back home. Relationships become monetized. According to a woman in her early twenties who has the training to teach school but has struggled to find a job, three of her friends with the same educational attainment and the same lack of employment went north. When she asked to join them, their response was, "It would be better for you to stay in Nebaj and die of hunger than come here. We're taking drugs. We have to get into bed with men, and at times they pay us very little."

In Pleasantville, in an alcohol-free apartment of evangelicals, I met an Ixil girl attempting to fend off motherhood. The recently arrived Cármen was taking care of a plump toddler who is an American citizen by birth. The child's mother showed up from her $7.50-an-hour job at a hamburger joint. The child's father was helping with expenses, but he had a wife and children back in Nebaj. Forewarned, Cármen wished to avoid romance and pregnancy in order to pay for her trip and save money as quickly as possible. As far as she knew, she was the only single Ixil woman in Pleasantville. "The others are pregnant or already have children," she said. "It's a lot that they have to do: the expense of food, shelter, and clothes. Many of the males here are just youth and don't stick around; they go somewhere else. I know my people, and the majority of the men don't respect the women. The majority just want to find a woman, take advantage of her, and go on to something else, without taking care of her. When I arrived here, the boys didn't respect me. Yes, the [local] police will intervene if there is physical abuse, but women don't want to denounce their husband. Our people are very vindictive. If you make a complaint, the man threatens that he will make you pay on another occasion." A few months later Cármen was pregnant by a fellow Nebajense, and she now has a toddler.

By this point, readers may wonder how many of Nebaj's wage migrants will come home again. This is an important question that could take many years to answer. My impression is that few Nebajenses go north without assuring their families they will return. Before border enforcement increased, Mexicans became famous for cycling between their work lives in El Norte and their families back home. The back-and-forth inspired an entire school of thought about migration, called transnationalism. The pattern is followed by some Guatemalans, including undocumented Nebajenses who have come home for a few months before returning to the United States, but border enforcement is making it exceptional. If Nebajenses going north ever tell their families they are leaving forever, I have not heard about it. The discourse is, instead, I am leaving you in order to help you and I will return. It would be difficult to say anything else given all the financial support migrants must obtain from their families. Once in the United States, they debate the issue of whether to hang on or return on a daily basis.

THE STRUGGLE FOR EQUALITY

Remittances are a clear source of empowerment for wives who receive them. In the absence of husbands, they become the decision makers, with the means to pay for better food, better clothes, school fees, and medical emergencies. But sociologists and anthropologists also find that the separation induced by transnational migration, as well as the ability of telephonic communication to magnify suspicion, can have the unfortunate effect of subordinating stay-at-home wives.[3] In the Q'anjob'al Maya town of Soloma, Stefanie Kron found that such women were subject to high levels of social control by their husband's relatives. Their movements were monitored and criticized. In a careful study of the impact of remittances on gender relations in the Jakaltek Maya town of Jacaltenango, Jocelyn Skolnik, Sandra Lazo de la Vega, and Timothy Steigenga (2012) found the transnational rumor mill so powerful that it was actually pressuring some wives to reduce their participation in community affairs—because even though their husbands were in the United States, a solo appearance in public would inspire gossip about adultery.[4]

Because anthropologists defend the legitimacy of indigenous cultures, we have been slow to focus on the second-class status of Mayan women. This is certainly my own case; I remember being shocked by Tracy Ehlers' *Silent Looms*, on the declining status of women in San Pedro Sacatepéquez in San Marcos Department. San Pedro is a boomtown of Mam Mayas who have prospered in commerce and moved into the professions. Paradoxically, modernization has undermined the ability of women to run their weaving businesses and other enterprises. According to Ehlers, Sanpedrana women enjoy complaining about men but also boast of the number of boyfriends each has had, real or imagined. Girls seem to enjoy romance. But in the behavior of their fathers toward their mothers, they also have seen enough of their own future that, "at one time or another, most *patojas* [teenage girls] swear they will never marry." Girls enter into courtship less because of their own erotic drives, Ehlers suspects, than because they wish to get out from under the authority of fathers and older brothers. The usual stimulus for marriage is pregnancy. What women expect from marriage is drunkenness, brutality, and betrayal. They are expected to face brutish behavior with equanimity and their powerlessness is reinforced by patrilocal residence, in which bride and groom live with the latter's parents for several years before establishing their own abode. One response to powerlessness is to bear large numbers of children, which emphasizes wives' contribution as mothers but collectively produces more workers than the economy can employ, encouraging yet more marginality in the new generation.

Only wealthier men can afford the de facto polygamy of *caseras* (mistresses), the second and sometimes even third households that are common in Guatemala and that often produce offspring. But Ehlers thinks that temporary hookups are also very common, and this requires the cooperation of married women as well as men. "Few families have not been scarred by one or more lurid extramarital episodes which are regularly recounted as lessons to the uninitiated," she reports. Women are not even supposed to enjoy sex, any sign of which would interfere with their assigned role as pillars of virtue. Given so many obvious negatives, Ehler asks, why would San Pedro women welcome irregular relationships with philandering men? The answer seems to be that they see extramarital relationships less as sexual releases than as transactions in which they will provide sex in exchange for resources.[5]

I am never going to produce my own ethnography of gender in Nebaj, but Ehlers' portrait resonates with what I see and hear. No one is paid very well in Nebaj, but pay for women is shockingly low. Standard wages for a *muchacha* (girl) who works as a live-in housekeeper, tortilla maker, and nanny is Q300 ($38.46) per month. This often includes food and shelter but works out to only Q10 or $1.28 per day. Older women make twice that, Q20 daily. By way of contrast, a male laborer earns a minimum of Q30 or $3.85 daily. Because of meal preparation from morning to night, women also seem to have a longer workday than men do; I met a tortilla maker who was making Q400 to Q600 ($51 to $77) per month by working seven days a week from seven in the morning until eight at night.

Little wonder, then, that women dealing with low wages and male irresponsibility might try to capitalize on sex—but as Ehlers points out, usually in the interest of bearing children and strengthening their family security net. This is an economic transaction that goes back a long way, and perhaps in every culture, but in Ixil country it was probably encouraged by the plantation era. Jackson Steward Lincoln was the first anthropologist to sojourn in Nebaj, in 1939–1940. He reported ladinos boasting that they could have sex with Ixil women whenever they wanted for ten cents, with the women apparently motivated by their need for money. Various plantation owners became known for siring dozens of unofficial offspring, who would be raised as Ixils or ladinos depending on the ethnicity of the mother. By the time I reached Nebaj in the 1980s, Ixil women seemed to be towers of virtue when it came to foreign men. I have witnessed more than one gringo (by definition, a person of wealth) fall in love with an Ixil woman and court her without success. Prostitution is not an obvious feature of Nebaj social life. I am told that it exists, but I have never seen it except for a few women—not indigenous and not local—who serviced soldiers in the late 1980s.

Getting back to Lincoln's report, a Nebaj boy was supposed to propose marriage by grabbing the corner of the girl's shawl and putting a few pesos down the back of her blouse. If she was game, she kept the money and a matchmaker negotiated the terms. If she wasn't interested, her father returned the money. Marriage entailed many exchanges which tilted in favor of the bride's family; a typical cumulative bride price was Q30 ($30 at the time), including gifts as well as cash, whose value can be gauged by the cost of a midwife attending a birth—twenty-five centavos. Brides were free to return to their parents as long as they returned the bride price and presents.[6]

Nowadays, I am told that Ixil bride prices have declined to the level of symbolism, in contrast to K'iche's, for whom they can still be substantial. Boys and their fathers are still expected to seek the permission of a girl's father for marriage, and some families still do this with considerable ceremony. But usually the couple have already agreed to marry and the girl is often pregnant. If the father shows any sign of rejecting the match, they will probably elope. Formal marriage in a church and at the civil registry usually follows cohabitation. *Juntarse* or "getting together" is the usual expression for the commencement of second unions; and children are considered a normal product of any sexual relationship, even if these are conducted simultaneously with an earlier union.

One disturbing aspect is that, when a woman embarks on a second marriage, she is expected to park the children of her first marriage with relatives and sideline them. As for fathers neglecting the children of their first marriage, this is considered so inevitable that it arouses little comment.

In the 1970s, Ixil marriage practices horrified Yolanda Colom, an organizer for the Guerrilla Army of the Poor. Colom's cover was the Catholic parish, through its house-building program, in which capacity she worked with the parish priest from Spain. Marriageable girls were cheaper than cows, she claimed, partly because fathers did not want the cost of raising them. The sixty quetzals (US$60 at the time) for a young girl was the same as for a donkey. Men had the prerogative of beating their wives for any number of reasons, with criticism reserved for men who did not. In 1975, Colom joined the guerrilla column as a political cadre and found that women's rights were an uphill struggle even among revolutionaries. For example, following one of her political talks on the need to liberate women, there was a long silence. Finally an Ixil leader suggested that, instead of beating their wives with a machete, men should use a switch. Indigenous women failed to realize that they were oppressed, instead focusing their pity on the girls who had become combatants. On one occasion, village women offered to buy one of the girls in Colom's unit. She never figured out how to change peasant attitudes toward women.[7]

In the 1990s, Guatemalan and foreign feminists had equally disillusioning experiences with the popular movement—the fraction of the peasant population that was still more or less aligned with the guerrilla organizations and that the left hoped would reorganize the far larger peasant population that, during the bloodbath of the early 1980s, sided with the army. Foreign activists placed particular hopes in the peasant refugees returning from Mexican camps to resettlement projects. The resettlements were financed by international donors, who also supported women's organizations such as Mamá Maquín, named in honor of an organizer killed by the army in 1978. Unfortunately, the return to peasant life in Guatemala became rife with competition for land and projects, and one of the most common backlashes was against women demanding equal rights. At Nueva Generación Maya, a resettlement in Huehuetenango Department, a dispute over salaries led to a community assembly that threatened to burn its Mamá Maquín members. Several took refuge in the United States.

The narrators of this incident, anthropologist Manuela Camus and Mamá Maquín activist María Mateo, are not enthusiastic about how the men and women of the resettlements have turned their hopes to the United States. The departure of the men and their occasional visits home encourage violence against women and make women vulnerable in other ways, report Camus and

Mateo. Women have had to drop out of Mamá Maquín to accompany their husbands to the United States, leaving their children as quasi-orphans. If on the other hand mothers stay with their children, they are so overwhelmed with work, and under so much surveillance because of their presumed inclination to adultery, that they stop attending Mamá Maquín meetings. When unmarried girls go north, they come under so much sexual pressure from men that they have to marry immediately and produce children, ending remittances to their mothers.[8]

A particularly grim note is Nebaj's reputation as a suicide capital, particularly for youth and especially girls. Guatemalan death registries do not record suicides as such, making it impossible to compare Nebaj with other towns. For what it is worth, in 2002 a newspaper reported that forty-eight Nebajenses had killed themselves in the previous four years.[9] If the figure is accurate and if the Nebajenses were a country, this would give them the thirteenth highest suicide rate in the world, not far behind Russians, Ukrainians, Japanese, and Chinese. They would also be killing themselves at almost nine times the recorded rate of other Guatemalans.[10] When the Archbishop's Office on Human Rights (ODHA) looked into Nebaj's suicides, it pointed the usual finger at the army's counterinsurgency campaign—except that youth killing themselves in the 1990s and 2000s would have experienced far less repression than their parents did. More to the point, when ODHA asked Ixil youth what they thought was needed to "improve the community," looming large in their answers were computers, electric guitars, Olympia mattresses, and large-screen Sony televisions. "Modern Mayan youth are both proud and ashamed of their culture, alternately valuing who they are and longing to be different," the report concluded. "Despite describing the ideal lifestyle in terms of traditional Ixil norms, they often act in ways inconsistent with community values. Some young women state that their traditional clothing is a crucial part of their identity yet long for Western styles. The confusion about and rejection of their own identity is one facet of the causes of youth suicide."[11]

Criticizing youth for failing to live up to the values of their family or culture is a reliable way to make them feel bad, but it is such a human universal that it hardly explains a suicide epidemic. A simpler explanation for girls killing themselves, and to me a more plausible one, is aggression by fathers and brothers. In the late 1980s, Sebastiana was a laughing teenager whom my wife and I hired to keep an eye on our toddler. Within a year, she gave birth to twins followed by eight more children. Toward the end of her reproductive career, Sebastiana's husband sold the solid house in town that her father had given her. He needed the money for his *negocios* (business deals), but his only visible investment was in alcohol. When his wife's capital was gone, he ran off with another woman, leaving Sebastiana and her children to fend for themselves in a shack at the edge of town. Sebastiana is twenty years younger than I am, but by this point, at the age of thirty-five, she looked older than me. Worse was to come. In 2008 her fifteen-year-old daughter, a good kid who did a lot for her mother and also did well in school, hung herself from a rafter. The trigger? Her drunk of a father, on a visit to the shack, had thrown her school certificates into the fire.

In a similar case, in Cantón Batzbacá in 2010, a young man came home from the United States in a bad mood; he was married to another immigrant, a U.S. citizen, which had not protected him from being deported. One day he was drinking and accused his little sister of being a slut. At the age of sixteen, while doing well at school, she already had a baby. The girl responded by drinking gramoxone, the local commercial name for paraquat, a herbicide which is on the shelf in many Ixil homes. Gramoxone destroys the ability of the lungs to absorb oxygen. It is a slow death that can take as long as a week. But it, along with hanging, is the most popular Nebaj technique for killing yourself.

Just as I was wrapping up this book in June 2012, Nebajenses were pondering another rash of adolescent suicides. I heard about seven, all apparently by hanging, but was able to confirm only three:

1. The daughter of two of José Domingo Sánchez's accomplices/victims hung herself near her old home in Cantón Julá.
2. The son of a failed moneylender hung himself at her house.
3. The son of a single mother who had gone to the United States also hung himself.

SETTLING SCORES IN LA PISTA

Just because the cultural ideal is for Nebaj women to be subordinate does not necessarily mean that this is how they behave. For example, while Ixils believe that siblings should receive equal shares of each parent's land, sisters are often shortchanged. But not Catalina, the woman who says she was raped by the Ixil men receiving her in Pleasantville. In another of the dramas characterizing Catalina's life, which in this case I was able to verify, she has used her position as the youngest sister, and the only one still living with her mother, to sell off her mother's substantial landholdings, one by one and for large sums without consulting her siblings or sharing the proceeds. To cover her tracks, she claims to have been cheated by a moneylender and a lawyer. When her siblings challenge her, she threatens to denounce them to the government's human rights ombudsman.

The position of women has improved in some ways. Evangelical churches teach that women should be subordinate to men, but they also have a lot to say about family responsibility, as does the Catholic Church. Both religions give women social space outside the home, hence more room for negotiating gender roles in the family. Aid projects are also making Nebaj women less subordinate. For two decades aid coordinators have labored to get women out of the home and into the public domain, to increase their income, and to get them, or at least their daughters, into school. Most girls as well as boys now attend at least a few years of primary school, and hundreds of girls are making it to the secondary level. This is no small accomplishment, of which Nebajenses can be proud, and in 2011 Catarina Pastor became the first Ixil woman elected to the national congress.

Now that Nebaj has become such a hub, the most enterprising women have been able to show that they have more commercial acumen than their menfolk. Not least of the new opportunities for emancipation is the borrowing and lending of money. But loans can be very tricky to collect, and large sums can ruin the creditor as well as the borrower. Consider the odds facing a female moneylender in the hurly-burly of La Pista, the village next to, and named after, Nebaj's little-used airstrip. La Pista originated as a refugee camp and benefitted from three decades of aid projects, so it boasts electricity and running water for its 470 households. But there are many things to disagree about in a village—from dogs that steal chickens to boys who impregnate girls to boundary markers that change location during the night. Then there is the thorny question of exactly who represents the community, and of exactly who will run aid projects, which in La Pista has led to the formation of two village governments, neither of which recognizes the authority of the other. Most households have partaken of the loan programs in the nearby municipal seat. So many La Pistans are in arrears that financial institutions have redlined the entire village. But some families have also been receiving remittances from El Norte, turning them into a target for kidnappers. Ransom kidnapping has yet to become an industry in Ixil country, but certain Ixils are trying to learn how, thus far at a high cost to themselves as well as to their victims.

The target of a La Pista kidnapping in 2008 was a campesino of no apparent means except for a son in the United States. He was seized as he tended his cow by men in face masks who cell-phoned his family and demanded Q100,000 ($12,800). The victim's family alerted neighbors, who called the national police, who called the local army detachment. Not coincidentally, the neighbors included the wife of one of the kidnappers. She quietly phoned her husband, whereupon he and his companions—fearing that the victim would be able to identify them—strangled him. But they were in a rush; he survived and was able to identify one. The suspect was arrested and whisked away to the department capital, the anti-lynching protocol that has become necessary to preserve the life of such persons. When the inevitable mob descended upon the Nebaj police station, what it wanted was not crystal clear. Some witnesses thought the mob wanted to *ajusticiar* (execute) the prisoner. But according to a town official, the mob consisted of the prisoner's friends and relatives insisting on his innocence. Whoever they were, they were not pleased when they were unable to take possession of him. They forced their way into the station, burned the office equipment and a motorcycle, and released the other prisoners. In response, all of Nebaj's justice personnel—police, judges, and other courthouse employees—left town on the grounds that it was too dangerous for them to perform their functions.

Seven months later, La Pista returned to the headlines with four more hostages. This time a Citizen Security Patrol, which reported to one of La Pista's two governments, took hostage (or arrested, if you thought it was legitimate) a ladino moneylender named Evidalia Hernández Martínez and three other La Pistans. Patrollers wearing face masks and carrying firearms pulled the four out of a passenger van and accused them of bringing *desconocidos* (strangers) into the village. Not a single *desconocido* was ever located; the patrollers focused their ire on Doña Evidalia but were unable to specify any law she had broken. When the national police arrived, the patrollers blockaded them. Eventually the combined authority of the police, the army, the human rights procurator, and the justice of the peace persuaded the patrollers to free the prisoners, but only on condition that Evidalia leave the village within a week.[12]

She never left, and months later she told me her side of the story. Evidalia lost her husband and child to army attacks in the early 1980s. Without a family to care for, she became a cook in base camps of the local guerrilla column, the Ho Chi Minh Front, and had three more children. Eventually, following one of the army's scorched-earth offensives, she and her children were starving, so she surrendered to the army and found sustenance on coastal plantations. Only in the late 1990s did her situation begin to improve, thanks to the new opportunities in El Norte. On a visit to relatives in Mexico, she met a man who suggested, "You send us people and for Q35,000 ($4,500) we'll take them to the United States." There was no shortage of men who wanted to go north; the problem was helping them finance the trip. Evidalia went to credit institutions, but they were not impressed with her collateral and loaned her only Q22,000. So she sold a hundred cuerdas—4.4 hectares of valuable land next to a growing village—and invested the resulting Q350,000 ($44,900) in a succession of migrants. These included two of her sons, each of whom went north at the age of fifteen and found their way to the construction boom in Las Vegas, Nevada.

By the time I met Doña Evidalia, she had a reputation as a swindler and she was destitute. I knew she was destitute because, unlike all the other female moneylenders of my acquaintance, she could no longer afford a cell phone. Everything she owned, by her account, had been lost to fourteen migrants who failed to repay her. The property documents they provided as collateral were no good. In one case, a deadbeat's brother persuaded her to bring the document to Chajul so that he could pay off the loan. Flanked by two other men, the brother took the document and then refused to give Evidalia her money. "My brother is not going to pay," he informed her. "Now he's in the United States, and why should he pay?" Evidalia went to Chajul's mayor to complain, but he chose to believe his constituent's version of events; Evidalia came home with nothing. In an earlier disaster, she arranged a Q280,000 ($35,900) travel package for seven kinsmen in the Chajul settlement of Santa Delfina. They went with an Ixil who claimed to be a coyote but who, at a critical moment, panicked and abandoned them. Stranded in Mexico, the Santa Delfinans rang up Evidalia. They said they were dying of hunger and, if they ever made it home, would kill her. Evidalia dispatched another coyote, who arranged their arrival in the United States, and she sent him the Q280,000. She was never repaid for this deal either.

In 2009, Doña Evidalia was living on a dirt floor under several roofs dating to different aid programs. Not knowing how to read and write, she depended upon her youngest child, a twelve-year-old boy, to decipher documents. She could not name the borrowers who had failed to repay her. In the course of losing her capital, Evidalia also lost two of her children. Her daughter Genara left for El Norte in 2005. Although only twenty when she left, Genara already had three small children by a youth from one of La Pista's leading families. He too was in the United States but recognized only the first of the children as his own, not the other two, and sent no money, even though he was sending remittances to his parents and they had purchased a small fleet of motor vehicles. Before Genara left, her in-laws used to poke fun at her. Since her departure she has never been heard from, but Evidalia thinks she is still alive and is raising her three children.

The other child Evidalia lost was her son Carmelito. Together with another youth, he was shot and killed in an episode which, like many in Guatemala, has never been clarified in a court of law. That the fifteen-year-old Carmelito was running around at 11:30 p.m. is, to many in La Pista, sufficient evidence that he (1) was a *marero* (gang member) and (2) received his just desserts as administered by other gang members. In Evidalia's opinion, her own nephew Juan was to blame because he was found with Carmelito's cell phone, along with other youths whom she persuaded the national police to arrest. According to Evidalia, this is one reason the Citizen Security Patrol went after her three months later—as a reprisal for seeking justice for her son. The other reason the patrollers went after her, Evidalia claims, is that they owe her money.

"They used to come to me asking for loans, I gave them a thousand quetzals, or two thousand quetzals, they owe me Q50,000 (in all, $6,400), and now they don't want to pay. I trusted them, I helped them, and how they treat me! The majority of the families who want to kill me are the ones who borrowed money from me. They are the families who owe me money, and they are the families who murdered my Carmelito and the other boy!" It was the son of one of the village's two mayors who held her hostage for eleven hours, and according to Evidalia this man's son was one of Carmelito's murderers. "They told me that if I didn't sign a document [agreeing to leave], they would burn me. I haven't brought a legal complaint because I'm afraid. [The village mayor] Benito told me, 'If you accuse us, we'll finish off your family. When your son returns from the United States, he'll come here for dinner before we finish him off. We don't obey human rights, we don't obey the [municipal] mayor, we don't obey the COCODES [the rival village government], because we are the ones who give the orders in this village.'"

The village mayor in question, Benito Cedillo, proved to be a frail old man with a kindly air. He denied any responsibility for taking Evidalia hostage in January 2009. Why did she get in so much trouble? I asked. "She spreads slanders, she blames me for the death of her son. She brought men to her house, she had guards. It was the village watch committee that arrested her when she showed up in a car. I defended her."

Subsequent to my conversation with Evidalia, she became known as an anti-eviction activist. She is credited with leading a crowd against a moneylender and house grabber in 2010, and soon thereafter she led a crowd resisting her own eviction. When I looked for her the following year, she was in prison, but not for fighting evictions, although she went to jail briefly for that as well. It seems that, when the boys indicted for killing her son went to trial and she showed up to rally her witnesses, the prosecutor instead grabbed her for fraud. Off she went to prison for a year—by her account because she had served as guarantor for another moneylender's loan. When I caught up with her in 2012, she was back in her accustomed premises, thanks to her sons in Las Vegas who had worked out a deal with the bank and who were now her lifeline. She was wondering how she could visit them.

ATTACK ON AN IXIL HUMAN RIGHTS DEFENDER

Nebaj women expect to be victimized by men, but their antagonist is often another woman, with whom they are competing for the dubious prize of a man. Confrontations can escalate quickly from verbal to physical. Ixil women have a reputation as *peleoneras* or fighters. No small number are familiar with the interior of the police station even though few are actually jailed. When a woman steals another woman's husband, legend has it, the wronged party organizes her friends to ambush the usurper, who is wrestled to the ground and has flour dough loaded with hot chili and chlorine cleanser shoved up her vagina. *Echarle chile* (stick chili in her) is the expression. When I asked for actual incidents, I was told that it is a joke—which is to say that it is a threat that comes up in altercations over straying husbands.

Thanks to their splendid apparel, the Ixil women of Nebaj have become a symbol of indigenous Guatemala. Regularly they are summoned to appear in full regalia to greet presidents, ambassadors, and delegations. "They always use us," I have heard Ixil women complain, but their striking garb is one of the reasons Nebaj has been showered with more projects than other towns. After the war ended and refugees came home, grant writers found that they could keep international donations flowing by invoking the needs of indigenous women, which are many. But the niche that Ixil women occupy is nastier than European and American feminists realize. While foreigners interpret Ixil culture as deeply communal, Ixil women deal with a reality in which everything is in short supply except babies. Land to inherit, men capable of providing income, opportunities to meet foreigners and benefit from their projects—all fall far short of the demand. While feminists envision their projects as a way for Ixil women to defend themselves from the usual suspects—the army, racism, capitalism, and men—Ixil women have learned from hard experience that the projects are yet another arena to compete with each other.

Consider the March 31, 2009, communiqué from a Nebaj women's organization that several international human rights groups relayed to their constituencies:

Yesterday around 4:30 p.m. Juana Bacá, leader of the Network of Ixil Women, was assaulted physically and verbally at Nebaj's town hall.

According to Juana Bacá, she arrived at the town hall to deliver a document and was surprised by three women who began to attack her verbally and then began to beat her all over her body. It's important to stress that the incident took place inside the town hall and that municipal police witnessed the events but did not intervene to defend the victim.

Subsequently Juana Bacá was transferred to the Nebaj hospital where she remains interned owing to the seriousness of the blows received. Because she is pregnant, she faces greater risk from this aggression.[13]

I knew one of the women whom Juana Bacá accused of assault. Teresa de Paz Sánchez is a single mother of four children because her husband left her for another woman. She makes refreshments for the town hall which is why she was there when up the stairs came Juana Bacá and Daniel Lopéz. Daniel Lopéz is the father of three of Juana Bacá's children. But he is not the man to whom Juana is married because Daniel is married to Teresa, who bore four of his children before he left her for Juana. According to Teresa, Juana spit out a remark and grabbed her by the hair. Teresa's estranged husband Daniel then punched her in the face and kicked her as she fell.

The municipal secretary was nearby and says the fight erupted so suddenly, with so little verbal sparring beforehand, that spectators never had the chance to gather before it ended. Juana and Daniel retreated down the stairs and into the latter's vehicle. On a videotape from a digital camera, a policeman obligingly holds open the door for Daniel as he steps in, before the camera then pans to Teresa's bruised and shocked face. Why didn't the policeman intervene? Perhaps because he knew Daniel López from his job at the courthouse as a conciliator.

Some Nebajenses dismissed the incident as another catfight between Ixil women. But most Ixil women are unable to persuade foreigners that their personal feuds are human rights violations. Juana Bacá Velasco is the first Ixil woman to earn a university degree in social work. She has been very successful at winning the friendship of international aid coordinators, persuading them to give their projects to her organization, and publicizing herself as a victim of human rights abuses. Here is how the Guatemala Human Rights Commission/USA (GHRC) informed its network of the incident:

> Juana was attacked in the town hall of Nebaj on March 30, 2009, and spent the next two days and nights in the hospital. Three local women beat, kicked, and punched her, throwing her down the steps. Her husband intervened to rescue her and is now accused of assaulting the assailants. "The women work for the mayor," Juana charges. "He is behind the attacks. I almost lost my baby."[14]

Eventually, a local judge determined that Juana had not been hospitalized, that the two other supposed assailants were never at the scene, and that Juana was guilty of *falta contra la persona* (offense against a person), for which she would have to spend twenty days in jail or pay a Q100 ($12.82) fine.[15] Juana appealed unsuccessfully to a higher court; Teresa de Paz says that her legal expenses have reached Q37,000 ($4,700). A judgment against her estranged husband is pending.

As the court case turned against her, Juana issued new denunciations which GHRC and other human rights networks distributed to their supporters. On July 3, 2009, according to Juana, "the mayor's car stopped to focus its head-

Women holding sky-rockets at a Catholic fiesta

lights on her" and someone shot a gun into the air six times. On July 6, she "received a threatening phone call from a man demanding money not to kill her. He said he was hired by the town council but was willing to negotiate a price for her life."[16] Should these latest denunciations be taken seriously? Perhaps not. Human rights groups did not have a clue that the March 30, 2009, incident was conjugal in nature because they relied solely on Juana Bacá and her organization for information. How did she achieve the trusted status of human rights worker, as GHRC characterizes her? The reason, essentially, is that she accused Nebaj's mayor of threatening her, an accusation which was taken seriously because the mayor has often been accused of threatening his enemies.

Virgilio Gerónimo Bernal Guzmán was elected mayor of Nebaj three times. The reason was not that he lacked opponents; in 2007, so many candidates ran against him that he needed only a plurality to win reelection. Enumerating all the conflicts surrounding Gerónimo would be an undertaking. He was one of the earliest Ixil schoolteachers, a post that required courage because, during the early stages of the army–guerrilla conflict, both sides demanded the cooperation of teachers and assassinated sixteen of them.[17] Gerónimo was also the first mayor elected by Nebaj when Guatemala returned to civilian government in 1986. He was a Christian Democrat, the political party that raised the highest hopes during this period, but his administration was marred by drunkenness and graft. Toward the end, a mob chased him out of town. After a decade attending to business investments, he staged a comeback with the Guatemalan Republican Front, the right-wing populist party led by the retired general and former dictator Efraín Ríos Montt. In Gerónimo's second and third terms, as a Riosmonttista, he brought his drinking under control, but not his penchant for making enemies. He dismissed village development committees that opposed him and appointed his own. An array of critics accused him of grabbing their funding and, when they resisted, threatening them.

Certain women's microloan groups were among those who feared Gerónimo. The *bancos comunales* (community banks) were solidarity groups supported by the national government through its Social Investment Fund (FIS). As to why they felt threatened, there was a personal angle. "Each woman was entrusted with seed capital for our activities," a member recalled. "The supervising firm CONSERTEP hired Juana Bacá as our trainer to give orientation sessions to the women. Each neighborhood and village had its banco comunal, and Juana Bacá was just an employee, not a founder or member. During this period she had a personal conflict with the FIS coordinator in Nebaj, Miguel Bernal." Some blame Miguel for pressuring the women to support his father Gerónimo in his campaign for mayor; others say Miguel was blameless and attribute the falling-out to Juana's capriciousness. Whichever is the truth, when Miguel's father won the 2003 election and became the new mayor, Juana warned the women that Gerónimo wanted to take their money.

To protect the money, Juana Bacá now ordered the women to pool all their cash so that it could be deposited in a bank. And so on the morning of June 3, 2004, from underneath their mattresses and other hiding places, the women of La Pista amassed Q133,000 ($17,100). In retrospect, Juana's order aroused wonderment because it invited the disaster that it was supposed to prevent. Recalls one of her supervisors, "When Juana phoned to tell me they robbed us, I couldn't believe it. I couldn't understand how it was possible. Because we had agreed on a rule that we were not going to collect cash in the communities." Sure enough, as the women transported their savings to town on a slow-moving truck, they were ambushed by three masked youth who were apparently local. The 2004 robbery was memorable not just for the amount, which was never recovered, but because Gerónimo's security chief was convicted of leading it. Juan Toma de la Cruz hails from Cotzal and is still known as Patricio, the nom de guerre under which he became one of the EGP's most feared combatants before surrendering to the army and becoming a trainer for its elite kaibil units. Why would the mayor of Nebaj need bodyguards? Because during the 2003 campaign Gerónimo was kidnapped and held for ransom. As for the La Pista robbery, Patricio always protested his innocence, but many Nebajenses accepted the court's verdict because of his wartime reputation and the acrimony surrounding his boss.

Gerónimo's mood was not improved by the indictment of his security chief. At a conciliation meeting in Guatemala City, he exploded in wrath. "When we entered," a participant recalled, Gerónimo "spoke to us in Ixil, then in Spanish. 'You're going to pay; I'm going to eliminate you,' he said. He was furious, shouting at us in front of many witnesses, including the human rights procurator, the judicial branch, and Peace Brigades International." Juana Bacá was not at the meeting. But she was on the list of twelve persons for whom, following this incident, the national government provided security guards—as many as four per person, with no end date. As time went on, the security measures dwindled to Juana because she was the only one who continued to report threats.

Throughout these troubles, the bancos comunales were beset by accounting problems, like most organizations in Nebaj, so Juana reorganized them into a more centralized women's association, the Network of Ixil Women, which would be led by herself. One of her opponents had this to say about the organization:

> We didn't realize that it was going to be dominated by Juana Bacá. The assembly ought to happen every three months, but there was no assembly for four years. When we asked for our money, Juana Bacá responded with accusations. "You want to rob the money," she told us. She didn't consult with us, and there were no more assemblies. The banco comunal of La Pista had savings of Q60,000 in Bancafé. Juana Bacá withdrew it and took it. She took away our records, and we had to sue her to get them back. She spent money but didn't account for it. She didn't allow the board of directors to participate.
>
> In 2008 we demanded an audit. Juana Bacá told us that she was too busy to meet with us, but we surprised her at her office. She was startled. She didn't have receipts. She had signed checks and emitted funds and spent lots of money without control. It was total disorder. In the next general assembly, Juana Bacá instigated the women against a señora asking for an audit. They even threatened to burn the señora. When the courthouse convened a conciliation meeting on July 7, Juana Bacá did not arrive and did not sign the agreement. Since 2004, Juana Bacá has counted with the services of two, and sometimes four, bodyguards paid by the Interior Ministry. She says that she is threatened by the Mayor Virgilio Gerónimo Bernal Guzmán, but we believe that she's making it up. It's she who has threatened us on repeated occasions, and the presence of the bodyguards makes people afraid.

In June 2009, a few months after Juana Bacá claimed to have been attacked at the town hall, one of her critics asked me to meet with several members of the La Pista banco comunal, including women who were on the truck when it was robbed in 2004. One woman recalled,

> In the road three masked men ambushed us with gunshots and shot one of us in the leg. The assailants immediately sought the señora who was carrying the bags of cash and grabbed them. They had hardly begun to fire when Juana Bacá said, "It's the security detail of the mayor." If they were masked, how could she know this? Red, red [with embarrassment] she turned, but she kept announcing that it was the security detail of the mayor. We told Juana Bacá to call the police [on her cell phone]. She called like mad, but really she was just pretending to call and the police never arrived. When we reached the police station in Nebaj, we wanted to make our declarations, but Juana Bacá did not want us to speak. So she shut herself in a room with the police and the police never interviewed us. Ten days later the prosecutor summoned one of us to identify the assailants. Juana Bacá told her that she would go to jail if she didn't identify them as the mayor's security detail. Because of everything that has happened since then, we now believe that Juana Bacá was the true author [of the robbery] and that the men in jail [Juan Toma de la Cruz and three young men from La Pista] are innocent.

At this point, the reader is doubtless wondering who to believe. As of 2009 there were at least nine different associations of women in Nebaj, and they seem to be a taxing experience for all concerned.[18] Consider the frustration expressed by the former president of the La Pista banco comunal who was fired by Juana Bacá:

> They're terrible with us. Q75,000 [$9,600] came from Japan for fifty members. The first time each of us borrowed Q500 [$64], the second time Q2,000 [$256]. The *técnico* Nicolás Brito Cedillo came to give us training, but he robbed Q10,000 [$1,280] from us here in La Pista. He took money from all of us [in the different bancos comunales], Q16,000 [$2,050] from Acul, and then he took off to the United States. I'm so stupid for lack of training. That's why I gave him my identity document. We women don't even know how to read. So we appealed to FIS, and it gave us Q4,000 [$513], which we turned over to Juana Bacá. And now Juana Bacá doesn't want to give back the Q4,000. We are the ones who suffer. I go to town on foot, I return on foot, and my husband gets angry with me. Juana Bacá became upset because we wanted the Q4,000 back. Then another man came to train us, Gaspar, and we went to [the mayor] Gerónimo so that he would help us. Juana Bacá was upset that we went to the mayor.

Paradoxically, while aid agencies have turned imagery of Ixil women into a source of legitimacy for fund-raising, Juana Bacá's critics, along with many other Ixil women, feel powerless to communicate with these organizations. Indeed, the only reason I learned of this tangled situation is that Juana Bacá's opponents sought me out and helped me obtain interviews. They beseeched me to investigate her and issue "an international denunciation" to counteract all the attention and funding she was getting, which they perceived was leaving them in the shadows. When I explained that I had no basis for doing so, that only they as Ixil women had the necessary legitimacy, they said they were too afraid to make their own declaration. Juana Bacá has never been shy about reminding her followers and enemies of her international backing. Groups that have invited her to represent Ixil women and/or have funded her projects include Hivos (Netherlands), the Presidential Secretariat for Women (SEPREM), the Defensoría of the Indigenous Woman, the Rigoberta Menchú Foundation, and the European Union's Tinamit civil society project.

The reason that Ixil women feel impotent is that, while foreign donors perceive them as profoundly communal, in actuality they are often competing with each other. When it comes to administering aid, determining who deserves help, and defining what constitutes a fair share, projects for women quickly give rise to competing versions of events. This is why aid functionaries gravitate to someone like Juana Bacá who, as a professional social worker, is adept at figuring out what they want to hear. Whoever you think is more credible, it is clear who has won. Juana Bacá now presides over Nebaj's first shelter for battered women, in a handsome new structure financed by the Italian embassy.

Part III

COMPARISONS AND EXTRAPOLATIONS

Chapter Eight

Dreams and Pyramid Schemes

Migration is but one manifestation of the appropriation of surplus value.

—Raymond Wiest, 1984

When I explain how Nebajenses struggle with debt, sometimes I'm asked whether I'm just collecting their stories, or am I also trying to help? That is a good question. Helping Nebajenses with their debts will require being useful to people like Juana. In 2005 this confident young woman and her husband owned more land than many Ixils. They lived in an excellent location, a short walk from town and a short walk from their cultivations. Juana had a good head for business, or so she thought. Borrowing from neighbors at 10 percent interest per month, she sent her husband north. She also bought two three-wheeled taxis and hired youths to drive them. When her husband's remittances could not keep pace with the interest, she borrowed again and fell prey to a get-rich-quick scheme. She lost every centavo, and the neighbors threatened to kill her. To pay them off, she went to banks and talked three of them into giving her large loans. They charged her less interest and their loan officers never threatened to kill her, but they did require collateral in the form of real estate. By the time I met Juana in 2008, she and her husband owed Q47,000 to Cotoneb, Q150,000 to Banrural, and Q175,000 to the Quetzal Foundation—$48,000 in all. Cotoneb was already in possession of three of her properties; Banrural was about to grab three more, including the house in which she and eight other women and children lived; and Quetzal was being patient—but it had the right to seize a seventh property belonging to an in-law.

Owing to all these reverses, Juana's marriage seemed to be at an end. She was still living under the same roof as her in-laws, but they were poking fun at her and pressuring her to move out. Her only consolation was that, unbeknownst to Banrural, it held the title to only half her crowded dwelling. The other half belonged to her in-laws who had mortgaged it to another financial institution. In the meantime, Juana was praying to the Lord, and he was sending her dreams. She had dreams about being overwhelmed by the sea, about me persuading her creditors to give her more time, and about paying all her debts by leaving for the United States.

Going north would require leaving her three children (aged twelve, nine, and four) behind in Nebaj. Could I help her obtain a visa? I could not, and I rained on her parade—entrusting her children to relatives and leaving for the United States would mark them for life.[1] Juana's next plan was to return to the capital and work twelve-hour shifts in a factory for Q2,400 ($308) per month. Without funds to send her children to school, she would have to lock them in a rented room every day. Visualizing the television set they would have for company, I told her that this too was a terrible idea. Instead, I urged her to organize her fellow victims, go to court, and obtain recognition as fraud victims. That would buy more time from the banks. Twice I found pro bono lawyers and set up meetings, but Juana was skeptical that any organization could help. She didn't buy my argument that the banks shared responsibility. "I lied to them. I didn't tell them I lost the money to a swindler. If I had said that, they wouldn't have lent me anything. I told them I was going to improve my house."

Juana blames herself. She hoped to make a pile of money and underestimated the risks, and now her lenders—mainly fellow Nebajenses—are holding her accountable. On the left we like to think of persons such as Juana as victims of neoliberal capitalism, but the Nebajenses who lent her money are also victims of neoliberal capitalism, and they will continue to blame her. Whoever is to blame, her situation illustrates a feature of our economy which affects everyone. Guatemalans are not alone in becoming agents of their own destruction. When we scrutinize how capitalism extracts value, we sometimes fail to capture its moth-to-the-flame quality, how it tantalizes people with dreams of a more exciting life, of a higher rate of consumption and higher status. Through an array of pressures ranging from privatization of crucial resources to rapid population growth and inflation, and through consumer advertising and other inducements, capitalism generates a competitive scramble that not only invites people to take risks; it pressures them to take risks, because if they don't they will fall behind their peers. Whatever a person's assets, he or she is expected to borrow against those assets in pursuit of a better future. So many people are doing the same thing that it becomes necessary to leverage assets—to place them at risk—just to stay in place.

In a scramble such as this, there is no safe place to remain at rest. Everyone must gamble. Many lose their gambles, and—as we shall see—all aspects of life, from work and investment down to family, become the functional equivalent of pyramid schemes. A pyramid scheme rewards initial investors at the expense of later investors, with the result that wealth travels up the pyramid until—in a town like Nebaj—it vanishes to another department or country. In chapter 6 we saw three possible pyramid schemes at work: the one run by the Mam zahorín José Domingo Sánchez, the one run by Licenciado Rolando Reyes y Reyes (AVIDESGUA), and the one led by Victor in La Pista, the Association to Support Needy People of a Single Heart and Faith (ANECOF). In this chapter, we will look at how Nebaj's migration stream to the United States, its moneylending schemes, and its large families can also be viewed as pyramid schemes—unsustainable business models that depend on the recruitment of new members who have little chance of recovering their initial investment.

HOW MIGRATION GENERATES CHAINS OF DEBT, RISK, AND EXTRACTION

But first let's broaden our horizon to low-wage migration streams from Mexico, Central America, the Caribbean, and Andean countries. Latin American migrants might seem to be merely responding to demand from U.S. labor markets. If so, the U.S. debt crisis, economic recession, and high unemployment should sharply reduce the flow. It is true that illegal border crossing by Mexicans dropped sharply with the 2008 recession. The loss of jobs on the U.S. side of the border, and extortion threats against migrants on the Mexican side of the border, were the most obvious reasons. Others included declining family size, rising wages in sending regions, and the U.S. government's quiet decision to grant more work visas to Mexicans.[2] But interest in coming to the United States remains keen in Guatemala, as it does in many other countries. While economic recession can have a dramatic effect on migration flows, these tend to bounce back even before the economy recovers.[3]

Researchers have long reported the self-sustaining quality of some migration streams even when demand for their labor seems to slacken. In the case of Nebaj, youth continued to rush north even after their relatives and neighbors warned of the difficulty of finding work. A sociological explanation for this paradox is network theory, also known as migration-stream theory, which explains the decision to migrate in terms of ties to previous migrants. The more migrants leave, the more want to follow. Why would this be so?

There are at least three reasons why a migration stream can get bigger even as employment dwindles:

1. Envy or imitation, which Americans call "keeping up with the Joneses" and Latin Americans refer to as "dollar mania." Remittance receivers enjoy sudden jumps in consumption which relatives and neighbors wish to imitate. If a critical resource such as land is in short supply, only persons receiving income from U.S.-level wages are able to buy it.
2. The longer migrants stay in the United States, the more obligations they develop there, and the fewer remittances they send home, so receiving households must send more migrants to maintain their level of consumption.
3. The migration process itself produces deficits that can be paid only through further migration.

Because this third reason is the most counterintuitive, let's burrow into it. When Nebajenses pull together $5,000 to go north, some sell land; others sell cows; one man sold his family's crypt in the cemetery. But usually Nebajenses borrow—from credit institutions, from relatives, and from earlier migrants. When you borrow money, you pledge to repay it with future earnings. Because each trip costs years of household income, the lenders want collateral in the form of real estate. Even when relatives are not loaning money to each other, the financing for expeditions to El Norte usually reaches into families because the collateral is a family inheritance or the property of a trusting relative. The "immigrant bargain" is a way of referring to these transactions—quid pro quos in which a family takes on debt and makes other sacrifices to establish a member in the United States.[4] The migrant is expected to pay the debt and, more often than not, help more members of his family migrate. And so the family becomes an export business, monetizing family relationships and taking on debt in the hope of placing more of its members in foreign labor markets and securing a higher income than before.

The crucial issue for migrants is whether they will find enough employment to pay off the loans. Well before the 2008 financial crisis led to a sudden drop in U.S. employment, traditional receiving areas and industries were clearly flooded with immigrant labor. In the single most popular destination of California, according to a sympathetic study, immigrants have not undermined the wages of native-born Americans. What they have undermined is the wages of immigrants who arrived earlier.[5] Wait a minute—isn't Latin American labor always in demand? Isn't the U.S. economy's need for Latin American labor why we should change our immigration policy? Not necessarily. Consider the following sequence of events:

1. The productivity and cheapness of Latin American immigrants raises the expectations of employers. They become convinced that they can no longer rely on native labor because it is less productive than immigrant labor, and also more troublesome. Native workers complain bitterly about conditions that immigrant workers accept with scarcely a word. Why are Latin American workers so productive? Why do they complain less than American workers? One reason is that so many are illegal, trapping them in a devil's bargain where insisting on their rights means they will lose their job.

2. To obtain more of this high-productivity labor, employers adopt the so-called referral system, which is also called network hiring.[6] When the employer has an opening or expands operations, he asks his most trusted Latin American employees to recruit from their social networks. Voilá! Magically appearing at the gate are brothers, nephews, cousins, and neighbors, just as disenfranchised and just as unlikely to complain.

So while there are no jobs for millions of Americans, there are still jobs for immigrants willing to work for less than a living wage—a wage insufficient to raise a family by American standards.[7] Historically, this pattern of events originated in farm labor. It has spread to meatpacking plants, janitorial service, the hotel industry, carpet mills, and the construction industry.[8] In the future it will probably spread to other industries as well. Notice that this is not an open-market hiring system. Instead, the hire is a personal favor, with the employer and his foremen taking on the attributes of Latin American patróns. Workers lose bargaining power because they have entered into a conspiracy of silence with their employer. Should they cause too much trouble, they are easy to fire and replace. If worse comes to worst, they can be reported to Immigration and Customs Enforcement. Now that the employer has a cheaper labor force, his competitors are under pressure to hire the same kind of workers. Entire industries come to rely on undocumented Latin American labor, which might sound like a good thing for Latin Americans except that these are also occupational ghettos where employers are not paying a living wage. Employers do not need to pay a living wage because their Latin American employees give them access to queues of potential replacements, stretching all the way back to towns like Nebaj.[9]

Hiring systems like this serve such powerful interests—ranging from corporate employers to middle-class homeowners, and from conservatives to liberals, not to mention immigrants themselves—that they have not received the scrutiny they deserve. Their very existence is often concealed by collusion between relatives, cronies, and employers, who find it to their mutual advantage to break U.S. immigration and labor law. It is when migrants work for fellow migrants, often their own countrymen and kin, that they face the highest probability of sublegal wages and other forms of wage theft. The most dramatic example is the Fujianese migration stream to New York City documented by the sociologist Peter Kwong. In this ethnic enclave with particularly strong boundaries, due to the history of discrimination against Chinese immigrants, Fujianese sweatshop operators turned the theft of their Fujianese workers' wages into a science. They also figured out how to trick the city government's social safety network into subsidizing their operations. Even though sweatshop operators were openly flouting U.S. labor laws, they succeeded in winning contracts from the garment industry and courting the Democratic Party. "Asian and Latino immigrants," Kwong warned, "are being used as a tactical weapon to restructure the American economy."[10]

Undocumented Latin Americans are usually not as deeply indebted as undocumented Chinese. But they too can find themselves in situations approaching indentured servitude. Anthropologist Sarah Mahler may have been the first to point this out in her early 1990s research with Salvadorans and Peruvians on Long Island, New York. Mahler was shocked by how her friends' quest for economic self-determination, in which they sacrificed many aspects of their previous lives to earn U.S. wages, could instead plunge them into debt. Worse, they found themselves indebted not to Americans of a different social class, but to their own friends and relatives—"people who were their social peers but are now more like patróns in a patrón-client tie." Immigrants found it far easier to profit from their own kind than from native-born Americans, Mahler found, because only with fellow immigrants did they have a power advantage. Thus earlier immigrants could become *raiteros* (ride givers) for newer immigrants without a car. They could buy a house and make the mortgage payments, hopelessly large for one immigrant's income, by subletting rooms to as many people as possible. Last but not least, earlier immigrants could become employers of more recent immigrants, often as contractors for an established firm.[11]

Immigrant workers carve out a niche in American society by offering to work harder and for less than native-born workers. But many are paid so little that the only way that they can achieve a stable middle-class income is by starting their own businesses, in which they employ more recent immigrants at sufficiently low rates of pay to undercut competitors. Granting legal status does not solve the problem because employment must stay off the books—that is, in violation of labor codes—to be economically viable in the larger economy. Indeed, immigrant employers who gain legal status have often used it to smuggle in more cheap labor.[12] Journalist Ted Conover noticed that a labor organizer, aside from trying to organize a union, was bringing in more labor from Mexico. He also found that Mexican Americans were making a living by bringing up Mexicans. In her study of Zapotec immigrants from Mexico, anthropologist Lynn Stephen found that labor contractors from the same ethnic group were using their command of the language to exploit their workers.[13] The ultimate in profitability is to turn one's co-ethnics or co-nationals into a captive labor force. Such cases are not typical, but they are not necessarily rare, and U.S. courts occasionally convict immigrant employers of human trafficking.[14]

Immigrant smuggling and debt peonage have long traveled with family and hometown ties in labor contracting for U.S. agribusiness.[15] In the 1990s anthropologist Fred Krissman interviewed twenty-four labor contractors in California who were recruited into performing this function by corporate farms that were busting labor unions. The labor contractors were all ex-farmworkers from Mexico who achieved legality in the 1986 amnesty. In their crews they employed an average of seven immediate family members. One contractor claimed to have brought to the United States more than two hundred members of his kin network. Another contractor employed siblings or in-laws as the foremen of each of his four crews, each of which was in turn a hierarchy of that person's kin. Back home his in-laws ran a store that was providing loans at 30 percent monthly interest for migrants who wished to join his labor force.[16] Wait! Don't family and hometown ties protect migrants from exploitation? This is what we would like to believe. But what you define as protection depends on your basis of comparison. If you're stuck in a menial job in Mexico and your uncle offers you a place on his harvesting crew in California, he's doing you a big favor—until you become sufficiently integrated into U.S. society to become aware of the labor code and expect your uncle to follow it.

The social glue holding together these arrangements is family obligation which becomes monetized. Monetizing family obligations doesn't necessarily destroy them, but doing so to join a precarious workforce puts them at risk. Some debts to your relatives turn out well, and others do not. In the words of Howard Karger, "[G]ood debt builds physical or social assets, such as mortgages that lead to home equity or student loans that enhance human capital. Bad debt is generated by purchases that consumers can't afford, or by loans for month-to-month living expenses that regularly exceed income."[17] In the broad sense of exchange, reciprocity, and obligation, debt is as old as the human condition. It is intrinsic to how humans engage with each other. Societies are built around reciprocal obligations which are never intended to be paid in full, which is why parents and children do not bill each other. Financial obligations *are* meant to be paid in full, however, and a market-oriented political order insists that such obligations take precedence over mere social obligations.[18]

In the case of Ixils and other Mayas, they organized their way of life around ritual obligations to ancestors and gods which traditional Catholics still honor. With the arrival of plantation capitalism at the end of the nineteenth century, the lure of cash as a medium of exchange, and the monetization of obligation in those terms, debt became a way to separate Ixils from their land. But monetized debt wasn't just a clever technique employed by ladino businessmen against indigenous peasants. It was the axiom of the system from top to bottom. Even the wealthiest families in Ixil country, the Arenas family who owned the Finca La Perla in Chajul and the Brol family who still own the Finca San Francisco in Cotzal, were chronically in debt to creditors. This was characteristic of the entire social class that owned coffee plantations. Planters were politically connected to the Guatemalan state and lived high off the hog, but they were always in debt to the European and North American brokers who bought their harvest. "The worker was indebted to the landowner; the landowner to the exporter; the exporter to the importer," notes Daniel Wilkinson. "When coffee prices dropped, the importers squeezed the exporters, the exporters squeezed the landowners, and the landowners squeezed the workers."[19]

Nowadays some Ixils still borrow cash advances from labor contractors before going to the plantations, but such debts are relatively small (rarely more than a few hundred quetzals) and easy to disown. A far deeper and more threatening deficit has emerged in the population growth that has overwhelmed the productive capacity of the coffee harvest, of subsistence maize agriculture, and of any other conceivable industry in Ixil country. Even in the 1960s the population of Ixil country surpassed the area's agricultural productivity, as measured by the fact that it was a net importer of its staple crop, maize. In 1973, when Horst Nachtigall studied Nebaj, 74 percent of his sample had worked on plantations.[20] We can take this to mean that roughly the same percentage of the population was unable to get through the year on the basis of their own agricultural efforts. Borrowing from labor contractors, and going to coastal plantations for several months a year, compensated for an underlying deficit in food production.

Currently Nebajenses are producing large numbers of children for another country's reserve army of labor. Pushed by their circumstances and guided by their dreams, they go north as the most obvious way to make up the deficit between the number of mouths to feed and the capacity to feed those mouths. El Norte requires heavy obligations to smuggling networks, and heavy obligations between family members, whose outcomes are far less predictable than the obligations that sustained the Ixils as peasant farmers. We have seen how exchanges feeding into migration to the United States can quickly degenerate into winner-take-all schemes that strip the assets of the most trusting or foolish. The cruelest of these expropriations occur within families, with the winners betraying parents and siblings, and they occasion much shaking of heads. Guatemalan peasants tend to be a lot less idealistic than middle-class Americans. But, like most human beings, they wish to think of parents and children as a stronghold of mutuality. During my 2011 visit, I heard about three situations in which sons were reportedly manipulating the title for the family residence in order to evict an elderly father, knock down a decrepit adobe, and build a new multistory dream house.

Such stories epitomize the fear that people are striving for a higher level of consumption by victimizing their near and dear. Seeking a higher income in the United States entails risks which the migrant transfers to his family by anchoring his debt to their collateral. If he fails, they will be dispossessed and pauperized. When this happens, chain migration stands revealed as a chain of exploitation that stretches from the employer back through the smuggling industry to the migrant's own family, with each person in the chain promising gain—but also transferring risk—to the next person in the chain. How do these chains form and lengthen? When a person is about to be swallowed by a debt, he figures out how to transfer it to another person. Thus a moneylender under siege from creditors obtains an infusion of cash by persuading a gullible relative to put up the document to her house as collateral for yet another loan. Or a migrant falling behind on loans decides that he must bring sons to help him, so he borrows even more. In either case, the supposed opportunity for gain, and the likelihood of loss, is extended to new potential victims. Cumulatively, this kind of decision making has the effect of saturating labor markets in the United States and increasing the number of people back home who will lose assets.

A fascinating attribute of debt chains is their siphon-like quality (pardon the mixed metaphor).[21] Thanks to *confianza*, trusting relatives loan their assets to migrants who pay coyote networks to take them to the United States. Whether or not the migrant finds enough work to pay back the loan, the coyote network remains with the cash. If the migrant succeeds, wealth flows from the United States in the form of remittances. If the migrant fails, the lack of remuneration means that the coyotes have siphoned off the assets of Nebaj households. The coyotes themselves are paying bribes to Mexican and perhaps U.S. officialdom. And of course the migrants are selling their labor to U.S. employers, many of them fellow immigrants who in turn become a source of profit for the commanding heights of the economy in real estate and finance. When the economy is expanding, the siphon quality can be difficult to locate because everyone seems to be winning their bets. The manifest benefits accruing to the most successful migrants and their families make losers hard to identify. Only when an economy crashes and large numbers of migrants are thrown out of work, as they resort to one unsuccessful expedient after another, and as they bring their moneylenders down with them, does siphoning of wealth away from the local level become impossible to deny.

The siphon also becomes evident when migrants are such failures that their families back home must send them additional funds—reverse remittances.[22] "Because of the apartment that he has, it's urgent that he pay for the apartment; he told us they were going to throw him into the street," a couple told me of their son in New Jersey. And so, after half a year in which he provided no remittances, they borrowed from neighbors at 10 percent per month to send him Q5,000 ($640). "He has to pay for the apartment every month; it doesn't matter if one doesn't have work. If one doesn't pay, they throw him out of the apartment. I don't want him to be in the street, let alone lose my son, but he doesn't find work and the interest increases every month. We're worried about the loan, every month, every month."

WHY LOWERING BORDER ENFORCEMENT WILL NOT END DEFICITS

Many people involved in the U.S. immigration debate, including many researchers with longer experience than I, believe that undocumented migrants would fare much better if it were not for U.S. border enforcement. If it were not for legal restrictions and border enforcement, undocumented migrants would have legal status—11.2 million of them in 2010 according to the most widely used estimate.[23] With full legal rights, as residents and citizens, they would not be trapped in the sublegal basement of the U.S. workforce. They would be under far less pressure to take advantage of each other.[24] Once no longer afraid of being deported, they would be in a better position to bargain with their employers, and if necessary to organize. Pay scales would rise. So isn't illegality the basic issue?

Certainly, Nebaj's wage pilgrims would be less in debt at the outset if they didn't have to each pay $5,000 to reach the United States. There is no doubt that immigration law and border enforcement raise the risk and cost of getting to the United States. Deportation features in many of the failure stories in this book. Without border enforcement, Nebajenses could come and go as demand for their labor waxes and wanes. But I doubt that illegality is the root of the problem. Whether low-wage immigrant workers are legal or not, they are not paid a living wage—that is, a wage sufficient to meet the cost of raising a small family in the United States. This is a problem they share with a growing percentage of the U.S. population.[25]

Consider the chronic indebtedness that the anthropologist Carlos Vélez-Ibáñez discovered in Mexican *colonias* or neighborhoods on the U.S. side of the border. Most of the inhabitants are U.S. citizens and legal residents who are chronically underemployed. At the end of the 1990s, Vélez-Ibáñez found that the average family of 6.2 persons had an average annual income of $22,578, with average annual expenditures of $26,240. How did the families make up the deficit? By "shuttling between informal and underground economies, pooling available resources and participating in [rotating-credit circles], borrowing from local banks and the local loan sharks or using credit cards, creating margins of favorable returns on goods purchased in pesos and sold in dollars, and finally, reneging on loans from the formal or informal credit sources."[26] Without a border, I would add, the colonia would lose its primary source of underground income, which is smuggling people and other contraband across it. If so, their primary problem is not the border; instead, it is the lack of demand for their labor.

Illegality is also not the basic issue if the lack of a living wage extends far beyond undocumented immigrants and their employers. Extremely low pay is also common in the H-2 guest-worker program which provides seasonal work visas.[27] Tree planting in U.S. national forests is an example. The U.S. Forestry Service accepts bids from U.S. firms, the firms hire Guatemalan labor contractors, and the contractors recruit workers from Huehuetenango Department. The Huehuetecos are desperate to reach the United States because they hope it will rescue them from their economic straits, and of course they would prefer to go legally. So they pay "an average of $2,000 in travel, visa and hiring fees" according to the Southern Poverty Law Center. To obtain the funds, many borrow from moneylenders at interest rates of up to 20 percent monthly. Once in the United States, they are paid by the number of trees they plant, which often works out to less than the minimum wage. Since the pine-planting season can be as short as three months, and since workers can earn less than $1,000 per month, at season's end some are still in debt.[28]

So debt chains are hardly confined to illegal immigrants. Usually only gruesome accidents bring the glare of publicity to these arrangements. In 2002, for example, a van carrying legally authorized H-2 forestry workers fell into a Maine river and fourteen men drowned. Four of the Guatemalans had been recruited by a man named Silvano Villatoro in their hometown of La Democracia, Huehuetenango. Silvano was a former civil patrol leader, which means that he was part of the Guatemalan army's counterinsurgency apparatus. Yet after moving illegally to the United States, he or his lawyer convinced an immigration judge that he was a victim of political repression, so he received political asylum. On the basis of legal residency, Silvano went to work for an American firm called Evergreen Forestry Services, and a year after the accident he was bringing up seventy Guatemalans a year—legally but enmeshed in debt to him as a labor contractor.[29]

Could these debt chains reflect foreign hiring patterns, brought to the United States by immigrants? I don't think so—what could be more American than the Pentagon and its reliance on the contractors who contribute so heavily to election campaigns? Supposedly to cut costs, the Department of Defense farms out an array of functions to private contractors. Corporations such as Fluor, DynCorp International, and the former Halliburton subsidiary KBR hire foreign subcontractors, which then hire manpower agencies to recruit "third-country nationals" from low-wage countries such as Nepal, Bangladesh, and Fiji to do service jobs on U.S. army bases. According to journalist Sarah Stillman, the agencies charge applicants exorbitant fees for the jobs. Applicants sell assets or borrow at high interest to pay the fees. If worse comes to worst, they find themselves in one of our fortresses in Iraq and Afghanistan where, aside from the risk of being blown up, they often earn much less than they were promised.[30]

Immigrant-rights advocates point out that if illegal immigrants were given legal status, they would have more bargaining power. But any relaxation of border enforcement would be very likely to attract fresh waves of immigrants, increasing the competition for jobs. In 2009, Zogby published a poll of Mexicans on their disposition to move to the United States for employment. Thirty-six percent of the 1,004 adults in the sample said they would go if they could. Of those who already had a member of their household in the United States, 65 percent "said a legalization program would make people they know more likely to go," even if they had to do so illegally. The Pew Global Attitudes Project obtained similar results. To the question "If, at this moment, you had the means and opportunity to go live in the United States, would you go?" 33 percent of Pew's sample of a thousand Mexican adults said yes. The same year Gallup published its first "world poll" on the disposition to migrate. Judging from a sample of 259,542 adults in 135 countries, "16% of the world's adults would like to move to another country permanently if they had the chance." If this is an accurate reflection of the desire to cross international borders in search of a better life, 700 million adults would like to do so. Of these, judging from the sample, 165 million regard the United States as their most desired future residence, with another 45 million preferring Canada.[31]

Such widespread interest in coming to the United States suggests that the problems facing immigrants cut far deeper than border enforcement. At bottom, immigrants attracted to U.S. wages face a worldwide shortage of gainful employment, with "gainful" increasingly being defined by how capitalism exaggerates the needs that people feel. Ultimately, it is not illegality that generates indebtedness but occupying the lower levels of the labor force and, particularly for youth, being deprived of status symbols. Owing to the allure of status consumption, the fecundity of rural populations, and the skill with which elites transfer risks to lower social classes, there are tremendous power differentials that will outlast any reform of border enforcement. For the people of Nebaj, the long and the short is that they are going into debt to join a chronic surplus of low-wage labor in El Norte. Under these conditions, allowing more immigrants into the United States is not likely to undermine exploitative patrón-client relationships. It is more likely to spread them.

The trap in which thousands of Nebajenses find themselves in U.S. labor markets is part of the wider "race to the bottom" that is undermining wages for a wide range of American workers, not just immigrants. Employers are gravitating to cheap foreign labor in two critical ways. First, corporate employers are offshoring production and service jobs to cheaper labor markets in Latin America and Asia. Second, employers are welcoming immigrants into the U.S. labor market where they undermine wages in a growing number of sectors.[32] In both cases, employers are transferring risks to weaker parties whose bargaining power is diminishing. Come adversity, workers pay the bill, in a sequence of indebtedness and dispossession which now extends to peasants in the Guatemalan highlands.[33]

Now let's see if this sequence of events can be analyzed as a financial pyramid. When migrants borrow large sums of money, they're making a speculative investment. When they attempt to repair their losses by recruiting more immigrants to follow them, their strategizing starts to look like a pyramid scheme. A financial pyramid is an unsustainable business model in which an instigator or "pharaoh"

1. induces investors to take on risk in the hope of high returns,
2. persuades them to recruit more investors into the scheme, and
3. enables midlevel investors to recoup some of their losses from investors below them before the scheme collapses.

By this definition, a pyramid scheme is more than a scam in which a swindler extracts money from suckers. To qualify as a pyramid, earlier participants must recoup their investment, or at least part of it, by recruiting more members. By this criterion, neither ANECOF nor AVIDESGUA in chapter 6 were necessarily pyramid schemes. Both made promises far and wide, and both encouraged the first members to become recruiters. But they are not pyramid schemes unless they enable the first members in Nebaj to profit from later members—of which I have little evidence. In the case of the zahorín José Domingo Sánchez and his office full of money, this may not be a pyramid scheme either—if we take the current penury of his followers as proof that they failed to recoup their losses. But if we look at the sunk-cost reasoning that impelled the zahorín's followers to continue giving him large sums of money, and how they could obtain these sums only by duping neighbors to loan them money on false pretenses, then the scheme starts to look like a pyramid—although one in which the midlevel investors ended up losing their shirts.

What distinguishes a pyramid scheme from more legitimate business investments is that there is no plausible strategy for creating a sustainable return. The only possible return is by attracting new investors who, because of the flimsiness of the business model, are certain to be victimized. Behind every financial pyramid is an appealing but mistaken premise. The mistaken premise of a migration pyramid is that gainful employment in the United States is available to all. Once people have been recruited into the pyramid and invested in it, the only way they can recoup their loss is by recruiting more people into it.

You may ask, how is this different from the financial legerdemain of Enron, American International Group (AIG), and New York investment banks? It is not. Nonsustainable business models are not confined to peasants and swindlers. They appeal to dreamers everywhere, they are an everyday feature of capitalism, and they take many different forms. One of these forms, I'm arguing, is low-wage migration from Central America.[34] This is not a Ponzi scheme with a single instigator who can be identified and indicted, even if certain figures on Wall Street and in Nebaj might deserve to be indicted. It is instead how the system works. It is a fateful convergence between immigrants attracted to American consumption levels, employers hungry for cheap labor, and visionaries who argue that bankers can help the poor by giving them credit. If so, then pyramid schemes can be hard to distinguish from the everyday workings of capitalism because the entire system sometimes seems to operate like a pyramid scheme.

HOW MICROCREDIT CAN MAKE THINGS WORSE

With this gloomy possibility in mind, let's look at the "microfinance revolution" (Robinson 2001) and how it has played out in Nebaj. Thus far I have refrained from scrutinizing the claims made for microcredit. If the poor are given access to credit, the argument goes, many will be able to bootstrap their way out of poverty—or at least ameliorate their situation and give their children a better chance of escaping poverty. This, anyway, is the pitch after it has been pared down for donors. In the global development industry, credit competes with other strategies that go in and out of fashion: building infrastructure, promoting new exports, making peasant agriculture more sustainable, providing income support for mothers with small children, encouraging migration to cities, and discouraging migration to cities. However contradictory the strategies may seem, each can alleviate poverty if backed by financial resources that, by definition, the poor always lack.

Here I wish to question only the assumption that cheap credit will enable large numbers of people to escape poverty. What follows is much obliged to scholars assembled by Thomas Dichter and Malcolm Harper. Their collection *What's Wrong with Microfinance?* should be read by anyone who still pins large hopes on the idea.[35] "Credit" is a reassuring word for debt, which is why "microdebt" has never caught on as a buzzword. Whatever term you prefer, everything hinges on the context in which the loan is made. That credit alone can alleviate poverty, and even create a path out of it, is a fairly new idea. In the ascendance of the United States and Western Europe, credit for the masses was pioneered by retailers, and its purpose was to encourage consumption. Credit for production was assumed to be the province of a specialized class of people who were particularly adept at divining market forces—businessmen.[36]

The idea that hundreds of millions of peasants will work their way out of poverty by gaining access to credit requires ignoring considerable historical experience, that they are more likely to mortgage themselves to the hilt and lose their land. In the American West, for example, mortgages and foreclosures led millions of farmers into bankruptcy. This is the predictable outcome if creditors seek to obtain profit, or just to get their money back, because commercial agriculture is inherently risky. If creditors don't really care about getting their money back, because they are actually philanthropists, then they are likely to face high default rates and miseducate borrowers about the consequences of borrowing from commercial lenders. The Nebajenses are far from unique in this regard. Rural credit schemes have a long history of high rates of default and rapid bankruptcy.

Away from the highly secularized West, using land as collateral cuts across the social obligations bound up with it. Morally, if not legally, land is often owned by a kin group rather than an individual or firm. If so, a man who claims to own private property is actually more like a trustee for an inheritance that he received from his forefathers, that he is supposed to bequeath to his descendants, and that may also be legitimately claimed by siblings and cousins. This is a point illustrated by the anthropologist Parker Shipton in his epic trilogy on obligation, debt, and aid projects among the Luo of East Africa. Consider a dilemma facing many Luo: if you have buried your parents outside the doorway of your house, as is the custom, what happens when this lineage patrimony is titled to a single member who then mortgages it and loses it? Hence "mortgaging the ancestors" in Shipton's apt phrase, a source of much trouble in Luo country.

Critics have little chance of deflating the mythic appeal of microfinance because, in the words of Ananya Roy, it "crystalliz[es] a multitude of aspirations, agendas, interests, and desires" and incarnates "the magic of private enterprise and self-help." It enables people who have been rewarded handsomely by capitalism to assume that more capitalism, of the right kind, will help poor people rather than hurt them. Aid planners have been learning otherwise for decades. In Bolivia, Elizabeth Rhyne reports, microlending started in the 1980s and was so successful that nonprofit aid agencies decided to turn themselves into licensed financial institutions. As the sector grew, so did the competition between lenders, and so did the practice of "bicycling"—in which borrowers pay off a loan by taking out a new one. During Bolivia's 1999 economic crisis, union organizers recruited borrowers into debtor's associations to oppose both for-profit consumer lending and nonprofit microlending. They demanded debt forgiveness for both. Street protests forced the government to intervene and set up a mechanism for debt relief. One debtor association turned out to be a pyramid scheme in which leaders collected their members' debt payments and used them to make new loans. "Clients are not good judges of their own debt capacity," concludes Rhyne. "Apparently, credit is like good food: when seated at the table in front of a feast, many people eat too much and regret it later. . . . If clients begin using one loan to pay off another, the game becomes . . . 'who collects first?' In short, the sector as a whole starts to become one big Ponzi scheme."[37]

The United Nations declared 2005 as the Year of Microcredit, and the Nobel Committee gave Muhammad Yunus, founder of the Grameen Bank in Bangladesh, its 2006 peace prize. But as microcredit was acclaimed in wealthy countries, its honeymoon in South Asia was over. By this time Grameen had abandoned its much-imitated solidarity model—making an affinity group liable for the loans of each member—because it was so burdensome and unfair to borrowers, who ended up hating it. In India, the state government of Andhra Pradesh shut down a microfinance showcase after it was accused of usury.[38]

Donors who become enthusiastic about microcredit often want to help women. Giving women control over a resource should increase their bargaining power with the men in their families. But just because a loan is made to a woman doesn't mean that she will necessarily retain control of it. Critics argue that the public transcript of alleviating poverty and empowering women masks a hidden transcript of patriarchal exploitation. That women are easier to collect from—because they are less mobile than men—might be good for the lending agency, but it does not demonstrate that women are being empowered.[39]

Still, how could such a simple, generous idea—giving women more access to credit, on easier terms than before—instead hurt them? The best argument for microcredit is that it protects households from emergencies and shortfalls. A cash-strapped household can, instead of selling assets or going without food, take out a temporary loan that serves as a bridge to its next income. Thus microcredit helps the poor manage their financial flows. The economist Jonathan Morduch and his colleagues have shown how even the poorest households in Bangladesh, India, and South Africa turn multiple sources of credit from relatives, neighbors, and agencies into a survival strategy. But these "portfolios of the poor," as Morduch and his colleagues call them, are also balancing acts.[40] One way the balancing act can be upset, judging from Nebaj, is a flood of easy credit.

Researchers who study microcredit's long-term impact on families and neighborhoods tend to paint a different picture than the success stories used to attract donations. The most appealing assumption of microcredit evangelism is that lack of cheap credit is a major contributor to poverty, and that providing it will enable poor people to bootstrap themselves to a better position. But most people in Third World countries are not potential entrepreneurs—no more than most people in well-off countries are potential entrepreneurs. When people borrow money, it is most often to survive an emergency or buy something they want, not to make an investment that will pay interest and generate profit.

In South Asia, researchers have learned that many microborrowers are unable to invest in a profitable enterprise. Because of structural constraints—such as the lack of productive potential, dependence on a few products for which there is little demand, or an oversupply of labor—many borrowers "are reduced to 'copycat' behavior, everyone selling the same thing," such that multiplying the amount of credit can reduce incomes.[41] When a loan fails to generate a new income stream, the most obvious way to pay it off is to take out a new loan, which over time deepens indebtedness. If borrowers end up being forced to sell assets, they are being stripped rather than bolstered. So discover Nebajenses who default on loans from their town's credit unions. These are nonprofit local institutions, whose intention is anything but stripping members of assets, but they are obliged to safeguard the capital of their other members.

In Latin America as well as South Asia, the profits to be made with microloans have attracted large commercial institutions whose profits suggest that they are siphoning wealth from the supposed beneficiaries. C. K. Prahalad (2006) has informed business-school audiences of the fortune to be made by selling and loaning to "the bottom of the pyramid." Even if the purchasing power of the poor is shockingly low, they are so numerous that the right product, such as cell phones or high-interest consumer loans to buy the coveted television, can make smart businessmen lots of money. I would like to know how the infatuation of Nebajenses with their cell phones, requiring the constant purchase of five- and ten-quetzal phone cards, has affected their expenditures on food.

Once we dispense with wishful terminology, it turns out that small-scale loans to the very poor—the rhetorical focus of microcredit evangelism—are tough to collect. The high repayment rates claimed by the Grameen Bank turned out to be fictional.[42] Profit is to be made only from people who are not very poor, or from poor people who are pressured into repaying, to the detriment of their survival strategies. This is what Catholic Relief Services (CRS) learned. It built successful microcredit programs and then decided to end them, after realizing that its host-country partnership organizations were profiting at the expense of the peasant farmers they were supposed to be helping. CRS learned that "credit management is a take-no-prisoners war against risk."[43]

At bottom, viewing microcredit as a panacea ignores the power relations within neighborhoods and families, through which even a modest loan can become an instrument of exploitation. For example, if high rates of repayment are achieved through solidarity groups, this is tantamount to group liability, which enables the most unscrupulous borrowers to offload their obligations onto cosigners. Because group liability is so exploitable, such programs are prone to undermine preexisting solidarity, not reinforce it.[44] Even if microloans are never collected, they habituate the needy borrower to further borrowing until she falls into the hands of nonphilanthropic lenders who take her assets.

So, has the "microfinance revolution" become a pyramid scheme in Nebaj? Without intending to, philanthropies loaning small amounts have encouraged their clients to borrow larger amounts from institutions that must recover their capital and make a profit. Certainly, a generous flow of credit has helped borrowers keep their heads above water. But given the underlying dearth of employment and productive potential, hence of plausible investments, the flow of credit has also encouraged them to lengthen their chains of debt to relatives and neighbors. For example, keeping up loan payments often depends upon borrowing from near and dear. Conversely, when Nebajenses receive loans from institutions, needy relatives pressure them for a share. In the absence of income-generating enterprises, how can interest and principal be paid except by sharing the burden or unloading it? Investments in El Norte, naturists, and zahoríns are often desperate attempts to climb out of debt traps by further borrowing. Nebajenses were facing serious deficits before their flings with bank credits, migration, and get-rich-quick schemes; now they are deeper in the hole than before. Under the circumstances, credit becomes a game of robbing Peter to pay Paul. If borrowers succeed in unloading their liabilities on others who incur the loss, they are winning in the functional equivalent of a pyramid scheme.

THE REPRODUCTIVE PYRAMID SCHEME

Given everything we've heard about indigenous people as cultures of resistance, their supposed insularity and durability, it might seem surprising that Nebajenses are so eager to acquire the comforts of modernity. But let us not forget all the outsiders who have offered them a better way of life. First the reformed Catholic Church of the 1960s and 1970s, and then Protestant evangelists, taught a new transcendent God, portable to one's purposes beyond the cornfield. Guerrilla cadres, then army officers, and ultimately a plethora of aid agencies, promised large improvements in material conditions. With the exception of the guerrillas and their vision of state socialism, each proposed improvement was premised on the ability of capitalism to multiply wealth. Each was attractive to people who spent their days working out in the elements and who had never ridden in the front seat of a car. This is the golden promise of capitalism, to provide a better life, and in Guatemala its most convincing manifestation is currently the American Dream, even if Guatemalans going north usually say they intend to come home some day.

In this parade of promises and reassurance, one issue that no one has wanted to confront is family size. Vaccination campaigns and other public health measures have reduced infant mortality, so most Guatemalan children now survive to adulthood. The assembled forces of cultural tradition, social stigma, and poor health care have prevented many Guatemalan women from using birth control until they affirm their worth by bearing armfuls of children. But birth control is far more accessible than it used to be, the Catholic clergy has refrained from opposing it, and population organizations credit Guatemalan women with reducing the number of live births to an average of 3.6 each. By 2011 the growth of the Guatemalan population has diminished to 2.4 percent a year. If sustained, this will double the population in twenty-nine years, but demographers expect the rate to continue falling. Unfortunately, if we look at the poorest fifth of the Guatemalan population—which would include the majority of the Ixil population—women are still averaging 7.6 live births.[45] This is not just a disappointing figure; in view of all the difficulties Nebajenses face in finding employment, it is a tragedy.

Family size is such a sensitive subject that few people, least of all wealthy Americans with our lavish consumption levels, want to tell Guatemalan peasants that they are having too many children. One common denominator, acceptable to just about everyone, is that giving girls more access to schooling, and more opportunity outside the domestic sphere, will bring down the number of children they bear. Finding employment, delaying the first pregnancy, becoming aware of options—all these salutary trends are encouraged by keeping girls in school. All are at work in Guatemala, and there is some sign of them in Nebaj's municipal seat. But out in the villages where the majority of Ixils and K'iche's live, it is difficult to keep the girls of impoverished families in school long enough for such things to happen. In the meantime, at an early age, girls start producing armfuls of children who will not be able to support themselves by farming (see table 8.1).

Why do people here have so many children if you don't have any land for them? I asked a leader at a development association. "It's our culture that we should not avoid pregnancy because it is according to God," he responded. "That's what my grandfather said: to avoid pregnancy is against God. That's what I believed, and now I have six children. But no more. I could get to eight or ten but no more." References to God's will are the most common response to questions about family size. Claims to be ignorant of contraception are also common. Less common is acknowledging children's value as labor, which starts as soon as they are old enough to help with chores. While I have witnessed women in dire poverty forcing five- and six-year-olds to carry firewood on tump lines, this is not typical. More often, sustained work is expected from the age of ten or so.

In the Tz'utujil Maya town of Santiago Atitlán, the most recent anthropologist to study population growth is my colleague Robert Carlsen. The Atitecos lost much of their land base to plantations in the nineteenth cen-

Table 8.1.   Projected Population and Land per Capita in Ixil Country, 1989–2020

Jurisdiction (area in km²)	1989 Population	Ha/ Capita	2011 Population	Ha/ Capita	2020 Population	Ha/ Capita
Nebaj (608)	45,438	1.34	82,101	.74	113,902	.53
Cotzal (182)	17,669	1.03	27,195	.67	34,180	.53
Chajul (1,524)	38,672	3.94	50,973	2.99	73,454	2.07
Ixil Country (2,314)	101,779	2.27	160,269	1.44	221,536	1.04
Quiché Dept (8,378)	539,669	1.55	953,027	.88	1,276,936	.66
Guatemala (108,890)	8,935,394	1.22	14,713,763	.74	18,055,025	.60

Source: Instituto Nacional de Estadística 1998 and 2012.

tury, when their population was a small fraction of what it is today. Now they have even less land per capita than the Ixils and have shifted to a mercantile economy, but not very successfully. "Atiteco existence is generally hand to mouth," Carlsen reports, "with the accumulation of economic surplus being impossible for most. Hence, children serve as one's old-age pension. Simply put, an aged Atiteco without children, or at least extended family members capable and willing to offer economic support, is likely to have to turn to begging as a means of subsistence." Children are also useful in the hewing of wood and the drawing of water, Carlsen points out, and they can be assigned to petty commercial endeavors such as selling peanuts to tourists.[46]

So progeny have economic value in three different stages:

1. From an early age, by helping with household chores.
2. From adolescence, by helping with agriculture, if the household still has any land to cultivate, and by bringing home money they have made elsewhere. Until children marry, they are expected to turn over a sizeable chunk of their income to their parents, which can turn a clutch of adolescents into an income spurt for their parents.
3. Later on, as old-age security for parents who have no other source of support.

One Ixil feminist ridiculed the "God's will" discourse with which Nebajenses answer questions about family size and told me it was a matter of cold calculation. "They think of their family like a machine of production," she scorned. "Many think like that. They look on their children as machines to exploit. They think, the more children I have, the more they can support me." Even if a man does not think in precisely these terms, he knows that there is no community or government safety net that will feed him once he becomes too old or crippled to work. Under the circumstances, having large numbers of children is survival-promoting behavior.

Once land has been fractionated, this hardscrabble strategy imposes a terrible price on the young. My impression is that most Nebaj children have socially stimulating childhoods. Troops of juveniles entertain each other and everyone else on afternoons and holidays. But as children mature, they become aware that

1. their parents have virtually no land to bequeath;
2. their parents are unable to pay for the education of more than one or two siblings, if that; and
3. they will not be able to earn enough to buy a lot for their own house, let alone build it.

Nebajenses don't use the term pyramid scheme, but I fear that many have been raised in one. They work for their parents and contribute to their welfare, but because of the number of siblings they have, they face even dimmer prospects than their parents did. They have been brought into the world as earners, on terms that will not enable them to assemble the resources necessary for their own reproduction—unless they engage in the same behavior as their parents, passing on the deficit and risk to their own quantity of children.

How do victims of a reproductive pyramid scheme escape familial exploitation? Emigration has long been a solution for surplus siblings. It is how Europe colonized the Americas. It is how capitalism has drawn labor from the countryside for industrial production. Nowadays the ease of communication and transport allows émigrés to conceive of their departure as a temporary expedient, an expedition from which they will return laden with dollars and vindication. This is how most Nebajenses conceive of their journey to El Norte; they are what scholars call sojourners or target earners, who say they will return home after saving enough for their goals.[47] Thus far many Nebajenses have indeed come home, although more of them in disappointment than flush. But the number of returnees could drop quickly. Once wage migrants are accustomed to the satisfaction of a wad of dollars in their pocket, once they are accustomed to the purchasing power of dollars and the day-to-day security these provide, it is painful to resume working for Guatemalan wages. And so many who come home to Nebaj are soon plotting their return, to rejoin the most entrancing pyramid scheme of them all—the United States of America.

The issue for Guatemalans pinning their hopes on El Norte is whether it can give them employment. From the 1980s to the 2000s, the U.S. economy absorbed increasing amounts of foreign labor. Whether that will continue is a big question. In the 1990s, Mexicans flooded California labor markets and fanned across the United States.[48] As this book goes to press, they face a wave of hostile state legislation supported by voters who fear that immigrants are taking jobs from citizens. Since 2006, stateside Nebajenses have found it more challenging to find employment, not just because of the construction downturn in 2007 and the wider economic downturn in 2008, but also because they have flooded local markets for their labor.

Even if we regard their job-seeking tribulations as temporary, any amnesty that makes it easier for them to stay in the United States will also make it easier for competitors to stay. If the United States is a healthy economy with ample room for growth, many of these people will sooner or later find enough work to improve their situation. But the American Century was produced by historical circumstances that will not be repeated. Thanks to deindustrialization, the country has lost many of the industrial jobs that enabled workers to

Village youth at the window of a passing car

experience upward mobility. Given the high cost of U.S. labor, it is hard to visualize how such jobs will be replaced with others paying as well.

In his ethnography of obligation among the Lou and what they have made of it under capitalism, Parker Shipton poses an important question: since this is capitalism, since capitalism runs on competition, and since competition creates losers as well as winners, who loses? For every microentrepreneur who builds a successful sales operation, there are others in the same line of work who lose sales. For every migrant who sends home enough remittances to buy agricultural land, what happens to the seller of that land and the seller's children?[49] Of course, there is a popular school of thought that no one has to lose. Businessmen and their media, such as *The Economist*, argue that capitalism is a tide that can lift all boats. Certainly there is no system that has multiplied private and public goods as rapidly as capitalism. Even if some classes of people lose in the short run, defenders of capitalism argue, the system functions in a way that will ultimately benefit the majority of people. One eloquent expression of this perspective is Doug Saunders' *Arrival Cities*, a defense of impoverished neighborhoods such as the Lower East Side in New York, East London, and South Los Angeles. Far from being nightmares of immiseration, Saunders argues, such neighborhoods are the only reliable escalator of the poor to higher incomes. If he is correct, encouraging Nebajenses to multiply in locales such as Homestead, with more and more new arrivals from Guatemala, will ultimately allow many of them to obtain secure livelihoods.

MINIMALIST VS. MAXIMALIST
INTERPRETATIONS OF NEBAJ'S INDEBTEDNESS

The travails of Nebajenses are not very different from what would happen to any human population that suddenly came into proximity with large amounts of cash. Any shock value in their stories would derive from our temptation, still strong in some corners of academia and political activism, to romanticize indigenous people. According to a minimalist interpretation of what I report in this book, Nebaj is a special case because of its peculiar attractiveness to the credit industry and because Ixils are so new to U.S. labor markets that they are especially vulnerable to recession. As for the two debt committees, they may represent only the most vulnerable (in some cases, self-destructive) members of the population. The 274 households in the two committees constitute less than 2 percent of the municipio's estimated 16,420 households. Even if we were to assume that debt is sinking every migrant to the United States (which is not the case), and even if we were to assume that every migrant is from a separate household (which is not the case either), my estimate of 4,041 Nebajenses in the United States would mean that only a quarter of households are being pulled down by migration debt.

Nebaj's debt committees would like to be viewed as victims of Banrural, of three savings-and-loan cooperatives, and of a swarm of microlenders and revolving-loan funds. However, blaming only financial institutions ignores the agency of the borrowers, including the considerable skill with which some Ixils have taken advantage of other Ixils. Once we bestow the term "community" on ourselves or an attractive population such as the Nebajenses, we expect the people in question to support each other. But an Ixil town is not a community in the warm, supportive sense evoked by writers of grant proposals. Ixil social life is extremely competitive, in ways that are very common among peasants. The most obvious compulsion is that land and employment are extremely scarce, and the most obvious reason for the scarcity is that the population has been growing so quickly. Population growth has ended any possibility of self-sufficient subsistence agriculture for most Nebajenses. The people of Nebaj face cruel choices, and I know many who have made deep sacrifices for each other. But when some choose narrow definitions of self-interest, exploitation reaches into the heart of neighborhoods and families.

A maximalist interpretation of Nebaj debt levels is that they are generated by the very process of seeking work in the United States. According to this reading, Nebaj's debt levels illustrate a much wider aspect of mass migration to the United States that usually escapes scrutiny but has become visible in Nebaj because Ixils are so accustomed to crafting their problems into aid appeals. Debt has escaped scrutiny not just because migrants are usually reluctant to talk about it, but also because many researchers seem to share the assumptions of the migrants themselves, that the U.S. economy has boundless capacity to employ them. As long as the U.S. economy can provide remunerative employment, debt should be a minor issue, even at exorbitant rates of interest. But Ixils were having trouble finding enough employment before the 2008 financial crisis, as were many other migrants from Central America and Mexico. It was when they began to spend long stretches on street corners that wage migration stood revealed as debt migration. In debt migration, debt not only enables the move but requires further migration, in a steady extraction of value from the sending population that probably will never be returned, appearances to the contrary such as new two- and three-story houses.[50]

It is tempting to ignore the implications of these extractions of value, or chains of debt, because of the importance of remittances to national economies, indeed the dependence of entire national economies upon them. The supposed imperatives of macroeconomics have made it easy to bypass the critical question of exactly who gets remittances, who does not get them, and the impact on the have-nots. When have-nots feel compelled to go deeply into debt to join the action, they take on great risk. And so wherever remittances have produced dependent inflationary economies, an inner ring of apparent success stories, symptomized by big spenders, could be surrounded by a less visible outer ring of losers who are unable to obtain enough employment in the United States and who could actually be losing assets back home.

Some of the most influential voices in migration scholarship seem to assume a smooth functionalism in the flow of Latin American labor, implying that American capitalism can be a win-win proposition for all concerned.[51] Fred Krissman has pointed out a crucial omission in the migrant network model of sociologist Douglas Massey that has been so popular with scholars. By focusing on symmetrical relationships between the migrants who come from the same hometown, the model takes at face value the normative ideals of the migrants themselves who, quite understandably, stress loyalty to family and locality. Focusing on migrant networks brings out the supportive, cooperative aspect of migration streams. But what about all the conflicts of interest that any serious ethnography reveals? The migrant-network model also sidelines key figures such as employers, human smugglers, and labor contractors. It implies a convergence of all relevant interests that anthropologists and sociologists have long put behind us in other realms. It underestimates the competitive quality of migration, as a chain of exploitation in which each actor—the employer, the coyote, and the migrant—passes along a risk or wager to someone else with less power who, when the wager goes bad, pays the price. Those passed-along risks or chains of debt are what are now taking the land and houses of Ixils who never set foot in the United States.[52]

In conclusion, I suggest that researchers—especially those of us viewing ourselves as immigrant-rights advocates—investigate whether migration and debt are generating each other in other Latin American localities. If the right to cross the U.S. border and seek employment is the main issue, then denying that right is how capitalism forces Latin Americans into the unregulated basement of the U.S. economy. Legalizing unauthorized immigrants should enable them to demand their rights. But if the rising number of migrants has flooded out the available employment, no amount of labor organizing is going to rescue them from their actual function in capitalism, which is to serve as the reserve army of the unemployed. To presume that more and more competing migration streams, and more and more surplus workers, will eventually achieve their place in the sun is to assume that the U.S. economy can offer near-limitless employment. This has become increasingly hard to believe.

Chapter Nine

The Right to Not Migrate

In 2004 my son Ben and I went to Tikal, the Classic Maya ruins in the Department of Petén. In the steamy lowlands of Izabal Department, the driveshaft of our bus clunked onto the pavement. With no help in sight, the driver's assistant found a machete, attacked a small tree, and cut out a forked section. This he employed to jam the drive-shaft back into place— the first time I have seen a motor vehicle repaired with a tree. Our next bus was packed. It was standing room only, with most of the seats occupied by sturdy youth whom I took to be a college excursion to a resort town ahead of us. These kids weren't rich, because if they were rich they wouldn't be on a bus. But they weren't poor either: the guys were buff and the girls were sleek.

Not a single one got off at the resort town. I wondered who they were. Our next stop was a fumigation station where everyone was ordered off so that the police could go through our luggage. Suddenly the police were not allowing the youth to reboard. There were twenty-five of them and they were from the neighboring country of Honduras. They were in Guatemala on seventy-two-hour tourist visas which prohibited them from approaching the border with Mexico. Ben and I were seeing U.S. border enforcement in action 850 miles south of the border, without U.S. immigration officials anywhere in sight. The Hondurans joined another thirty young men who had been pulled off earlier buses and who were awaiting transport in the other direction. "I'll get to the United States or die trying," one told me.

A year later, one of the first Ixils to enter the U.S. labor market, Adán, whom we met in chapter 3, decided to come home after a decade. Jobs were becoming scarce for men like him, and Americans had removed the welcome mat. "I went to the United States three times in all," Adán told me in 2007.

217

"I crossed the border fourteen times and was arrested seven times. They have me registered as a Mexican, through my fingerprints. When at last I told them that I was a Guatemalan and wanted to be repatriated to my country, they told me that I was a liar and I was a Mexican. But I have a driver's license from North Carolina, plus a Social Security number in my own name, plus English. In the end I lost my political asylum case and received a deportation order. Every year I had to visit a lawyer and pay him one or two thousand dollars. At last the lawyer just said, 'Look, there are millions like you.' So I just stopped visiting the lawyer and went ahead working like everyone else. In 2005 my wife and I were without work for two months. In 2006 we were without work for two weeks and living in a hotel, debating whether to go or stay. If we went, we would lose our life in the United States. If we didn't go, if we stayed in the United States, we would lose our business here in Nebaj, which was going downhill. Many friends advised us, stay in the U.S. because a new law will allow us to arrange our papers. Get your papers in order! But I'm a political analyst. [The U.S. authorities] are going to favor their own people, not outsiders like us. Those who stayed have still not arranged their papers. And I don't think they ever will.

"For me there are two classes of Americans—those who did not graduate from high school and those who kept going, to the universities. Those who did not graduate from high schools are the ones who do not like the immigrants, because they are on the same level. The difference is that the immigrant comes with a dream. He is only a housekeeper now, like the ones who did not graduate from high school. But he is not going to miss days, he's not going to stop working because he has a headache, and soon he's going to be the manager, unlike the Americans working on the same level.

"The Americans who like the immigrants are the doctors and lawyers, because immigrants give them lots of money. For lack of insurance, I have to pay lots of cash for medical care. The lawyers too, I have to give them lots of money. Also the business owners, those who give jobs, because we are very grateful to have work and I'm going to give my hundred percent to it. In North Carolina, at the Galey & Lord textile plant near Greensboro, there were 150 Americans—most of them white—and two Hispanics. My first month, I earned the minimum wage of six dollars an hour. After three months, I earned nine dollars an hour. After six months, I earned twelve dollars an hour and applied for a mechanic's job. After a year I earned $14.95 an hour. There were Americans who had waited more than ten years without reaching this level.

"I had many advantages in comparison with those who go north now. One is that I had a Social Security number. Many have come back. Many are still going, up to forty or fifty at a time. I tell them that they are going to suffer hunger. I tell them that there isn't work like before. It changed a lot eight or ten years ago. It used to be, you walked along the street and Americans greeted you. They said good morning, how are you? It was like here [in Nebaj]. Americans were *amable* [pleasant]. Now they look at you as a foreigner; it's turned ugly. But the guys here do not want to believe me. They think that I want to keep it just for myself. And so they go. They dream of what they see on television. They dream of buying a car. They dream of seeing what it's really like. After being there a month, they tell me that I was right."

The national police of Guatemala are usually not an imposing sight, but anti-riot squads with their helmets, shields, and billy clubs make an impression, and lately they have been descending on Nebaj more often. They showed up in the greatest number after the 2011 election, to prevent street battles for control of the town hall, but they also show up to overawe anyone who might try to stop an eviction. Here are the four evictions about which I heard the most:

- In July 2010 my friend Onofre, the one presiding over the T'al Ka'b Association and its loan program, evicted a family from its home in Cantón Xemamatzé. The house belonged to an aged man with a blind eye and a withered arm. Pedro Brito López never actually received the loan; instead, he allowed his sister to use his house document as collateral, for one of her attempts to borrow her way out of previous debts. Unlike several earlier evictions, this time Onofre played by the rules. At the courthouse, his lawyer persuaded the judge that this was a legitimate property sale, not a usurious loan. And so now, backed by seven carloads of police and judicial authorities, Onofre took possession of the house. A small decrepit adobe, it detracted from the value of the lot, so he ordered his workmen to level it. Several hours later, after the police and authorities departed, Onofre was leaving on his motorcycle when he collided with a crowd. Some say the crowd consisted of neighbors incensed at the destruction of a family's dwelling. Others say it consisted of anti-eviction activists. When I tried to clarify this point with neighbors and then with anti-eviction activists, they were both firm in pointing the finger at the other. Whoever was in the crowd, someone clubbed Onofre in the head and knocked him off his motorcycle. To defend himself, he pulled a revolver out of his backpack and fired shots in the air before fleeing on foot. When I asked him about the incident, he denied that it had occurred.
- In August 2010, Evidalia Hernández Martínez summoned supporters to stop the Multiplier credit union from seizing her house in La Pista. Come her supporters did, from Cambalám, Las Violetas, and Xemamatzé as well as La Pista. "Bring your machete, bring your club, bring your firearm," she reputedly told them, and some brought canisters of gasoline; Evidalia armed herself with a bullhorn. By the time her paltry furniture was being

removed by thirty police, they were outnumbered. Rocks flew, the police set off tear gas, and four protesters were arrested including Evidalia.

- In October 2010 sixty police, twenty soldiers, and a judge evicted Sebastián Sánchez Terraza and his family from their house in Cantón Tu Manzano for a debt to Banrural. The size of the force may have been due to the fact that, like Evidalia, Sebastián was active in one of the debt committees. When the street filled with uniformed personnel, he was not at home, and his fifteen-year-old son refused to open the door. As the police broke down the door, they set off smoke grenades and arrested the just-arrived Sebastián along with his son and wife (they were soon released as was Evidalia).

- In December 2010 thirty police, ten soldiers, and a judge evicted Rafael Chel and his family from their house in Cantón Xemamatzé for a debt to the San Miguel Chuimequená credit union. Like Evidalia and Sebastián, Rafael Chel was a leader in one of the debt committees.

I was surprised by the small number of evictions, but for financial institutions this is a last resort; they would prefer to pressure borrowers into selling a house themselves. I was even more surprised to find three evicted families back home again. I can only guess at why the banks were apparently leaving them alone. From 2010 to 2012, real estate prices were showing no sign of recovery, so if banks wanted to avoid registering an embarrassing loss, they would have to postpone selling the property. Maybe there were no buyers at any price. The banks also seemed to be treading lightly because they were afraid of violent reactions. Yet while Nebaj was full of organizations dedicated to social justice, none gave public support to the two debtor committees.[1] People facing eviction always had sympathizers, but if they owed large sums to one of the town's credit unions, whose depositors were fellow Nebajenses, they also had strong critics.

"Evidalia doesn't behave herself, she's not easy to get along with, she doesn't apologize; instead she speaks evil and gets involved with bad organizations," a neighbor remarked of La Pista's anti-eviction leader. "If you apologize because you can't pay, if you ask for more time saying that you will pay, then it's acceptable; there's no problem. But Evidalia borrowed here, she borrowed there, she asks for documents from one and then another until she has borrowed Q150,000, and then she doesn't pay. The bank, the cooperative, is helping us. If we don't pay, the cooperative is finished. He who pays his debt is doing his duty to the law of Christ. He who does not, he does not respect the Lord. That is what the Bible says." "You found that in the Bible?" I asked. "Yes, I read it in my Bible," the man replied.

Nebajenses make frequent reference to their American Dream as do migrants from elsewhere in Latin America. What they usually mean is what researchers call "target earning"—working in El Norte to amass the savings needed for a better life in Guatemala. This is the plan anyway. What Nebajenses quickly learn at the bottom of the U.S. labor force is that their goal will take longer than expected. Even if they find stable employment, two years becomes three or four, then five years or more. When they finally come home, moreover, men who earned $50 to $100 per day find it very difficult to live on wages of five dollars a day. So the only way they can maintain their customary level of expenditure is to go north again. How many will eventually finish their lives in the United States is impossible to say. But the number will include some who have promised their families to come home. Of another Guatemalan stream that began earlier than Nebaj's, from the municipio of Zacualpa, Quiché, the anthropologist Ricardo Falla estimates that 19.3 percent of Zacualpa's population has gone north, mainly to Providence, Rhode Island. He also believes that only a small percentage of this estimated emigration of 5,480—some two hundred people, or 4 percent—have come home.[2]

Any way you run the numbers, remittances are hard to argue against, not just because of their purchasing power, but because they bypass chronic limitations of aid projects.[3] Community projects always require the selection of beneficiaries, generating resentment among nonbeneficiaries. Community projects also require group finances, which become a source of contention and require management by administrators, who tend to become a privileged class living off the presumed communal idealism of the recipients. Despite the rhetoric of self-determination, aid is a subsidy that tends to produce petitions for further subsidies. Because of the tremendous wealth differences between donors and recipients, it is difficult for the latter to reciprocate, so the destructive psychology of the handout is difficult to avoid. In contrast, a microcredit is supposed to be repaid. This is one of the best things about it. Yet once generous flows of microcredit saturate a population, they mirror prevailing relations of power and add to preexisting deficits.

Another form of exchange that is more balanced than donations are remittances. Remittances are the fruit of toil, they have individual owners, and they go to the people whom the owners designate—usually kin—which spreads them more widely than any other form of international transfer. In Guatemala, according to survey research by the International Organization for Migration, a third of the population (4.5 million people) is receiving remittances from 1.4 million Guatemalans abroad, 97 percent of whom are in the United States.[4] Remittances have come to surpass any of Guatemala's exports. Everyone seems to agree that they are crucial to the country's economy.

Should we conclude that remittances are necessary for the survival of Guatemala's poor? The World Bank estimates that, from 2000 to 2006, remittances reduced the number of Guatemalans living in extreme poverty from 20.4 to 15.2 percent. For the poor who get them, remittances were paying for

38.1 percent of their consumption, which is a lot—they have become crucial. But what about the majority of the poor who do not receive remittances? Scrutiny of the World Bank data reveals that in 2006, only 23 percent of households in the bottom quintile of the Guatemalan population were receiving remittances, and only 31 percent of the households in the next higher quintile, whereas 35 percent of the households in the next two higher quintiles were recipients, along with 32 percent of the households in the top quintile.[5] So remittances are very rewarding, but their distribution could be causing income gaps to become wider. This may be even more pronounced in terms of ethnicity. Given that ladinos began migrating to the United States earlier than Mayas, remittances could be widening the difference between indigenous and nonindigenous Guatemalans.[6]

For Americans who prioritize human rights, the most salient fact about Guatemalans asking us for jobs is that they have the right to seek a better life. However, just because we are accustomed to thinking of immigrants as poor because we see them in low-paid jobs, we should not leap to the conclusion that most are poor in the context where they decide to go north. In Nebaj, the quest for higher wages in El Norte passes along risks, costs, and deficits to the most vulnerable. The most obvious example is how remittances inflate the price of real estate. If so, are remittances a solution for any except the lucky few? Not if remittances force every household who wishes to buy land to send one or more members to a foreign country. This means adding a new gauntlet to the competition for land.

According to the labor journalist David Bacon, indigenous delegates at an assembly in Oaxaca, Mexico, have demanded the "right to not migrate," the right to stay at home.[7] What that will require is an important question, and not one that will have a comfortable answer. In 2007 I assumed that the main obstacle facing Nebajenses in the United States was border and workplace enforcement. Now I believe it is lack of employment. Many more of Nebaj's migrants have been brought low by the lack of steady employment than will ever be arrested by the Migra. In 2007 I assumed that the main problem they faced was exploitative Anglo employers; now I believe that the majority of the employers who pay them sublegal wages are fellow immigrants. In 2007 I assumed that the main problem they faced was racism; now I think the main problem they face is flooded labor markets. In 2007 I assumed that the main force pulling Nebajenses north was American wages; now I think they are being pushed by debts and inflationary spirals that are being worsened by earlier migrations northward. If this is the case, the right to not migrate cannot be guaranteed simply by channeling more investment into rural livelihoods. The right to not migrate will also require preventing remittances and reproductive decisions from pressuring people to go north.

REMITTANCES BOUNCE BACK IN 2011

I am grateful to the Nebajenses for helping me analyze how aid projects, credit, land scarcity, and migration interact in their difficult lives. Anthropologists like to believe that our methodology of burrowing into a particular social group tells us about wider situations. This is what I would like to believe as well. But my argument is not based upon survey research and statistical extrapolation. Instead, my primary form of evidence consists of tales of woe. In the stories that migrants themselves tell, as Sarah Mahler has pointed out, they often exaggerate their success because they are ashamed to report failure.[8] The bias in this book has been the opposite. My methodology of tracing rumor and gossip to failed migrants led me to more tales of failure. Looking up one failed moneylender usually led to another, as did one repentant swindler to another.

This is what survey researchers call snowball sampling. It does not produce representative samples, and it can quickly lead to exaggerated estimates of

Repairing Nebaj's sixteenth-century
Catholic church

a problem because it excludes everyone who does not share in the condition being tracked from one case to the next. But my methodology did lead me to first one and then a second debt committee. The two committees represent 274 households who have fallen so far behind on their loans that they are losing property or afraid of same. We can also be sure that the migration-debt equation is not confined to Nebaj. In the Department of Chimaltenango, debt suddenly became visible when 287 Guatemalans, mainly Kaqchikel Mayas, were deported after the 2008 raid on a meatpacking plant in Postville, Iowa. According to the National Council for Attention to the Migrant, 158 returned to debts ranging from Q5,000 to Q100,000 which threaten their land and houses.[9]

Looking back on who my snowball sampling missed, I know that at least one important group is underrepresented: Nebajenses who stayed in the United States, who were stably employed there, and who continued remitting between 2007 and 2011, the years when I searched for ruination in their hometown. Such remitters would be underrepresented in the two debt committees and their households. They would also have different stories to tell than all the disappointed and injured returnees I met. Consistent remitters exist in the Baltimore–Washington corridor, in Ohio, and in southeastern Florida, and through all the despair in these pages they continued to send substantial sums. In April 2008, according to a Cotoneb director, his savings-and-loan cooperative processed 315 remittances that averaged a respectable Q4,193 or $538. Three years later, from January to April 2011, Cotoneb processed a total of 1,575 remittances that averaged Q4,989 or $640.

Impressively, this average remittance is double the average remittance ($280–$283) estimated by the World Bank and the Organization for International Migration.[10] My calculation suggests a fierce determination to remit, which can be attributed to strong family loyalty and deep indebtedness. If we apply OIM's estimate that 65.7 percent of the remittances are arriving monthly, that is, twelve times a year, then two-thirds of Nebaj migrants' families would be receiving an average of $7,680—enough to pay off a smuggling debt or to finance another migrant's trip north. Alternatively, three or four years of remittance at this level would be enough to buy a lot and build a medium-sized house.

My arithmetic, even if crude, suggests that the remittance era is not finished in Nebaj. Judging from what moneylenders and other coyotes say, fewer Nebajenses are going north because fewer are able to borrow the necessary funds. Now that lenders have lost confidence in El Norte as an investment, trips can be financed only by selling assets or borrowing from a successful relative who is already there. Successful or not, several thousand Nebajenses must still be in the United States. This seems to be the case because in 2011 they may have sent home even more money than they did three years earlier, before the crash described in chapter 5.

During my 2009 and 2010 visits, bank managers said that remittances had plunged, although by how much they did not want to say. A year later in June 2011, they were cheerful. Focusing just on Banrural, which processes the lion's share of remittances, it was receiving eleven million quetzals a month at the previous height of late 2007 and early 2008. Sustaining that rate for a year would bring Q132,000,000, or $16.9 million. Three years later, in June 2011, a Banrural manager claimed to be receiving fifteen to eighteen million quetzals a month. If the average was Q16.5 million per month, this would mean Q198,000,000, or $25.4 million, per year just to Banrural.

This is encouraging and could belie the pessimism of this book. Doomsayers such as myself have been prophesying the collapse of capitalism since the nineteenth century. Thus far we have gone to our graves but capitalism has not. The system that has destroyed so many livelihoods has an uncanny way of creating new ones. What is good about migration to the United States is that it has boosted the income of hundreds of Nebaj families, perhaps thousands. Remittances mean better food, warmer and drier houses with cement floors, and school expenses for the lucky recipients. Migrants' *suerte*, their term for luck or destiny, hinges on whether they arrive early in an economic boom or late, as the boom goes bust. I never would have heard most of the stories in this book if my interviewing had occurred before 2007. By the time I began canvassing Nebajenses about El Norte, many were running out of luck. What they have told me would also be rather different if the United States had not gone into a major recession and if the demand for their labor had not suddenly dropped. Boom-and-bust cycles magnify the difference between the lucky and unlucky, winners and losers. If a significant number of Nebajenses can withstand these cycles and achieve stable employment in the United States, some of the sad stories in this book will have more encouraging outcomes than I can give them at present.[11]

However, remittances will not necessarily continue to rebound. They could instead be spiking. The position of remitters in El Norte is so tenuous that I do not know of a single undocumented Nebajense who has obtained legal residency. The U.S. government's commitment to workplace enforcement through verifying identity could mean that, as returned migrants warned me in 2012, *papeles chuecos* (phony documents) will no longer suffice. If this is already affecting Nebajenses, a possible explanation for the remittance bounce is that the sturdiest remitters are cleaning out their U.S. bank balances before coming home. If that were not enough, getting through the Arizona desert is becoming harder. In 2012 a trio of brothers told me how they spent eight days walking from the Mexican border to within sight of

Tucson, guided by experienced coyotes from San Marcos Department, only to be picked up by a surveillance camera and nailed by a helicopter. I also heard that Mexican smugglers have stopped offering three tries across the border—supposedly they now offer just two or one.

THE NEXT STEP IN A LONG CONVERSATION

Back home, the biggest losers of the last five years will not recover their savings, land, and houses. "The sunk are going to stay sunk," one loan officer predicted. But borrowers who do not have meaningful collateral will sooner or later have their debt forgiven; they will merely return to their previous state of penury. Households raising numerous wage earners will experience income spurts as their children mature and bring home money. The prospect of earning U.S. wages, so much more profitable than any other source of income, will continue to tantalize Nebajenses. Even if it is just a mirage for all but the lucky few, remittances will keep it shimmering in the distance.

So the United States will continue to fascinate Nebaj, just as Nebaj continues to fascinate well-off Americans and Europeans. Nebaj entrances so many visitors that it has been touted as a model for just about everything. For the Guerrilla Army of the Poor, the *pueblo combatiente* (fighting people) of Ixil country incarnated a prolonged popular war that was supposed to liberate Guatemala from capitalism. Other visionaries have touted Nebaj as a stronghold of Mayan tradition, as a brave outpost of liberation theology, and as a people being transformed by the Holy Spirit. In the midst of these religious advertisements, it also became a showcase for the army's counterinsurgency program, in the form of the model villages. Simultaneously, the guerrilla movement advertised the refugees it controlled in the mountains as the Communities of Population in Resistance. Nowadays, Nebaj serves as a showcase for aid projects too numerous to enumerate. Not wishing to end the tradition, I am nominating Nebaj and its financial bubble as a showcase for the paradoxical outcome of two panaceas.

For researchers familiar with microcredit and migration, my findings will come as no great surprise. Nebaj's combination of the two merely throws their paradoxical aspects into high relief. Some anthropologists have lionized indigenous communities as bulwarks of resistance to capitalism. But the indigeneity of a town like Nebaj can make the extraction of productive assets and surplus easier, not harder. For example, the attachment of many Nebajenses to their particular locale means that, instead of just moving away from a bad situation, they will pay dearly to cling to it. Hence, for youth whose families are losing the last of their agricultural land, the consuming struggle to buy a house lot even though the price has risen to absurd levels. The very indigeneity of a place like Nebaj sets up special opportunities for exploitation. For example, because many Ixils feel insecure about their command of Spanish and distrust Spanish-language institutions, they allow more confident Ixils to step into the breach and serve as intermediaries. That makes them easier to depredate, and the depredators are often their fellow Ixils.

The influx of donations, credit, and remittances, and the shock of inflation, has heightened the contrast between haves and have-nots, and with it feelings of competition, isolation, and envy that have attracted a tidal wave of fraud. Con men target people who dream of riches in El Norte and have no way of getting there. Other victims have children in the north and more cash on their hands than before. Still other victims have sent wage earners to the United States but, paradoxically, continue to fall further behind. And so, beneath its polite and dignified exterior, Nebaj seethes with schemes to acquire wealth, which are conveyed in the language of friendship but prove to be cutthroat.

Beyond presenting Nebaj as a case for the comparative study of migration and microcredit, I have a broader ambition, to push a wider hypothesis about low-wage migration to the United States in the twenty-first century. I argue that, however beneficial chain migration is to some, it becomes a chain of exploitation of enormous cost to others. As long as the magnet economy in the United States absorbs new foreign labor, it looks like everyone can be a winner. But the Nebaj bubble was collapsing even before the U.S. bubble did. Once many migrants fail to find stable employment, it becomes apparent that inner rings of beneficiaries—employers, smugglers, and creditors who are often fellow immigrants—have been offloading risk on outer rings of migrants. These risks, conveyed through a chain of debt, cause the outer rings of migrants to lose their assets.

The world's current financial crisis is hardly the first time that the distinction between sound investments, pyramid schemes, and alchemy has suddenly vanished. Charles Kindleberger's (1989) "manias, panics and crashes" go back as far as capitalism does. The devastation wrought by Guatemalan peasants, almost exclusively upon each other, is nothing compared to the devastation wrought by our Wall Street financial wizards.[12] The magical schemes that I report in this book are an attempt to gain access to, and benefit from, the economic mysteries enriching elites. They require our attention not just because they are cultural cognition of the kind beloved by anthropologists. They require our attention because they have tragic consequences.

When people become recruiters for get-rich-quick schemes, they cash in their social relationships. Knowingly or unknowingly, they turn what Guatemalans call *confianza* and what anthropologists call trust, their lifelong relationships with relatives and neighbors, into potable wealth which is then lost. Unfortunately, seeking work in the United States can have the same consequences as seeking wealth from a volcano. Failure can quickly separate families from their assets. The colorful swindles in chapter 6 are a mere sideshow, a mere redistribution, of what really brings money into Nebaj: donations, credit, and remittances from the production and export of surplus workers. Credit, remittances, and ultimately children as a source of future remittances, are all resources being pyramided. That is, each is being leveraged in order to attract a higher rate of return. Unfortunately, the U.S. economy cannot fulfill all the hopes it arouses because it cannot provide employment for everyone attracted to it. This is how the speculative bubble surrounding migration to the United States can (pardon the mixed metaphor) vacuum a population's assets into the hands of swindlers and traffickers.

I opened this book with the long conversation that began when Europe came to America. Lately this long conversation has turned to the question of whether the poor of Central America can defend themselves from capitalism by moving to the United States and joining its reserve army of labor. The immigrant-rights movement frames the question in terms of human rights, without worrying overmuch about what awaits Central Americans who seek their rights in the United States. Ironically, this is the same question that the Sanctuary movement bracketed in the 1980s when it struggled, with some success, to legalize the flow of Salvadorans to Los Angeles. In actuality, there was precious little "sanctuary" for Salvadorans in the inner-city neighborhoods open to them. The neighborhoods were so poor and mean that Salvadoran youth, beleaguered by hostile gangs, organized the Mara Salvatrucha. At the bottom of the U.S. labor force, Central American immigrants are so likely to have their rights violated that we need to return to Parker Shipton's question at the end of the last chapter, namely, who is losing? If capitalism tends to become a pyramid scheme at the expense of newcomers in the newest bottom layer, who is coming into the scheme too late to recoup his cost by recruiting new investors?

My first inkling of this subject, some twenty-five years ago, was spotting a Mayan teenager as I sped along an endless strip of Florida retail. The kid looked unhappy and lost, but he was probably applying for a job at one of the innumerable chain restaurants. And he may have found it—this was Jupiter, north of Palm Beach, where Mayas from Huehuetenango Department have become another stripe in the American rainbow. For me, and for Guatemalans like this boy, the most important issue is whether the U.S. economy can give them a living wage. Employment is the key: if they can find a job at something like a living wage, then most of the problems raised in this book will resolve themselves or at least be manageable. Thus if you think the U.S. economy can provide tens of millions of good jobs for a rapidly growing population, then immigrants like the Nebajenses have a good chance of paying their debts, contributing to the U.S. economy, and helping their families back home. If on the other hand you think the U.S. economy faces serious constraints, that it will be an uphill struggle to provide living wages for our existing population let alone large numbers of immigrants, then our low-wage migration streams have become yet another unsustainable business model.

The "Walmartization" of the Central American poor is how one sociologist characterizes this model. According to José Luis Rocha, Central American elites collaborate in the export of large numbers of their citizens to the United States because this is the only way they can generate economic growth. Absent more productive alternatives, the upper classes of Central America are presiding over a commercial bonanza fueled by remittances. Shoppers throng to Walmart and other big-box retailers in car-strangled imitations of American suburbia. But pumping up Central American economies with remittances is rife with contradiction, Rocha argues. To compete with each other, capitalists must reduce costs, including what they pay for labor, so there are definite limits to the employment they can provide. Yet the only way to sell all the goods they produce is by increasing demand, which can be accomplished only by extending massive amounts of credit. This is the same strategy that U.S. elites have used to pump up the U.S. economy, at the cost of creating so much debt that it threatens the future of the system. Encouraging more Central Americans to come to the United States has other paradoxical implications, Rocha adds. For example, if undocumented immigrants receive amnesty, they will use legal residency to bring their closest relatives to the United States and stop remitting. That will cut off the economic transfusions on which Central American economies depend, pressuring even more people to go north.[13]

Under these difficult circumstances, is there anything outsiders can do to help people like the Nebajenses? I have probably given the impression that aid projects are pointless. For all their problems, aid projects are a worthier endeavor than many other ways that well-off people like myself spend our money. On the particular subject of aid projects in Nebaj, I tell anyone who asks that their idea will probably fare better in another town that has received less attention. This is especially true of any scheme involving credit. In 2004, I was interviewing an Ixil administrator when he suddenly argued that the entire idea of microcredit, as a bootstrap for the poorest of the poor, is a mistake. In his experience, the bulk of the poor in Ixil country (that is, below-subsistence farmers) are so unlikely to mount productive enterprises, of the kind that can pay back loans, that they would be better off with a food security strategy. Such a strategy would focus on housing upgrades, sustainable-farming projects, and incentives to encourage parents to have fewer children.[14]

The most reliable industry in Nebaj, which absorbs more labor than any other and which still provides partial sustenance to much of the population, is peasant agriculture. The U.S. and European financial crisis, still unfolding as of this writing in 2012, should remind us that our global economy is not as inevitable as exponents have claimed. It is instead the result of profit seeking by elites who have made very serious mistakes even from their own point of view. Our supposedly inevitable global economy is contingent on schemes, alliances, and structures that are anything but stable. Currently, the majority of Guatemalans are losers. They are becoming more dependent on remittances from the United States. Their country can attract investment only by keeping wages competitively low with other export platforms around the world.

But what happens in the case of a global economic collapse? Because the majority of Guatemalans are accustomed to physical labor, because many of them are still knowledgeable about agriculture, because of the tropical climate and its year-round growing season, such a denouement could turn Guatemala into a more fortunate country than the United States. Guatemala's potential for becoming sustainable, its capacity for resilience in the face of disaster, resides in its indigenous and nonindigenous farmers. That the youth of Nebaj are currently mesmerized by the dancing screens of global capitalism could prove to be as ephemeral as their supply of electricity. I'm not suggesting that a collapse of the current economic order will resurrect indigenous civilization or create a happier social order; far from it. It will be a disaster of unprecedented magnitude, with steep population declines. But peasants are likely to do better than most of the people reading this page. So even if peasant agriculture does not look very appealing at present, it is well worth supporting as an investment in the survival of the human race.

Notes

PREFACE

1. "Sobreviviente identifica pueblo arrasado en 1982 por el Ejército," *Prensa Libre*, January 26, 2012.

2. "Etnias por departamento," 2002 census, Instituto Nacional de Estadística (www.ine.gob.gt, accessed March 29, 2012), and England 2003: 733.

3. The remaining 5 percent of the municipio's population are Q'anjob'al Mayas. They live in the north and are little seen in the municipal seat. Percentages courtesy of Jacinto Matom Ceto, Unidad Técnica del Municipio, Nebaj town hall, June 18, 2012.

CHAPTER 1: GREAT EXPECTATIONS IN A GUATEMALAN TOWN

1. Researchers who have attended to debt as a critical issue in Latin American migration streams include Sarah Mahler (1995: 77–79) on Salvadoran and Peruvian immigrants on Long Island, David Kyle (2000) and Ann Miles (2004) on Ecuadorian immigrants, Sonia Nazario (2006) on Honduran immigrants, Jan and Diane Rus (2008) on Mexican immigrants from the state of Chiapas, and David Griffith (2006) on H-2 guest workers from Mexico and Jamaica. Griffith provides the broadest analysis of how American employers impose peonage-like conditions on immigrant labor to boost productivity, as well as how remittances generate further debt in sending populations and further migration. Indentured servitude has been a more obvious feature of illegal immigration from China (Kwong 1997 and Keefe 2009) than from Latin America. However, even in the case of the Fujianese who became notorious for human trafficking in the 1990s, indenture has largely been replaced by loans from relatives and friends according to the anthropologist Julie Chu (2010: 122).

I know of just two film documentaries focusing on debt in Latin American migration streams. One is Olivia Carrescia's "Una Vida Mejor" (A Better Life, 2011) on the Mam Maya town of Todos Santos Cuchumatán. The other is Greg Brosnan and Jennifer Szymaszek's "A Tale of Two Villages," about the impact of the Postville, Iowa, raid on Kaqchikel Maya migrants and their families in Chimaltenango Department (*Frontline*, Public Broadcasting Service, July 30, 2009, available at http://www.pbs.org/frontlineworld/watch/player.html?pkg=rc82guat&seg=1&mod=0, accessed February 4, 2012).

2. Prahalad 2006; Roy 2010: 64; and Elyachar 2005: 28–29.

3. Elyssa Pachico, "'No Pago' Confronts Microfinance in Nicaragua," North American Congress on Latin America (NACLA), October 28, 2009 (nacla.org/node/6180, accessed February 8, 2012), and Neil MacFarquhar, "Big Banks Draw Profits from Microloans to Poor," *New York Times*, April 13, 2010.

4. Camus 2008: 47.

5. "Race and Hispanic Origin of the Foreign-Born Population in the United States: 2007," American Community Survey Reports, U.S. Census Bureau, issued January 2010.

6. A World Bank study (Cheikhrouhou 2006: 7) has estimated that 70 percent lack legal status.

7. "Envío de remesas creció 6% en 2011," *Prensa Libre*, January 6, 2012.

8. International Organization for Migration 2011: 64. Deportations number 30,855: Eliane Portillo, "Steep Rise of Guatemalans Deported from U.S., Mexico," *Latin Daily Financial News*, December 31, 2011.

9. Sandra Valdez, "Van más de mil muertos en unidades," *Prensa Libre*, June 15, 2011.

10. Paola Hurtado, "Si la tierra se abriera y nos tragara," *El Periódico*, March 18, 2007.

11. Luis Tax, "Instan a no emigrar a EE.UU.," *Prensa Libre*, February 14, 2007, per Patrick Daniels' blog (http://jocote.org/2007/02/coming-and-going-the-great-migration-paradox).

12. "EE.UU., principal emisor: Van 281 repatriados," *Prensa Libre*, June 3, 2007.

13. "Baleado en zona 2," *Prensa Libre*, June 16, 2007.

14. "Abandonados por traficantes," *Prensa Libre*, June 13, 2007.

15. Agencia EFE, "Capturan en Chiapas a 159 chapines ocultos en tráiler," *Siglo21*, November 13, 2007.

16. "La otra puerta al sueño americano," *Prensa Libre*, November 5, 2007.

17. "Atribuyen violencia a deportados," *Siglo21*, June 1, 2007.

18. Estuardo Zapeta, "Menores de edad ¿Inimputables?" *Siglo21*, June 1, 2007.

19. "Sumidos en la pena," *Siglo21*, May 29, 2007.

20. Sullivan 1989: xxv–vi.

21. Martin Barillas, "The First Wetbacks Were Jesus, Mary, and Joseph," http://www.speroforum.com (accessed January 20, 2012).

22. Associated Press, "Ruling on Women May Spur Asylum Claims," *New York Times*, July 15, 2010. For ethnographic context on the production of asylum claims in sending populations, see Kwong 1997; Chu 2010; Piot 2010; and Mathews 2011.

23. Karger 2005: xi–xv. Immigrants hit hard by subprime fraud: Rivera 2009: 102–13.

24. Strange 1997.

25. Camus 2008: 46, 146, 157, 168; Kron 2007: 60; Burrell 2005: 16.

26. The seven are Barillas, Soloma, San Mateo Ixtatán, Santa Eulalia, San Juan Ixcoy, San Rafael La Independencia, and San Miguel Acatán.

27. Burns 1993: 7–8, 44–45, 119, 132; Burns 2000.

28. Burns 1993: xii–xiv, xlv, 28–29, 90–91.

29. Burns 1993: 115, 145, 148.

30. Burns 1993: 180–82.

31. John Lantigua, "Unraveling the Mystery of Petrona," *Palm Beach Post*, November 24, 2002; Dana Canedy, "After Conviction of Boy, Prosecutor Switches Sides," *New York Times*, November 18, 2002; Pedro Pop, "Una pesadilla con final feliz para Petrona Tomás," *Prensa Libre*, January 2, 2005.

32. Anne Marie Apollo, "Lee Trafficking Cases a Recent Chapter in County's History," January 29, 2006, and Janine Zeitlin, "The Guatemala Connection: Impoverished Nation the Root of Human Trafficking," *Naples Daily News*, January 30, 2006, plus twenty-one other stories between January 29 and February 3, 2006.

33. Judging from a 2010 survey of three thousand Guatemalan households by the International Organization for Migration (2011: 20–21), 6.9 percent of the Guatemalans benefitting from remittances were planning to emigrate in the next twelve months, which would be 277,000 people. In a book titled *Suburban Sweatshops*, the lawyer and organizer Jennifer Gordon (2005: 34–36) identifies a "two-year myth" which many Guatemalans share; they assume that, because U.S. wage levels are so much higher, they will need just a few years to earn enough money to come home in triumph. The realities at the bottom of the U.S. workforce, in Gordon's words, make them "settlers in fact but sojourners in attitude."

For a portrait of Akatek Mayas and their work in a poultry-processing plant in Russellville, Alabama, in 2008, see Thompson 2010. For a wider spectrum of Mayan experiences in the United States, see the essays in Loucky and Moors 2000.

CHAPTER 2: A TOWN OF MANY PROJECTS

1. Colby and van den Berghe 1969.

2. Ball, Kobrak, and Spirer 1999: 37–38; but see Sabino 2008: 322–25 for an argument to the contrary. The worst massacres in Ixil country occurred two weeks after Ríos Montt took power on March 23, 1982 (Stoll 1993: 111). The personable major who turned Nebaj into an army showcase was Otto Pérez Molina, who rose to the top of the army's command structure. After retiring, Pérez Molina organized the Patriot Party and in 2011 was elected president until 2016. During his first weeks in office, in January 2012, the attorney general (a holdover from the previous administration) indicted Ríos Montt for genocide.

3. Stoll 1993: 186–87.

4. For anyone who needs help with nomenclature, the key doctrines of evangelical Protestant churches are (1) the need for evangelism to save the lost from hell; (2) salvation through Jesus Christ alone, which some evangelicals call being "born

again"; and (3) biblical inerrancy. The insistence on these three points distinguishes evangelical Protestants from the leadership of the "historical" or "mainline" Protestant denominations, which are declining in the United States and have little influence in Latin America. Most Guatemalan evangelicals belong to Pentecostal denominations. That is, they accept the three doctrinal imperatives of evangelical Protestants but add a fourth of their own: the gifts of the Holy Spirit, which include speaking in tongues, faith healing, and prophecy. Some Pentecostal churches describe themselves as charismatic, but in Latin America this term usually refers to Catholics who adopt Pentecostal forms of worship and continue to identify with Roman Catholicism. Latin American Protestants rarely use the terms *protestante* and *pentecostal*; they prefer to call themselves *evangélicos* or *cristianos*.

5. Stoll 1993: 146–51, 289–94; Stoll 1996.

6. Philpot-Munson 2009: 49, 52.

7. De Leon Ceto 2006: 42–46, 88–89, 102.

8. By way of comparison, more than half the K'iche' Maya municipio of Almolonga, Quetzaltenango, identifies as evangelical (Goldin 2009: 105). For the country as a whole, a 2007 sample found that 35 percent of Guatemalans identified themselves as such (Steve Crabtree, Latin America's Entrepreneurs: Catholics vs. Protestants, July 15, 2008, http://www.gallup.com, accessed January 30, 2012).

9. Personal communication, November 22, 2011.

10. Cf. Barmeyer 2009: 220–21.

11. Cf. Kowal 2008.

12. Sampson 2003: 312–13; Sampson 2002: 4, 6. For a thoughtful ethnography of project society, although not in Sampson's terms, see Nora Haenn's (2005) book about the Calakmul Biosphere Preserve in Mexico.

13. For the implications of the religious "free market" in Latin America, see Andrew Chesnut's (2003) analysis of the competition between Pentecostal Protestants, charismatic Catholics, and African-inspired spiritists in Brazil.

14. For the Ixil area between 1978 and 1996, three different truth commissions tabulating incidents and body counts came up with totals of 4,609, 4,028, and 5,423 killings (Ball 1999: 238). On the basis of a sampling procedure, which Carlos Sabino (2008: 376–78) questions, Patrick Ball (1999: 250) estimates a total of 16,655 victims in the Ixil area between 1981 and 1983. When I analyzed census shortfalls in the Ixil area (Stoll 1993: 232–33), I came up with a missing population of 15,000. One source of ambiguity is the term *asesinatos* (killings) and whether it includes people who died of hunger and illness while hiding from army offensives.

15. A 1999 analysis by the Ministry of Agriculture and Grazing found that 85 percent of Nebaj's surface area should be kept in forest, 10 percent was suitable for agroforestry, and 5 percent was suitable for "cultivation subject to limitations." More than half of the municipio's surface was being cultivated, however (Aubry and Servado 2004: 14). Even in 1979, when Nebaj's population was less than half what it is in 2012, only 12 percent of the 4,142 farms in the national agrarian census were classified as *familiares*: that is, at seven hectares or larger, considered sufficient to support a family (Stoll 1993: 226).

I have an agronomist friend who dissents from pessimistic assessments of Ixil country's agricultural potential. He argues that, with careful organic techniques focusing on local varieties, many Ixil farmers could live far better than they do at present. For a spirited defense of the sustainability of traditional Mayan agriculture (although in a very different biological zone), see Liza Grandia (2012: 83–116) on Q'eqchi' Maya lowlanders in Petén Department. Grandia argues that the imposition of private property on customary management is responsible for much of the environmental degradation attributed to population growth.

CHAPTER 3: NEBAJ GOES NORTH

1. Benjamin Colby and Pierre van den Berghe (1969: 131–32) estimated that a fifth of the adult male population was leaving for the plantations every month, with as much as 30 to 40 percent absent at any one time.

2. Steverlynck 2003: 43.

3. Steverlynck 2003: 29, 35, 42–44, 47, 61.

4. Here is how I arrive at my estimate. According to managers, in April 2008 the Banrural branch in Nebaj received 2,338 remittances, and the Cotoneb cooperative received 315, for a total of 2,653. Estimates from two other financial institutions and two private agents would add 1,225 more remittances that month, for a total of 3,878. If half the remitters are sending money twice a month, one-quarter are sending once a month, one-eighth are sending four times a month, and one-eighth are sending once every two months, the sending population would be 3,031. If a quarter of the Nebajenses in the north are unable to remit any money at all, the total population in the United States would be 4,041. The slightly different estimate I made in Stoll 2010: 141 was due to a computational error.

Obviously this calculation hinges on my estimate of the frequency of remittance and the percentage of migrants who never remit. For another go at this problem, let's take the frequency of remittance reported by the International Organization for Migration on the basis of its 2010 survey of three thousand Guatemalan households. According to the survey, 65.4 percent of households receiving remittances said they received remittances once a month, 6.8 percent said they received remittances every two months, 4.9 percent said they received remittances every three months, 3.7 percent said they received remittances every four months, 4 percent said they received remittances every six months, and 3.7 percent said they received remittances less than once a year. If Nebajenses remitted in the same proportions, the 3,878 remittances received in April 2008 would have been sent by a total of 3,162 people.

According to the same table (2011: 141), IOM estimates 1,263,764 remitters. Elsewhere in the same report (2011: 54), it estimates 1,409,548 remitters. Factored into IOM's estimate of 1,637,119 Guatemalans living abroad, either 77 percent or 86 percent would be remitting. Applying these two percentages to 3,162 people remitting to Nebaj, the total number of Nebajenses living abroad would be 4,106 or 3,677.

According to IOM, 97 percent of Guatemalans living abroad are in the United States; so are most Nebajenses living abroad.

5. Based on a survey of three thousand households, the International Organization for Migration (2011: 54) estimates that 72.4 percent of Guatemalans living abroad are male and that 77.7 percent are between fifteen and thirty years of age. In the case of Nebaj, with its comparatively recent migration stream, an even higher percentage are probably male.

6. My calculation is based on the information that Nebaj bank managers have shared with me. In April 2008, Banrural received 2,338 remittances and Cotoneb received another 315, for a total of 2,653. The total amount received by Banrural that month was Q10,843,000 and by Cotoneb Q1,321,000, for a total of Q12,164,000. These same figures give an average remittance of Q4,584, or $588. If this monthly total was an average total for the peak year June 2007–May 2008, it would mean that Q145,968,000 was received by just these two institutions. During the same period, other Nebaj agencies estimated that they were receiving an additional 1,225 remittances every month. Thus, of the estimated 3,878 remittances Nebaj was receiving monthly, 68.4 percent corresponded to Banrural and Cotoneb, and 31.6 percent to the other agencies. If these other agencies were receiving the same size remittances as Banrural and Cotoneb, the total remittances would be Q213,404,000, or $27,359,000, for the peak year in 2007–2008.

7. Per the 2008 population of 73,216 estimated by the Instituto Nacional de Estadística (2012). For comparison, consider the K'iche' Maya municipio of Zacualpa in southern Quiché Department. The anthropologist Ricardo Falla (2008: 28–38) estimates that by 2006, 4,603 men and 877 women had left Zacualpa for the United States. This would be 19.3 percent of the estimated population of 28,391. Falla also estimates that the 5,480 Zacualpans in the United States sent home Q138 million ($17.7 million) from July 2005 to June 2006. This would represent $623 for each man, woman, and child in the municipio. Migration from this corner of Quiché Department to the United States began much earlier than migration from Ixil country, around 1984 (Foxen 2007: 97).

8. Per capita income is challenging to estimate. It is especially misleading when peasants are growing much of their own food supply. For what it is worth, a credit study (Faceta Central Desarrollo Empresarial 2002: 3) estimated the per capita income of Nebajenses in the year 2000 as $140 to $175. If so, remittances could have tripled the amount of money in circulation.

9. Nebajenses refer to U.S. immigration enforcement as the Migra, and so will I. Near the border this would usually mean the U.S. Border Patrol. In the interior it would usually mean Immigration and Customs Enforcement (ICE). Both agencies report to the Department of Homeland Security.

10. One of the brokers sentenced in a 2009 Chamblee case, Lin Chen, "testified that only 1 in 100 workers for whom she found jobs were legal. She also testified that restaurant owners liked more recently arrived workers as they did not know as much about the system and could be paid less than illegal immigrants who had been in the United States for a longer period of time" (Department of Justice Press Release, U.S. Attorney's Office, Northern District of Georgia, April 28, 2009).

11. Steverlynck 2003: 43.

12. Angee and Hernández 2007: 21–22.

13. L. Ismatul, "De Estados Unidos a los Cuchumatanes," *Siglo21*, August 15, 2003.

14. Deborah Sontag, "Immigrants Facing Deportation by U.S. Hospitals," *New York Times*, August 3, 2008, and "Jury Rules for Hospital that Deported Patients," *New York Times*, July 28, 2009.

15. Eliane Portillo, "Steep Rise of Guatemalans Deported from U.S., Mexico," *Latin Daily Financial News*, December 31, 2011.

16. Julia Preston, "Illegal Worker, Troubled Citizen and Stolen Name," *New York Times*, March 22, 2007.

17. Another example of stateside impunity is the lack of punishment for the murderers of Vicente "Chente" De Leon Brito, Nebaj's most well-known homicide victim in the United States. In 2006, Chente lived with four Nebajenses in the Washington suburb I'm calling Pleasantville. He was an ex-soldier of thirty-seven years, with a wife and four children back home, which made him older than the majority of Nebajenses on the scene. A housemate named Diego was outside drinking with three friends when an altercation started and Diego took refuge inside. When the other three came to the door, Chente told them to get lost. They pounded on the door, so he confronted them a second time, whereupon one of the three slipped a knife through the opening and stabbed him repeatedly in the stomach. One of the three, Andrés Terraza Brito, spent six months in jail before the U.S. authorities let him go. Nebajenses differ over whether it was he or another of the drunks that night who sank the knife into Chente. Both men were back in Nebaj by 2012, but no charges have been filed.

18. *Times Reporter* (New Philadelphia, Ohio), July 19, 2007, and March 25, May 28, and December 18, 2008.

19. *Times Reporter*, February 23 and March 11, 2008.

CHAPTER 4: INDENTURE TRAVEL

1. In Antonio's village of Acul, two girls who were pregnant identified him as the father. With the help of his family, I forwarded photographs and hair samples to the Forensic Science Center at the Pima County Office of the Medical Examiner in Tucson, Arizona. The Pima County morgue receives hundreds of bodies from the border-crossing routes south of Tucson. It is also known for its efforts to identify those remains. In this case, the center was unable to make the match. In 2011 Antonio's mother heard from the Nebaj rumor mill that Antonio had been spotted in Miami. Supposedly he was *tomando* (drinking, for Nebajenses a sufficient explanation of failure), but he identified himself and said that he wasn't communicating with his family because "for them I am now dead." I was unable to trace the rumor because the people spreading it said that their stateside relatives were afraid of giving out their telephone numbers and being deported.

Some Nebajenses in the United States just disappear, and one possible explanation is that they view their debts as hopeless. Given that some moneylenders will forgive interest if a migrant dies, a youth's decision to stop communicating with his family is arguably in the same category as altruistic suicide to collect life insurance. But cutting off contact also means abandoning a financial obligation. In another case that I have yet to figure out, a failed Nebaj moneylender sent a son north in a last-ditch effort to reestablish her cash flow; another son had gone north earlier, only to brawl with other migrants and be deported. In June 2010, the youth telephoned his father to say that he was sending money for Father's Day. Then he failed to call again with the code needed to pick up the remittance. When his parents called his cell phone, it was answered by an unknown Ixil youth who said he knew nothing. Two years later the son had yet to communicate; the local police have no unidentified bodies matching the son's description. The only rumor I could pick up from the Ixil grapevine was that the son was living in Alexandria, Virginia, and drinking.

2. Cf. Sarah Mahler (1995: 78) who uses the term "life-price" and Ruth Gomberg-Muñoz (2011: 54) who notes that the result is "much like an indentured servant."

3. A *huevón*, derived from the colloquial *huevo* (egg) for testicles, is a man who is worthless. *Hombres hombres* are manly men or real men.

4. "They take the house, they take the land, leaving the poor without anything," exploded an Ixil elder during a conversation. "And when migrants reach the United States, they are arrested by Migration. Why doesn't the United States arrest the coyotes? I read *Prensa Libre* every day, and I've never seen a report of this happening. Why doesn't the United States come to Aguacatán to investigate? That's where the anthill is."

5. Spener 2009: 90–91, 145–46, 154, 171.

6. Steverlynck 2003: 46.

7. Nebajenses were victimized for years before they worked out reliable arrangements for tiptoeing into the United States. Around 2001 the cooperatives of Quiché Department—organized by Catholic activists, repressed during the violence, and chronically in arrears—hosted a big impressive Guatemalan who claimed to be a labor contractor recruiting seasonal guest workers for agribusinesses from California to Florida. With him everything would be legal; each worker would get a visa and go to the United States seated with dignity in an airliner. Two hundred people showed up at a single meeting, and many of them handed over their personal documents and Q3,500 application fees. None of them ever went because it was a scam.

For years I heard about schemes to trick tourist visas out of the U.S. embassy. In one case around 2002, a ladino from Antigua named Elwyn offered to obtain invitations from the United States in exchange for Q4,000 in advance and another Q45,000 once the visa was in hand. The pitch was probably that the Nebajenses would tour as a cultural and/or human rights delegation. Six people joined the scheme and actually reached the United States, including my source, but not the next group, who lost their advance payments.

Paying in advance was an open invitation to being cheated. One woman ruined in this way was Doña Elena, a housekeeper who in October 2006 met an appealing foreigner named Señor Jesús. Señor Jesús said that he came from Spain. His accent was not Guatemalan; he looked like a gringo but was short and bald. He had a nice car; a K'iche' Maya assistant from Almolonga, Quetzaltenango; and a housekeeper from Cotzal with whom he lived in a rented house. Señor Jesús had two propositions for Elena and other Ixil clients. First, if they gave him Q100,000, he would give them back Q500,000. Second, he would take them to the United States. In Elena's case, he would take her two nieces and her two daughters to the United States in an airplane, without subjecting them to the dangers of walking through the desert. Even though the four were village girls without much schooling or experience outside the house, Jesús happened to have a brother and sister in the United States who would give them a home and find them work, probably in agriculture.

To send her two nieces and her two daughters north, Elena gave Señor Jesús Q200,000 ($25,600), more than she could hope to earn for the rest of her life. Where did she get all this money? The K'iche' from Almolonga helped her turn the only land that she owned into collateral for a Q50,000 loan from Banrural. Elena borrowed the rest from friends and moneylenders. When Señor Jesús took delivery of the cash, he put it between his thumbs and kissed it as he presented it to his household saint—a desk-size image of Christ carrying the cross. Señor Jesús said that he would return to Nebaj on November 9 in order to take the girls. Elena and her brood waited all day on the 9th of November, then on the 10th, 11th, and 12th, and of course he never returned. Why didn't she go to the courthouse to file a complaint? The only document that she had was her three-year loan agreement with Banrural. She had no receipt from Jesús, nor any idea of his surname or location.

8. Spener 2009: 180, 186, 189.

9. Jacinto de Paz is struggling to support a wife and five children on eighteen cuerdas of land (.8 hectares) that is too steep to grow anything. In 2009 a prosperous-looking Huehueteco in a pickup truck promised him a job in El Norte. "I'm going to find you work," he told Jacinto. After coming all the way through Mexico and the desert, Jacinto spent three days at a safe house in Phoenix. After he and five other men from Quiché Department paid for their trip, the Mexican in charge of the safe house drove them to a busy commercial avenue and told them he would come right back. He never did. After four hours, their plight (no money, food, or orientation) attracted the Migra. The men told the officers exactly who they were, and within a few days they were back in Guatemala. Jacinto does not know the name or even the town of the Huehueteco who took his money. All he has is a telephone number that no one answers. Now he owes Q2,100 every month to a savings-and-loan coopera-tive for the next two and a half years. He has no way of earning more than half this amount, he's not giving his wife money for expenses, his children are going hungry, and he's falling further behind with Q20-per-day late fees. It looks like he will lose his house. A few days before Jacinto told me of his plight, another Huehueteco was in the town square, telling him and his friends that he could get them to the United States in twelve days and place them in a job at a company.

10. Spener 2009: 145–46, 156–58.

11. Randal C. Archibold, "Victims of Massacre in Mexico Said to Be Migrants," *New York Times*, August 25, 2010, and Jason Beaubien, "Drug Cartels Prey on Mi-grants Crossing Mexico," National Public Radio, July 7, 2011. Mexico's National Commission on Human Rights estimates that some twenty thousand migrants, mainly Central Americans, are being kidnapped and held for ransom each year (Fernández de Castro 2012).

12. Pedro Ricardo Santiago Raymundo (1968–2010) was an ex-EGP combatant. During his sojourns in Mexico in the 1980s and 1990s, he learned how to pass as a Mexican.

13. Foxen 2010: 77–78 and Foxen 2007: 98, 100, 138, 147–50.

14. Taylor, Moran-Taylor, and Rodman Ruiz 2006: 58–59.

15. Rus and Rus 2008; Mines 1981: 128–29; Reichert 1981: 61; Wiest 1984: 123, 129, 132; Quinones 2007: 11, 205.

16. Cf. Fletcher 1999.

17. Personal communication, June 6, 2011. For the debate over the impact of remittances on rural Mexicans, see Massey et al. 1987: 236–41; Binford 2003; the response to Binford by Cohen, Jones, and Conway 2005; Cohen 2004; and Heyman et al. 2009. For the impact of remittances sent by H-2 guest workers in Jamaica as well as Mexico, see Griffith 2006. For the astonishing case of Intipucá, El Salvador, the majority of which has decamped to Washington, D.C., see Villacrés 2009. For a perceptive analysis of how proletarianization in the United States supports middle-class consumption patterns in Central America, confusing all concerned as to their social class, see Baker-Cristales 2004 and Schmalzbauer 2008.

18. Nevins 2002: 169; Griffith 2005: 55–56; Valentine 2005: 9–13; Castañeda 2007: 29; Rodríguez 2007: 239.

CHAPTER 5: BORROWERS, MONEYLENDERS, AND BANKS

1. As quoted in "La familia en Guatemala pasa por tiempos duros," *Prensa Libre*, May 18, 2008.

2. Colby and van den Berghe 1969: 133; Nachtigall 1978: 141–42.

3. Economists refer to this problem as moral hazard—the tendency to disregard risk if someone else will absorb the losses. In 2002, aid consultants noted the problem of multiple borrowing, as well as a widespread attitude that borrowers were not obliged to repay loans, and the obvious need for a credit bureau. They counted fourteen institutions in Nebaj giving credit. Successful programs were loaning to individuals, not groups, and they were requiring property as collateral. As for loans between individuals, a close friend would charge 5 percent per month, a known person (*conocido*) 10 percent per month, and one with less relationship 15 percent per month. The fifty-page report never mentioned using loans to go to the United States (Faceta Central Desarrollo Empresarial 2002: 14, 34, 40).

4. "While there were guidelines that mothers should not be participating in other [microcredit] projects," an aid coordinator told me of her time in Nebaj, "I observed that many women who were in our project were also receiving loans from other institutions. Payback rates were fairly low, and many women just couldn't make their payments. Some confessed that they were waiting for relatives in the United States to send money to them so that they could make their payments. This was not the intention of our organization. We were hoping that the small loans would be able to aid them in creating a sustainable business, not become dependent on a chain of loans.

... My experiences have led me to believe that 'lending' in general in poor regions is a very difficult concept to teach and perhaps not the best way to go about creating change."

5. Petition to President Alvaro Colom, dated October 13, 2008, and signed by seven officers. The group changed its name several times, but the most descriptive is "the Organization of Women Affected by the Economic Crisis in the Ixil Area."

6. The other debt committee was still extant in June 2011. The Asociación de Desarrollo Integral para Familias Afectadas por la Crisis Económica en el Area de Ixil (ADIFACE) was affiliated with the Coordinadora Nacional Indígena y Campesina (CNOC or CONIC). ADIFACE asked the Colom administration for debt relief, without success, and also solicited income-generating projects. According to a March 7, 2011, petition, its fifty-three families claimed a cumulative debt of Q2,657,556 (or an average of Q50,142.57 per family). But this figure included only debts to institutions. ADIFACE decided to exclude its members' debts to moneylenders, according to the group's president Rafael Chel, because the government has no right to intervene in debts between individuals. Actually, Guatemalan law is the reverse: while institutions try to operate within legal parameters so their loans will be recoverable through a court of law, the 10 percent rate charged by moneylenders is illegal, even if it has never been prosecuted by a Nebaj court.

7. I should not have been surprised—anthropologists have long reported the wheeling and dealing of peasants. Just for Guatemala, see Smith 1977; Smith 1984; Sol Tax's (1951) *Penny Capitalism*; and Sheldon Annis' (1987) *God and Production in a Guatemalan Town*, the last for its *de suelo al cielo* ("from dirt to heaven") stories told by the evangelical entrepreneurs of San Antonio Aguas Calientes, a Kaqchikel Maya town near Antigua.

8. Vélez-Ibáñez 2010: 44–45, 54.

9. Many Nebajenses do not want to borrow from a bank, in the words of an evangelical pastor, "because the bank demands many requirements including your NIT number; your SAT number, which many do not have because it requires making four tax payments a year; a commercial license, which costs money; how much you've taken in and how much you've spent; and an inventory of your merchandise. Also because, when there's an emergency, getting money out of a bank requires lots of time." In the pastor's case, he owns a passenger van whose operation he entrusted to a son. One day the son was fighting off sleep and gave the wheel to his fare collector, who ran over a child. The police arrested the son, not the fare collector, who was a juvenile. Getting the son out of jail required Q15,000 for the dead child's parents and Q15,000 for the lawyer, which the pastor borrowed from friends before taking out a bank loan.

The anthropologist Thomas Dichter (2007a: 13) explains why moneylenders have more legitimacy than reformers think they should: "In a world of relative isolation, based on a family economy ... whatever is 'outside' is alien. Trust can only exist among known and familiar entities. Thus the law, and formal institutions such as banks, are distant abstract strangers. To be in debt to such outsiders is thus fundamentally different from being in debt to a friend, a family member, or even a landlord. With these creditors one understands the rules of the game and thus, even though one gives up a degree of control, it is better than the total loss of control involved in a debt to a large, formal, far away institution such as a bank. . . . Thinking about debt in this socio-cultural way might also reveal . . . that moneylenders are not the villains they seem, at least not to those they are presumed to 'exploit.' . . . [M]oneylenders are often viewed benignly because they combine several things at once. They are near and distant, known entities but not 'friends.' As a result there is less loss of face incurred in dealing with a moneylender, less ambiguity, less ambivalence. Most important, they give fast service and are available. In an emergency moneylenders may even lend needed cash in the middle of the night."

10. Easy credit did not just pull down Nebajenses who lost their wager on El Norte. It also ruined people who succumbed to their desire for bigger houses, furnishings, sound systems, computers, and motor vehicles. They pledged their real estate as collateral, then took out more loans to pay for the first loans, this time against the real estate of their spouse and other trusting relatives, until the monthly payments sucked away their incomes, property, and social relationships.

11. For Mexico, see Mines 1981: 128–29; Reichert 1981: 61; Massey et al. 1987: 236; Grimes 1998: 77; Bacon 2006: 137; Smith 2006: 38–39; and Quinones 2007: 11, 206. For Ecuador, see Kyle 2000: 71, 103, and Jokisch 2002: 526. For Pakistan, see Ballard 2003: 41. For Guatemala, see Rodríguez and Hagan 2000: 205; Steverlynck 2003: 50; Foxen 2007: 98, 288; Camus 2008: 182–83; and Steigenga, Palma, and Girón Solórzano 2009: 163.

12. Unfortunately there is no registry that accurately records sale prices. Tax declarations are undervalued to reduce tax assessments. A cuerda in Ixil country is equivalent to .108 acres and .044 hectares, with a hectare equivalent to 22.72 cuerdas and an acre equivalent to 9.26 cuerdas.

13. How much is due to background inflation? If we compound annual inflation rates recorded by the Banco de Guatemala (http://www.banguat.gob.gt/inc/ver.asp?id=/pim/pim01&e=98846, accessed July 15, 2012), Q1 in 1979 inflated to Q19.58 by 2007. Thus a cuerda of land in Vicalamá selling for Q10 in 1979 would be worth Q195.8 by 2007. If the cuerda sold for Q50,000 in 2007, this indicates an additional inflation rate of 25,540 percent. In 1973, Horst Nachtigall (1978: 92–93) heard about a wider range of land prices in Nebaj, from Q5 to Q100 per cuerda depending on location and quality. Thus if the cuerda of land in Vicalamá was so attractive that it actually sold for Q100 in 1979, background inflation would raise its price to Q1,958 by 2007. If the cuerda then sold for Q50,000 in 2007, this would indicate an additional inflation rate of 2,554 percent.

14. Faceta Central Desarrollo Empresarial 2002: 4.

15. Aside from Banrural, Cotoneb, and T'al Ka'b, the most active foreclosers were the San Miguel Chuimequená and Multiplicador savings-and-loan cooperatives, which opened handsome new offices just before the 2008 crash. Given how freely Nebaj's credit institutions loaned money, you may ask, were they intending to grab property? With the possible exception of T'al Ka'b, I detected no interest in acquiring or speculating in real estate. After 2008, lenders tightened their rules to include scrutinizing spouses to make sure that they were not heavily indebted, accepting only houses as collateral for loans rather than agricultural land, and requiring relatives to

assume full responsibility for any loan backed by their property. For elderly parents who were about to lose the family land they had pledged as collateral, Cotoneb started asking their adult children to protect their inheritance by taking on the debts—but now with the added guarantee of a compra-venta agreement.

CHAPTER 6: PROJECTS AND THEIR PENUMBRA—SWINDLES

1. Personal communication, January 6, 2010.

2. Licenciado = a person who holds a license, in Latin America a university degree between a bachelor's and a master's.

3. One of Nebaj's first Ixil lawyers, Pedro Santiago De León, investigated AVIDESGUA at the request of two Ixil building contractors. According to the contractors, the president of the Kumool ("Compañero" or "Comrade") Association, Joel Maximiliano Itzep, extracted more than Q100,000 ($12,800) from each of them. Their "commissions" were to secure the contracts to build hundreds of houses, on each of which the contractors stood to earn Q20,000 ($2,550). After this scam was exposed, the officers of the four other associations also came under suspicion of profiting from AVIDESGUA, but without any evidence of which I am aware. According to Santiago De León, Reyes also obtained large sums from victims in Chajul, Cunén, Chimaltenango and Cobán.

4. For a rich analysis of migration as a network of family obligations and troubles, see the anthropologist Karen Richman's (2005: 64) ethnography of Léogane, Haiti, and its migration stream to the United States. The families of Ti Rivyè "organize themselves as producers of people for export, consumers of migrants' remittances and managers of migrants' assets in people and things." So onerous are the obligations incurred by migrants that her principal informant, Little Caterpillar, abandons Vodou for Protestantism, which does not protect him from being killed by the sorcery of his feuding relatives.

5. "Occult economy" is the term chosen by anthropologists John and Jean Comaroff (1999: 284, 297) to describe the explosion of pyramid schemes, witchcraft scares, and Pentecostal revivals in post-apartheid South Africa. Occult economies seek material gain through magical means. According to the Comaroffs, they are powered by "glimpses of . . . vast wealth" multiplying in mysterious ways and a "dawning sense of chill desperation" that one is being left behind. Hence the fantasies of escape captivating Togo, an overpopulated dictatorship in West Africa where remittances have become as much as half the gross national product. According to Charles Piot (2010: 4, 77), cybercafes are "filled night and day with people connecting to various elsewheres," and the U.S. government's visa lottery has inspired an entire industry of speculation. As many as one in six of every Togolese applied for the 2004 lottery. "Affinity fraud," of which the largest example is Bernie Madoff's swindling of his fellow Jews of up to $20 billion, is particularly rife in the American Bible Belt and the heavily Mormon state of Utah ("Fleecing the Flock," *Economist*, January 28, 2012).

6. The Millionaire is identified as José Grave Gómez in the only press report on the Zacualpa uprising I have been able to find (Oscar Toledo, "Estafan a más de 5 mil

campesinos," *Prensa Libre*, September 15, 2007). However, the Millionaire becomes José Grave Simaj in Enrique Naveda's later and more detailed account ("La gran estafa," *El Periódico*, February 17, 2008). Four years earlier, two ANECOF representatives from Zacualpa who reported being robbed were identified as José Grave Gómez and Manuel Grave Simaj (*Prensa Libre*, October 23, 2004).

7. According to Naveda as well as Diane Nelson (2009) and Patricia Foxen (2010), the contributions demanded by El Millonario escalated from Q500 to much larger sums. Simultaneously, his vision evolved from a development project funded by foreigners into a deal with the Devil at a local hilltop shrine. He demanded not only larger contributions—to obtain which, followers mortgaged their properties—but ever more exhausting religious devotions, such as peregrinating on knees, an old folk Catholic ritual which sent some of his followers to the hospital. Pilgrims arrived from all over southern Quiché Department. At the center of the movement in the municipios of Zacualpa, Joyabaj, and Chinique, followers sold off timber and land and took out loans, with the result that some lost their houses (Foxen 2010: 79–80). When I visited in June 2012, various Zacualpans remembered José Grave as a shoeshine boy from the hamlet of Pasajoc who opened a small pinball/video parlor before disappearing for several years and returning as a man of wealth and allure.

The first social researchers to happen upon ANECOF may have been Jan and Diane Rus in Chiapas, Mexico. In 2007 they learned that a young friend in the Tzotzil Maya municipio of Chamula had personally signed up 1,100 friends and neighbors for a strange organization of which they'd never heard—the Asociación de Apoyo a los Necesitados de un Solo Corazón y Fe. What their confidant told them was not reassuring. He was promising his new members a huge financial reward that would come from supposed benefactors in Europe—but only after they gave him a substantial fee and only if they met regularly to pray. The young man's family smelled a rat; they were afraid that 1,100 friends and neighbors would show up at their house to demand a refund. If worse came to worst, their boy could get lynched.

As this situation unfolded, journalist Abenamar Sánchez (2008) broke the story in the Chiapas newspaper *Cuarto Poder*. In a house without a sign, in the sleepy village of Bochil, the reporter found a man who could explain ANECOF. Lorenzo López Ruiz, a short man with a cell phone and three assistants, identified himself as the local coordinator for a network of affiliates in thirty-eight municipios as well as across the border in Guatemala. With the help of a laminated sheet of frequently asked questions, he explained that Germany has given other countries like Japan and the United States a boost through gifts of money. Now it's the turn of Chiapas and Guatemala because these are the poorest places in the world. A hundred thousand people had signed up in Chiapas and more in Guatemala, López Ruiz claimed.

ANECOF continues to be headquartered in the border settlement of Pacayalito where it seems to have originated at the end of the 1990s. Judging from what neighbors told Sánchez, the organization was started by two coffee pickers. One, a Guatemalan named José Pascual Vicente, came to Pacayalito as a war refugee. Judging from the name, he is a Q'anjob'al from Huehuetenango Department. I have heard nothing of his whereabouts. The other, Manuel García Silvestre, continues to serve as ANECOF's president and is now a wealthy man (Sánchez 2010). Back in Nebaj, the village coordinator Victor told me that his local committee was retaining Q50 of every Q500 application fee it received for travel expenses. The *sub-jefatura* in San Juan Ixcoy, Huehuetenango, was retaining another Q50 for expenses, while Q400 was going to the *jefatura* (headquarters) in Pacayalito, Chiapas.

At a 2004 conference sponsored by the Organization of American States, ANECOF was credentialed as a representative of the Mayan people (Consejo Permanente de la Organización de los Estados Americanos, Comisión de Asuntos Jurídicos y Políticos, Grupo de Trabajo encargado de elaborar el Proyecto de Declaración Americana sobre los Derechos de los Pueblos Indígenas, Tercera Reunión de Negociaciones para la Búsqueda de Consensos, April 28 to 30, 2004).

8. "Liberan a seis retenidos: Comunitarios de Raxruhá los acusen de estafa," *Nuevo Diario*, May 9, 2012. According to this story, thousands of inhabitants held four Guatemalans and two Mexicans hostage for four days in the municipio of Raxruhá, Alta Verapaz, just south of Petén Department, before they were liberated by the police. The story does not mention ANECOF, but Victor assured me the hostages were ANECOF leaders.

9. For an ethnography of the appeal of multilevel marketing in Latin America, particularly the vitamin scheme Omnilife, see Cahn 2011.

10. I say "usually" because, in the case of AVIDESGUA, the president of the Kumool Association was collecting commissions from the two building contractors. In Chiapas, Abenamar Sánchez reports that ANECOF leaders are displaying wealth in the form of large houses, motor vehicles, and business enterprises.

11. Charges were dropped against Vinicio Cerezo, but as of 2012, Alfonso Portillo is fighting extradition to the United States, and Jorge Serrano Elías has found haven in Panama.

CHAPTER 7: LOSING HUSBANDS TO EL NORTE

1. Patricia Foxen (2007: 101) also has come across the failure to inform close relatives in the "highly secretive and swift" departures of K'iche' Mayas from southern Quiché Department to Providence, Rhode Island.

2. For a detailed portrait of a wife's decision-making process, including how debt propelled her to follow her husband northward but landed her in a crowded labor market where she was exploited by fellow migrants, prompting her return to Zacualpa, Quiché, with meager results, see Falla 2008: 189–314. For an ethnography on how the departure of male wage earners for El Norte leads to the abandonment of mothers and children and motivates their own journeys northward, see Nazario 2006.

3. For the growing literature on women in Mesoamerican migration streams to the United States, see the work of Victoria Malkin (2004), Denise Segura and Patricia Zavella (2007), and Michelle Moran-Taylor (2008a). Patricia Foxen (2007), Manuela Camus (2007), and Judith Hellman (2008) are eloquent on how stay-at-home wives deal with the lack of remittances and other conflicting demands. Turning to a comparable migration stream from highland Ecuador, Brad Jokisch (2002: 542) describes the "unsteady remittance economy" for stay-at-homes in the following terms: "[W]hile migrants are paying down the debt and making substantial purchases, remittances commonly

range between $250 and $1,000 per month. After money is dedicated to these priorities, remittances may provide only $50–$125 monthly for daily expenses. Numerous women reported that migrant remittances decline after major purchases have been made, dwindling to a mere subsistence remittance. If the migrant does not send a minimum of $100 per month, then the value of his labor in Ecuador has not been replaced, and his family will continue to lead meager lives. In other words, international migrant households may not receive many of the expected benefits. . . . Notably, hundreds of women in the region have been abandoned by their husbands living in the United States; some women have not heard from their spouses for years, or receive only annual holiday gifts."

4. Kron 2007: 77; Skolnik, Lazo de la Vega, and Steigenga 2012.

5. Ehlers 1990: 133–35, 149–52.

6. Lincoln 1945: 78–79, 166, 172–78.

7. Colom 1998: 47–48, 52–54, 86, 90, 111, 130–31, 275, 287.

8. Camus and Mateo 2007: 136–37, 141–48.

9. "El Suicidio en Guatemala," *Al Día*, September 7, 2002, as cited in Mely Roxana Elizabeth Juàrez Oliva and Brenda Judith Palma Alvarado, "Suicidio: Estudio de Tres Casos Ocurridos en la Capital," thesis for licenciatura, Escuela de Ciencias Psicològicas, Universidad de San Carlos de Guatemala, November 6, 2006, p. 16.

10. Nebaj's population reached the level of sixty thousand in 1998–2002. Forty-eight suicides would be an average of twelve per year, and twelve suicides per year among sixty thousand people would be equivalent to twenty per hundred thousand. The Guatemalan suicide rate of 2.3 per 100,000 per year comes from the World Health Organization and places Guatemala 87th on a list of 103 countries according to "List of Countries by Suicide Rate," http://www.wikipedia.org.

11. Lockhart and Recondo 2001.

12. "Retienen a cuatro," *Prensa Libre*, January 30, 2009.

13. "Ataque a lideresa Ixil," March 31, 2009.

14. "Rural Women's Network Leader Attacked and Robbed," *El Quetzal* (Guatemala Human Rights Commission/USA, Washington, DC), no. 4, September 2009.

15. Apelación 02-2010, Organismo Judicial Guatemala, Lic. José Reynaldo Galván Casasola, Juez de Primera Instancia Penal, without date. Attached notice is dated March 5, 2010.

16. "Rural Women's Network Leader Attacked and Robbed."

17. Stoll 1993: 207.

18. Alida Juliani, "Artistas españolas apoyan a mujeres indígenas en su lucha contra la violencia," Agencia EFE, May 19, 2009.

CHAPTER 8: DREAMS AND PYRAMID SCHEMES

1. Nazario 2006; Moran-Taylor 2008a; Heymann et al. 2009.

2. Damien Cave, "Better Lives for Mexicans Cut Allure of Going North," *New York Times*, July 5, 2011.

3. "Migration after the Crash: Moving Out, On and Back," *Economist*, August 27, 2011.

4. Smith 2006: 123.

5. Peri 2007. According to a press release on these findings, "the actual losers in the equation are prior immigrants, whose wages are hurt by the newcomers. In 2004, immigrants who had entered California before 1990 lost between 17 and 20 percent of their real wages due to the entry of new foreign-born workers." Benefits for native-born workers accrue to those in a position to manage, organize, and train immigrant workers, while the costs fall on native-born workers who are the least attractive to employers— those with the least education, experience, and habituation to routine (Public Policy Institute of California, February 27, 2007). For an argument that low-wage labor migration hurts native-born workers, not just immigrants, see Borjas 1999.

6. Referral system: Valentine 2005: 20–21. Network hiring: Waldinger and Lichter 2003.

7. According to research for the Pew Hispanic Center (Kochhar 2012: 4, 7, 19), more rapid job growth for Hispanics and Asians is keeping pace with the growth of their working-age populations. But the 2008 recession and a weak economic recovery has widened employment shortfalls for black and white workers. As of the end of 2011, black employment was 12 percent below potential (about two million jobs), and white employment was more than 7 percent below potential (seven million jobs). Hispanic employment was less than 6 percent below potential (one million jobs), and Asian employment was 5 percent below potential (half a million jobs). The most remarkable difference in employment shortfalls was between foreign-born and native-born workers. Foreign-born employment was 1.4 percent below potential at the end of 2011. Native-born employment was 8.9 percent below potential according to Pew.

For research on the preference of employers for immigrant rather than native-born labor, see Johnson et al. 2000: 327; Millard and Chapa 2004; Zúñiga and Hernández-León 2005; Izcara Palacios 2010; and Anderson 2004: 362. For two remarkable case studies, see Brent Valentine's (2005: 20–21, 47–48, 57) report on the open preference of Wisconsin dairy farmers for Mexican labor and Laura López-Sanders' (2009) account of how a manufacturing plant in South Carolina hired her to replace African American workers with Latino workers. This is not the only case in which low-income black Americans have been the most affected by employer preference for hiring immigrants; see Johnson et al. 2000 and Shulman 2004.

Terry Repak (1995: 11, 86–87, 156–57) has documented the active recruitment of foreign workers, particularly Central American women for child care, by Washington, D.C.'s government, diplomatic, and professional elites. Is it valid to talk of a labor shortage, asks Repak, when the jobs filled by immigrants are notoriously underpaid and the city's black unemployment rate is high? Philip Moss and Chris Tilly (2001: 17) have documented the correlation between employers praising the work ethic of immigrants and paying their workers less. In California lettuce production, the sociologist Robert Thomas (1985: 125) found that employers had a particularly strong preference for undocumented workers because they were so much more productive even than green-card holders.

8. According to research for the Pew Hispanic Center (Passel and Cohn 2009: 31), undocumented workers have risen to 5.4 percent of the U.S. labor force. But in particular states they comprise 8 to 12 percent of the labor force—Florida, New Jersey, Arizona, California, and Nevada. In 2008, 17 percent of construction workers were undocumented, including 40 percent of all drywall installers and 37 percent of all brick-

layers. Jennifer Gordon (2005: 12) portrays the "disturbing renaissance of sweatshop work" that is moving out of urban cores into the suburbs. Pierrette Hondagneu-Sotelo (2001) describes the rebirth of domestic service on the East and West Coasts owing to the rising supply of female immigrants.

9. Robert Thomas (1985: 139–48) found network hiring through Mexican coyotes in his study of the California lettuce industry. Rachel Adler (2004: 89–90) describes an Italian immigrant in Dallas paying his Yucatec Maya employees to bring up their relatives and friends; they worked off the debt in his restaurant. Jacqueline Hagan (1994: 62–64) has published a fascinating ethnography of a K'iche' Maya migration stream pulled to Houston by referral hiring. Five-sixths of the men in an enclave of a thousand Guatemalans were working for a single retail chain, where they controlled hiring because they knew about vacancies—members of their group planning to go home—before management did. Even before the jobs could be advertised, the Guatemalans had replacements offering to fill them. Ruth Gomberg-Muñoz (2011: 53, 67, 116) provides another fine ethnography of referral hiring, in a network of Mexican busboys from Guanajuato working for Italian restaurants in the Chicago suburbs. Each member of the network is brought up by a sponsor, usually a brother or close friend, who fronts them the money for the coyote. "Many U.S. employers have become quite adept at tapping into undocumented social networks to recruit new workers," she notes. Contrary to the usual portrayal of undocumented workers as excluded and marginalized, Gomberg-Muñoz points out, this is actually preferential hiring. In Judith Hellman's (2008: xx) interviews with a wide range of Mexican migrants, she was surprised to learn that most were not employed by Anglos. Instead, they worked for fellow Mexicans or non-WASP ethnic groups who were typically first-generation immigrants themselves.

10. Kwong 1997: 15, 103, 177.

11. Mahler 1995: 77, 90, 138–213.

12. See Mahler 1995: 53 on what she calls "chain migration," as well as Spener 2005: 69–71 and Krissman 2000: 291 on how the 1986 Immigration Reform and Control Act facilitated rather than curtailed undocumented migration. In a comparison of Chinese and Ecuadorian smuggling networks to the United States, David Kyle and John Dale (2001: 40) found that U.S. green-card holders (immigrants who have been granted legal residence) were turning into coyotes who were making their living by bringing in more immigrants. Liliana Suárez-Navaz (2012: 49) reports Ecuadorians moving to Spain through "chains of debt" in which domestic workers refinance their own loans by making loans to new migrants. Of Chinese from Fujian Province, Peter Kwong (2001: 241–42) refers to the "family migration project." Operating like a relay team and producing an exodus to the United States, the family migration project has a strong economic as well as cultural and moral rationale. Namely, the cheapest and most dependable labor for an immigrant-owned enterprise in the United States is to bring more workers from China, and often from one's own family.

13. Conover 1987: 38–39, 55; Stephen 2007: 165–67.

14. "Around the world, the role of family and community members in recruiting victims into trafficking is especially prevalent and discouraging," reports an authority on human trafficking (Bales 2005: 142–43). "At the most personal level are those recruiters who visit individual homes in order to encourage emigration and to reassure other family members of the safety of the process. In West Africa, Thailand, and Central America, older women are known to recruit young people of the same ethnic

and language group. They bring to local villages the consumer goods and nice clothes that they know will help entice the young. To older family members, the recruiters make promises about the money that can be earned abroad and remitted to the home village. They weave a picture of wealth, comfort, sophistication, and prestige that can be irresistible to the poor and isolated."

In 2011 the Human Trafficking Database at the University of Michigan Law School (http://www.law.umich.edu/clinical/HuTrafficCases/Pages/searchdatabase .aspx) included six cases of Mexicans and Guatemalans in the United States enslaving co-nationals for the purpose of prostitution, domestic service, and forestry work.

15. Spener 2005.

16. Krissman 2000: 284–88.

17. Karger 2005: 42.

18. Exchange is one of the core issues of sociocultural anthropology. For an overview of the anthropology of credit and debt, see Gustav Peebles 2010. For an ambitious historical analysis of how debt has evolved under state societies and capitalism, see David Graeber 2011.

19. Wilkinson 2002: 77.

20. Colby and van den Berghe 1969: 31; Nachtigall 1978: 143.

21. Debt chains: cf. Vélez-Ibáñez 2004: 130.

22. Cf. Marc Lacey, "Money Trickles North as Mexicans Help Relatives," *New York Times*, November 16, 2009.

23. Passel and Cohn 2011.

24. The anthropologist Josiah Heyman (1998: 174–75) has studied enforcement along the U.S.-Mexican border. He points out that "conspiracies to avoid the law" make it harder to define the difference between mutuality and exploitation. "When undocumented immigrants construct reciprocal exchanges, they may appear to follow egalitarian idioms but their choices are limited and channeled by the need to reduce disruption by [U.S. immigration enforcement]. The restriction of alternatives adds power to the superordinate partner. Debts may then be called in for use in exploitative domains. Superexploitative results flow up a channel of obligations from the immigrant to the immigrant-helper, on to the foreman and employer."

25. Vyse 2008; Porter 2012. In a poultry-processing plant in Russellville, Alabama, labor journalist Gabriel Thompson (2010: 177) was unable to find any Americans who were worried that immigrant workers (mainly Akatek Mayas from San Miguel Acatán) were taking their jobs. The plant's labor force consisted of equal proportions of whites, blacks, and immigrants, with the latter concentrated in the most debilitating jobs. The work was so poorly paid that only desperate Americans would take it, but of these there was quite a supply—many so stripped of assets that they seemed little better off than undocumented immigrants.

26. Vélez-Ibáñez 2004: 137, 146.

27. Griffith 2006.

28. Southern Poverty Law Center 2007: 10, 13, 18.

29. Bacon 2008a: 97–99.

30. Stillman 2011: 58. For other examples of how guest-worker programs generate debt and servitude, see Audrey Macklin 2003 (strippers in Canada) and Pardis Mahdavi 2011 (servants in Dubai).

31. Zogby poll: Reuters 2009. Pew Global Attitudes Project 2009: 9. Gallup poll: Esipova and Ray 2009. In most countries the Gallup samples were between one thousand and three thousand, with sampling errors ranging from 3 to 6 percent and a confidence level of 95 percent.

32. Lind 1996: 206.

33. For an analysis of how this chain of risk and exploitation operates in H-2 recruitment of seasonal agricultural workers from Tamaulipas, Mexico, see Izcara Palacios 2010 and 2011.

34. Cf. Kyle and Dale 2001: 40; "[I]t is also common for return migrants to lend money to regional intermediaries . . . who in turn lend money to professional *chulqueros* [moneylender/smugglers], who in turn lend to the new migrant at the highest rate, thus forming a pyramid scheme that requires a constant influx of new migrants to keep capital circulating to the top."

35. Another valuable collection of experiences is Lont and Hospes 2004. For the most detailed review of the growing debate over microcredit, by a scholar who has attended the conferences and parses the competing paradigms, see Roy 2010. For summaries of the issues, see Bond 2006; Dichter 2006; and Cons and Paprocki 2008. The term "microcredit" tends to be applied to the most altruistic programs that tolerate loss; "microfinance" tends to be applied to programs that oblige repayment, either because they are for-profit or because they must protect the capital of contributors.

36. Dichter 2007b: 185.

37. Roy 2010: 188; Rhyne 2001: 144–46, 155. Even in developed countries, microfinance strategies can be injurious. In Bosnia-Herzegovina, following the civil war with Serbia and Croatia, the aid community's decision to push profit-oriented commercial microfinance justified a bias against large-scale investment to restore the country's industrial capacity. The result was a trade-based economy focusing on, not production, but schemes for buying cheap and selling dear. Economist Milford Bateman (2007: 210, 212, 218–20) compares the Bosnian commercial microfinance model to "a rapidly growing weed that hogs the nutrients and sunlight needed by the slower growing crops around it." He suggests that, by encouraging secrecy, distrust of government, and individualistic cost-recovery instead of collective endeavor, microfinance destroyed social capital rather than built it.

38. Affinity groups unfair: Rahman 2007: 194. Andhra Pradesh: Ghate 2007: 165.

39. Hidden transcript: Rahman 1999. Does not demonstrate empowerment: Roy 2010: 107–110.

40. Collins et al. 2009.

41. Dichter 2006. In the Grameen heartland of Bangladesh, reports Milford Bateman (2010: 68), "all of the most simple business areas have already been colonized by swarms of microenterprises, with any initial income gains made by the 'first movers' largely wiped out later on as the local competition rapidly balloons."

42. Pearl and Phillips 2001.

43. Wilson 2007: 102–4. Some critics (Elyachar 2005: 11; Rahman 2007; Roy 2010: 167) argue that microfinance has produced a new rentier class living off the presumed beneficiaries. Agencies are customarily directed by networks of relatives and cronies. Registered as nonprofits and supported by philanthropists, they become proprietary concerns with lifelong benefits for the people running them, in contrast

to the temporary benefits for borrowers. For a person who faces severe structural disadvantages, it is important to stress the temporary, at best ameliorative, nature of extending credit. According to S. M. Rahman's (2007: 200) assessment of the microcredit experience in Bangladesh, the mother of the industry, recipients of microcredit continue to use moneylenders as they do in Nebaj.

44. Rahman 1999; Lazar 2004: 308–9.

45. These figures are from the Population Reference Bureau (2007: 12; 2011). For the PRB's overview of family planning on the national level, see Haub and Gribble 2011. Nebaj's government hospital now offers birth control to every mother after she gives birth, free of charge, and says that more village women are using it. According to two maternity nurses, Nebaj women prefer Depo-Provera injections and under-the-skin implants to intrauterine devices and birth control pills.

46. Carlsen 2011: 134–36. For an analysis of producing large families as an adaptive mechanism, despite worse poverty than the Ixils face and in the face of ecological disaster, see Timothy Schwartz's (2009) analysis of Jean Rabel, Haiti. For an analysis of how family size is affected by the interaction between development programs and peasant cognition, see Liza Grandia's (2012: 83–116) analysis of Q'eqchi' Mayas and their demographic overshoot in Petén Department. Grandia also provides an excellent sketch (205–9) of the challenges posed by monetization, the slippery slope of consumerism, the attempt to escape the land per capita squeeze by investing in children's education, and fear that children will fail to support parents in their old age—all of which rings true for Nebaj.

47. For a good review of the ideology of return as it manifests itself among Guatemalans in Phoenix, see Moran-Taylor 2001.

48. Tobar 2005.

49. Shipton 2010: 195.

50. "There is no denying that most villagers and their overseas relations have become deeply enmeshed in financial debt over the past two decades of mass migration," reports Julie Chu (2010: 169) of a Fujianese sending population—even though many have obtained legal status in the United States. "By the time I was doing research in Longyan, debt had become such a pervasive mediator of social relations that one could hardly find someone in the village . . . who was not either in the process of securing financing for emigration, paying off loans for past smuggling ventures, or lending funds to others. In fact, it was not at all unusual to find villagers or their overseas relatives simultaneously playing both debtor and creditor, lending money to someone while still paying off a long-standing smuggling debt to someone else."

51. Massey, Durand, and Malone 2003; Castañeda 2007.

52. Krissman 2005: 14.

CHAPTER 9: THE RIGHT TO NOT MIGRATE

1. An exception was the National Coordination of Indigenous Peoples and Campesinos (CONIC), which accepted one of the debt committees as an affiliate but does not have an office in Nebaj.

2. Falla 2008: 37–38.

3. For an overview of the debate over remittances on a global level, see Ghosh 2006.

4. Lorena Alvarez, "Encuesta: 4.5 millones de personas reciben remesas," *El Periódico*, March 31, 2011, citing International Organization for Migration 2011.

5. World Bank 2009: 85, 91–92, 111.

6. Among the few researchers to deal with this issue are the geographer Michelle Moran-Taylor (2008b) and the anthropologist Manuela Camus (2007: 39). According to Camus' compilation of the national census and a 2002 survey by the International Organization for Migration, 39.53 percent of the ladino population benefits from remittances. But when we look to the four largest Mayan groups, which constitute three-quarters of Guatemala's indigenous population, only 18.32 percent of the K'iche', 10.22 percent of the Kaqchikel, 5.79 percent of the Q'eqchi', and 26.76 percent of the Mam population benefit from remittances. Only one small Mayan language group exceeds ladinos in benefitting from remittances—the Akatekos, with 60.17 percent. The figure for the Ixils is 15.52 percent. One explanation for the rapid migration streams from indigenous municipios is that they are trying to catch up with ladinos. For Mayas hoping to close an income gap with ladinos, going north is an obvious strategy.

7. David Bacon and Gaspar Rivera-Salgado attribute the demand for the "right to stay home" (*derecho de no migrar*) to a 2008 assembly of Triqui, Mixtec, and Zapotec delegates of the Binational Indigenous Front of Organizations in Juxtalahuaca (Bacon 2008b). But the phrase may have an earlier provenance in the Catholic Church (see Bingham 2007). In 2011 the "right to not migrate" was taken up by the Global Forum on Migration and Development in Geneva.

8. Mahler 1995: 85–89.

9. Marcela Fernández and Cristina Bonillo, "Estafan a migrantes deportados de Postville," *Prensa Libre*, August 26, 2009.

10. Cheikhrouhou 2006: 5, and Organization for International Migration 2011: 20.

11. The economists David Mckenzie and Hillel Rapoport (2007) argue that, as a migration stream matures, it offers opportunity to a wider spectrum of the sending population. Even if the first migrants tend to come from the upper levels of a sending community, the bridgehead they establish tends to reduce risks and costs for the people who follow them, enabling poorer households to send workers north. One sign of the recency of Nebaj's migration stream is that its stateside migrants have not established a hometown association of the sort that contributes to community projects as well as repatriation of the dead.

12. Lewis 2011.

13. Rocha 2011: 469, 476.

14. One step in limiting family size could be Guatemala's adoption of an idea pioneered by the Brazilians and Mexicans, the cash-transfer strategy for fighting malnutrition. Every low-income mother with a child below the age of five receives a government stipend of Q150 (US$19) per month, which increases to Q300 if and when the child starts school. The amount does not increase with more births.

Bibliography

Adler, Rachel H. 2004. *Yucatecans in Dallas, Texas: Breaching the Border, Bridging the Distance*. Boston: Pearson.

Anderson, Warren O. 2004. "P'urépecha Migration into the U.S. Rural Midwest: History and Current Trends." In *Indigenous Mexican Migrants in the United States*, edited by Jonathan Fox and Gaspar Rivera-Salgado, 355–84. San Diego: Center for U.S.-Mexican Studies, University of California at San Diego.

Angee, Alejandro, and Cynthia S. Hernández. 2007. "Seeds of Justice: Community Action and Social Research Working Together to Combat Wage Theft in South Florida's Plant Nurseries." Unpublished paper, Florida International University, October 1.

Annis, Sheldon. 1987. *God and Production in a Guatemalan Town*. Austin: University of Texas Press.

Aubry, Laura, and Charlotte Servado. 2004. "Intensificación y migraciónes temporales frente a la presión hipotecaria: Diagnóstico agrario de dos valles altos del municipio de Nebaj, area ixil, Guatemala." Thesis, Instituto Nacional Agronómico Paris-Grignon, October.

Bacon, David. 2006. *Communities without Borders: Images and Voices from the World of Migration*. Ithaca, NY: Cornell University Press.

———. 2008a. *Illegal People: How Globalization Creates Migration and Criminalizes Immigrants*. Boston: Beacon Press.

———. 2008b. "The Right to Stay Home." New America Media, July 9. http://news.newamericamedia.org (accessed January 1, 2012).

Baker-Cristales, Beth. 2004. "Salvadoran Transformations: Class Consciousness and Ethnic Identity in a Transnational Milieu." *Latin American Perspectives* 31 (5): 15–33.

Bales, Kevin. 2005. *Understanding Global Slavery: A Reader*. Berkeley: University of California Press.

Ball, Patrick. 1999. "Metodologia Intermuestra." In *Memoria del Silencio*, Comisión de Esclarecimiento Histórico, Anexo III. http://shr.aaas.org/guatemala/ceh/mds/spanish/anexo3/aaas/aaas.html (accessed July 24, 2012).

Ball, Patrick, Paul Kobrak, and Herbert F. Spirer, eds. 1999. *State Violence in Guatemala, 1960–1996: A Quantitative Reflection*. Washington, DC: American Association for the Advancement of Science.

Ballard, Roger. 2003. "A Case of Capital-Rich Under-development: The Paradoxical Consequences of Successful Transnational Entrepreneurship from Mirpur." *Contributions to Indian Sociology* 37:25–57.

Barmeyer, Neils. 2009. *Developing Zapatista Autonomy: Conflict and NGO Involvement in Rebel Chiapas*. Albuquerque: University of New Mexico Press.

Barrera Nuñez, Oscar. 2009. "Desires and Imagination: The Economy of Humanitarianism in Guatemala." In *Mayas in Postwar Guatemala: Harvest of Violence Revisited*, edited by Walter E. Little and Timothy R. Smith, 110–23. Tuscaloosa: University of Alabama Press.

Bateman, Milford. 2007. "De-industrialization and Social Disintegration in Bosnia." In *What's Wrong with Microfinance?* edited by Thomas Dichter and Malcolm Harper, 207–23. Rugby, Warwickshire: Practical Action Publishing.

———. 2010. *Why Doesn't Microfinance Work? The Destructive Rise of Local Neoliberalism*. London: Zed Books.

Binford, Leigh. 2003. "Migrant Remittances and (Under)Development in Mexico." *Critique of Anthropology* 23 (3): 305–36.

Bingham, John K. 2007. "To Leave or Not to Leave: The Right to Not Migrate and What the Church Is Doing to Help People to Stay at Home." Geneva: International Catholic Migration Commission. http://www.migrationanddevelopment.net/perspectives-positions (accessed January 2, 2012).

Bond, Patrick. 2006. "Beyond Microcredit Evangelism." http://www.pambazuka.org/en/category/comment/38007/print (accessed July 24, 2012).

Boo, Katherine. 2004. "Letter from South Texas: The Churn." *New Yorker*, March 29.

Borjas, George. 1999. *Heaven's Door: Immigration Policy and the American Economy*. Princeton, NJ: Princeton University Press.

Burns, Allan F. 1993. *Maya in Exile: Guatemalans in Florida*. Philadelphia: Temple University Press.

———. 2000. "Indiantown, Florida: The Maya Diaspora and Applied Anthropology." In *The Maya Diaspora: Guatemalan Roots, New American Lives*, edited by James Loucky and Marilyn M. Moors, 152–74. Philadelphia: Temple University Press.

Burrell, Jennifer L. 2005. "Migration and the Transnationalization of Fiesta Customs in Todos Santos Cuchumatán, Guatemala." *Latin American Perspectives* 32 (5): 12–32.

———. 2010. "In and Out of Rights: Security, Migration, and Human Rights Talk in Postwar Guatemala." *Journal of Latin American and Caribbean Anthropology* 15 (1): 90–115.

Cahn, Peter S. 2011. *Direct Sales and Direct Faith in Latin America*. Basingstoke: Palgrave Macmillan.

Camus, Manuela, ed. 2007. *Comunidades en movimiento: La migración internacional en el norte de Huehuetenango*. Huehuetenango, Guatemala: Centro de Documentación de la Frontera Occidental de Guatemala (CEDFOG).

Camus, Manuela. 2008. *La sorpresita del Norte: Migración internacional y comunidad en Huehuetenango*. Antigua Guatemala: Editorial Junajpu.

Camus, Manuela, and María Mateo. 2007. "Una mujer q'anjob'al de Mamá Maquín." In *Comunidades en movimiento: La migración internacional en el norte de Huehuetenango*, edited by Manuela Camus, 119–50. Huehuetenango, Guatemala: Centro de Documentación de la Frontera Occidental de Guatemala (CEDFOG).

Carlsen, Robert S. 2011. *The War for the Heart and Soul of a Highland Maya Town*. 2nd edition. Austin: University of Texas Press.

Castañeda, Jorge G. 2007. *Ex Mex: From Migrants to Immigrants*. New York: New Press.

Chacón, Justin Akers, and Mike Davis. 2006. *No One Is Illegal: Fighting Racism and State Violence on the U.S.-Mexico Border*. Chicago: Haymarket Books.

Cheikhrouhou, Hela, et al. 2006. "The U.S.-Guatemala Remittance Corridor: Understanding Better the Drivers of Remittances Intermediation." World Bank Working Paper 86. Washington, DC: World Bank.

Chesnut, Andrew. 2003. *Competitive Spirits: Latin America's New Religious Economy*. New York: Oxford University Press.

Chu, Julie V. 2010. *Cosmologies of Credit: Transnational Mobility and the Politics of Destination in China*. Durham, NC: Duke University Press.

Cohen, Jeffrey H. 2004. *The Culture of Migration in Southern Mexico*. Austin: University of Texas Press.

Cohen, Jeffrey, Richard Jones, and Dennis Conway. 2005. "Why Remittances Shouldn't Be Blamed for Rural Underdevelopment in Mexico: A Collective Response to Leigh Binford." *Critique of Anthropology* 25 (1): 87–96.

Colby, Benjamin N., and Pierre L. van den Berghe. 1969. *Ixil Country: A Plural Society in Highland Guatemala*. Berkeley: University of California Press.

Collins, Daryl, Jonathan Morduch, Stuart Rutherford, and Orlanda Ruthven. 2009. *Portfolios of the Poor: How the World's Poor Live on $2 a Day*. Princeton, NJ: Princeton University Press.

Colom, Yolanda. 1998. *Mujeres en la Alborada: Guerrilla y participación femenina en Guatemala*. Guatemala: Editorial Artemis & Edinter.

Comaroff, Jean, and John L. Comaroff. 1999. "Occult Economies and the Violence of Abstraction: Notes from the South African Postcolony." *American Ethnologist* 26 (2): 279–303.

Conover, Ted. 1987. *Coyotes: A Journey through the Secret World of America's Illegal Aliens*. New York: Vintage.

Cons, Jason, and Kasia Paprocki. 2008. "The Limits of Microcredit—A Bangladesh Case." *Food First Backgrounder*, 14 (4).

De Leon Ceto, Miguel. 2006. "Las Fuentes de Poder del Movimiento Evangélico en Nebaj, Guatemala." Master's thesis, Ciencias Politicas, Universidad Rafael Landivar, October.

Dichter, Thomas. 2006. "Hype and Hope: The Worrisome State of the Microcredit Movement." http://www.saiia.org.za/archive-eafrica/hype-and-hope-the-worrisome-state-of-the-microcredit-movement.html (accessed July 23, 2012).

———. 2007a. "Can Microcredit Make an Already Slippery Slope More Slippery? Some Lessons from the Social Meaning of Debt." In *What's Wrong with Microfinance?* edited by Thomas Dichter and Malcolm Harper, 9–17. Rugby, Warwickshire: Practical Action Publishing.

————. 2007b. "The Chicken and Egg Dilemma in Finance: An Historical Analysis of the Sequence of Growth and Credit in the Economic Development of the 'North.'" In *What's Wrong with Microfinance?* edited by Thomas Dichter and Malcolm Harper, 179–92. Rugby, Warwickshire: Practical Action Publishing.

Dichter, Thomas, and Malcolm Harper, eds. 2007. *What's Wrong with Microfinance?* Rugby, Warwickshire: Practical Action Publishing.

Ehlers, Tracy Bachrach. 1990. *Silent Looms: Women and Production in a Guatemalan Town.* Boulder, CO: Westview Press.

Ellerman, David. 2007. "Microfinance: Some Conceptual and Methodological Problems." In *What's Wrong with Microfinance?* edited by Thomas Dichter and Malcolm Harper, 149–61. Rugby, Warwickshire: Practical Action Publishing.

Elyachar, Julia. 2005. *Markets of Dispossession: NGOs, Economic Development, and the State in Cairo.* Durham, NC: Duke University Press.

England, Nora. 2003. "Mayan Language Revival and Revitalization Politics: Linguists and Linguistic Ideologies." *American Anthropologist* 105 (4): 733–43.

Esipova, Neli, and Julie Ray. 2009. "700 Million Worldwide Desire to Migrate Permanently." November 2. http://www.gallup.com/poll/124028/700-million-world wide-desire-migrate-permanently.aspx (accessed July 23, 2012).

Faceta Central Desarrollo Empresarial. 2002. "Informe Final, Misión de Apoyo: Realización de un inventario y tipificación de la oferta—demanda de crédito en el Triángulo Ixil." April 29, to U.S. Agency for International Development, Convenio n. GUA/B7-2120/98/482.

Falla, Ricardo. 2008. *Migración transnacional retornada: Juventud indígena de Zacualpa, Guatemala.* Guatemala City: Asociación para el Avance de las Ciencias Sociales en Guatemala (AVANCSO).

Fernández de Castro, Rafael. 2012. "Transmigration in Mexico: The Invisible Victims." *Revista: Harvard Review of Latin America* 11 (2): 63–65.

Fink, Deborah. 1998. *Cutting into the Meatpacking Line.* Chapel Hill: University of North Carolina Press.

Fink, Leon. 2003. *The Maya of Morganton: Work and Community in the Nuevo New South.* Chapel Hill: University of North Carolina Press.

Fletcher, Peri L. 1999. *La Casa de Mis Sueños: Dreams of Home in a Transnational Mexican Community.* Boulder, CO: Westview Press.

Foster, George M. 1965. "Peasant Society and the Image of Limited Good." *American Anthropologist* 67 (2): 293–315.

Foxen, Patricia. 2007. *In Search of Providence: Transnational Mayan Identities.* Nashville, TN: Vanderbilt University.

————. 2010. "Local Narratives of Distress and Resilience: Lessons in Psychosocial Well-Being among the K'iche' Maya in Postwar Guatemala." *Journal of Latin American and Caribbean Anthropology* 15 (1): 66–89.

Gardner, Katy, and Zahir Ahmed. 2009. "Degrees of Separation: Informal Social Protection, Relatedness and Migration in Biswanath, Bangladesh." *Journal of Development Studies* 45 (1): 124–49.

Ghate, Prabhu. 2007. "Learning from the Andhra Pradesh Crisis." In *What's Wrong with Microfinance?* edited by Thomas Dichter and Malcolm Harper, 163–76. Rugby, Warwickshire: Practical Action Publishing.

Ghosh, Bimal. 2006. "Myths, Rhetoric and Realities: Migrants' Remittances and Development." Geneva: International Organization for Migration.

Goldin, Liliana R. 2009. *Global Maya: Work and Ideology in Rural Guatemala*. Tucson: University of Arizona Press.

Gomberg-Muñoz, Ruth. 2011. *Labor and Legality: An Ethnography of a Mexican Immigrant Network*. New York: Oxford University Press.

Gordon, Jennifer. 2005. *Suburban Sweatshops: The Fight for Immigrant Rights*. Cambridge, MA: Harvard University Press.

Graeber, David. 2011. *Debt: The First 5,000 Years*. Brooklyn, NY: Melville House.

Grandia, Liza. 2012. *Enclosed: Conservation, Cattle, and Commerce among the Q'eqchi' Maya Lowlanders*. Seattle: University of Washington Press.

Griffith, David. 2005. "Rural Industry and Mexican Immigration and Settlement in North Carolina." In *New Destinations: Mexican Immigration in the United States*, edited by Victor Zúñiga and Rubén Hernández-León, 50–75. New York: Sage.

———. 2006. *American Guestworkers: Jamaicans and Mexicans in the U.S. Labor Market*. University Park: Pennsylvania State University Press.

Grimes, Kimberly. 1998. *Crossing Borders: Changing Social Identities in Mexico*. Tucson: University of Arizona Press.

Haenn, Nora. 2005. *Fields of Power, Forests of Discontent: Culture, Conservation, and the State in Mexico*. Tucson: University of Arizona Press.

Hagan, Jacqueline Maria. 1994. *Deciding to Be Legal: A Maya Community in Houston*. Philadelphia: Temple University Press.

Hamilton, Nora, and Norma Stoltz Chinchilla. 2001. *Seeking Community in a Global City: Guatemalans and Salvadorans in Los Angeles*. Philadelphia: Temple University Press.

Haub, Carl, and James Gribble. 2011. "The World at 7 Billion." *Population Bulletin* 66 (2).

Hellman, Judith Adler. 2008. *The Lives of Mexican Migrants: The Rock and the Hard Place*. New York: New Press.

Heyman, Josiah McC. 1998. "State Effects on Labor Exploitation: The INS and Undocumented Immigrants at the Mexico-United States Border." *Critique of Anthropology* 18 (2): 157–80.

Heymann, Jody, et al. 2009. "The Impact of Migration on the Well-Being of Transnational Families: New Data from Sending Communities in Mexico." *Community, Work & Family* 12 (1): 91–103.

Hondagneu-Sotelo, Pierrette. 2001. *Doméstica: Immigrant Workers Cleaning and Caring in the Shadows of Affluence*. Berkeley: University of California Press.

Instituto Nacional de Estadística. 1998. "Guatemala: Población Estimada Por Departamento y Municipio 1985–90."

———. 2012. "Guatemala: Estimaciones de la Población total por municipio Período 2008–2020."

International Organization for Migration. 2011. "Encuesta sobre Remesas 2010, Protección de la Niñez y Adolescencia." Guatemala: Organización Internacional para las Migraciones y UNICEF.

Izcara Palacios, Simón Pedro. 2010. "La Adicción a la Mano de Obra Ilegal: Jornaleros Tamaulipecos en Estados Unidos." *Latin American Research Review* 45 (1): 55–75.

———. 2011. "Redes migratorias versus demanda laboral: Los elementos que moldean los procesos migratorios." *Convergencia: Revista de Ciencias Sociales* 18 (57): 39–59.

Jaffee, Daniel. 2007. *Brewing Justice: Fair Trade Coffee, Sustainability and Survival.* Berkeley: University of California Press.

Johnson, James H., et al. 2000. "African American Males in Decline: A Los Angeles Case Study." In *Prismatic Metropolis: Inequality in Los Angeles*, edited by Lawrence D. Bobo et al., 315–37. New York: Sage.

Jokisch, Brad D. 2002. "Migration and Agricultural Change: The Case of Smallholder Agriculture in Highland Ecuador." *Human Ecology* 30 (4): 523–50.

Jokisch, Brad, and Jason Pribilsky. 2002. "The Panic to Leave: Economic Crisis and the 'New Emigration' from Ecuador." *International Migration* 40 (4): 75–99.

Jones, Richard C. 1998. "Remittances and Inequality: A Question of Migration Stage and Geographic Scale." *Economic Geography* 74 (1): 8–25.

Karger, Howard. 2005. *Shortchanged: Life and Debt in the Fringe Economy*. San Francisco: Berrett-Koehler.

Kaufman, Kathy A. 2000. "Outsourcing the Hearth: The Impact of Immigration on Labor Allocation in American Families." In *Immigration Research for a New Century: Multidisciplinary Perspectives*, edited by Nancy Foner, Ruben G. Rumbaut, and Steven J. Gold, 345–68. New York: Sage.

Keefe, Patrick Radden. 2009. *The Snakehead: An Epic Tale of the Chinatown Underworld and the American Dream*. New York: Doubleday.

Kindleberger, Charles P. 1989. *Manias, Panics, and Crashes: A History of Financial Crises*. Revised edition. New York: Basic Books.

Kochhar, Rakesh. 2012. "The Demographics of the Jobs Recovery: Employment Gains by Race, Ethnicity, Gender and Nativity." Washington, DC: Pew Hispanic Center, March 21.

Kochhar, Rakesh, C. Soledad Espinoza, and Rebecca Hinze-Pifer. 2010. "After the Great Recession: Foreign Born Gain Jobs; Native Born Lose Jobs." Washington, DC: Pew Hispanic Center, October 29.

Kowal, Emma. 2008. "The Politics of the Gap: Indigenous Australians, Liberal Multiculturalism, and the End of the Self-Determination Era." *American Anthropologist* 110 (3): 338–48.

Krissman, Fred. 2000. "Immigrant Labor Recruitment: U.S. Agribusiness and Undocumented Migration from Mexico." In *Immigration Research for a New Century: Multidisciplinary Perspectives*, edited by Nancy Foner, Ruben G. Rumbaut, and Steven J. Gold, 277–300. New York: Sage.

———. 2005. "Sin Coyote Ni Patrón: Why the 'Migrant Network' Fails to Explain International Migration." *International Migration Review* 39 (2): 4–44.

Kron, Stefanie. 2007. "El estilo solomero no tarda mucho: Negociando la frontera en la transmigración q'anjob'al." In *Comunidades en movimiento: La migración internacional en el norte de Huehuetenango*, edited by Manuela Camus, 57–94. Huehuetenango, Guatemala: Centro de Documentación de la Frontera Occidental de Guatemala (CEDFOG).

Kwong, Peter. 1997. *Forbidden Workers: Illegal Chinese Immigrants and American Labor*. New York: New Press.

———. 2001. "Impact of Chinese Human Smuggling on the American Labor Market." In *Global Human Smuggling: Comparative Perspectives*, edited by David Kyle and Rey Koslowski, 235–53. Baltimore, MD: Johns Hopkins University Press.

Kyle, David. 2000. *Transnational Peasants: Migrations, Networks, and Ethnicity in Andean Ecuador*. Baltimore, MD: Johns Hopkins University Press.

Kyle, David, and John Dale. 2001. "Smuggling the State Back In: Agents of Human Smuggling Reconsidered." In *Global Human Smuggling: Comparative Perspectives*, edited by David Kyle and Rey Koslowski, 29–57. Baltimore, MD: Johns Hopkins University Press.

Kyle, David, and Rey Koslowski, eds. 2001. *Global Human Smuggling: Comparative Perspectives*. Baltimore, MD: Johns Hopkins University Press.

Lazar, Sian. 2004. "Education for Credit: Development as a Citizenship Project in Bolivia." *Critique of Anthropology* 24 (3): 301–19.

Lee, Jennifer. 2000. "Immigrant and African American Competition: Jewish, Korean and African American Entrepreneurs." In *Immigration Research for a New Century: Multidisciplinary Perspectives*, edited by Nancy Foner, Ruben G. Rumbaut, and Steven J. Gold, 322–44. New York: Sage.

Levitt, Peggy. 2001. *The Transnational Villagers*. Berkeley: University of California Press.

Lewis, Michael. 2011. *Boomerang: Travels in the New Third World*. New York: Norton.

Lincoln, Jackson Steward. 1945. "An Ethnological Study on the Ixil Indians of the Guatemala Highlands." Microfilm Collection of Manuscripts on Middle American Cultural Anthropology No. 1. University of Chicago Library.

Lind, Michael. 1996. *The Next American Nation: The New Nationalism and the Fourth American Nation*. New York: Free Press.

Lockhart, Shannon, and Olivia Recondo. 2001. "Crisis of Identity among Ixil Youth." *Report on Guatemala* (Washington, DC), Winter.

Lont, Hotze, and Otto Hospes, eds. 2004. *Livelihood and Microfinance: Anthropological and Sociological Perspectives on Savings and Debt*. Amsterdam: Eburon Delft.

López-Sanders, Laura. 2009. "Trapped at the Bottom: Racialized and Gendered Labor Queues in New Immigrant Destinations." Working Paper 176. San Diego: Center for Comparative Immigration Studies, University of California.

Loucky, James, and Marilyn Moors, eds. 2000. *The Maya Diaspora: Guatemalan Roots, New American Lives*. Philadelphia: Temple University Press.

Macklin, Audrey. 2003. "Dancing across Borders: 'Exotic Dancers,' Trafficking, and Canadian Immigration Policy." *International Migration Review* 37 (2): 464–500.

Mahdavi, Pardis. 2011. *Gridlock: Labor, Migration, and Human Trafficking in Dubai*. Stanford, CA: Stanford University Press.

Mahler, Sarah. 1995. *American Dreaming: Immigrant Life on the Margins*. Princeton, NJ: Princeton University Press.

Malkin, Victoria. 2004. "We Go to Get Ahead: Gender and Status in Two Mexican Migrant Communities." *Latin American Perspectives* 31 (5): 75–99.

Massey, Douglas S., Rafael Alarcón, Jorge Durand, and Humberto González. 1987. *Return to Aztlán: The Social Process of International Migration from Western Mexico*. Berkeley: University of California Press.

Massey, Douglas S., Jorge Durand, and N. Malone. 2003. *Beyond Smoke and Mirrors: Mexican Immigration in an Era of Economic Integration.* New York: Sage.

Mathews, Gordon. 2011. *Ghetto at the Center of the World: Chungking Mansions, Hong Kong.* Chicago: University of Chicago Press.

Mckenzie, David, and Hillel Rapoport. 2007. "Network Effects and the Dynamics of Migration and Inequality: Theory and Evidence from Mexico." *Journal of Development Economics* 84:1–24.

Miles, Ann. 2004. *From Cuenca to Queens: An Anthropological Story of Transnational Migration.* Austin: University of Texas Press.

Millard, Ann V., and Jorge Chapa. 2004. *Apple Pie & Enchiladas: Latino Newcomers in the Rural Midwest.* Austin: University of Texas Press.

Mines, Richard. 1981. *Developing a Community Tradition of Migration to the United States: A Field Study in Rural Zacatecas, Mexico, and California Settlement Areas.* Monographs in U.S.-Mexican Studies, 3. San Diego: Program in United States–Mexican Studies, University of California.

Moran-Taylor, Michelle J., 2001. "Nostalgia por la tierra, nostalgia por el dolar: Guatemalan Transnational Lives and Ideology of Return Migration." *Estudios Fronterizos* 2 (4): 93–114.

———. 2008a. "When Mothers and Fathers Migrate North: Caretakers, Children, and Child Rearing in Guatemala." *Latin American Perspectives* 35 (4): 79–95.

———. 2008b. "Guatemala's Ladino and Maya Migra Landscapes: The Tangible and Intangible Outcomes of Migration." *Journal of Human Organization* 67 (2): 111–24.

Moran-Taylor, Michelle J., and Matthew J. Taylor. 2010. "Land and Leña: Linking Transnational Migration, Natural Resources, and the Environment in Guatemala." *Population and Environment* 32 (2–3): 198–215.

Morduch, Jonathan. 1999. "The Microfinance Promise." *Journal of Economic Literature* 37:1569–1614.

Moss, Philip, and Chris Tilly. 2001. *Stories Employers Tell: Race, Skill, and Hiring in America.* New York: Sage.

Nachtigall, Horst. 1978. *Die Ixil: Maya-Indianer in Guatemala.* Berlin: Dietrich Reimer Verlag.

Nazario, Sonia. 2006. *Enrique's Journey.* New York: Random House.

Nelson, Diane M. 2009. "Mayan Ponzi: A Contagion of Hope, a Made-off with Your Money." *e-misférica* (Hemispheric Institute, New York University). http://hemisphericinstitute.org/hemi/en/e-misferica-61/nelson (accessed July 16, 2012).

Nevins, Joseph. 2002. *Operation Gatekeeper: The Rise of the "Illegal Alien" and the Making of the U.S.-Mexico Boundary.* New York: Routledge.

Passel, Jeffrey, and D'Vera Cohn. 2009. "A Portrait of Unauthorized Immigrants in the United States." April 14. Washington, DC: Pew Hispanic Center.

———. 2011. "Unauthorized Immigrant Population: National and State Trends." February 1. Washington, DC: Pew Hispanic Center.

Pearl, Daniel, and Michael M. Phillips. 2001. "Grameen Bank, Which Pioneered Loans for the Poor, Has Hit a Repayment Snag." *Wall Street Journal*, November 27.

Peebles, Gustav. 2010. "The Anthropology of Credit and Debt." *Annual Review of Anthropology* 39:225–40.

Peri, Giovanni. 2007. "How Immigrants Affect California Employment and Wages." *California Counts: Population Trends and Profiles* (Public Policy Institute of California), 8 (3).

Pew Global Attitudes Project. 2009. "Troubled by Crime, the Economy, Drugs and Corruption: Most Mexicans See Better Life in U.S.—One-in-Three Would Migrate." September 23. http://www.pewglobal.org/2009/09/23/most-mexicans (accessed July 31, 2012).

Pfeiffer, James. 2004. "Civil Society, NGOs, and the Holy Spirit in Mozambique." *Human Organization* 63 (3): 359–72.

Philpot-Munson, Jailey. 2009. "Peace under Fire: Understanding Evangelical Resistance to the Peace Process in a Post-War Guatemalan Town." In *Mayas in Postwar Guatemala: Harvest of Violence Revisited*, edited by Walter E. Little and Timothy R. Smith, 42–53. Tuscaloosa: University of Alabama Press.

Piot, Charles. 2010. *Nostalgia for the Future: West Africa after the Cold War*. Chicago: University of Chicago Press.

Popkin, Eric. 1999. "Guatemalan Mayan Migration to Los Angeles: Constructing Transnational Linkages in the Context of the Settlement Process." *Ethnic and Racial Studies* 22 (2): 267–89.

Population Reference Bureau. 2007. "Population and Economic Development Linkages." Washington, DC.

———. 2011. "Data Sheet." Washington, DC.

Porter, Katherine. 2012. *Broke: How Debt Bankrupts the Middle Class*. Stanford, CA: Stanford University Press.

Prahalad, C. K. 2006. *The Fortune at the Bottom of the Pyramid*. Upper Saddle River, NJ: Wharton School Publishing.

Quinones, Sam. 2007. *Antonio's Gun and Delfino's Dream: True Tales of Mexican Migration*. Albuquerque: University of New Mexico Press.

Rahman, Aminur. 1999. "Micro-credit Initiatives for Equitable and Sustainable Development: Who Pays?" *World Development* 27 (1): 67–82.

Rahman, S. M. 2007. "A Practitioner's View of the Challenges Facing NGO-based Microfinance in Bangladesh." In *What's Wrong with Microfinance?* edited by Thomas Dichter and Malcolm Harper, 193–205. Rugby, Warwickshire: Practical Action Publishing.

Reichert, Joshua S. 1981. "The Migrant Syndrome: Seasonal U.S. Wage Labor and Rural Development in Central Mexico." *Human Organization* 40 (1): 56–66.

Repak, Terry A. 1995. *Waiting on Washington: Central American Workers in the Nation's Capital*. Philadelphia: Temple University Press.

Reuters. 2009. "Poll: Mexicans Say Amnesty Would Increase Illegal Immigration." October 14. http://www.reuters.com/article/2009/10/14/idUS39829+14-Oct-2009+PRN20091014 (accessed July 31, 2012).

Rhyne, Elizabeth. 2001. *Mainstreaming Microfinance: How Lending to the Poor Began, Grew, and Came of Age in Bolivia*. Bluefield Hills, CT: Kumarian Press.

Richman, Karen E. 2005. *Migration and Vodou*. Gainesville: University Press of Florida.

Rivera, Geraldo. 2009. *The Great Progression: How Hispanics Will Lead America to a New Era of Prosperity*. New York: Celebra.

Robbins, Richard. 2009. "Anthropologizing Growth: Lessons from the Latest Crisis." *Anthropology News*, October 11–12.

Robinson, Marguerite. 2001. *The Microfinance Revolution*. Vols. 1 & 2. Washington, DC: World Bank.

Rocha, José Luis. 2011. "Remittances in Central America: Whose Money Is It Anyway?" *Journal of World-Systems Research* 17 (2): 463–81.

Rodríguez, Gregory. 2007. *Mongrels, Bastards, Orphans, and Vagabonds: Mexican Immigration and the Future of Race in America*. New York: Pantheon Books.

Rodríguez, Nestor P., and Jacqueline Maria Hagan. 2000. "Maya Urban Villagers in Houston: The Formation of a Migrant Community from San Cristóbal Totonicapán." In *The Maya Diaspora: Guatemalan Roots, New American Lives*, edited by James Loucky and Marilyn M. Moors, 197–209. Philadelphia: Temple University Press.

Rouse, Roger. 1992. "Making Sense of Settlement: Class Transformation, Cultural Struggle, and Transnationalism among Mexican Migrants in the United States." In *Towards a Transnational Perspective on Migration: Race, Class, Ethnicity and Nationalism Reconsidered*, edited by Nina Glick-Schiller, Linda Basch, and Cristina Blanc-Szanton, 25–52. New York: New York Academy of Sciences.

Roy, Ananya. 2010. *Poverty Capital: Microfinance and the Making of Development*. New York: Routledge.

Rus, Diane, and Jan Rus. 2008. "La migración de trabajadores indígenas de Los Altos de Chiapas a Estados Unidos, 2001–2005: El caso de San Juan Chamula." In *Migraciones en el Sur de México y Centroamérica*, edited by Daniel Villafuerte Solís and María del Carmen García Aguilar, 343–82. Mexico: Miguel Angel Perrúa.

Sabino, Carlos. 2007–8. *Guatemala, la historia silenciada* (1944–1989), Tomos I and II. Guatemala: Fondo de Cultura Económica.

Sampson, Steven. 2002. "Weak States, Uncivil Societies and Thousands of NGOs: Western Democracy Export as Benevolent Colonialism in the Balkans." http://www.anthrobase.com/Txt/S/Sampson_S_01.html (accessed July 10, 2012).

———. 2003. "'Trouble Spots': Projects, Bandits and State Fragmentation." In *Globalization, the State and Violence*, edited by Jonathan Friedman, 309–42. Walnut Creek, CA: AltaMira Press.

Sánchez, Abenamar. 2008. "Bochil, en el fraude," "Red Anecof reconoce fraude," and "Opera Anecof tras reconocer fraude." *Cuarto Poder* (Tuxtla Gutiérrez, Chiapas), September 25, October 4, and October 29.

———. 2010. "La oferta de un paraiso: El fraude de Anecof." January 14. http://anecof.blogspot.com/2010/01/la-oferta-de-una-paraiso-anecof.html (accessed July 31, 2012).

Saunders, Douglas. 2011. *Arrival City: How the Largest Migration in History Is Reshaping Our World*. New York: Pantheon Books.

Schmalzbauer, Leah. 2008. "Family Divided: The Class Formation of Honduran Transnational Families." *Global Networks* 8 (3): 329–46.

Schwartz, Timothy T. 2009. *Fewer Men, More Babies: Sex, Family and Fertility in Haiti*. Lanham, MD: Lexington Books.

Scott, James C. 1976. *The Moral Economy of the Peasant: Rebellion and Subsistence in Southeast Asia*. New Haven, CT: Yale University Press.

Segura, Denise, and Patricia Zavella, eds. 2007. *Women and Migration in the U.S.-Mexico Borderlands*. Durham, NC: Duke University Press.

Shipton, Parker. 2007. *The Nature of Entrustment: Intimacy, Exchange, and the Sacred in Africa*. New Haven, CT: Yale University Press.

———. 2009. *Mortgaging the Ancestors: Ideologies of Attachment in Africa*. New Haven, CT: Yale University Press.

———. 2010. *Credit between Cultures: Farmers, Financiers, and Misunderstanding in Africa*. New Haven, CT: Yale University Press.

Shulman, Steven, ed. 2004. *The Impact of Immigration on African Americans*. New Brunswick, NJ: Transaction Publishers.

Simon, Jean-Marie. 1987. *Guatemala: Eternal Spring, Eternal Tyranny*. New York: Norton.

Skolnik, Jocelyn, Sandra Lazo de la Vega, and Timothy Steigenga. 2012. "Chisme across Borders: The Impact of Gossip in a Guatemalan Transnational Community." *Migraciones Internacionales* 6 (3): 9–38.

Smith, Carol. 1984. "Does a Commodity Economy Enrich the Few While Ruining the Masses? Differentiation among Petty Commodity Producers in Guatemala." *Journal of Peasant Studies* 11 (3): 60–95.

Smith, Robert Courtney. 2006. *Mexican New York: Transnational Lives of New Immigrants*. Berkeley: University of California Press.

Smith, Waldemar R. 1977. *The Fiesta System and Economic Change*. New York: Columbia University Press.

Southern Poverty Law Center. 2007. "Close to Slavery: Guestworker Programs in the United States." Montgomery, AL: Southern Poverty Law Center.

Spener, David. 2001. "Smuggling Migrants through South Texas: Challenges Posed by Operation Rio Grande." In *Global Human Smuggling: Comparative Perspectives*, edited by David Kyle and Rey Koslowski, 129–65. Baltimore, MD: Johns Hopkins University Press.

———. 2005. "Mexican Migration to the United States, 1882–1992: A Long Twentieth Century of Coyotaje." Working Paper 124. San Diego: Center for Comparative Immigration Studies, University of California.

———. 2009. *Clandestine Crossings: Migrants and Coyotes on the Texas-Mexico Border*. Ithaca, NY: Cornell University Press.

Steigenga, Timothy J., Silvia Irene Palma, and Carol Girón Solórzano. 2009. "Lived Religion and a Sense of Home: The Ambiguities of Transnational Identity among Jacaltecos in Jupiter." In *A Place to Be: Brazilian, Guatemalan, and Mexican Immigrants in Florida's New Destinations*, edited by Philip J. Williams, Timothy J. Steigenga, and Manuel Vásquez, 151–69. Piscataway, NJ: Rutgers University Press.

Stephen, Lynn. 2007. *Transborder Lives: Indigenous Oaxacans in Mexico, California, and Oregon*. Durham, NC: Duke University Press.

Steverlynck, Cécile. 2003. "Del otro lado del Norte." Unpublished report for Bernard van Leer Foundation, The Hague, Netherlands.

Stillman, Sarah. 2011. "Invisible Army." *New Yorker*, June 6, 56–65.

Stoll, David. 1993. *Between Two Armies in the Ixil Towns of Guatemala*. New York: Columbia University Press.

———. 1996. "To Whom Should We Listen? Human Rights Activism in Two Guatemalan Land Disputes." In *Human Rights, Culture and Context: Anthropological Perspectives*, edited by Richard Wilson, 187–215. London: Pluto Press.

———. 2009a. "Harvest of Conviction: Solidarity in Guatemalan Scholarship, 1988–2008." In *Mayas in Postwar Guatemala: Harvest of Violence Revisited*, edited by Walter E. Little and Timothy R. Smith, 167–80. Tuscaloosa: University of Alabama Press.

———. 2009b. "Human Rights, Land Conflict and Memories of the Violence in the Ixil Country of Northern Quiché." In *Human Rights in the Maya Region: Global Politics, Cultural Connections, and Moral Engagements*, edited by Pedro Pitarch and Shannon Speed, 187–204. Durham, NC: Duke University Press.

———. 2010. "From Wage-Migration to Debt-Migration? Easy Credit, Failure in El Norte, and Foreclosure in a Bubble Economy of the Western Guatemalan Highlands." *Latin American Perspectives* 37 (1): 123–42.

Strange, Susan. 1997. *Casino Capitalism*. Manchester: Manchester University Press.

Stull, Donald D., Michael J. Broadway, and David Griffith, eds. 1995. *Any Way You Cut It: Meat Processing and Small-Town America*. Lawrence: University Press of Kansas.

Suárez-Navaz, Liliana. 2012. "Kichwa Migrations across the Atlantic Border Regime: Transterritorial Practices of Identity and Rights within a Postcolonial Frame." *Journal of Latin American and Caribbean Anthropology* 17 (1): 41–64.

Sullivan, Paul. 1989. *Unfinished Conversations: Mayas and Foreigners between Two Wars*. Berkeley: University of California Press.

Tax, Sol. 1953. *Penny Capitalism: A Guatemalan Indian Economy*. Publication No. 16. Washington, DC: Institute of Social Anthropology, Smithsonian Institution.

Taylor, Matthew J., Michelle J. Moran-Taylor, and Debra Rodman Ruiz. 2006. "Land, Ethnic, and Gender Change: Transnational Migration and Its Effects on Guatemalan Lives and Landscapes." *Geoforum* 37:41–61.

Thomas, Robert J. 1985. *Citizenship, Gender and Work: Social Organization of Industrial Agriculture*. Berkeley: University of California Press.

Thompson, Gabriel. 2010. *Working in the Shadows: A Year of Doing the Jobs (Most) Americans Won't Do*. New York: Nation Books.

Tobar, Hector. 2005. *Translation Nation: Defining a New American Identity in the Spanish-Speaking United States*. New York: Riverhead Books.

Valentine, Brent Eric. 2005. "Uniting Two Cultures: Latino Immigrants in the Wisconsin Dairy Industry." Working Paper 121. San Diego: Center for Comparative Immigration Studies, University of California.

Vélez-Ibáñez, Carlos G. 2004. "The Political Ecology of Debt and Class Formation among Mexican Colonias in the Southwestern United States." In *Livelihood and Microfinance: Anthropological and Sociological Perspectives on Savings and Debt*, edited by Hotze Lont and Otto Hospes, 129–51. Amsterdam: Eburon Delft.

———. 2010. *An Impossible Living in a Transborder World: Culture, Confianza, and Economy of Mexican-Origin Populations*. Tucson: University of Arizona Press.

Vila, Pablo. 2000. *Crossing Borders, Reinforcing Borders: Social Categories, Metaphors, and Narrative Identities on the U.S.-Mexico Frontier*. Austin: University of Texas Press.

Villacrés, Daniela. 2009. "A View from the Inside: Grounding the Development-Remittance Link." *Migraciones Internacionales* 5 (2): 39–73.

Vyse, Stuart. 2008. *Going Broke: Why Americans Can't Hold on to Their Money.* New York: Oxford University Press.

Waldinger, Roger, and Michael I. Lichter. 2003. *How the Other Half Works: Immigration and the Social Organization of Labor.* Berkeley: University of California Press.

Wiest, Raymond E. 1984. "External Dependency and the Perpetuation of Temporary Migration to the United States." In *Patterns of Undocumented Migration: Mexico and the United States,* edited by Richard C. Jones, 110–35. Totowa, NJ: Rowman and Allanheld.

Wilkinson, Daniel. 2002. *Silence on the Mountain: Stories of Terror, Betrayal, and Forgetting in Guatemala.* Boston: Houghton Mifflin.

Williams, Philip J., Timothy J. Steigenga, and Manuel Vásquez. 2009. *A Place to Be: Brazilian, Guatemalan, and Mexican Immigrants in Florida's New Destinations.* Piscataway, NJ: Rutgers University Press.

Wilson, Kim. 2007. "The Moneylender's Dilemma." In *What's Wrong with Microfinance?* edited by Thomas Dichter and Malcolm Harper, 97–108. Rugby, Warwickshire: Practical Action Publishing.

World Bank. 2009. "Guatemala Poverty Assessment: Good Performance at Low Levels." Report No. 43920-GT, March 18. Washington, DC.

Zúñiga, Victor, and Rubén Hernández-León, eds. 2005. *New Destinations: Mexican Immigration in the United States.* New York: Sage.

Index